WAR

Bob Woodward

Simon & Schuster

New York   London   Toronto   Sydney   New Delhi

100 YEARS

SIMON & SCHUSTER

Simon & Schuster
1230 Avenue of the Americas
New York, NY 10020

First Simon & Schuster hardcover edition October 2024

SIMON & SCHUSTER and colophon are registered
trademarks of Simon & Schuster, LLC.

Simon & Schuster: Celebrating 100 Years of Publishing in 2024

For information about special discounts for bulk
purchases, please contact Simon & Schuster Special Sales at
1-866-506-1949 or business@simonandschuster.com.

The Simon & Schuster Speakers Bureau can bring authors to
your live event. For more information or to book an event,
contact the Simon & Schuster Speakers Bureau at 1-866-248-3049
or visit our website at www.simonspeakers.com.

Maps by David Lindroth

Manufactured in the United States of America

1   3   5   7   9   10   8   6   4   2

Library of Congress Cataloging-in-Publication Data is available.

ISBN 978-1-6680-5227-3
ISBN 978-1-6680-5229-7 (ebook)

*For my lifelong friend and reporting
partner Carl Bernstein*

Contents

"Mechanical and scientific creations of modern man tend to conceal from him the nature of his own humanity and to encourage him in all sorts of Promethean ambitions and illusions."

George Kennan, American diplomat and the father of the policy of containment theory that the U.S. firmly block the expansion of the Soviet Union

Author's Personal Note

"I'm going to keep going," Claire McMullen, my remarkable full-time assistant on this book, tells me all the time. Going to keep going is her motto.

A brilliant, gifted writer and lawyer from Australia, Claire, 30, made this book possible. Without her, there would be no book. Period. She is a genius. Always good-natured and joyful, Claire is also tough. She challenges me to pursue the hard stories, confirmation and evidence. Her push is kind but never-ending. She regularly reminds me of the new reporting paths that must be explored. She may understand these wars in Ukraine and the Middle East better and more than I do. She knows our files, the public record, and is always connecting them. When my energy stalls out, she shows up early, stays late and comes in weekends. She is always thinking. Never stumped. Claire manages the hundreds of files and interview transcripts which she makes personally with marathon speed and accuracy.

I many times think, Why am I not more like her? The honest answer is that there is only one Claire McMullen. She will write her own books soon. Her contribution to this one cannot be overstated. With affection, friendship and overwhelming admiration.

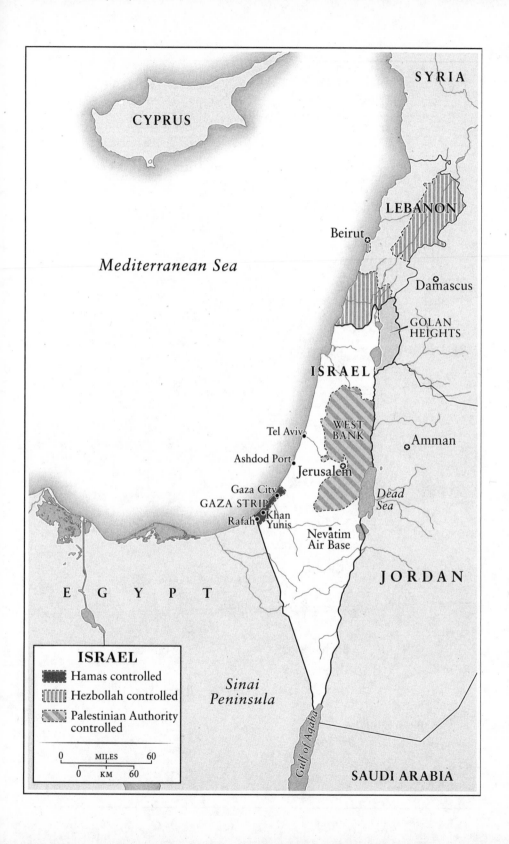

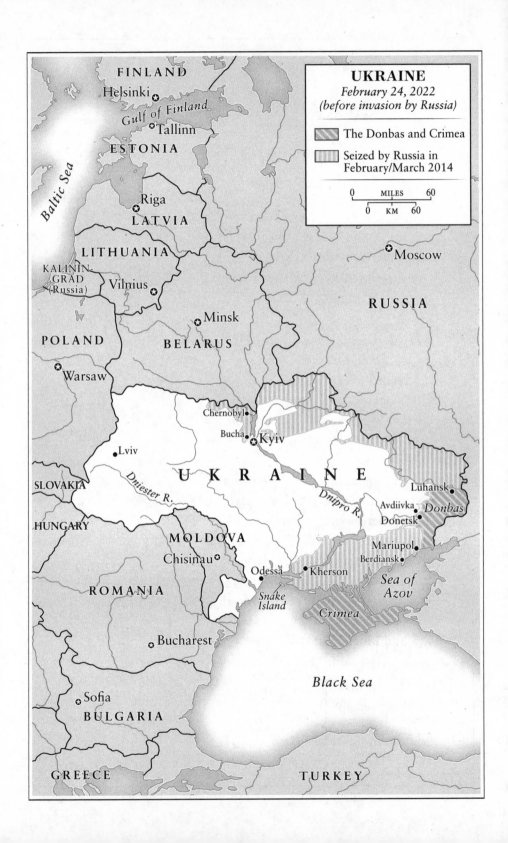

UKRAINE
February 24, 2022
(before invasion by Russia)

The Donbas and Crimea

Seized by Russia in
February/March 2014

0 — MILES — 60
0 — KM — 60

FINLAND
Helsinki
Gulf of Finland
Tallinn
ESTONIA

Baltic Sea

Riga
LATVIA

LITHUANIA

Moscow

KALININ-
GRAD
(Russia)
Vilnius

POLAND

Minsk
BELARUS

RUSSIA

Warsaw

Chernobyl
Bucha Kyiv

Lviv

UKRAINE

Luhansk

SLOVAKIA

Dniester R.

Dnipro R.

Avdiivka *Donbas*
Donetsk

HUNGARY

MOLDOVA
Chisinau

Mariupol
Berdiansk

Odessa
Kherson

*Sea of
Azov*

ROMANIA

*Snake
Island*

Crimea

Bucharest

Black Sea

Sofia
BULGARIA

GREECE

TURKEY

Prologue

One evening in February 1989, my Watergate reporting partner Carl Bernstein bumped into Donald Trump at a dinner party in New York City.

"Why don't you come on up," Carl urged me on the phone from the party, hosted by Ahmet Ertegun, the Turkish American socialite and record executive, in his Upper East Side townhouse. "Everybody's having a good time," he said. "Trump is here. It's really interesting. I've been talking to him."

Bernstein was fascinated with Trump's book, *The Art of the Deal*. Somewhat reluctantly I agreed to join him, in large part, as Carl often reminds me, because I needed the key to his apartment where I was staying at the time.

"I'll be there soon," I told him.

It had been 17 years since Carl and I first collaborated on stories about the Watergate burglary, June 17, 1972.

Trump took a look at us standing together, then age 45, and he came over. "Wouldn't it be amazing if Woodward & Bernstein interviewed Donald Trump?" he said.

Carl and I looked at each other.

"Sure," Carl said. "How about tomorrow?"

"Yeah," Trump said. "Come to my office at Trump Tower."

"This guy is interesting," Carl assured me after Trump was gone.

"But not in politics," I said.

I was immediately intrigued by Trump, a hustler entrepreneur and his unique, carefully nurtured and cultivated persona, designed even then to manipulate others with precision and a touch of ruthlessness.

The Trump interview, taped on a microcassette and transcribed with a typewriter, was deposited into a manila envelope with a copy of Trump's book and eventually lost in piles and piles of records, interview notes and news clippings. I am a pack rat. For over thirty years, Carl and I looked for it.

I joked with President Trump about "the lost interview" when I interviewed him in the Oval Office in December 2019 for the second of my three books on his presidency, *Rage*.

"We sat at a table and we talked," Trump recalled. "I remember it well." He said I should try to find it because he believed it was a great interview.

Last year, 2023, I went to a facility where my records are stored and sifted through hundreds of boxes of old files. In a box of miscellaneous news clippings from the 1980s, I noticed a plain, slightly battered envelope—the interview.

It's a portrait of the young Trump at age 42, focused exclusively on his real estate deals, on making money and his celebrity status. But he was hazy about his future.

"I'm really looking to make the greatest hotel," Trump told us in 1989. "That's why I'm doing suites on top. I'm building great suites.

"You ask me where I'm going and I don't think I could tell you at all," Trump said. "If everything stayed the way it is right now I could probably tell you pretty well where I'm going to be." But, he emphasized, "The world changes." He believed that was the only certainty.

He also spoke about how he behaved differently depending on who he was with. "If I'm with fellas—meaning contractors and this and that—I react one way," Trump said and then gestured to us. "If I know I have the two pros of all time sitting there with me, with tape recorders on, you naturally act differently.

"Much more interesting would be the real act as opposed to the façade," Trump said about himself. I wondered about "the real act."

"It's much more interesting. It's an act that hasn't been caught," Trump added.

He was constantly performing and, that day, we were the recipients of his full-on charm offensive.

"It's never the same when there's somebody sitting with you and literally taking notes. You know, you're on your good behavior, and frankly, it's not nearly as interesting as the real screaming shouting."

Trump also appeared preoccupied with looking tough, strong.

"The worst part about the television stuff when we do it is they put the makeup all over you," Trump said. "This morning I did something and they put the makeup all over your face and so do you go up and take a shower and clean it off or do you leave it? And in the construction business you don't wear makeup. You got problems if you wear makeup."

We asked Trump to take us through the steps of one of his real estate deals. How are they done?

"Instinctively," he said immediately. "I cannot tell you what it is, you understand. Because instinct is far more important than any other ingredient if you have the right instincts. And the worst deals I've made have been deals where I didn't follow my instinct. The best deals I've made have been deals where I followed my instinct and wouldn't listen to all of the people that said, 'there's no way it works.'

"Very few people have proper instincts," he said. "But I've seen people with proper instincts do things that other people just can't do."

Is there a master plan?

"I don't think I could define what the great master plan is," he said referring to his life. "You understand that. But it somehow fits together in an instinctual way. I'll tell you what, if you find out let me know. I'd be interested. I might be actually interested."

I asked about his social conscience. Could it "lead you into politics or some public role?"

"Well, you know, to me it's all very interesting," he said. "The other week I was watching a boxing match in Atlantic City and these are rough guys, you know, physically rough guys. And mentally tough in a sense, okay. I mean they're not going to write books but mentally tough in a certain sense.

"And the champion lost and he was defeated by somebody who's a very good fighter but who wasn't expected to win. And they interviewed the boxer after the match and they said, 'How'd you do this? How'd you win?'

"And he said, 'I just went with the punches, man. I just went with the punches.' I thought it was a great expression," Trump said, "because it's about life just as much as it is about boxing or anything else. You go with the punches."

To look back over Trump's life now—his real estate deals, his presidency, impeachments, investigations, civil and criminal trials, a conviction, attempted assassination, campaign for re-election—it is exactly what he has done. Roll with the punches.

"Anybody that says where they're going to be in ten years is a schmuck," Trump added. "The world changes. You'll have depressions. You'll have recessions. You'll have upswings. You'll have downswings. You'll have wars. Things that are beyond your control or in most cases beyond people's control. So you really do have to go with the punches and it's bad to predict too far out in advance, you know, where you're going to be."

At the time he was almost obsessed with critical news headlines about him losing deals.

"You make more money as a seller than you do as a buyer," Trump explained. "I found that to be a seller today is to be a loser. Psychologically. And that's wrong.

"I'll tell you what. I beat the shit out of a guy named Merv Griffin," Trump said. Griffin was a television talk show host and media mogul. "Just beat him. And, you know, he came in—you talk about makeup. He came in with makeup and he was on television, you know, he comes into my office. He made a deal to buy everything I didn't want in Resorts International," Trump said. "I kept telling him no, no, no, no, and he kept raising the price, raising the price, raising the price. All of a sudden, it turns out to be an incredible deal for me. An unbelievable deal.

"Plus," Trump added, "I got the Taj Mahal, which is the absolute crown jewel of the world." He was referring to the Taj Mahal Atlantic City casino, not the sacred mausoleum in India.

"The point is that people thought I lost," he said. "So what's happened is there's a mood in the world for the last five years that if you're a seller, you're a loser, even if you're a seller at a huge profit."

I asked Trump, When you get up in the morning, what do you read? Who do you talk to? What information sources do you trust?

"Much of it is very basic," Trump said. "I read *The Wall Street Journal* and *The New York Times*. I read the *Post* and the *News*, not so much for business, just to sort of I live in the city and you know, it's reporting on the city." The *New York Post* was a tabloid that covered Trump almost obsessively.

"I rely less on people than I do just this general flow of information," he said. "I also speak to cab drivers. I go to cities and say what do you think of this? That's how I bought Mar-a-Lago. Talking to a cab driver, and asking him: 'What's hot in Florida? What's the greatest house in Palm Beach?'

"Oh, the greatest house is Mar-a-Lago," the cab driver said.

"I said where is it? Take me over." Trump then added, "I was in Palm Beach, I was in the Breakers and I was bored stiff."

Trump eventually bought Mar-a-Lago for $7 million.

"I talk to anybody," he said. "I always call it my poll. People jokingly tell me you know that Trump will speak with anybody. And I do, I speak to the construction workers and the cab drivers, and those are the people I get along with best anyway in many respects. I speak to everybody."

Trump claimed he bought 9.9 percent of a casino company, Bally Manufacturing, and in a short period of time made $32 million.

He then said he spent "close to 100 million on buying stock" in Bally which led to a lawsuit against him. The lawyers for the other side wanted Trump's records.

"They were trying to prove that I did this tremendous research on the company, that I spent weeks and months analyzing the company," Trump said. "And they figured I'd have files that would be up to the ceiling. So they subpoenaed everything and I ended up giving them no papers. There were virtually no files. So I'm being grilled by one of their high-priced lawyers."

Trump impersonated the lawyer: "How long did you know about this, Mr. Trump? And when?"

"In other words, they're trying to say like this is this great plot," Trump said. "I said, I don't know, I just started thinking about it the day I bought it."

The lawyer was incredulous. "Well, how many reports did you do?"

"Well, I really didn't, I just had a feeling."

"They didn't believe that somebody would take 100 million bucks and put it into a company with no real research," Trump said. "Now I had research in my head, but beyond that, you know, they just had not thought that happens. And the corporate mind and the corporate mentality doesn't think that happens. Those are my best deals."

Carl asked Trump if he ever sees himself in a public service role?

"I don't think so but I'm not sure," Trump said. "I'm young. In theory, statistically, I have a long time left. I've seen people give so much away that they don't have anything when bad times come."

He said he was setting up a Donald J. Trump Foundation. "When I kick the bucket—as the expression goes—I want to leave a tremendous amount of money to that foundation. Some to my family and some to the foundation. You have an obligation to your family."

Trump spoke about "bad times" as if they were inevitable. "I always like to sort of prepare for the worst. And it doesn't sound like a very particularly nice statement," he said. "I know times will get bad. It's just a question when."

He brought up his private 282-foot yacht that he bought from the wealthy Saudi businessman and arms dealer Adnan Khashoggi. Trump had renamed it *Trump Princess*. "To build new today would cost 150 to 200 million dollars. If you guys want we'll go on it or something. . . . It's phenomenal. If you read *Time* magazine I do nothing but float around on this boat all day long. It's not the way it is."

Who is your best friend? I asked.

He listed some names of businessmen and investors, people who worked for him, that neither Carl nor I recognized, and his brother Robert. "I guess in all cases business related," he said. "Only because that's the people I deal with.

"But friendship is a strange thing. You know, I'm always concerned with friendship. Sometimes you like to test people; right now everybody wants to be my friend for whatever reason. Okay for the obvious reasons.

"Sometimes you'd like to test and say one day just for a period of a week that Trump blew it, and then go back and call 'em up and invite 'em for dinner and see whether they show up. I've often wanted to do that. Take a period of a month and let the world think that I blew it just to test whether or not in fact the friends were friends.

"I'm a great loyalist. I believe in loyalty to people. I believe in having great friends and great enemies. I've seen people who were on top who didn't stay on top and all of a sudden . . . the same people who were kissing their ass are gone. I mean like gone.

"One example was a banker. He was really a great banker, for one of the big banks—Citibank. And he was in charge of huge loans to very substantial people.

"He made a lot of people rich loaning money and he called me like two years after the fact. He said, you know, it's incredible, the same people that were my best friends, that were calling me up all the time and kissing my ass in every way, I can't even get through to 'em on the telephone anymore. . . . When he left the bank they wouldn't take his calls anymore.

"I would."

Trump described his strategy of refusing to pay the property violations he received from inspectors until they disappeared or forgot about them.

"From day one, I said fuck them," Trump said of the inspectors.

"When I was in Brooklyn, inspectors would come around and they'd give me a violation on buildings that were absolutely perfect," Trump recalled. "I'd say, 'fuck you.' And they'd give me more violations. And more. And for one month it was miserable. I had more violations—and they were unfounded violations. But they give it because what they wanted was if you ever paid 'em off they'd always come back. So what happened to me, in one month they just said, 'fuck this guy, he's a piece of shit.' And they'd go to somebody else.

"The point is if you fold it causes you much more trouble than it's worth," Trump said.

"You can say the same thing with the mob. If you agree to do business with them, they'll always come back. If you tell 'em to go fuck themselves—in that case, perhaps in a nicer way. But if you tell them 'forget it man, forget it, nothing's worth it,' they might try and put pressure on you at the beginning but in the end they're going to find an easier mark because it's too tough for them. Inspectors. Mobs. Unions. Okay?"

This was Trump's basic philosophy.

Carl asked, who are your greatest enemies?

"Well, I hate to say because then you're just going to go and interview 'em. I hate playing the role of a critic."

Trump in fact loved it. "The obvious one is Ed Koch," he said. "Ed Koch was the worst mayor in the history of New York City."

Thirty-five years later, Trump still criticizes opponents with the same exaggerated effect. "Joe Biden is the worst president in the history of the United States," he said after President Biden announced in July 2024 that he would not be seeking re-election.

Even in 1989, Trump's character was focused on winning, fighting and surviving. "And the only way you do that," he said, "is instinct.

"If people know you're a folder," he said, "if people know that you're going to be weak, they're going to go after you."

Trump said it was "a whole presentation. It's a way of presenting.

"You've got to know your audience and by the way, for some people be a killer, for some people be all candy. For some people be different. For some people both."

Killer, candy, or both. That's Donald Trump.

What a remarkable time capsule from 1989, a full psychological study of a man, then a 42-year-old Manhattan real estate king. I never expected Donald Trump to become president or a defining political figure of our time. The same instincts I reported on during his presidency are just as much a trademark of his character back then. Here, in this interview 35 years ago, we see the origin of Trumpism in the words of Trump himself.

ONE

Thirty-five Years Later

———— ◆ ————

As rioters stormed the Capitol on January 6, 2021, President Donald Trump watched on television from his private dining room next to the Oval Office. His supporters climbed the walls of the historic building, shattered windows and attempted to force the front doors open with a battering ram.

Gallows were being set up outside. "Hang Mike Pence. Hang Mike Pence. Hang Mike Pence," Trump's supporters called for the vice president, who had refused to overthrow the certification of Biden's 2020 election win.

"Where is the president?" Republican House Minority Leader Kevin McCarthy was calling the White House, asking aides to connect him with Trump. McCarthy's office was being vandalized. House Speaker Nancy Pelosi's was being ransacked. Supporters took pictures with their feet on her desk. They left a note on her keyboard: WE WILL NOT BACK DOWN.

Congressional leaders, including McCarthy and Pelosi, had been rushed out by Capitol security and driven to a secure location, Fort McNair, a U.S. Army post a few blocks from the Washington Nationals baseball stadium. But their staff were still in there, hiding in various offices with the lights switched off, desks barricading the doors.

President Trump finally got on the phone.

"You've got to get out and tell these people to STOP! We've been run over," McCarthy said. He was intense. "Someone just got shot."

At 2:44 p.m., Air Force veteran Ashli Babbitt was shot and killed by a police officer inside the Capitol as she and others tried to breach a door near lawmakers. Among the rioters were leaders of pro-Trump, far-right militia groups, the Oath Keepers and the Proud Boys, as well as conspiracy theorists from groups like QAnon. What began as a Trump rally had escalated into a violent attack on the constitutional order of the United States.

"I'll put a tweet out or something," Trump replied.

"They've taken over the Capitol!" McCarthy yelled at him. "You've got to tell them to stop. You've got to get them out of here. Get them out of here. Now."

The president seemed not to grasp the gravity of the situation. "Well, Kevin, I guess these people are more upset about the election than you are," Trump said.

The FBI later estimated that over 2,000 people entered the Capitol on January 6, 2021. Five people died, 172 police officers were injured, and more than 500 were arrested. The cost of the damage to the historic Capitol building exceeded $2.7 million.

It took President Trump *187 minutes* to post a tweet telling his supporters to "go home."

Two months earlier, Donald Trump had lost the 2020 election to Joe Biden. But he rejected the loss. Instead, he said it was "rigged," "a fraud on the American public," and "stolen."

Even now, 35 years after our interview, Trump was convinced any loss—even a presidential election loss—could be brushed aside if he simply *didn't fold.*

At Trump's "Save America" rally on January 6, he urged his supporters to "fight like hell."

"We won this election, and we won it by a landslide.

"We will never give up. We will never concede.

"We are going to the Capitol."

The House Select Committee investigating the January 6 attack later concluded that Trump "engaged in a successful but fraudulent effort to persuade tens of millions of Americans that the election was stolen from him."

Garret Miller, a Trump supporter who brought a gun to the Capitol on January 6, said, "I believed I was following the instructions of former President Trump."

Another supporter, Lewis Cantwell, testified that he had watched President Trump on TV "telling the world" the election was stolen. "What else would I believe, as a patriotic American who voted for him?"

Stephen Ayres, who also stormed the Capitol that day, said he was "hanging on every word [Trump] was saying." Ayres had posted on social media that "Civil War will ensue" if Trump did not stay in power for a second term.

"You need to call Joe Biden and you need to do it today," House Minority Leader Kevin McCarthy told Trump shortly after the attack.

No, Trump said. He claimed Biden only won because of fraud.

"Stop saying that," McCarthy said. "Just stop saying that. You need to leave Joe Biden a letter in the desk."

A tradition.

"Well, I haven't decided," Trump said.

McCarthy was emotional and exhausted. The violence on January 6 carried a shocking, traumatizing weight.

"Your legacies will be different now because of that day," McCarthy warned him. "Call Joe Biden."

No, Trump said.

McCarthy told him it was important for the country for some sort of conversation between the outgoing and incoming leader to take place. A president should acknowledge his successor.

"Okay, okay, okay," Trump finally said. He wanted off the call with McCarthy, but McCarthy stayed on.

"What do you think your grandchildren are going to think of you if you don't do this?" McCarthy said.

"Okay, okay," Trump repeated.

The phone call to Biden never happened.

But on his last night in the Oval Office, January 19, 2021, Trump hand-wrote a two-page letter to Joe Biden. He finished it at 10:00 p.m., signed it *Donald J. Trump* and placed it inside the desk. Biden would later tell his White House press secretary Jen Psaki it was "shockingly gracious."

Trump, with First Lady Melania, left the White House early on January 20, 2021, for their club and Palm Beach estate, Mar-a-Lago. On board Air Force One, Trump took a call from Republican National Committee chairperson Ronna McDaniel. It was a farewell message on behalf of the committee.

"I'm done," Trump said, cutting her off. "I'm starting my own party."

McDaniel balked.

"You cannot do that," McDaniel implored Trump on the phone. "If you do, we will lose forever."

"This isn't their Republican Party anymore. This is Donald Trump's Republican Party," Trump's eldest son, Don Jr., had declared onstage at the "Save America" rally on January 6.

"Exactly. You lose forever without me," Trump snapped at McDaniel. "This is what Republicans deserve for not sticking with me." He wanted to take down the Republican Party.

The Republican National Committee leadership would later make clear to Trump's advisers that the former president's lust for revenge would hurt not only his legacy but his finances. The Republican Party threatened to cease paying Trump's legal bills and destroy the value of his campaign's email list that contained 40 million Trump voters. Trump had been selling the list to other Republican candidates. If he tried to use it they would give it away for free.

Trump backed down. He later denied to ABC News journalist Jonathan Karl that he'd ever even thought about starting his own party. "Oh, that is bullshit. It never happened," Trump said. Karl later released the tape of his interview with McDaniel recounting Trump's threat.

On Air Force One, the Trump family sat at the front of the plane, a bunch of his closest senior and junior staff at the back.

"They never came back," a Trump aide said. Not the president, nor any of his family. Even among his closest aides, there was a sense of almost overwhelming shell shock. Many did not have a plan for what they would do next. Some didn't know where they would live. Usually staff had about two and a half months, from the election to January 20, to prepare for life after the White House.

"For a lot of people that was compressed into 13 days," an aide said because it wasn't clear to them that Trump would leave the White House until after January 6.

At 11:59 a.m., January 20, Trump was in his cavernous apartment at Mar-a-Lago. No tweets. No speeches. At 12:01 p.m., as Biden was sworn in as the 46th president of the United States, Secret Service agents began shrinking the fortified security set up around Trump's estate.

Trump didn't like it. He stayed in his quarters the rest of the day.

"Hey, it's your all-time favorite president," Trump said on the phone to House Republican leader Kevin McCarthy a few days later. "Look, I want to talk," he said. "I'm down in Florida."

McCarthy had said on the House floor on January 13 that Trump "bears responsibility" for the Capitol riot and called on him to "accept his share of responsibility." Trump exploded with anger when he saw the TV replay but appeared to have gotten over it.

"I'll stop by," McCarthy said. He didn't tell anyone he was

going, not even his staff. McCarthy knew Trump had not been seeing many Republicans. He was moping. The media spotlight had dimmed over Mar-a-Lago.

Republican strategist Ed Rollins once said of Trump, "There's only one thing you need to know about him. He watches television all day and then at night goes on television."

Trump was now fighting for attention. He no longer had his Twitter feed or Facebook, having been kicked off the sites after his torrent of election lies. He began making surprise appearances at wedding receptions at Mar-a-Lago.

President Trump, in a dark suit and yellow tie, was grinning as McCarthy walked into Mar-a-Lago on January 28. "You know Melania said this has more press than when I met Putin," he said. "There are four TV helicopters outside!"

McCarthy's visit to the former president was all over the news. Having the top House Republican come for lunch showed Trump was still in control of the Republican Party.

"You know it's good for you and me, right?"

"All right," McCarthy said. "Whatever."

McCarthy came with the hope of keeping Trump involved with the House GOP so Republicans could retake the majority in 2022. He needed to steer Trump away from stoking unnecessary primary fights and to lend his name to winnable seats. They sat down for lunch.

"You know, being off Twitter has kind of helped me," Trump said.

"Oh, really?"

"Yeah, a lot of people would say they liked my policy, didn't like my tweets."

"Yeah, like everybody."

"My numbers have kind of gone up."

Trump asked about his upcoming Senate impeachment trial. He was charged with inciting an insurrection.

"I don't think it's going anywhere," McCarthy said.

It didn't. On February 13, 2021, Trump was acquitted. While a majority of senators, including seven Republicans, voted to convict the former president, they failed to reach the two-thirds needed for conviction. It was merely symbolic since Trump was no longer president.

President Biden's chief of staff, Ron Klain, 59, with dark brown hair and a friendly, high-charging demeanor, had counseled Biden for more than 20 years. When Biden decided to run for president, he called Klain up to his home in Wilmington in early March 2019.

"I just feel like I have to do this," Biden said. "Trump represents something fundamentally different and wrong about politics."

Biden's next words would stick forever with Klain: *"This guy just isn't really an American president."*

On the campaign trail, Biden had gone after Trump's character and policies relentlessly. From his first day in the White House, Biden barely mentioned Trump's name, referring to him in public as "my predecessor" and often in private as "that fucking asshole."

Biden told his advisers he wanted his own presidency. Trump's four years, his handling of the coronavirus pandemic and the January 6 insurrection, were a trauma on the presidency.

The mission now, as Klain saw it, was to fix what Trump broke and move the country forward.

"We as a country still need to process this Trump thing a bit," Klain said. "The way we're doing it is by showing the American people that the presidency can work again. That they can have a decent person in the White House.

"In the end Donald Trump lost because he didn't control the pandemic and the economy. Notwithstanding the stock market, the real economy, where people live got worse on his watch.

"Obviously there are some hard-core Trump supporters that are what they are and they're not going to go away and that's part of our country," Klain said. But Biden "was elected to move this country forward post-Trump and that's what he's doing. That's his mission.

"Donald Trump can stand in as many arenas as he wants and raise his arms as loudly as he wants," Klain declared. He believed Trump's early attempts at a shadow presidency would die out by the fall of 2021.

"Donald Trump will be a sideshow," Klain said confidently.

TWO

"Chekhov's gun" was National Security Adviser Jake Sullivan's immediate thought as he reviewed overhead satellite photos that showed an unprecedented 110,000 Russian troops massing on the border of Ukraine.

If a pistol appears conspicuously in the first act of a play it is there for a reason and will be fired at some point, the 19th-century playwright Anton Chekhov had famously written.

It was April 2021, only the third month of Biden's presidency. Sullivan had barely settled into his new office in the White House West Wing.

At 44, Sullivan, thin and fair-haired, was the youngest national security adviser since Henry Kissinger. With the discipline of a former marathon runner, Sullivan was the operational coordinator of Biden's foreign policy. When Biden appointed him, Biden called Sullivan, a former Rhodes Scholar and Yale Law School honors graduate, "a once in a lifetime intellect" and had entrusted him with extraordinary decision-making authority.

The intelligence also showed Russian naval forces were actively deploying to the Black Sea, a vast inland body of water bordered by Ukraine and Russia. Flatbed trucks could be seen hauling huge rocket launchers and old Soviet armored personnel carriers. More satellite photos showed Russian tanks, artillery, missiles and naval landing craft being moved into Crimea, on the northern coast of the Black Sea, and along the 1,200-mile land border between Russia and Ukraine.

According to the latest CIA psychological profile, Vladimir Putin, the autocratic Russian leader, was defined by his extreme insecurity and imperial ambition. Putin was convinced that he was the only person that could restore Russia to the old Russian empire. He was fixated on Ukraine.

What was Putin doing? Sullivan wondered. Was this just an exercise, a war game? Was it purely coercive to gain leverage on Ukraine or to force the United States and Europe to back off any talk that Ukraine might eventually join NATO, the world's most powerful military and diplomatic alliance?

It was also possible, Sullivan thought, that Putin was planning to use the troops to seize more territory in the Donbas.

Russia and Ukraine had been fighting in the Donbas, a region in the east with sizable coal reserves, since 2014 when Russia seized neighboring Crimea and control of about a third of the Donbas. Nearly 14,000 people had been killed on both sides. There had been 29 cease-fires, all of which had failed, a sign of festering instability.

Sullivan worked in a state of near constant intellectual anxiety. And yet he couldn't look past the obvious: You don't move that amount of men or matériel to another country's border if you are not at least thinking about using them.

Was Putin hanging his pistol on the wall?

President Biden and Sullivan had debated what the administration's Russia policy should look like. Biden was clear.

"I'm not looking for a reset," Biden said during his first weeks as president. "I'm not looking for some kind of good relationship, but I want to find a stable and predictable way forward with Putin."

But so far the relationship with Russia was neither good, stable, nor predictable. From their first days in office, Biden and Sullivan had been responding to various acts of Russian aggression. The near fatal poisoning of Russian opposition leader Alexei Navalny, Russian interference in the 2020 U.S. elections, suggestions that Russians may have paid the Taliban to kill Americans in Afghanistan, and the massive SolarWinds cyberattack on more than 16,000 computer systems worldwide, including U.S. government departments and key private industries. It was one of the worst data breaches in U.S. history.

Biden had also upped the tension in an ABC television interview on March 16, when he was asked if he thought Putin was a "killer"?

"I do," Biden said.

The Kremlin had called the insult "unprecedented." Putin withdrew the Russian ambassador from Washington in a show of displeasure.

Now Putin was undertaking some grandiose movement of his military.

"Is it actually possible to have a stable and predictable relationship with Russia?" Sullivan asked Deputy National Security Adviser Jon Finer with slight exasperation, standing in the cramped national security suite.

Finer, 45, with cropped light brown hair, a half-beard and mustache, was low on the Washington visibility pecking order but central to the White House national security strategy. Finer had worked as chief of staff to Secretary of State John Kerry and previously spent three years embedded as a *Washington Post* journalist during the 2003 Iraq invasion and occupation. Like Sullivan, Finer was also a Rhodes Scholar and Yale Law School graduate.

The odds are weighted against success, Finer said candidly but agreed they ought to keep trying. U.S. intelligence indicated that Russia had not as yet signaled an intention to use the forces to invade Ukraine. But their purpose remained unclear. While it could just be a pressure tactic, they couldn't be sure.

"Putin cares a lot about dignity and respect," Sullivan mused. A summit meeting would be on brand for Biden, who placed great value in personal relationships.

Sullivan went down the hall to the Oval Office to discuss the idea with the president.

"He wants to be a big player on the big stage," Biden said of Putin. "This is what this guy's all about."

Sullivan suggested Biden meet with Putin in person. He knew the president preferred to meet face-to-face with everyone, especially world leaders.

Biden agreed instantly. "I know people are going to criticize me and say if you meet with Putin, you're elevating him, you're legitimizing him," he said. "But this guy has been a major figure on the global scene for two decades. Me meeting with him is not transforming him into something he's not.

"Look, I'm not going to sweet-talk this guy out of this or that but maybe you can change the dynamic of it," Biden said.

But when to meet?

"If we make the offer to meet for June," two months away, Biden said, "it gives Putin some incentive to say hey, what have the Americans got? You know? That might lead Putin to reduce pressure on Ukraine's border and deter the likelihood of a potential military operation in the spring."

Ukraine played a dramatic, outsized role in American politics. During a phone call with newly elected Ukrainian president Volodymyr Zelensky in September 2019, then-President Trump asked Zelensky to investigate Joe Biden and his son Hunter, who was on the board of a Ukrainian energy company, in exchange for security aid from the United States. A transcript of the call was released and Trump was impeached by the House of Representatives. He was later acquitted in the Senate. Republicans, however, continued to press for an investigation into Biden, who was in charge of the Ukraine portfolio during the Obama administration and had been particularly engaged.

Dr. Colin Kahl, an academic and Defense Secretary Lloyd Austin's undersecretary for defense policy at the Pentagon, had been Vice President Biden's national security adviser from 2014 to 2017. Intensely cerebral, he had his own distinctive intellectual flair, often adding bright red-framed glasses, a patterned tie or colorful socks to his daily wardrobe. Kahl remembered Biden working the Ukraine account for the Obama administration with relish and visiting Kyiv, the capital, four times during his vice presidency.

"Hey Petro," Biden said in one call to then-president Petro Poroshenko. Ukraine's fledgling democracy was particularly fragile and large portions of its governance system remained rotten and corrupt.

"I know this is hard," Biden said sympathetically. "I know that your politics is a den of vipers over there, I get it. I know this is hard and I have confidence in you doing the right thing. But I'm telling you, it's going to be really hard for us to maintain the confidence of the West, who don't want to give you the benefit of the doubt.

"You've got to help me help you by doing the right things," Biden said to Poroshenko, urging him to act to address corruption. "That could be reforms on procurement, it could be reforms on the banking system, it could be setting up new anti-corruption entities, it could be pushing the prosecutor general to be more aggressive.

"If you don't do these things," Biden emphasized, "it's going to be hard for you to maintain the support of our Congress, of our president, of the Europeans, and the Russians are going to eat you for lunch."

Biden said his goal was to keep Ukraine's leadership moving on the path of democratization, precisely what Putin didn't want.

"I sat in the room with Joe Biden every single day and he called the Ukrainians probably once or twice a week as vice president," Kahl recalled. "Just to do marriage counseling between [President] Poroshenko and [Prime Minister Arseniy] Yatsenyuk or whoever happened to be prime minister at the time and there was never a call where he did not push the Ukrainians beyond their comfort zone on anti-corruption issues."

Biden's approach to Ukraine was "big hugs, little punches," Kahl said.

———

Now on April 13, 2021, as president, Biden phoned President Putin.

"I'm upset you called me a killer," Putin said, almost immediately.

"I was asked a question. I gave an answer. It was an interview on a totally different topic. And it was not something premeditated," Biden said, as if that negated his "killer" remark.

U.S. intelligence analysts who profiled Putin had listed among the Russian leader's main character traits that he was "thin-skinned," "extremely insecure" and even "sadistic."

During the call, Putin flatly denied the accusations on election interference, the poisoning of Navalny and Russia's cyberattacks.

Biden reminded Putin of the United States' unwavering commitment to Ukraine's sovereignty and warned Putin not to start a new military incursion into Ukraine.

"You're wrong about everything," Putin said matter-of-factly. "You have no evidence. We didn't interfere in your election. We didn't do any of these things."

Biden dismissed the denials. "I'm warning you we are coming at you with these responses."

He then described to Putin the series of costs that would be imposed on Russia, including formally naming the Russian Foreign Intelligence Service (SVR) as the perpetrator of the Solar-Winds attack. He would also be expelling 10 Russian diplomats from Washington and placing a series of economic sanctions on Russia for its 2020 election interference and ongoing occupation of Crimea.

"They will happen this week and I want you to hear it from me directly. And it's because of the specific things you've done. I've said I would respond and I'm responding."

Biden switched gears. "Let's meet," Biden said, trying to cut through the tense atmosphere and shift his tone.

"Let's you and I sit down. You bring your concerns, and I will bring mine," Biden said. On any and all topics. "And we'll sit face-to-face, and we'll talk about all of it."

"Let me get this straight," Putin said, a note of astonishment in his voice. "You want to meet and talk about all the issues in our relationship? All of them?"

Sullivan, who was listening on the call, thought Putin, always suspicious, wanted to make sure it was not some kind of trap.

Biden assured Putin it would be an open dialogue. He knew Putin realized a meeting on the global stage would show he was respected by the American president.

They had met in person once before a decade earlier, in 2011, when Biden was vice president and Putin was temporarily serving as prime minister.

Biden had later claimed during that meeting he said to Putin, "I'm looking into your eyes and I don't think you have a soul." Putin smiled and told Biden, through an interpreter, "We understand one another."

For Biden, it was standard for an American president to meet with a Russian leader as his predecessors had. Though a declining economic power with less than 10 percent of the U.S. GDP, Russia had more than 4,400 nuclear warheads, the largest arsenal in the world.

"Okay," Putin finally replied, "I would like to have the summit also. Let's have our teams work on it."

Biden knew he needed to be prepared. Vladimir Putin, a 68-year-old former KGB spy who had led Russia as president or prime minister for more than two decades, was a master at using big public events as a stage to play games or seize the upper hand with the leaders of Western countries.

In 2007 during a bilateral meeting with German chancellor Angela Merkel at Putin's palatial home in Sochi on the Black Sea, the Russian president called his large black Labrador, Konni, into the room in front of journalists and cameras. Merkel had a well-known terror of dogs.

As the dog sauntered over to sniff the German chancellor, she froze in her chair, lips pursed and one ankle tucked tightly behind the other. Watching her unease, Putin leaned back in his chair, his legs sprawled comfortably in front of him.

"I'm sure it will behave itself," he said with a smirk.

"It doesn't eat journalists, after all," Merkel said not missing a beat.

Merkel later talked to the press about the incident.

"I understand why he has to do this—to prove he's a man," she said. "He's afraid of his own weaknesses. Russia has nothing, no successful politics or economy. All they have is this."

American presidents had also been a target of Putin's theatrics. In 2018, a week before then-President Trump's summit with Putin in Helsinki, 12 Russian military intelligence agents were indicted in the U.S. for hacking the presidential campaign of Democratic candidate Hillary Clinton in her race against Trump.

In a joint press conference following the summit, Putin played to Trump's ego, flattering him. When Trump was asked about Russian interference in the 2016 election, Putin was rewarded with one of the most extraordinary statements by an American president.

"He just said it's not Russia," Trump said. "I don't see any reason why it would be."

Standing side by side, Trump appeared to strongly defend the Russian president and wave off the conclusions of U.S. intelligence agencies, which had unanimously determined that Russia had interfered. Condemnation was swift. Some senior Trump advisers still recoil at the memory of the president siding with Putin over the American intelligence agencies. Putin had again won the moment. Trump's carelessness was on full display.

After returning to the U.S., Trump tweeted, trying to fix the blunder: "I have GREAT confidence in MY intelligence people."

Trump's unwillingness to criticize Putin was not a one-off incident but a consistent character trait.

"I want Putin to respect our country, okay?" Trump told me during an interview with him before the 2016 election.

"What would he respect?" I asked.

"Well, first of all, it's sort of interesting. He said very good things about me," Trump said. "He said, Trump is brilliant, and Trump is going to be the new leader and all that. And some of these clowns said, 'you should repudiate Putin.' I said, why would I repudiate him?"

THREE

N o adviser felt the sting of Helsinki more than Dr. Fiona Hill, a former intelligence analyst specializing in Russian affairs for Presidents Bush and Obama. The coauthor of the book *Mr. Putin: Operative in the Kremlin*, she had served on the National Security Council under President Trump and was his chief Russia expert.

Backstage in Helsinki, Hill had watched with dismay as Trump walked right into Putin's trap. She even contemplated pulling the fire alarm at the venue. Hill would later testify against Trump in his first impeachment trial.

She said there was no doubt that Russia interfered in the 2016 election. "President Putin and the Russian security services," she testified, "operate like a super PAC. They deploy millions of dollars to weaponize our own political opposition research and false narratives."

Trump idolized Putin, Hill believed, and that made him extremely vulnerable to manipulation. "He had a very fragile ego," Hill said of Trump. "When you're the president of the United States, it becomes a fatal flaw, because President Trump couldn't disassociate or disentangle himself from many of the issues that were the critical ones to address. So, when people were concerned about Russian influence in the United States election, he only thought about how that affected him."

Hill was walking her dog in the park when President Biden called her out of the blue. She was surprised at the informality.

The president said he wanted to talk about Putin and get a feel for the Russian's thinking.

Soon after the call, the president gathered a group of Russia experts, including Hill, in the Roosevelt Room of the White House.

Biden had entered presidential office with more than three decades of foreign policy experience, having chaired the Senate Foreign Relations Committee from 2001 to 2003 and then again from 2007 to 2009. He had met three Soviet leaders and two Russian presidents. As vice president, Biden had spoken with Putin in person and by phone. He felt he had a good sense of the man but wanted a gut-check and to debate his view of Putin's intentions.

He asked the group: Have I got it wrong? I haven't seen this guy in a while. Does my assessment of him still hold true? What am I missing?

If there was something really wrong with Biden's assessment of Putin, the president wanted to know. Hill found Biden's approach refreshing. Usually consulting an expert was a paint-by-numbers exercise for most presidents—a formality without real purpose other than so the president could say they had talked to experts.

Hill had plenty of times experienced the "I'll take that under advisement," when in reality a president had already made up their mind. But here, Biden had gathered together a group of experts with very different views on Russia. He wanted a debate.

The last time she had been in the Roosevelt Room, President Trump had spent the entire briefing glowering at a picture of Teddy Roosevelt's Nobel Peace Prize on display, unable to concentrate. "Trump hated it," Hill thought. Did he think it was unfair? Did he think he deserved his own?

Biden posed more questions to the group: What should this summit be about? Should the agenda be the U.S. bilateral relationship with Russia, strategic stability and arms control? Or is there something else going on? Why does Putin have 110,000 troops massed on Ukraine's border?

"Is he going to back off?" Biden asked. "He's not, is he?"

"Putin is probing," Hill said. He is probing to see if he can negotiate with you. He wants you to negotiate away Ukraine.

Essentially, abandon Western support for Ukraine so Russia can take control of it.

Putin, Hill believed, was watching Biden closely—the domestic issues in the U.S. and the plans for a full U.S. withdrawal from Afghanistan negotiated by Trump—and trying to figure out: Is Biden someone who will put Ukraine to one side and move on?

Several of the experts around the table agreed.

The Russian leader was looking for a big, strategic negotiation about Ukraine and the future of European security. Putin had been fixated for years on Ukraine, which he claimed was part of Russia.

But Biden told the group he wasn't about to let Russia just swallow up an independent country.

Biden also worried aloud that deep political divisions in the United States meant there was now little consensus on anything, not even on matters of foreign policy. In the past, a president could go abroad and meet with adversaries knowing the other political party would back him and his predecessor wouldn't meddle. No more. Putin knew that and would use it to Russia's advantage to deflect criticism. Part of Putin's disinformation game was to stoke divisions in the United States.

Given the troops on Ukraine's border, Hill was struck that President Biden's biggest concern was not that Russia might be about to invade Ukraine but that the disunity in the United States would weaken his influence with Putin. Putin would try to exploit it.

Hill agreed, that's exactly what Putin would do.

Russian troops continued to move in plain sight covering extraordinary distances across the country from Siberia and the Urals in the west to the Ukraine border. Air defense systems, trainloads of military vehicles and heavy artillery moved into Crimea. Field hospitals were being built.

Russian drones glided into Ukraine at night dropping land mines. Russians were digging new trenches and Russian amphibious assault ships were spotted surveilling the coast.

FOUR

Putin gave his annual state of the nation address on April 21, 2021. Thousands of Russians had gathered along Tverskaya Street, a main road leading to the Kremlin, shouting chants of "Freedom for Navalny," "Putin is a thief."

Former Russian opposition leader Alexei Navalny had been poisoned in August 2020 with a Soviet-style Novichok nerve agent. Navalny blamed Putin for the attempted assassination. After Navalny received life-saving medical treatment in Berlin, he had returned to Russia in January only to be imprisoned. He was on the third week of a hunger strike as Putin delivered his address to the Russian nation.

On foreign policy, Putin was combative. "Some countries have taken up an unseemly routine where they pick on Russia for any reason, most often, for no reason at all," Putin said. "We behave in an extremely restrained manner, I would even say, modestly, and I am saying this without irony.

"As I said, every now and then they are picking on Russia for no reason. And of course, all sorts of petty Tabaqui are running around them like Tabaqui ran around Shere Khan," Putin said, referring to Rudyard Kipling's *The Jungle Book* where Tabaqui, male jackals, lived in the jungle and fed on scraps from tiger Shere Khan—in this case, the United States.

"Everything is like in Kipling's book," Putin said, "howling along in order to make their sovereign happy.

"Those behind provocations that threaten the core interests of our security will regret what they have done in a way they have not regretted anything for a long time," he warned.

"But I hope that no one will think about crossing the 'red line' with regard to Russia," he said. "We ourselves will determine in each specific case where it will be drawn."

The next day, a week after Biden and Putin's phone call, Russian defense minister Sergei Shoigu announced that Russian troop units would withdraw from the Ukraine border by May 1. Russian media, however, reported that weapons and equipment, including tanks, artillery, trucks and armored vehicles, would remain at "training grounds" along the land border with Ukraine in preparation for the joint Russian-Belarusian Zapad 2021 exercise scheduled for the coming fall.

Russia also permanently relocated large troop units to Crimea, meaning that tens of thousands of troops would not withdraw at all.

By mid-May there were still at least 80,000 troops near the border. Ukraine's minister of foreign affairs Dmytro Kuleba warned publicly that Russia's so-called withdrawal was not what it seemed.

"What is happening cannot be called a withdrawal of troops," Kuleba said publicly. "The threat has not passed.

"What we are seeing today is the withdrawal of troops without a withdrawal of troops," Kuleba said.

NATO's Special Operations adviser to Ukraine, U.S. Major General Michael Repass, was also wary of the supposed withdrawal.

"They have retained a rather lethal force in the region and have only pulled back some forces," Repass said.

"That tells me they may want to come back later when timing and circumstances are more advantageous to Russia," he said. "This will happen again."

Ukraine's president Zelensky invited Putin to meet in the Donbas region of Ukraine to discuss peace. Putin responded that Zelensky ought to come to Moscow, a not so thinly veiled threat.

FIVE

◆ ◆

Retired Army Lieutenant General Keith Kellogg, a loyal Trump adviser and national security adviser to Vice President Mike Pence, had left the White House on January 20, 2021, and not lost any sleep over Ukraine.

"When we left the administration, Ukraine was not on the real problem list," Kellogg said. "You had Iran, which was on the problem list. You still had North Korea. You had China because of what had happened with Covid. But Ukraine wasn't there."

Putin, Kellogg believed, had been far too concerned about the coronavirus—about contracting it himself and about his small circle of loyalist advisers contracting it.

President Trump had secretly sent Putin a bunch of Abbott Point of Care Covid test machines for his personal use as the virus spread rapidly through Russia.

"Please don't tell anybody you sent these to me," Putin said to Trump.

"I don't care," Trump replied. "Fine."

"No, no," Putin said. "I don't want you to tell anybody because people will get mad at you, not me. They don't care about me."

"Ukraine wasn't on the top of his hit list at all," Kellogg repeated. Trump's national security advisers had seen no indications that Russia was preparing for aggression in Ukraine.

Zelensky, who became president in 2019, was a new guy on the political scene. Trump was still trying to feel Zelensky out. So was Putin, Kellogg believed.

"To him, Putin, Trump was an unknown," Kellogg said. "Hell, we didn't know how Trump would react at times.

"Trump was basically Jekyll and Hyde."

SIX

President Biden and President Putin met at Villa La Grange, an 18th-century French-style manor house on the shores of Lake Geneva in Switzerland, on June 16, 2021.

"Mr. President, I'd like to thank you for your initiative to meet today," Putin said to Biden as they took their assigned seats in the library in front of floor-to-ceiling shelves lined with leather-bound books. A large globe stood prominently between them.

"It's always better to meet face-to-face," Biden said. He was surprised, and pleased, that Putin, who usually liked to make world leaders wait, had arrived on time. Putin had been 45 minutes late to his first formal meeting with Trump.

Secretary of State Antony Blinken and Foreign Minister Sergey Lavrov joined the two leaders. Trump had not allowed advisers to be in the room during his meeting with Putin in Helsinki, only their interpreters. On another occasion, Trump even insisted on confiscating his interpreter's notes after a meeting with Putin in Germany.

Unlike Trump's secretive, free-wheeling discussions with the Russian president, Biden's meeting with Putin was highly scripted.

Top of Biden's agenda was cybersecurity. A recent attack by Russian cybercriminals on Colonial Pipeline had disrupted the fuel supply to almost half of the East Coast. Another attack had temporarily shut down JBS, America's biggest meat supplier, until JBS paid an $11 million ransom.

"Put yourself in my shoes," Biden said. "I mean, with the attacks on our infrastructure. Imagine if something happened to your oil infrastructure . . ."

"It would matter," Putin replied.

"Why did you leave Afghanistan?" Putin, the black belt judo

master, asked Biden in an attempt to unbalance him. Trump had promised the Taliban all U.S. troops would withdraw by May 1.

"Why did you leave?" Biden taunted back, a reference to the Soviet Union's embarrassing withdrawal from Afghanistan in 1989, after 10 years of occupation.

Afghanistan, Biden said, is "the graveyard of empires."

Curiously, Ukraine was barely a footnote in the conversation. Later, some would wonder if the failure to focus on it was a colossal mistake.

The conversation about Ukraine was like dozens before: U.S. talking points versus Russian talking points.

Presidents Putin and Biden agreed to hold separate press conferences after the meeting—the approach recommended by Biden's national security advisers and Russia experts who wanted to see what Putin had to say before Biden responded. Trump's advisers had made a similar recommendation, but Trump had disregarded it.

Secretary Blinken and State Department spokesperson Ned Price watched Putin's press conference from Blinken's hotel room suite at the InterContinental in Geneva. Price, a former CIA analyst, had left the CIA in 2017 because he did not want to work for Trump.

Putin, who rarely traveled beyond Russia's borders, especially since the coronavirus pandemic, stood at a podium adorned with the Russian crest in a nondescript conference room. This was his first international trip in 17 months since January 2020. Even more unusual was the Russian president appearing before Western journalists.

Sitting at a distance from Putin in spaced-out chairs, nearly all the journalists wore masks, making it clear the coronavirus was still a top concern for the Russian president.

"Did you commit in these meetings to stop threatening Ukraine?" a reporter asked the Russian president.

Putin gave an accusatory answer, couching Russia's buildup of 100,000 troops as regular military exercises.

"We are not bringing our equipment and personnel closer to the state borders of the United States of America when we conduct our exercises. Unfortunately, this is what our U.S. partners are doing. So, the Russian side, not the American side, should be concerned about this," Putin said.

NATO had conducted annual military exercises in May, involving some 28,000 personnel from 26 countries. The exercises were spread across a dozen European countries.

Putin took another jab. "People, including leaders of various organizations, are killed in American cities every day," he said. "You can barely say a word there before you are shot in the face or the back, regardless of who is nearby, children or other adults.

"The CIA prisons that were opened in many countries, including Europe, where they subjected people to torture—what is this? Is this respect for human rights? I don't think so, do you?

"The U.S. concerns regarding militarization are absolutely groundless," Putin said.

It was the classic deflection tactic that Biden had been wary of.

When asked about Biden, the Russian president unleashed a carefully calibrated charm offensive.

"He recalled some things about his family," Putin said of Biden. Then gently sticking the knife in, "They do not seem to be directly related to the subject, but they still show the level and quality of his moral values. That was quite endearing, and I did feel like we generally spoke the same language.

"This does not mean we have to peek into each other's souls, look into each other's eyes and swear eternal love and friendship— not at all. We defend the interests of our countries, our peoples, and our relations are always primarily pragmatic in nature."

Another reporter asked, "Do you consider it possible at this stage to reach a new phase in bilateral relations?"

"You know," Putin said, "Leo Tolstoy said once, there is no happiness in life, only flashes of it—cherish them. I believe there cannot be family trust in this situation, but I think we have seen flashes of it."

The Russian president's press conference had run for just under an hour.

Blinken and Ned Price were surprised that Putin didn't come out swinging. He sounded many of the right tones, all the sorts of things that Biden wanted to hear. He was smooth, relaxed, articulate and conveying astonishing self-confidence.

Putin gave the impression that maybe the Russians are seeking to do what we are seeking to do, Price said, build a relationship that is stable and predictable.

"Let's see how this plays out," Blinken said. "This is about testing the proposition. We won't know the results of that test for six months or a year because it's not so much what's said in the moment but how it's acted upon.

"Too soon to tell," Blinken said, quoting, as he often did, what Henry Kissinger was told about the French Revolution by Chinese premier Zhou Enlai.

Biden followed with his own press conference outdoors, the sun shining on Lake Geneva in the background.

"I communicated the United States' unwavering commitment to the sovereignty and territorial integrity of Ukraine," Biden said.

"I think the last thing he wants now is a Cold War," Biden said of Putin. "He still, I believe, is concerned about being quote, 'encircled.' He is still concerned that we, in fact, are looking to take him down, et cetera. He still has those concerns, but I don't think they are the driving force as to the kind of relationship he's looking for with the United States."

On the plane, Biden told Blinken he came away with a better understanding of Putin. This was a man Biden had known for a long time from a distance but who he had not spent much time in a room with. Biden's sense of the relationship was measured. He was not optimistic Putin would change his behavior, or Russia's. "This is going to be hard," Biden concluded.

On Fox News, Trump declared that Biden's summit with Putin was "a good day for Russia."

"I don't see what we got out of it," Trump said to Fox News anchor Sean Hannity. "We didn't get anything. We gave a very big stage to Russia, and we got nothing."

In the White House the mood had lifted. There was a sense they had dodged a bullet from Russia on Ukraine.

"Whatever Putin was thinking in April about Ukraine, he's at least for some time set it aside," Sullivan said.

As Russia's aggressive rhetoric tamped down, Sullivan and his deputy Finer turned their focus to other things, namely the withdrawal from Afghanistan.

But for Sullivan, a central question remained. Was Chekhov's gun still on the wall?

SEVEN

A lmost six months into Biden's presidency, Trump continued to claim that the 2020 election had been rigged and stolen from him. There was zero credible evidence to support this claim, but Trump only needed people to believe him.

Polls showed that 53 percent of Republicans believed Trump to be the "true president" even though Biden sat in the Oval Office.

During my interview with Trump before the 2016 election, he told me, "Real power is, I don't even want to use the word, *fear*."

Now Trump had tapped into another real power: instilling doubt.

"I wouldn't be surprised if they found thousands and thousands and thousands of votes," Trump yelled to a crowd at Mar-a-Lago, his lavish estate in Palm Beach, Florida. "This was a rigged election, everybody knows it!"

Once audits of the election counts were completed in key states like Georgia, Wisconsin and Arizona this summer, Trump said he would make his return to the Oval Office. He believed if he could get a swing state to find that he had actually won the state then all the other states he lost would have to begin probes.

"If a thief robs a jewelry store of all of its diamonds, the diamonds must be returned," Trump said in a statement in May, referring to the 2020 election.

But more than 60 court cases, dozens of investigations, audits and ballot recounts in numerous states found no evidence of widespread fraud. Again and again the validity of the 2020 election result was upheld.

Trump ignored the findings and claimed massive fraud would materialize.

Prominent Republican election lawyer Benjamin Ginsberg later testified to the House Committee investigating the January 6 attack on the Capitol that "in no instance" did a court find that Trump's allegations of fraud were real.

Senator Lindsey Graham blamed Mar-a-Lago for Trump's inability to put the results of 2020 behind him.

"It's just, it's the culture," Graham told colleagues. "It's the attitude down in Mar-a-Lago of all the people that go. You know, all the people he hangs around with down there. They constantly feed this narrative.

"He keeps talking about Arizona," Graham said, where an audit was still underway. "You know, he lost Arizona because he beat on John McCain and just went too far." The late senator John McCain of Arizona had been a prisoner of war in Vietnam and Republican nominee for president in the 2008 election.

"He thinks he lost because of all these bizarre conspiracies," Graham said. "He didn't.

"Biden won fair and square," Graham added. "Trump doesn't like to hear that."

Graham was focused on the 2022 political races where Republicans needed to put their best candidates forward to take back the House and Senate majorities.

"There are very few Republicans that can get out of the whirlwind of dealing with Trump to think ahead," Graham said. "Wishing Donald Trump away is not a viable strategy. Donald Trump's not going away. There are millions of people in the Republican Party who believe in him, and the goal is to try to take the magic he has with our base and make it 'Trump Plus.'

"Once you get in a general election if you repeat some of the things that the president's saying, you don't have a snowball's chance in hell," Graham said. "Some of our candidates are going to have to break from Trump on certain issues to get the 'plus' part."

Graham rejected the notion that Trump was a wound that could not heal in the Republican Party.

"Trump represents a real part of the American family," Graham said. "It's not a wound. It's part of who we are."

But Trump would not, or could not, let his "stolen election" mantra go. In June 2021, the former president pushed Republicans to support reinstating him as president. He told his aides he would move back into the White House by August, a date QAnon conspiracy theorists had latched on to in online forums.

"He had an army. An army for Trump. He wants that back," Brad Parscale, Trump's former campaign manager, said privately in July. "I don't think he sees it as a comeback. He sees it as vengeance."

Trump phoned Republican representative for Alabama Mo Brooks, a staunch Trump supporter, and asked him to publicly call for a special election to reinstate him as president.

Brooks, who had supported the plan by Trump and conservative lawyer John Eastman to challenge the certification of Biden's win, pointed out that Joe Biden was president. Brooks said Biden's victory had been certified and there was no legal pathway for Trump to rescind it. The Constitution provided no mechanism to reinstate a president.

Trump was enraged. He later withdrew his endorsement of Brooks in the Alabama Senate race. Brooks lost in the Republican primary.

In the 2020 election, Trump received 74 million votes, more than any presidential candidate in history with the exception of Joe Biden, who won 81 million votes. Biden secured the Electoral College with 306 votes to Trump's 232.

Biden won the 2020 election, but six months in he was still in a battle for his own presidency.

EIGHT

A month after the Geneva summit, Putin placed another gun on the table.

In a starkly personal and bellicose 5,000-word diatribe published on July 12, 2021, Putin argued Ukraine had never existed as an independent country.

National Security Adviser Jake Sullivan read the Russian president's manifesto as a declaration of the inner Putin, who he was and what he wanted to do.

"Russians and Ukrainians are one people—a single whole," Putin began. "Russians, Ukrainians and Belarusians are all descendants of Ancient Rus, which was the largest state in Europe." And since the 9th century, he continued, Kyiv was considered "the mother of all Russian cities."

"The formation of an ethnically pure Ukrainian state," Putin said, "is comparable in its consequences to the use of weapons of mass destruction against us."

His tone self-righteous and academic, Putin erased the existence of Ukraine as a separate country, a people with their own history, beliefs, culture and language.

"Therefore, modern Ukraine is entirely the product of the Soviet era. We know and remember well that it was shaped—for a significant part—on the lands of historical Russia," Putin said. "Russia was robbed."

When Sullivan read through Putin's manifesto his first thought was "Covid."

U.S. intelligence reporting showed that during the pandemic, Putin had been changed by intense and prolonged isolation. He had surrounded himself with a small coterie of trusted people of similar nationalistic views who became almost a feedback loop. Those who wanted to see him in person had to quarantine for weeks. He was physically and metaphorically separated from Russian society for nearly three years.

One of the central figures in Putin's inner circle was Yury Kovalchuk, a Russian billionaire reputed to be Putin's personal banker. He had known Putin since the 1990s and appeared to share the messianic worldview that Putin espoused in his manifesto.

Another Putin confidant was Father Tikhon, an Orthodox priest with a similarly imperialistic view of Russia. Then there were the Rotenberg billionaire brothers—Arkady Rotenberg and Boris Rotenberg, who owned the largest construction company for gas pipelines in Russia.

Other people learned Irish step dancing in quarantine, Jake Sullivan joked, but Putin went deep into Russian history.

Sullivan had heard that during a phone call between Putin and German chancellor Angela Merkel, Putin said you wouldn't believe the stuff that I've been finding in the Russian archives.

It was clear to Merkel that Putin had spent a lot of his time in isolation just digging around in the archives, taking things out, studying ancient maps.

Taking Ukraine had become kind of a fever dream during his Covid isolation. But the fever didn't pass. It didn't break.

Sullivan and his deputy Jon Finer took the manifesto seriously, but it didn't strike them as an alarm bell or a declaration of war. More than anything they viewed it as typical Putin. The Russian leader was known for his long philosophical rants, historical fabrications, and absolute refusal to acknowledge Ukraine's independent existence. But still it was puzzling and unsettling for its intensity. A topic of curiosity and even disgust.

Sullivan had spent the last year reading up on Russian history and trying to understand Putin's almost neurotic obsession with Ukraine. The formation of Russia, the deeply rooted grievances, the chip on Putin's shoulder, the relationship with Europe, with NATO, the sense of needing central control, the Mongols taking Moscow in the mid-13th century, Putin's desire to be a messiah in Russian history like Peter the Great, Catherine the Great. All of it.

After reading Putin's manifesto, National Security Council Russia director Eric Green found it unusual for a sitting Russian president to go into such depth. Was Putin just trying to get something off his chest? Was this something he wanted to use as an exercise or a way of explaining Russia's view of things? Or would Putin's essay actually inform Russia's actions?

"I think it speaks to Putin's disillusionment with the Ukrainian government and his attempt to start to delegitimize it," Green said. "Putin wants his prophecy about Ukraine being a failed state, he wants that to come true."

"Ukraine used to possess great potential," Putin said in his essay. "Step by step, Ukraine was dragged into a dangerous geopolitical game aimed at turning Ukraine into a barrier between Europe and Russia, a springboard against Russia."

The biggest country in Europe, Ukraine was also an important buffer between Russia and Europe.

Putin called Ukraine's leaders "neo-Nazis"—President Zelensky was Jewish—and leveled a long list of accusations against them and the West for pursuing an "anti-Russia project."

"We will never allow our historical territories and people close to us living there to be used against Russia," Putin warned. "And to those who will undertake such an attempt, I would like to say this way they will destroy their own country."

For CIA director Bill Burns, who had served as ambassador to Moscow from 2005 to 2008, the manifesto was reminiscent of many of his conversations with Putin over the years. "There was nothing really new in it," Burns believed. Some of it is dressing up a conviction which is mostly at its core about power and what Russia believes it is entitled to do, he said. Then you dress it up with a lot of history—selectively.

Over in the Pentagon, Undersecretary for Defense Colin Kahl

had read intelligence that Putin actually believed the things he had written—that Ukraine is not a real country and Ukrainians are all just Russians.

"Putin was not a fan of the Soviet Union," Kahl said, "but he still saw the collapse of the Soviet Union as the biggest crime of the 20th century and believed that the Russians had been serially stabbed in the back since then."

Kahl saw the essay as another showcase of Putin's imperial ambition. "He dreams of reconstituting a Russian empire and there is no Russian empire that doesn't include Ukraine," he said.

"It's always weird to read things like that as an American," Kahl added, "because our history doesn't go back very far. So the notion that countries would give a shit about what happened 9,000 years ago or whatever or, you know, 2,000 years ago or 1,000. Americans don't think like that."

NINE

◆———◆

In Washington, Biden was also preoccupied with an increasingly tenuous withdrawal of American troops from Afghanistan, a fulfillment of Biden's campaign promise to end the 20-year war.

It was a cornerstone belief of Biden's foreign policy that America's presence in Afghanistan was a classic case of mission creep. Too many troops for an unclear purpose.

A decade earlier while vice president, Biden had urged President Obama not to add another 30,000 U.S. troops to Afghanistan despite U.S. military insistence.

Biden had cut short his family vacation in Nantucket to plead his case to Obama directly. "Listen to me, boss," Biden said. "Maybe I've been around this town for too long, but one thing I know is when these generals are trying to box in a new president." He leaned in toward Obama and stage-whispered, "Don't let them jam you."

Obama had been rolled and fed "bullshit" by his military generals, who in Biden's view had executed a tragic power play against a young, inexperienced president.

The initial U.S. invasion of Afghanistan in 2001 had been intended to destroy Osama bin Laden's Al Qaeda terrorist group responsible for the 9/11 attacks in New York and Washington, D.C. But once Al Qaeda had effectively been driven from Afghanistan, the mission had expanded into nation-building. Mission creep, Biden said, and "fucking illogical."

Biden's primary argument was that the mission had shifted from its original intent and it was unclear what the U.S. mission was now.

Also hanging over Biden was a deal Trump had signed with the

Taliban in February 2020 promising to withdraw American troops by May 2021. The Taliban agreed not to attack American forces if they withdrew by May 1, 2021.

In his first months as president, Biden directed Sullivan to run a full interagency review on withdrawing from Afghanistan.

"I absolutely want to hear arguments to the contrary," Biden told Sullivan, "and I'm going to keep an open mind about this because if there is a compelling reason to stay, I will certainly consider it and listen to it." A presidential promise of open-mindedness was often thwarted by presidential will.

The options presented to Biden were to execute a full orderly withdrawal of all remaining troops as quickly and safely as possible; undertake a slow, gated withdrawal in three or four stages to allow time and space for political negotiations; or approve an indefinite U.S. troop presence in Afghanistan.

If the U.S. stayed, the intelligence forecast was that the Taliban would resume their attacks. Should that happen, Biden reasoned that he inevitably would be asked to send more troops.

"If we have 3,000 troops there and they're attacked, you guys"—he pointed to Defense Secretary Austin and Chairman of the Joint Chiefs Mark Milley—"will come in and say okay, we need 5,000 more." And they would be off to the races.

Biden knew a troop presence became a magnet for more troops because the military leaders naturally would want to protect their own force.

The president was clear: He wanted out.

"Don't compare me to the Almighty," Biden said to Blinken, "compare me to the alternative."

Sullivan did not think Biden anguished over the decision. The president seemed at peace with his choice.

President Biden had given a 16-minute address to the nation on April 14. Instead of the high drama of an evening Oval Office address, he spoke from the Treaty Room in the afternoon, the same

setting President George W. Bush had used in 2001 to launch the
U.S. military operation in Afghanistan.

"I'm now the fourth United States president to preside over
American troop presence in Afghanistan: two Republicans, two
Democrats," he said. "I will not pass this responsibility on to a
fifth.

"For the past 12 years, ever since I became vice president, I've
carried with me a card that reminds me of the exact number of
American troops killed in Iraq and Afghanistan.

"As of this day, 2,448 U.S. troops and personnel have died in
our Afghanistan conflicts, 20,722 have been wounded.

"It's time to end the forever war," he said.

In an unusual public display, Biden then visited Arlington National Cemetery and walked alone through Section 60 where the
dead from Afghanistan and Iraq are buried.

"I have trouble these days even showing up at a cemetery and
not thinking of my son Beau," Biden said of his oldest son, who
had died of a brain tumor in 2015 at the age of 46. Beau, an Army
officer and lawyer, had received a Bronze Star for his military service in Iraq and served two terms as Delaware's attorney general.
The son who had been following his father's path into politics.
Biden turned to the hundreds of white tombstones, extended his
arms, and said, "Look at them all."

Biden was immediately blasted for the decision to withdraw.
He had not expected to see on television and in the newspapers so
much critical commentary. People who had been clamoring to end
the longest war were now fixated on the future of various groups
in Afghanistan, including women and girls.

"I do expect a civil war that will be brutal, bloody and have all
the terrible manifestations of uncivil war," retired General David
Petraeus said publicly. Petraeus had commanded U.S. forces in Afghanistan and been the modern architect of the counterinsurgency
strategy Biden loathed. "We have an administration that talks
about bringing back support for democracy and human rights.
Well, so much for that," Petraeus said.

Former president George W. Bush, in a rare public comment, said Biden's decision to withdraw was a mistake. "I'm afraid Afghan women and girls are going to suffer unspeakable harm."

Biden was standing by the Resolute Desk taking in the avalanche of criticism. Blinken could see that the president was stung by it.

The president lightly tapped the desk. "Yeah," Biden said, "the buck really does stop here."

The troop withdrawal was one of the rare agreements between Biden and his predecessor, Donald Trump, who continued to claim the election was stolen. In Wellington, Ohio, on June 26, 2021, at his first campaign rally since leaving office, Trump gloated that he was responsible for bringing the American troops home because Biden could not stop the process he had started through his deal with the Taliban.

"All the troops are coming back home," Trump said. "They [the Biden administration] couldn't stop the process. 21 years is enough, don't we think? 21 years.

"It's a shame," Trump said, "21 years, by a government that wouldn't last. The only way they last is if we're there. What are we going to say? We'll stay for another 21 years, then we'll stay for another 50. The whole thing is ridiculous. . . . We're bringing troops back home from Afghanistan."

Despite more than 50 planning meetings, the Biden administration's withdrawal from Afghanistan spiraled into devastating chaos. They had failed to anticipate contingencies and plan for the worst-case scenarios. When they did plan, it was too late.

On July 6 the remaining U.S. forces secretly withdrew in the dark of night from Bagram Air Base, an hour from Kabul and the largest airstrip in Afghanistan. Bagram at one time had hosted up to 100,000 U.S. soldiers. This left the American embassy in Kabul still operating with more than 1,400 Americans protected by just 650 marines and soldiers.

If Kabul fell to the Taliban, the exit from Bagram shut off the only avenue for a possible evacuation of noncombatants, many of whom the U.S. promised to protect after years of service.

On July 23, Biden spoke to Afghanistan president Ashraf Ghani about the rapidly deteriorating situation, and pressed him to change the worldwide perception that the fight against the Taliban was going poorly.

"You clearly have the best military, you have 300,000 well-armed forces versus 70–80,000 [Taliban] and they're clearly capable of fighting well," Biden said.

"Mr. President," Ghani said, "we are facing a full-scale invasion, composed of Taliban, full Pakistani planning and logistical support, and at least 10–15,000 international terrorists."

The Taliban surge swept through the country like a tidal wave, with district after district falling with shocking speed, taking Biden and his administration by surprise. Afghan forces offered little resistance and in some instances simply laid down their weapons.

As the Taliban closed in on Kabul, Secretary of State Blinken spoke to President Ghani on the phone on August 14. Ghani declared defiantly that he would defend Afghanistan until the end. The next day Ghani was in the United Arab Emirates. He had fled.

Kabul fell swiftly and spectacularly. Taliban fighters took control of the Presidential Palace and posed for photographs around Ghani's desk holding rifles.

Thousands of desperate Afghan civilians swarmed the tarmac at Kabul International Airport. People climbed onto the wings of U.S. evacuation planes as they took off, some tumbling to their deaths.

In an about-face, Trump called on Biden to "resign in disgrace for what he has allowed to happen in Afghanistan" and criticized Biden for his handling of Covid, the southern border and the economy. "It shouldn't be a big deal because he wasn't elected legitimately in the first place," Trump added, persisting with his unsupported mantra that the election had been stolen from him.

President Biden blamed the Afghan government for the situation. In a speech on August 16 from the East Room, Biden said, "I do not regret my decision to end America's warfighting in Afghanistan.

"The truth is," he said, "this did unfold more quickly than we had anticipated. So what's happened? Afghanistan political leaders gave up and fled the country. The Afghan military collapsed, sometimes without trying to fight.

"If anything, the developments of the past week reinforced that ending U.S. military involvement in Afghanistan now was the right decision," Biden added.

Ten days later on August 26, an Islamic State (ISIS) suicide bombing at Abbey Gate on the outskirts of the airport killed more than 170 people, including 13 American servicemembers, marking it one of the deadliest days for U.S. forces in the last decade of the 20-year war.

On August 29 the U.S. conducted a drone strike in Kabul targeting a suspected ISIS operative with a car full of explosives. Instead, in another tragic mistake, they killed 10 civilians, including a longtime aid worker for the United States and seven children.

After evacuating more than 120,000 people in the final few days, on August 31, 2021, Biden announced the end of "the longest war in American history."

His speech, which hailed the "extraordinary success of this mission," fell flat. No language could disguise or dress up the failure of the withdrawal. Kabul had fallen in 11 days to the Taliban. Thirteen American soldiers had been killed.

"There are those who would say we should have stayed indefinitely for years on end," Biden said. "Why don't we just keep doing what we were doing? Why did we have to change anything?"

Biden shifted blame onto Trump.

"The fact is: Everything had changed. My predecessor had made a deal with the Taliban. When I came into office, we faced a deadline—May 1. The Taliban onslaught was coming.

"To those asking for a third decade of war in Afghanistan, I ask: What is the vital national interest? In my view, we only have one: to make sure Afghanistan can never be used again to launch an attack on our homeland.

"The fundamental obligation of a President, in my opinion, is to defend and protect America—not against threats of 2001, but against threats of 2021 and tomorrow.

"I give you my word," Biden concluded. "With all of my heart, I believe this is the right decision, a wise decision, and the best decision for America."

The calamitous withdrawal hammered Biden and his principal advisers. Critics in op-ed pieces and on television leveled blame on National Security Adviser Sullivan, calling for his resignation. And this time, it wasn't just coming from Republicans.

"The national security adviser has two jobs. As the name suggests, they are the last and ideally closest counselor to the president in the Situation Room," former Obama adviser Brett Bruen said in *USA Today*.

"Their second duty is to translate the commander in chief's decisions and direction into practical policies. Sometimes that requires speaking truth to power. On all of these scores, the current occupant of the office appears to have failed.

"President Biden needs to fire his national security adviser and several other senior leaders who oversaw the botched execution of our withdrawal from Afghanistan," Bruen said.

Sullivan, who was accustomed to laudatory reviews of his competence and performance, was shell-shocked. "All of our nerves had been exposed to sunlight and frayed and raw and burned," he said, especially his.

Chairman of the Joint Chiefs Mark Milley and Vice Admiral Frank Whitworth, a three-star career Navy intelligence official and Milley's J2—the top military intelligence adviser in the Pentagon—pored over the second-order and third-order effects of the withdrawal to see what threats could be ahead.

Milley and Whitworth were close. They had served together in Afghanistan. When Trump appointed General Milley to be his next chairman of the Joint Chiefs, Admiral Whitworth had spent every day in the run-up briefing Milley to take over the role.

When Admiral Whitworth was ready to move from his two-star role into a three-star position, Milley stepped in and personally petitioned the Pentagon to make the J2 intelligence post into a three-star role so General Milley could keep Whitworth alongside him.

Now both felt the sting of Kabul's swift fall. For months they had chewed on tabletop exercises, tweaking preparations, and been briefed on the latest intelligence.

They had seen a degradation in the ability of the Afghans to defend themselves, but not how swiftly the collapse would be.

"To me it was a cascading event that was much faster than I had anticipated," Whitworth said frankly. He had been on a family holiday in Hawaii when the first province fell to the Taliban, another province an hour later and then a third.

"I could see what was happening," he said. He wasn't in a SCIF, a sensitive compartmented information facility, but sent a note to the Pentagon: "Get our folks to safety." They needed to speed up the withdrawal.

His holiday was over. Admiral Whitworth was in Washington, D.C., standing beside Chairman Milley and Defense Secretary Austin when the last plane left Afghanistan. A trio who had served together in Afghanistan all those years before.

"I'll treasure forever our being there together as we finally got our last people out," Admiral Whitworth said. "Speed is what keeps Americans alive and so speed had to be employed."

He believed the military had done the best job they could in a worst-case scenario.

"I don't think anyone in uniform, in the intelligence community could say we knew it was going to fall in 10 to 14 days," Admiral Whitworth lamented. "I personally think corruption and the power of social media are the two biggest X factors."

The real culprit was the untamed, impulsive desire to insert U.S. troops into a foreign country believing they were a fix and ignoring the lessons of Vietnam.

TEN

In Maidan Square at the center of Ukraine's capital, Kyiv, British Navy Admiral Tim Woods held his two-year-old daughter up to see the Ukrainian jets flying low overhead. It was August 24, 2021, the 30th anniversary of Ukraine's independence from the Soviet Union. President Zelensky, who previously had criticized military parades, decided it was time to send Putin a message.

The parade displayed Ukraine's growing military power. Upgraded battle tanks, missiles and air defense systems rolled through the main street. Appearing near the end of the parade was the centerpiece, their new Bayraktar TB2—a sophisticated attack drone with a four-lane-wide wingspan unlike any in the Russian arsenal—recently purchased from Turkey. Ukrainian soldiers marched in uniform. Army representatives from partner countries like the United States, Great Britain and Poland also joined the parade.

An emotional President Zelensky had tears in his eyes as he addressed the crowd in a speech that celebrated the power of Ukraine's independence and promised an independent future.

"New tanks and helicopters with Ukrainian blades are being built for the army this year," Zelensky said. He said Ukraine was "reviving its naval fleet, naval bases" and adopting "a missile program for 10 years.

"Such a country becomes a NATO partner with enhanced opportunities," Zelensky promised his people. NATO membership for Ukraine was a red line for Russia with its vast 1,200-mile land border.

As Ukraine celebrated its independence and its military advancement, Woods believed Putin saw a country moving further away from Russia's imperial grip.

"Putin does his numbers," Woods said. "He saw a closing window."

A fluent Russian speaker, Rear Admiral Woods had been part of the United Kingdom's military training mission in Ukraine since 2018—helping to transition Ukraine's military into a NATO-standard force and address corruption in Ukraine's Ministry of Defense. He lived in Kyiv with his wife, a British Intelligence officer who was working to strengthen Ukraine's ability to defend against Russian hybrid or gray-zone warfare—including cyber, disinformation, Russian bribery and psychological warfare.

His family were intimately familiar with the Russian Intelligence Service psychological games. On a number of occasions they had uninvited guests at their apartment in Kyiv. One evening, their young daughter had strewn big pieces of a children's floor puzzle across the floor of their play room. His wife, exhausted, had left the mess and gone to bed. The next morning she came out to find the puzzle, about 30 pieces, had been beautifully completed.

"Pretty standard of Russian intelligence services," Woods said. "They want to scare you: We can do this anytime we want." There were other occasions they found candelabras turned upside down.

"We weren't fazed by it," Woods said. "We were quite amused."

A friend of theirs had left boots out one night and the next morning all of the laces had been strung the opposite way round so the laces were coming out the bottom of the boots.

"We just assumed as well that the apartment was wired for sound and video, that any conversation there was recorded," Woods said.

Woods had traveled out to the border with Ukrainian colleagues to see the Russian buildup in March 2021. While Russian defense minister Shoigu had withdrawn the troops, the Russian equipment, "the kit," had remained sitting there.

Now, in late August, Woods noticed the kit was starting to build up again.

ELEVEN

"**C**hairman, you're not going to believe what I'm about to show you," said Admiral Frank Whitworth, bursting into General Milley's office one morning a few weeks after the Afghanistan withdrawal.

"I think we've got some indications that could change the rest of, certainly your chairmanship," he said.

New pieces of intelligence were coming in that suggested Russia was planning a large-scale military attack on Ukraine. The warning was not singular but multifaceted.

Milley and Whitworth were thunderstruck.

"And by a nuclear nation," Admiral Whitworth said. "You're talking about by a nuclear nation. Conquest by a nuclear nation."

In the President's Daily Brief every morning Biden was presented with an extraordinary intelligence trove on what the Russians were visibly doing with their military forces, but also what the Russians were talking and thinking about doing with those forces.

Putin's ultimate intentions remained unclear. There was an unsettling sense of déjà vu. Biden had been vice president and Blinken was President Obama's deputy national security adviser when Russian forces swiftly annexed Crimea in southern Ukraine and seized a portion of the Donbas in 2014. Obama and their team had failed to spot Putin's brazen land grab for what it was and adequately push back on it in time. It had been an easy win for Putin, with few lasting negative ramifications for Russia.

Tony Blinken, 5-foot-10 with a neat wave of once brown, but now gray, hair had been Biden's trusted foreign policy adviser and close friend for 20 years. They had spent countless hours work-shopping foreign policy: in the Senate, on international trips, in the vice president's office, in the White House Situation Room, and over joint family dinners, forming a genuine bond.

Blinken did not want to believe what the Russians were contemplating could be serious. But Biden did not want to be surprised by Putin again. Surprise was a weapon that gave an immediate battle-field advantage to the aggressor. The president didn't want to start out on the back foot this time.

Biden told his principals, including Sullivan, Blinken, Austin and Milley, that his first priority was avoiding a direct conflict with Russia. Their strategy, he said, would have two prongs: Work over-time to try to *prevent* some sort of Russian invasion of Ukraine. Work equally hard to *prepare* for it.

He told them their task was prepare us, prepare Ukraine and prepare the allies. What does Ukraine need to defend itself? He did not want anything that might be a replay of the Afghanistan disaster.

Biden was clear that whatever the U.S. did for Ukraine, it would do bilaterally with Ukraine, not through NATO. Putin saw NATO as an absolute, direct threat to Russia. Ukraine's desire to join, en-shrined in its constitution, was a constant threat to Putin. The U.S. had to be careful to not antagonize tensions and speed up Putin's preparations to attack Ukraine.

Less than two weeks after the fall of Kabul, on August 27, Biden authorized an additional $60 million defense package for Ukraine. Biden, Sullivan and Blinken wanted to get weapons delivered to Ukraine quickly and as quietly as possible.

They did not make a big fuss about it. They didn't want head-lines to play into Putin's propaganda machine. Putin was continu-ing to slander Ukraine's president Zelensky as a Nazi and continued to claim that Russia was being threatened by NATO.

The package included Javelins, the world's best shoulder-fired anti-armor missile that automatically guides itself to the target after launch, allowing a gunner to take cover. Called a "fire and forget" weapon, it can be operated by a single person and destroy tanks and other battle armor.

The Javelin, configured with a high-explosive anti-tank (HEAT) warhead, has a range of one to two miles and climbs high over a target enemy tank and dives down to strike where the armor is weakest.

Each Javelin launch system with one missile costs about $200,000, which the Pentagon helpfully noted is about the cost of a Ferrari Roma automobile.

In a brief notification to Congress, the Biden administration said the security assistance package for Ukraine was necessary because of a "major increase in Russian military activity along its border" and because of mortar attacks, cease-fire violations and other provocations.

TWELVE

O n September 1, 2021, President Biden welcomed Ukraine's president Volodymyr Zelensky to the White House for the first time. Zelensky, formerly an actor and comedian, had won Ukraine's 2019 presidential election in a historic landslide over incumbent president and billionaire Petro Poroshenko, whom Biden had counseled when he was vice president. Zelensky won a crushing 73.17 percent of the vote, compared with 24.5 percent for Poroshenko.

Elected at age 41, Zelensky came into office with no political experience—the complete contrast to Joe Biden. Zelensky had owned a successful television production company Kvartal 95, and become a household celebrity playing the fictional president of Ukraine in a hugely popular television series *Servant of the People*, a political satire that aired from 2015 to 2019.

In the TV show, Zelensky's character, a high school history teacher, is accidentally elected president after his rant about government corruption goes viral on the internet. His approval ratings as the actual president, however, had sunk to an abysmal 38 percent in the spring of 2021.

Zelensky's surprising arrival on the political stage in many ways mirrored that of his fictional character. Zelensky was an outsider with no political acumen but he embodied the role of an everyman.

In a dark slim-fitted suit and polished shoes, Zelensky had walked to the Rada—the Ukrainian parliament building in Kyiv—on May 20, 2019, waving, shaking hands and taking selfies with supporters before being sworn in as president.

"Dear Ukrainians," Zelensky said in his inauguration address. "After my election win, my six-year-old son said: 'Dad, they say on

TV that Zelensky is the president. . . . So, it means that I am the President too?!' At the time, it sounded funny, but later I realized that it was true. Because each of us is the president.

"From now on, each of us is responsible for the country that we leave to our children," Zelensky said. "Each of us, in his place, can do everything for the prosperity of Ukraine."

He raised his first priority: a cease-fire in the Donbas where Russian-backed separatists and Ukrainian forces had been fighting since Putin's 2014 invasion. "I have been often asked: What price are you ready to pay for the cease-fire? It's a strange question," Zelensky said. "What price are you ready to pay for the lives of your loved ones? I can assure that I'm ready to pay any price to stop the deaths of our heroes. I'm definitely not afraid to make difficult decisions and I'm ready to lose my fame, my ratings, and if need be without any hesitation, my position to bring peace, as long as we do not give up our territories.

"History is unfair," Zelensky added. "We are not the ones who have started this war. But we are the ones who have to finish it.

"I really do not want you to hang my portraits on your office walls. Because a president is not an icon and not an idol. A president is not a portrait. Hang pictures of your children. And before you make any decision, look into their eyes," he said.

"And finally," Zelensky concluded, "all my life I tried to do all I could so that Ukrainians laughed. That was my mission. Now I will do all I can so that Ukrainians at least do not cry anymore."

In Washington, D.C., however, Zelensky was not known for being the TV star who became president, but for the controversy surrounding President Trump's first impeachment trial.

During a July 25, 2019, call President Zelensky asked to purchase more Javelin antitank missiles from the United States. Trump replied, "I would like you to do us a favor though because our country has been through a lot."

Trump then asked Zelensky to investigate Joe Biden and his son

Hunter, saying "whatever you can do with the Attorney General would be great."

When I interviewed Trump at Mar-a-Lago, Florida, on December 30, 2019, about his impeachment, Trump said: "There's nobody that's tougher than me. Nobody's tougher than me. You asked me about impeachment. I'm under impeachment, and you said you just act like you just won the fucking race. Nixon was in a corner with his thumb in his mouth. Bill Clinton took it very, very hard. I just do things, okay? I do what I want."

I asked Trump if he thought the call with Zelensky had given his political opposition a sword.

"It's a perfect phone call!" Trump said. "I didn't give them a sword."

The phone call, Trump said, "talked about *us*. It talked about help *us*, comma, the country. Our country. And then I talked about see the attorney general.

"Let me just tell you about Zelensky," Trump added. "They never in a million years thought I was going to release the call, number one. Number two, they never in a million years thought that we had it transcribed. I want my calls transcribed."

Zelensky later told *Time* magazine journalist Simon Shuster that Trump had indeed blindsided him with the release of the transcript and it had destroyed his trust in Ukraine's allies. "On the question of who I trust," Zelensky said to Shuster for his book, *The Showman*, "I told you honestly: No one."

Zelensky told Shuster he felt like a pawn trying to avoid Ukraine getting crushed by great powers.

"I would never want Ukraine to be a piece on the map, on the chessboard of big global players, so that someone could toss us around, use us as cover, as part of some bargain," Zelensky said.

Trump's repeated claim that Ukraine was corrupt had also been a slap to Ukraine's reputation and economy as investors hesitated or pulled out.

"When we're giving vast amounts of money to a country, I think you have to say if they're corrupt, where is this money coming from?" Trump said during my interview with him in December 2019 about U.S. aid to Ukraine. "Why is it that there's such corruption when we're giving it? And you know, there's another thing that I also talk about. And I talk about why isn't Germany, France, the European nations who are much more affected by Ukraine than us, because Ukraine is like a massive wall. Think of it as a wall between Russia and Europe, okay?"

Trump continued, "I said, why isn't Germany? Why isn't France? Why aren't these other countries putting up money? Why is it always the foolish United States?"

Zelensky was, perhaps unsurprisingly, not invited to the Trump White House.

When Zelensky visited President Biden at the White House, he pressed Biden to help Ukraine get NATO membership, something Biden was not prepared to push in the short term.

Bill Burns, Biden's CIA director, had worked actively for years to tamp down any U.S. efforts to push Ukraine along a path to NATO.

When Burns was U.S. ambassador to Moscow in 2008 he had sent then–Secretary of State Condoleezza Rice a long personal email through secure channels.

"Ukrainian entry into NATO is the brightest of all redlines for the Russian elite (not just Putin). In more than two and a half years of conversations with key Russian players, from knuckle-draggers in the dark recesses of the Kremlin to Putin's sharpest liberal critics, I have yet to find anyone who views Ukraine in NATO as anything other than a direct challenge to Russian interests."

Even preliminary steps would be seen as "throwing down the strategic gauntlet," Burns said. "Today's Russia will respond. Russian-Ukrainian relations will go into a deep freeze.

"I can conceive of no grand package that would allow the Russians to swallow this pill quietly," Burns concluded.

THIRTEEN

In October 2021 Director of National Intelligence Avril Haines and CIA director Bill Burns presented to President Biden, Vice President Kamala Harris and their principal cabinet advisers top secret U.S. intelligence showing conclusively that President Putin had developed a war plan to invade Ukraine with 175,000 troops. It was an astonishing intelligence coup from the crown jewels of U.S. intelligence, including a human source inside the Kremlin.

It is the intelligence community's unanimous conclusion that Putin plans to invade Ukraine, Director Burns said.

Burns and Haines shared exacting details of how Russia planned to conquer certain cities and then divide responsibilities within Russia's military and security services to maintain control of them. It was as if they had secretly entered the enemy commander's tent and were hunched over the maps, examining the number and movement of brigades and the entire planned sequence of the multifront invasion.

Secretary of State Tony Blinken was stunned by the level of the intelligence detail they now had. The new breadth and specificity of Russia's war plan for territorial conquest was alarming. A global disruptive event.

Russia's war plan was to take control of the entire country of Ukraine, eliminate Ukrainian president Zelensky, and control the capital, Kyiv.

They could see the choreography, the preparation of Russian forces, and how they would use them to attack and conquer Ukraine. Most importantly, they had information from inside the Kremlin that Putin actually intended to do it.

"This isn't just a contingency plan in an abundance of caution," thought Jon Finer, the deputy national security adviser. "This is something that Russia is looking to do."

Despite the compelling evidence, the plan was confounding. If Putin followed through with the boldest attempt at territorial conquest since World War II, it would obliterate Russia's economic and diplomatic relationship with the United States and Europe, and maybe even China and India. Biden's principals in the room struggled to see Putin's logic. Why would he go through with this?

"There was really nothing leading into October, other than Putin's manifesto," Sullivan said, "that led us to think, okay, something has really swerved here."

Putin's war plans were not being reflected in Russia's public posture or rhetoric. There was no preparation of Russia's public for war.

Something had changed dramatically, Sullivan realized.

"But all is quiet," Sullivan said. "All is quiet." It was more perplexing than comforting.

Putin was about to attempt to forcibly take another sovereign country and make it part of Russia. "When we put our frame of reference on it, our logic on it, it sounds crazy," Blinken said to Biden.

"If you put yourself in Putin's mindset, maybe not so much and there's a fairly consistent line," Blinken said, "if you read and take some of his speeches at face value.

"Putin's profound philosophical conviction or theological conviction is that Ukraine needs to be erased from the map and subsumed into Russia," Blinken said, thinking of Putin's manifesto.

Biden agreed. "You read these things, he's telling you why he's doing what he's doing," Biden said.

Jon Finer wondered, Did Putin comprehend the obstacles?

Ukraine was not about to just relinquish sovereignty and let Putin take over. That was certain. Ukraine had declared independence from the Soviet Union in 1991. Putin's invasion of Crimea in 2014 had hardened Ukrainian sentiment against Russia and contributed to the creation of a stronger Ukrainian national identity.

Prior to 2014 only 20 to 30 percent of Ukrainians favored joining NATO. In 2019, a constitutional amendment committed

Ukraine to pursuing NATO membership. In 2021, before Putin's first spring troop buildup, support for NATO membership had risen to 56 percent. Putin was creating his own problems.

Let's just say Putin wins comfortably and easily at what he views as an acceptable cost, Finer reasoned. Then he is occupying this enormous country with a relatively small number of troops for the geography. Ukraine, which covers nearly the land area of Texas, is the second largest country in Europe after Russia and has a population of about 44 million, 14 million more than Texas.

Does he just think the Ukrainians are going to acquiesce to that? That there won't be some sort of insurgency?

There would be violent uprisings, rebellions, and years of ongoing conflict, Finer said.

The intelligence seemed on the one hand to be of such tectonic significance, Finer thought, but on the other hand, so illogical.

Despite the uncertainty, the president and his cabinet unanimously agreed Russia's war plan was "dead serious."

"It's very highly developed, the actual decision to pull the trigger hasn't been made but is primed," Blinken said.

A plan, however, is not a decision. They could see a very serious consideration by Russia, but not a decision. That was an important distinction.

It was also Putin's style, CIA director Burns noted. "He likes to keep his options open."

"What are the alternative explanations for all this intelligence other than just the straightforward interpretation?" President Biden asked.

"Is this a war game? Is this an option? Are we meant to be seeing this so that it scares us into doing something?"

Burns said there were no alternate explanations. The intelligence was conclusive.

Avril Haines, who as director of national intelligence oversaw all the U.S. intelligence agencies, including the CIA, had a trove of intelligence about Putin's reasoning and walked them through the new data points they had collected.

Insecurity and confidence are two sides of the same coin with Putin, Haines said. "He can be insecure, he can also be somebody who believes that he's the *only* person that can restore Russia to its former glory."

Putin had long lamented the breakup of the Soviet Union, which he called the greatest catastrophe of the 20th century. Ukraine's lands, Putin believed, were "the cradle of Russia."

"He believes that Ukraine has to come back to Russia and that has to trump everything else," Haines said. There was an absolute assumption of ownership.

Yet, Ukraine was clearly distancing itself from Russia while deepening its engagement with the West and NATO. The Ukrainian military was getting stronger and better with assistance from the West. The longer Putin waited to invade, the more formidable the Ukrainian pushback would be.

Putin's assessment was that military action would be the best option to prevent Ukraine from integrating more with the West. This was something Putin believed he had to stop at all costs. "For Putin, losing Ukraine is in effect an existential threat," Haines said.

By his calculations, an invasion would be successful and quick, bringing Ukraine once again under Russian control.

Haines had a frankness and intensity when she spoke that held the room's attention.

His war plan sounds crazy if you are thinking about what makes sense for the Russian people, Haines said, but Putin prioritizes *his* vision well over the health and wealth of the Russian people.

Putin believed that Russia would be welcomed by most Ukrainians, Director Haines summarized. He sees Ukrainians as lesser people than Russian people. "He is one of the most racist leaders that we have."

The Russian president reasoned that any consequences for his country would be short-lived. Economic sanctions from the West would be mitigated by Russia's strong national wealth fund and favorable economic indicators in the next few years before Putin would face his next election. Current high energy prices would make it difficult for Europe to join the United States in issuing significant economic sanctions that would hurt European domestic economies.

European and U.S. resolve would weaken with time and with worsening food shortages, inflation and energy shortages. Russia would be better at maintaining resolve and Putin's judgment was that time was on his side. At least that was what the U.S. intelligence showed.

"This is what Putin plans to do," Burns repeated. It was unusual for intelligence agencies to be so definitive.

"This would be so crazy," Biden said. "I know leaders. Leaders tend to think a lot more about downside risk than upside gain and Putin is opportunistic but pretty risk-averse. He's only at the lower, narrow end of risk acceptance. This is so radically different from what I know about him," Biden said. "And also for a leader to decide to do this without a particular match lighting the fuse." It would be crazy.

"I see the intel," Biden added. The president was not disbelieving of it.

The sense of incredulousness—and destiny—hung in the room.

"Jesus Christ!" Biden finally said. "Now I've got to deal with Russia swallowing Ukraine?" He had just had the Afghanistan ordeal. Now this?

Finer could see this would transform Biden's presidency, the administration's goals, and global stability.

"This is going to be the next year of our lives if not the rest of this term," Finer said. "This is going to be the thing that animates it, dominates it."

Continue looking at the situation from 360 degrees, Biden directed, think of every possible angle.

Biden repeated his main charge: "Number one, prevent it.

"But," he added starkly, "our ability to prevent this is limited." An aggressor, willing to launch an invasion, had a substantial initial advantage. This was the reality of global disruption they might face.

Nonetheless Biden's directive was: "Try. We'll run a play and see."

Number two, full preparation: "If it happens," Biden said, "we need to be positioned as effectively as possible so that our response enhances rather than depletes our interests." They wanted to avoid the scramble of paperwork and months of bureaucratic delays on funding and weapons delivery after Putin invaded.

Sullivan could see how Biden was applying his decades of foreign policy experience. The president had spent a considerable amount of time thinking about alliances, NATO, U.S.-Russia relations, great power politics.

Sullivan kept in regular communication with Fred Kagan, an expert on military history and strategy, who wrote regularly for the Institute for the Study of War, an independent think tank considered the gold standard for providing independent assessments of the strategic landscape of conflicts around the world.

"He's not going to do a big invasion," Kagan said flatly to Sullivan. He sounded certain. ISW was counting the Russian brigades and monitoring Russia's military buildup.

"It's war 101," Kagan said. "You need to prepare the public ground for war and there's none of that. None of it."

Kagan's point gave Sullivan pause.

In their never-ending talks, Sullivan and Finer debated whether Putin could be engaging in some kind of mental experiment.

If the expectation is for a massive invasion and only a more minor one occurs, Putin might be banking on less U.S. and European pushback. "So you scare people about the big thing to negotiate the grabbing of a smaller thing," Finer said.

The biggest problem with that theory was it did not match the intelligence which showed Putin's plan was to fully invade.

Hanging over the intelligence was the fallout from Biden's chaotic withdrawal from Afghanistan. It was an area Putin only saw weaknesses in Biden and his administration, according to intelligence of conversations inside the Kremlin. That weakness suggested Biden would not know what to do when Putin invaded.

President George W. Bush, who had ordered the invasion of Iraq in 2003, in part because the CIA had said the intelligence that Iraq had weapons of mass destruction was a "slam dunk," sympathized with Biden's Afghanistan fiasco.

During a phone call after the Afghanistan withdrawal, Bush said to Biden, "Oh boy, I can understand what you're going through. I got fucked by my intel people, too."

"We have to consider the human psychology at play here," Defense Secretary Austin's principal adviser Colin Kahl said. His team at the Pentagon was tracking the substantial Russian troop movements and preparations along Ukraine's border. "This is more than just a bluff," Kahl said. As they studied the intelligence, it seemed remarkable in its depth and clarity, but what it suggested seemed insane. "We are not going to compound what happened in Afghanistan with us not being on the ball on this crisis," Kahl directed.

Since Afghanistan was a NATO mission, not just a U.S. one, the chaotic withdrawal had also created turbulence among NATO allies who were critical of the U.S. execution. "Seeing this intelligence we have to work overtime," Kahl said, "to get the allies on side, to get them to trust in the intelligence, to see the oncoming train that we are seeing and get ready to respond.

"This was the crown jewels of U.S. intelligence," Kahl said. They had to find a way to share it with allies.

Blinken began right away to build an international coalition to support Ukraine and impose costs on Russia through sanctions and export controls.

For Blinken, the political implications were far bigger than Ukraine. If Putin could get away with naked aggression against another country, redrawing another country's borders by force, Blinken believed the peace and stability in Europe and around the world that grew out of the ashes of World War II would be obliterated.

He worried about the risk of potential reverberations in the Indo-Pacific where China was threatening Taiwan. If Russia simply got away with this, other more powerful countries could take it as a green light to redraw their own borders by force.

After initial outreach, Blinken updated President Biden and Sullivan: Most of the allies really think this is unlikely, Blinken said. He had heard a lot of skepticism. Some outright denied the U.S. analysis.

Sullivan and Finer also started approaching allies, including the Ukrainians, to gauge how others responded to the idea that Russia was seriously preparing to invade Ukraine.

"We just had to really pressure-test the theory before we were comfortable believing it," Finer said.

"I mean even we, the ones who were out beating the drum the loudest—inside our government, with our partners—that this was going to happen, I think even in the back of our minds on some level up until the end, it seemed so crazy that there at least felt like there was a chance that Putin wouldn't go through with it even with all the information staring us in the face.

"We were full speed ahead starting in the early fall period. But it just never made sense."

FOURTEEN

◆ ◆

O n the sidelines of the G20 in Rome on October 30 and 31, President Biden chaired a private meeting with a small group of world leaders.

Prime minister of the United Kingdom Boris Johnson, French president Emmanuel Macron and German chancellor Angela Merkel sat around a small table with President Biden in a conference room. Merkel also brought her soon-to-be successor, Olaf Scholz. On chairs behind each leader were their foreign minister and national security adviser. Blinken and Sullivan sat behind Biden. The room was swept to ensure the 12 people in the room were not being covertly listened to.

"We've all seen that the Russians have re-massed forces on the border as they did in April," Biden said. "We now have information about what they are actually thinking, planning and plotting.

"What we don't know is whether they've actually decided to pull the trigger," Biden said. "But the gun is cocked."

This was the first time Biden had directly engaged the core European partners on what Russia was planning to do in Ukraine.

French president Macron and the two German leaders voiced skepticism. It didn't seem Putin was that crazy. Maybe the Russian leader was seeking to gain leverage.

Boris Johnson found the intelligence that Putin was going to invade Ukraine completely credible. MI6 and Defense Minister Ben Wallace had been providing Johnson with a similarly worrying portrait of Putin's war plans. Perhaps it was Putin's bluff, but Johnson believed Putin was monstrous to even be thinking about it.

In a phone call, Johnson confronted Putin.

"You have no reason to invade Ukraine," Johnson said. "There is no way Ukraine would be joining NATO anytime soon."

"Boris," Putin said, "what do you mean by anytime soon? When is that? Next month?"

"No," Johnson said, "look, I mean, the reality is Ukraine is not going to join in the foreseeable future."

Johnson believed that Putin knew that. It was nonsense, Johnson felt, this was Putin's paranoia about NATO.

It was also a game for Putin. The Russian leader wanted to goad Johnson and other Western leaders into saying publicly: There is no way Ukraine will join NATO.

"He has us in a trap," Johnson thought with frustration. Johnson couldn't say it publicly because that would have contradicted NATO's open-door policy and seemed like Putin had imposed a Russian veto on a sovereign country's decision to apply for NATO membership.

"It would be a massive concession and an admission of defeat, a surrender to Putin's pressure and quite wrong," Johnson believed.

Johnson, a member of the British Conservative Party and the product of prestigious Eton and Oxford, found the conversation with Putin "very creepy," later confiding to an associate that the Russian autocrat was a "small, puckish, lowlife."

FIFTEEN

◆ ◆

In several close-hold meetings in the second half of October, Biden, Sullivan and Burns weighed how best to confront Putin with the intelligence the U.S. had collected—to credibly and unambiguously send the message "We know." And, in similarly direct terms, to lay out the consequences for Russia.

They decided to hold the president in reserve. Should the president personally travel to Russia to warn Putin and try to talk him out of it, and Putin went ahead and invaded, Biden would be seen to have failed and look weak.

Confronted with the possibility of a war that could threaten the entire international order, Biden could have met the moment and delivered the warning to President Putin in person himself. The Russian autocrat wanted the respect of world leaders. Anyone else was an underling, a bureaucrat. The only messenger from the United States with the weight and influence to stop Putin was the president.

When President Reagan wanted to warn Russian leader Gorbachev about the isolation of Berlin, he did not send a top official from his administration. He went himself against advice from some of his staff who said it would be too provocative.

Standing at the Brandenburg Gate in Berlin on June 12, 1987, Reagan said, "Mr. Gorbachev, tear down this wall." It was Reagan's most memorable statement. Two years later the Berlin Wall fell.

Leaders have to risk looking weak, especially in efforts to stop war. Often these are remembered in history as great strengths. Maybe Putin was immovable but it would have been worth trying. Leadership is often about making risky big plays.

President Biden decided to send the person who arguably had more experience with Putin than anyone in the U.S. government. Biden called Bill Burns his Putinologist and believed he was the natural choice for the mission.

Burns, a trim, straitlaced 65-year-old with snowy hair and a mustache, had served 32 years in the foreign service, including as ambassador to Moscow. He knew Putin. Burns was in his seventh year as head of the Carnegie Endowment for International Peace when Biden called and asked him to be his CIA director. He was both floored and thrilled at the chance to return to government, especially in the high-profile and coveted post. No career diplomat had ever been appointed CIA director.

President Biden said he would send Burns to Moscow to meet with Putin. But Biden was not going to stand completely in reserve. Burns would carry a private letter from Biden to Putin. The letter matched closely with what Burns would say to Putin. Each point had been crafted carefully by the NSC in collaboration with the intelligence agencies to send the message "we know" without disclosing everything or how they knew it.

The CIA director was acutely aware of the importance of protecting their intelligence sources and methods, which had produced such exquisite insight into Putin's planning. He had not only a sharp, detailed picture of Russia's military plans but Putin's preparations for political control of Ukraine as well.

Burns traveled from Joint Base Andrews on a military 737 plane to Moscow on Tuesday, November 2. Eric Green, the NSC Russia director, and Karen Donfried from the State Department accompanied him along with a small team from the CIA.

When they arrived 12 hours later a thick fog had descended on Moscow so their plane spent another two hours circling the city's three principal airports looking unsuccessfully for an opening.

At 2:00 a.m. they landed in Riga, Latvia, 500 miles from Moscow. Burns slept for two hours before the plane was in the air again, arriving finally in Moscow later that morning.

Burns first went to the Kremlin to meet with the secretary of the

Kremlin's Security Council, Nikolai Patrushev, a close Putin ally going back to their days in Russia's Security Service, the KGB, in St. Petersburg. He was also the former head of the FSB—Russia's internal security and counterintelligence service.

Patrushev, hardline and hawkish, looked like a balding European businessman, but he is the most powerful figure among the intelligence officials in Putin's inner circle. For practical purposes and given the importance of the intelligence portfolio in Putin's Russia, Patrushev was the equivalent to a national security adviser—overall master coordinator for policy. Burns found him to be a dour character.

The CIA director confronted Patrushev about Russia's war plans.

He appeared both surprised and irritated. Burns had not given the Russians a heads-up about his message for Putin. Patrushev believed Burns was visiting to begin preparations for another meeting between Biden and Putin.

Patrushev was not in any way apologetic or defensive, and made no effort to rebut the points Burns made. The CIA director noted that Patrushev was defiant but did not tell him he was wrong.

U.S. intelligence indicated that the number of people around Putin who were involved in his decision-making for a war was extremely small. Burns knew Patrushev was one of the people in that inner circle.

"Well," Patrushev said, "you know we Russians may not be able to compete economically with the United States, but don't underestimate our military modernization. We have modernized our military over the last two decades. We can compete militarily."

"I would not underestimate the seriousness of the message that I'm conveying," Burns said. He was not about to get into a tit-for-tat over whose military was superior.

Another wave of the coronavirus had just hit Moscow, which was under a strict curfew. Putin, described by U.S. intel as fearful and almost paranoid about contracting the virus, was isolating in

his high-security palace complex in Sochi on the coast of the Black
Sea, about 1,000 miles south of Moscow. Putin, Burns was told,
would speak with him by phone.

Putin's chief foreign policy adviser Yuri Ushakov met him in
his office adjacent to the Kremlin. Ushakov left Burns alone in the
room. The phone rang.

Burns recognized Putin's voice instantly. Putin recalled when
Burns had been ambassador to Moscow, 14 years earlier, and then
appeared to wait for Burns to deliver his message. He almost certainly had been tipped off by Patrushev about what was coming.

Burns wanted to be straightforward with the Russian president.

"We are alarmed that you are seriously contemplating a major
invasion of Ukraine," Burns said. "That would be a mistake.

"If you do that, this is what we will do," Burns continued, laying out as the president had directed him to do what they were
seeing and the severe actions Biden would take in response.

Putin didn't interrupt. He seemed to listen carefully as Burns
laid out the consequences.

"We are going to rally the West, we are going to impose severe economic penalties, crushing economic sanctions," Burns
said. Ukraine is a sovereign state. We would continue to support
Ukraine. We would adjust our force posture in Europe.

"I'm not threatening you, I'm just saying this is what we will do
in response and you need to know that," Burns said. "The types of
consequences you faced in 2014 will be nothing compared to what
we are prepared to do now." In 2014, when Putin invaded Crimea,
the West's response was slow, weak and divided. The intelligence
indicated Putin was expecting much the same this time.

The United States will make sure that the whole Russian banking system is removed from Swift, Burns continued, referring to
the global communications system used by banks for the smooth,
secure coded rapid transfer of money.

Swift sends about 40 million messages a day as trillions of dollars are transferred reliably among thousands of banks. Removal

from the Swift system would harm Russian banks severely because they'd have to develop their own banking communications
system—a laborious and almost impossible task.

"We're going to isolate you diplomatically and we're going to
help Ukraine defend itself," Burns said.

Putin's side of the conversation was fairly lengthy, and to Burns,
a familiar recitation of Putin's convictions about Ukraine and his
cockiness about Russia's ability to enforce its will on Ukraine.

"Ukraine is weak and divided," Putin argued. "Not a real country. Russia's interests require us to control Ukraine's choices."

Putin completely dismissed Zelensky as a political leader and repeated his usual complaints about the illegitimacy of the Ukrainian
government and possible NATO expansion. He argued that ethnic
Russians in Ukraine were being discriminated against and perse-
cuted.

The Russian president's tone wasn't defensive or apologetic.
Putin also made no effort to take issue with the CIA director's
description of Russia's preparations for the conflict. It seemed to
Burns as though Putin really believed everything he said about
Ukraine and that his risk appetite had grown.

Burns asked Putin, "With a force of 180,000 to 190,000 how
are you going to control a country of 44 million that doesn't want
to be controlled by Russia? How are you going to deal with that?"

Putin did not answer.

Burns had always found with Putin a fixation on controlling
Ukraine. Putin seemed to not believe he could be a great Russian
leader unless he made Ukraine part of Russia.

In Moscow, Burns also met with Alexander Bortnikov, the head
of the FSB, who intelligence showed was intimately involved in the
decision-making for a war. He also appeared unmoved by U.S.
clarity about their war plans.

Others Burns met with like Sergei Naryshkin, the head of the
Foreign Intelligence Service, appeared not to know about Russia's
invasion plans.

Eric Green and Karen Donfried, who attended some of the

meetings with Burns, picked up a sense that the Russians were feeling kind of full of themselves after the U.S. withdrawal from Afghanistan.

"I think it reinforced Putin's conceptions about how easy it would be," Green noted. The fiasco of the U.S. withdrawal was a centerpiece of Putin's disdain. "Here's a military force that's been supported by the U.S. for decades at that stage. They just collapsed. The Americans didn't back them up."

Burns stayed one night at Spaso House, the U.S. ambassador's large yellow house in Moscow where Burns had lived for three years. He left Russia the next day feeling even more troubled than when he arrived. On the plane he sent a highly classified cable to President Biden.

"I came away with a very strong impression that Putin has just about made up his mind to go to war," Burns reported.

The CIA director said that this was both because of what he could see in the hard intelligence in terms of Russia's preparations for war, and his own sense of Putin's absolute conviction that without controlling Ukraine's choices, Russia can't function as a great power.

Burns believed Putin had come to the conclusion that strategically his window of opportunity to exert control over Ukraine was closing. The winter of 2021–2022 provided a favorable landscape. Putin believed Europe was distracted. The French had elections coming up in early 2022. Chancellor Merkel was about to be succeeded by Olaf Scholz as the new German leader.

Also, Burns noted, Putin seemed convinced that he had modernized the Russian military to the point that they would not face much of a challenge in Ukraine. Putin saw President Zelensky as weak and thought the Ukrainians would roll over.

Putin expressed almost a sense of entitlement for dominance over Ukraine, Burns said.

"None of that was new," Burns added, "but there was a purposefulness, a conviction, brutish as it was in a lot of ways that he was unmistakable in what he was saying."

Nothing Burns had heard from Putin or the people around him suggested to him that the Russians were looking for a way out of war.

The CIA director concluded, "It is shaping up to be the biggest ground war in Europe since World War II."

Burns called Jake Sullivan on a secure line and summarized his cable to the president. He also called President Zelensky and laid out exactly what he had conveyed to Putin and what the Russian leader had said in return.

Burns's to-do list was headed by his insistence that the Ukrainians understand what was coming.

While Burns was in Moscow, Secretary of State Tony Blinken and his deputy chief of staff for policy, Tom Sullivan, brother of Jake Sullivan, were in Glasgow, Scotland. On the sidelines of the United Nations Climate Change Conference, Blinken met with Zelensky to convey a warning from President Biden.

"The president asked me to share this with you," Blinken said to Zelensky. They sat almost knee-to-knee facing each other.

Zelensky showed no indication that he knew what the U.S. secretary of state was about to say.

"We all know and you know better than anyone the Russians have their forces re-massed on your border," Blinken said. "But we have information in great detail about what they are actually planning to do with those forces. We have the plans, the preparations, all the stuff that's not visible and we believe there is a very high risk that the Russians will re-invade your country."

Zelensky listened carefully.

"We're going to link you up with our intelligence people," Blinken said. "They'll give you chapter and verse about what we know and what we don't know. But I wanted you to hear it from me on behalf of the president. This is what we're concerned about and what we're seeing happen."

Zelensky was skeptical.

The Ukrainian president called in a few of his close senior advisers and asked Blinken to repeat the message so they could hear directly.

A buildup of Russian forces did not necessarily mean that the Russians were coming in, the Ukrainians said. Zelensky was doubtful the Russians would pull the trigger.

"Look," Blinken said, "none of us want to believe that they would do something that foolhardy but we see this as dead serious." He hedged, "If not a certainty, a probability."

"You need to be prepared and we're getting prepared," Blinken said. The Pentagon's grim calculation was that if Putin invaded Ukraine with its far larger, superior military, Ukrainian territory would quickly fall to the Russians.

"We're going to be by your side," Blinken added. "We are going to be with you in the coming months whatever is to come. We are going to do everything we can to deter this and we're going to do everything we can to support you."

"Thank you for letting me know," Zelensky said.

Eric Green and Karen Donfried flew from Moscow to Kyiv to share intelligence with Zelensky's chief of staff Andriy Yermak and Minister of Foreign Affairs Dmytro Kuleba.

Their reception was polite but restrained. Green sensed suspicion on the part of the Ukrainians and an element of "hello, yes, the Russians are out to get us. We know that. We live that reality. What else?"

Finally, it was Secretary of Defense Lloyd Austin's turn to bang the drum. Austin, age 68, a retired Army general, was America's first African American secretary of defense. He had graduated from West Point in 1975 on the heels of a humiliating U.S. withdrawal from Vietnam and served more than four decades in the Army—unmatched warfighting experience for a secretary of defense.

He was the only defense secretary to have held combat commands in the U.S. wars in Afghanistan and Iraq at the one-, two-, three- and four-star levels. He was a soldier's soldier and had known Biden for more than a decade. During the Obama years, Austin had been director of the Joint Staff, one of the most important stepping-stones in the military, and later had been sent to Iraq as the commanding general of U.S. forces. Biden's eldest son, the late Major Beau Biden, was a lawyer on Austin's staff and they had developed a strong relationship.

Austin met with Ukraine's defense minister Oleksii Reznikov in Washington to go over the latest Russian troop movements along Ukraine's borders.

Just like Zelensky, Reznikov was dubious that Russia would actually invade. Putin, he reminded Austin, had sent the same number of troops to their border in the spring.

"And what did Putin get?" Reznikov said. "He got two phone calls with Biden and a personal meeting in Geneva." The Ukrainian defense minister was convinced Putin was merely trying to get more attention and concessions from Biden and NATO.

Austin set up a battle rhythm of 8:00 a.m. meetings a few times a week. The Pentagon needed to be prepared for an invasion, even if Putin bluffed. They were in a period of ambiguous warning.

"This is one of the dilemmas that the principals faced and that the president faced," Undersecretary of Defense for Policy Colin Kahl said. "If Putin hasn't made the final decision, could we inadvertently make him do things that provoke him?"

It was a classic foreign policy and military dilemma. In trying to deter a bad thing from happening you inadvertently create the conditions for an adverse move against you, bringing about the thing you were working so hard to avoid.

Kahl likened the daily meetings to the old television show *Hollywood Squares*. Around the virtual table, filling the squares on his large screen was the senior military and civilian leadership of the Pentagon along with his commanders across the world.

Austin began each meeting by reviewing the "North Stars," their overall objectives: Bolster Ukraine to defend itself. Be prepared with forces on alert. Reinforce NATO to make sure any conflict in Ukraine does not spill over. Keep the allies united and avoid steps that would lead to a direct conflict with Russia. If it happens, prevent a military conflict from becoming World War III.

SIXTEEN

Vice President Kamala Harris traveled to Paris to repair White House relations with French president Emmanuel Macron, who was still seething after a U.S. deal with Australia for nuclear-powered submarines stripped France of its $60 billion submarine contract with Australia. Macron had recalled the French ambassador from Washington in a dramatic display of displeasure. France's foreign minister said publicly they had been "stabbed in the back."

Biden also gave his vice president a second assignment: brief Macron on the latest U.S. intelligence about Russia's war plans.

"Be clear with Macron that this is going to happen," Biden told her. "We need a plan and we need alliance solidarity."

"We are highly confident that Russia is going to do this," Vice President Harris said to French president Macron at the Élysée Palace during their two-hour meeting on November 10.

Macron was skeptical Putin would actually invade but took the threat seriously. His advisers were telling him: Putin's planning, blustering, moving troops. It doesn't mean he will actually do it.

If we are to have any chance of deterring it, Putin needs to know the Europeans will step up, Harris said.

The U.S. intel shows Putin's thinking, she said. Putin sees the Europeans as "weak." He believes Europe doesn't want to deal with a conflict, is divided, and doesn't have confidence in United States leadership. Putin believes Europe will "just swallow this."

Harris appealed to Macron to lead the European charge. Putin viewed France differently to other European allies, she said, because the French had not always been aligned with the U.S. on transatlantic and NATO issues.

Bring the other Europeans on board, Harris urged, and show Putin that NATO will be united and that there will be severe economic costs if he invades.

With German chancellor Angela Merkel stepping down, it was no secret that the French president aspired to be the next great leader of Europe, the powerhouse at the center of European decision-making and foreign policy. This was a tantalizing opportunity.

Macron took up the mantle. He would order the French military to reinforce Eastern European allies—send striker brigades to Romania and boost forces in Poland.

"France is prepared to impose costs," Macron assured Harris. "I'm on board for that."

He would also personally confront Putin.

If there is a country that might be a risk to alliance unity, it is not France, Macron said adamantly. He pointed to Germany's Nord Stream 2 pipeline project and their reliance on Russian oil and gas. France is not the weak link in the alliance, he repeated.

"If there was a weak link it would be Germany," Macron said.

While the discussion was serious, the tone of the meeting was good-natured. That evening the French president escorted the vice president to dinner where she was given the seat of honor. When Harris delivered her address at the Paris Peace Forum the next day, Macron sat in the front row. A strong public signal that while the U.S. and France could have their disputes, even fiery ones, the two countries remained firm, committed allies.

On foreign trips, the vice president would send her own reports to President Biden, often including Sullivan and Blinken in the secure email exchange. As she departed Paris, Harris reported that she felt good about the meeting with Macron. There had been "no lingering acrimony over the AUKUS submarine deal." The French president did not even bring it up.

SEVENTEEN

$\mathbf{B}$linken flew to Stockholm, Sweden, for the December 2, 2021, meeting of the OSCE—the Organization for Security and Co-operation in Europe. It operated as the world's largest forum for cooperation on regional security, which included the United States and Russia as members.

He watched Russia's foreign minister Sergey Lavrov, whom he had known for years, address the Ministerial Council in the flag-lined auditorium. Ned Price, his top aide, was sitting next to him.

Lavrov is highly intelligent, Blinken said to Price. "He is a great polemicist. He is extremely good at what-about-ism, in that you'll go down one path and he says well, what about when you did this or did that?"

"Sergey," as Blinken called him, was a 6-foot-2, 71-year-old career diplomat and Russia's longest-serving foreign minister since the fall of the Soviet Union. Putin had personally appointed him in 2004. Lavrov spoke multiple languages fluently, including English, French and Sinhalese, and had served for a decade as Russia's ambassador to the United Nations. With perfectly fitted suits and thin, rimless glasses that punctuated his stern, inquisitorial gaze, Lavrov was careful to maintain a public presence manicured to Putin's liking. He smoked regularly and could be quite cunning.

"The OSCE is in a depressing state today," Lavrov said to the OSCE Ministerial Council. "It has become hostage to the bloc-based discipline within the European Union and NATO and is mired in petty agendas.

"Our Western partners seek to replace international law with a rules-based order, which they themselves are establishing on the basis of their own exceptionalism," Lavrov said. "Liberal values are being instrumentalized for shameless interference in the internal affairs of sovereign States."

Russia's accusations were familiar to Blinken but with up to 100,000 Russian troops congregating on Ukraine's borders, the "Russia is the victim" card seemed phonier than usual. Still Blinken listened carefully for anything that hinted at a legitimate security concern or opening for real negotiation.

"The fall of the Berlin Wall marked the end of the Cold War and the cessation of the struggle between two systems," Lavrov continued dramatically. "Now, new walls are being erected by those who proclaimed themselves 'civilized democracies' and consider it their mission to contain 'authoritarian regimes.'"

He moved on to directly accuse NATO of threatening Russia. "The Alliance's military infrastructure is being irresponsibly moved closer to Russia's borders, and anti-missile defense systems that could be used for missile strikes are being deployed in Romania and Poland. U.S. medium-range missiles can appear any day now on European territory." Blinken knew this was not true.

"Europe remains silent. Ukraine is being pumped up militarily, which fuels the Ukrainian government's desire to sabotage the Minsk agreements"—the security agreements negotiated and originally signed by Russia, Ukraine and the OSCE after Putin's 2014 invasion—"and fosters the illusion that the conflict can be resolved by force."

The Minsk agreements had failed to stop ongoing military clashes between Russia and Ukraine in the Donbas since 2014. Russia and Ukraine blamed each other for the failure of the agreements.

"The decision of the NATO Bucharest Summit of April 2008 that Georgia and Ukraine will become members of NATO was like a landmine placed beneath the very foundations of the European security architecture," Lavrov said. "It has already exploded once, in August 2008, when Mikheil Saakashvili, euphoric about the prospect of joining NATO, took a gamble that had dire consequences for Georgia itself and brought the security situation in Europe to a knife-edge."

Blinken blanched. This was a loosely veiled reminder that Russia had successfully invaded Georgia in 2008 to prevent it from pursuing a path to joining NATO. And Saakashvili, Georgia's former president who had put the country on a democratic reform agenda toward EU and NATO membership, was now wasting away in a Georgian prison cell.

"Third countries"—meaning, the United States—"have no right to express their position on the issue of NATO enlargement and are playing with fire," Lavrov warned. "I am convinced that they cannot be unaware of this."

When it was Blinken's turn to speak, he addressed Russia's aggression in a cool, comfortably diplomatic tone.

"The seizure by force of Crimea has brought relentless abuses against Crimean Tatars, ethnic Ukrainians, and others who peacefully oppose this occupation," Blinken said. "And as I said yesterday at the NATO foreign ministers meeting, we are deeply concerned by evidence that Russia has made plans for further significant aggression against Ukraine, and so we call on Russia to respect Ukraine's sovereignty and territorial integrity, to de-escalate, reverse the recent troop buildup, return forces to normal peaceful positions, and to implement the Minsk commitments."

Blinken cornered Lavrov for a private talk on the sidelines of the forum.

"Tony," Russia's foreign minister said, "do you really think we're going to invade? Are you really serious with this stuff?

"We have no plans to invade Ukraine and we're not trying to threaten Kyiv," Lavrov said.

NATO was continuing to build up a security threat to Russia, he said. The real threat is directed at Russia, not directed at Ukraine, he argued.

"Kyiv is placing advanced weapons in Ukraine close to Russia's borders that they could use to strike deep within Russia in a matter of minutes," he said.

"Sergey, that's not true," Blinken said, "and you know it's not true so unless you are being misinformed by your own people, you have to know that that's not true." President Zelensky had been careful not to place weapons close to the border out of fear of giving Russia an excuse to attack Ukraine.

Lavrov then segued their conversation to alleged persecution of ethnic Russians and Russian speakers inside Ukraine.

"As best I can tell," Blinken said, "the rights of ethnic Russians in Ukraine are greater than the rights of ethnic Russians in Russia."

Blinken could see Lavrov didn't appreciate the comment. "Tony," Lavrov scoffed, "you know that's not true."

They went back and forth on the Minsk agreements.

The Russians had an entire narrative about the Minsk process that was basically Alice in Wonderland, Blinken thought. A fantasy.

Blinken conveyed President Biden's deterrence message, warning that the U.S. and allies would impose severe costs and consequences on Russia if it takes further aggressive action against Ukraine, "including high-impact economic measures that we've refrained from taking in the past."

The strategy was still to hold President Biden in reserve. Lavrov replied with Russia's own threats. "Drawing Ukraine into the geopolitical games of the United States," he said, "will have the most serious consequences."

Blinken left the meeting convinced that his Russian counterpart was not fully aware of the extent of Putin's war plans. He had a sliver of sympathy for how far outside Putin's confidence Lavrov was.

"First of all, I think we had pretty good information that this"— the invasion plan—"was extremely closely held among Putin and a very small handful of people—three to four people," Blinken said. "Not to include Lavrov.

"Second," Blinken said, "to some extent his declarations in these meetings were mostly bluster but it's also entirely possible that we knew more about the war plan than he did. I actually believe that we did."

At the official dinner that evening, the 57 foreign ministers and secretaries of state sat at one of the biggest dining tables Blinken had ever seen. He was seated next to Ukraine's foreign minister Dmytro Kuleba and directly across from him was Lavrov.

Lavrov lost no time launching into a diatribe about the origins of 2014, claiming there had been a coup perpetrated by the United States and others in Ukraine that caused the rightly elected president Viktor Yanukovych to be deposed.

Having lived through that period himself, Blinken felt he had to correct Lavrov as he attempted once again to replace history with the Putin-preferred narrative.

"That's not what happened," Blinken interjected, "and you know it and everyone at this table knows it."

Blinken went through the litany of what actually had happened in 2014.

Lavrov, unfazed, raised the Minsk process.

Blinken interjected again, "Sergey, we can talk about the Minsk process.

"Here"—Blinken held a piece of paper in his hand. "Here are the requirements that Russia had under the Minsk process.

"Immediate and full cease-fire in particular districts of Donetsk and Luhansk Oblasts of Ukraine and its strict fulfillment as of 00.00 midnight (Kyiv time) on Feb. 15, 2015.

"You didn't do it," Blinken said.

"Withdrawal of all heavy weapons.

"You didn't do it," Blinken said.

"Allow OSCE monitoring.

"You didn't do it," Blinken said.

"All-for-all political prisoner exchange.

"You didn't do it.

"Ensure delivery of humanitarian assistance.

"You didn't do it.

"Restore control of the state border to the Ukrainian government in the whole conflict zone.

"You didn't do it," Blinken said. "I could go on. I think you get the point."

Lavrov responded with bluster, flagrant denials and condescension. But he sounded convincing. That was the problem with Lavrov in these large meetings. He was a showman and he had an attentive audience.

"The conviction when he speaks," Blinken said afterward to Ned Price. "If you are uninformed or weren't participating in something, you might actually say oh, maybe this is accurate."

While in Stockholm, the secretary of state also met with Swedish intelligence officials to deliver the U.S. warning about Ukraine. By now, Blinken had delivered his presentation so many times he had it down pat.

"We have information dating back several weeks now that President Putin has ambitions to undertake an invasion of Ukraine," Blinken said. "He is mobilizing forces to position them to be able to launch a large-scale invasion of Ukraine at his order. We don't know precisely when this will take place but our intelligence officials are confident that he is putting himself in a position to be able to do this in the relatively near term."

The Swedish intelligence leader was puzzled. "We've seen nothing to corroborate that type of information. And you know we have a close relationship but we just don't have anything that speaks to the concern that you all are putting forward."

Blinken understood the skepticism. Putin's plan wasn't logical and even the secretary of state carried a lagging sense of disbelief.

"Look," Blinken said, "we need to make sure that you're seeing what we're seeing and that you have what we have.

"Our intel officials are competent in what they assess," Blinken added, "but we need to make sure that our intelligence services are linked up so that we're dealing with the same set of information."

Part of diplomacy had become covert salesmanship.

EIGHTEEN

"**W**e have got to get the allies on board because we can't do this effectively alone," Biden urged his top advisers and the vice president during a President's Daily Brief. Despite the efforts to ring the alarm bell on Russia's plans, the allies remained deeply skeptical of the U.S. warnings and intel assessments.

"We've seen how Putin has been capable of just lying, bald-faced lying," Director of National Intelligence Haines said, "to presidents.

"He's lying to people on a very consistent basis," Haines added. "That is hard for Western leaders to absorb."

Sullivan and his deputy, Jon Finer, suggested they take a more dramatic approach to intelligence sharing, almost a Madison Avenue marketing campaign.

Quiet intelligence sharing was not proving persuasive and that was dangerous when faced with an adversary like Russia that was so highly skilled in the art of disinformation. It gave Putin an opportunity to divide public opinion using carefully crafted pretexts and lies to explain away an invasion. Russian media outlets were already full of propaganda suggesting that Ukraine was a neo-Nazi state and that NATO was using Ukraine to threaten Russia. Doubt among allies, the public and among Ukrainians meant valuable time and space for Putin to maneuver.

Letting someone in on something private or even top secret is attention-grabbing, Jon Finer said, drawing on his prior experience as a *Washington Post* reporter.

"People are much more interested in the accounts of things that normally are only available to people inside the room," he added. Let's declassify some of the intelligence on Russia's war planning and strategically share it. In short, dominate the information space so that Putin would lose the element of surprise.

Initially the intelligence community was reluctant, maddeningly cautious, according to Sullivan. But after several more meetings with CIA director Burns and his deputy, and DNI Haines and her deputy, they developed a new approach which they called a "strategic downgrade."

It was an unfortunate label. "Downgrade" suggested that the information was somehow less, almost fire-sale material. It was anything but.

Biden directed Haines to start sharing downgraded intelligence with allies and partners on a weekly, even daily basis—an unprecedented pace of intelligence sharing. Haines traveled to brief the North Atlantic Council more than half a dozen times. The intelligence agencies built technology that made it easier to share the information quickly. It was an in-your-face, all-out bulletin focused on Russia.

The next step was a public warning.

The *Washington Post* headline on December 3, 2021, read: "Russia Planning Massive Military Offensive Against Ukraine Involving 175,000 Troops, U.S. Intelligence Warns." The front page of the paper prominently displayed a large map of Russia and Ukraine superimposed with satellite photographs that showed Russia's buildup along Ukraine's border. It was the National Security Council's first public downgrade.

Instead of using highly classified government satellite images, the NSC's director for intelligence programs, Maher Bitar, pulled commercial satellite photos that showed the exact same formations of 70,000 Russian troops massed in four locations near Russia's border with Ukraine as well as newly arrived tanks and artillery in Crimea.

Putin continued to publicly dismiss the notion he intended to invade Ukraine with the troops on the border. But there was little sign that Russia was pulling back. The story noted that Russia's war plans indicated that the 70,000 troops pictured on November 9, 2021, could increase to 175,000 by as soon as early 2022, a signal to allies and media outlets around the world to watch for further buildup.

It was intended to be a Cuban Missile Crisis–style laydown similar to the dramatic visual presentation made by United Nations ambassador Adlai Stevenson in 1962 to show the Soviets were lying when they said they had not placed missiles in Cuba. In televised hearings at the United Nations, watched by millions, Stevenson displayed satellite photos on easels.

The Russians brushed off the *Washington Post* story as nonsense, claiming the troops were there for routine training exercises.

But inside the White House and U.S. intelligence agencies, quiet whoops were shared. They had broken from outdated, rigid intelligence sharing procedure, and created a new mode of informational warfare intended to beat Putin at his own game.

But making public what Putin knew already to be true was not going to deter him.

NINETEEN

◆ ◆

"If you do this there are going to be enormous costs to Russia," President Biden said to Putin during a videoconference at 10:00 a.m. on December 7, 2021. "We're going to ensure that."

Putin flatly denied Russia had any plans to invade Ukraine. He demanded security guarantees to rule out NATO's eastward expansion.

"We have a team," Biden said. "They've prepared documents. We're ready to discuss them with you. They go to broader questions of European security not just Ukraine." Biden was searching to see if there were real Russian security concerns they could negotiate, or was all this just cover?

"You know, you've asked for things that we don't think are totally beyond the pale," Biden said. "Like no long-range weapons systems being placed inside Ukraine. We think these are things we can negotiate and discuss.

"You say that you're worried about a NATO combat presence inside Ukraine. There is *no* plan for a NATO or U.S. combat presence in Ukraine," Biden underscored. "We do this training mission. It's way over in western Ukraine, not up against your border, not a threat to you," he said.

Similar to his conversation with British prime minister Boris Johnson, Putin wanted the United States to prevent further NATO enlargement, close the open-door policy. In other words, guarantee that Ukraine would never be a part of NATO.

Putin's requests were maximalist and he appeared disinterested in negotiating any practical security arrangements like weapons placements.

So Biden tried turning to shared history and reminded Putin that during the Cold War, the U.S. and Soviet Union had a special responsibility for ensuring security in the world. Their predecessors had avoided direct war between their two countries.

Sullivan and Finer listened in on the call.

What surprised Finer was that he always thought of Putin as a thug but his demeanor with Biden was calm. More in the mode of a lawyer arguing a case for why Russia was the aggrieved party and why the U.S. and Europe needed to address his grievances.

"His presentation is not forceful. It is casual," Finer said. "He doesn't shout. He doesn't use harsh language. He's very matter-of-fact."

How ordinary it seemed. "It was tonally not a conversation that you would imagine befitting of this seminal moment," Finer said. U.S. intel still persuasively indicated Putin would invade no matter what the U.S. did to try to deter him.

"Just the air of tension was diminished by the way Putin operates, the way he presents," Finer said. "But at the same time it was quite clear he was not backing off, not all that interested in a diplomatic off-ramp, and that he heard very clearly what the president said."

Biden left the call convinced the invasion was coming. A diplomatic off-ramp had no appeal with Putin. He was on a war path. Strangely, it was not as much from what Putin said but from all he had not said. Sometimes more truth could be found in Putin's silences than in his rhetoric.

During an interview with President Trump at Mar-a-Lago a year earlier, Trump had told me about his relationship with President Putin.

"Getting along with Russia is a good thing, not a bad thing, all right? Especially because they have 1,332 nuclear fucking warheads," Trump said. "And they work!

"Nobody ever has been tougher on Russia than me," Trump added. "Putin respects me. And I respect Putin. I think Putin likes me. I think I like him.

"I do like him," Trump concluded.

Trump's national security adviser Robert O'Brien had given me a different assessment. I told Trump, "O'Brien says we can't have good relations with Russia if they are invading the neighbors, like Ukraine, Georgia."

"Well, I don't like that. No," Trump said. "But if you look at, because of us, they just did a big prison swap with Ukraine. A lot of things are happening, Bob. A lot of things.

"Take a look at all the things that I've done," Trump declared. "Obama sent them pillows. I sent them tank-busters."

President Obama had provided Ukraine with more than $120 million in security assistance but refused to send lethal weapons. Trump was the first president to approve the sale of U.S. lethal weapons to Ukraine, including Javelin antitank missiles.

TWENTY

———— ◆ ◆ ————

"**I** am not sending U.S. troops to Ukraine," Biden said to Sullivan as the two sat alone in the Oval Office. This was his firm position, his red line not to be crossed—no American troops.

U.S. troops in Vietnam had led to catastrophe. The same problem in Afghanistan when Biden as vice president had unsuccessfully opposed adding 30,000 troops.

So Biden and Sullivan decided to ask the intelligence leaders what they thought: Should Biden leave open the possibility that the U.S. would send troops?

"The intelligence community," Sullivan reported, "came as close as the intelligence community comes in writing to you, are you fucking crazy? If you threaten to use U.S. troops in Ukraine, Putin will go faster and bigger, not back off." Putin would move before the U.S. could be prepared to deploy.

CIA director Bill Burns strongly agreed with this assessment. "Burns's view," Sullivan said, "was that saying the United States is going to send troops to Ukraine to defend Ukraine would have hastened the invasion, not forestalled it. Because Putin would have wanted to move before we could be prepared to mobilize."

Burns also said it would complicate the U.S. effort to build a coalition of countries to support Ukraine since many countries would be deeply uneasy if the U.S. started talking about putting boots on the ground in Ukraine.

Biden knew it was a matter of time before he was asked the question by a reporter and wanted to debate his response with Sullivan.

For years Biden had always said, "Great powers don't bluff." Sullivan had heard it many times. Biden wanted his policy position to be clear, not ambiguous.

Let's look at the other side, Sullivan said. Was there strategic value in bluffing? Could bluffing work? Churchill, for one, bluffed all the time.

"You have the big stack of chips, you have huge room to bluff," Sullivan said. As in poker, the U.S. had the biggest stack of chips given its military and economic preeminence. "If you have the big stack you can afford to lose some chips and not be out of the game. If you've got the big stack, yeah, you can bluff all the time."

Sullivan thought there could be a deterrent value in keeping the possibility of U.S. troop involvement unknown.

But a bluff, whether you're caught at it or not, Biden said, would impact overall U.S. credibility.

"If you're a big country with interests everywhere and you bluff here," Biden said, "it has an impact, say, on how the Japanese look at you over there with respect to China." The bleeding of credibility would not be limited to one circumstance.

Bluffing was off the table, Biden said. Since he knew he wasn't going to send U.S. troops, he thought he ought to say so publicly.

For Sullivan it was a difficult 51–49 call whether to say publicly and categorically that the U.S. was not going to send troops to fight in Ukraine. Sullivan still leaned toward using the large stack of chips they had. Bluffing was an available tool in the national security policy bag. Why not try?

Biden remained a firm: No.

Bluffing, even about U.S. troops, was the biggest strategic disagreement between the president and Sullivan.

In a national security crisis or when an issue came up, presidents often, even routinely, said publicly: "All options are on the table." Such a stance sounded tough and even threatening. It gave them much more flexibility.

But it wasn't Sullivan's call to make. Biden wanted clarity.

On December 8, a day after Biden's tense two-hour secure video call with Putin, Biden answered questions from reporters as he walked across the White House lawn to Marine One.

"I made it very clear, if in fact he invades Ukraine there will be severe consequences," Biden said of his meeting with Putin.

Biden then repeated to reporters what he had said privately to Sullivan: He would not send U.S. troops to Ukraine.

"That is not on the table," Biden said categorically. "We have a moral obligation and a legal obligation to our NATO allies if they were to [come under] attack under Article 5, it's a sacred obligation. That obligation does not extend to . . . Ukraine," which was not a member of NATO.

Fred Kagan, who was tracking Russia's military buildup with the Institute for the Study of War, called Sullivan in disbelief.

"You guys shouldn't take troops off the table," Kagan said. Ambiguity could be a deterrent. Why answer a hypothetical?

It was standard doctrine in tense diplomatic and military relations to keep all options available for discussion and negotiation.

"We had this exact debate," Sullivan said, "and it's legitimate.

"The problem is," Sullivan said, "if you keep open 'will you send U.S. troops? Well, we'll see' and the war starts, the pressure on you to send U.S. troops is through the roof and not sending them is basically like abandoning the country in their moment of need.

"So being clear," Sullivan added, "about what you're prepared to do and not do up front changes it from 'Biden whiffed' to 'wow, Biden's response was quite robust.'"

Deputy National Security Adviser Jon Finer was surprised by how directly Biden answered the question, but later told others he thought the president had made the right call.

"I felt like it was a relief and the right thing," Finer said. "It made the Ukrainians realize that they were going to have to do this themselves," he said, "with a ton of support but there was no cavalry coming to rescue them."

The remaining question not immediately answered was: Had this statement of "no U.S. troops" encouraged or even given Putin a green light believing that he would not directly or in any way face the largest and most experienced military force in the world?

Biden, however, told Sullivan and Finer that he would send American weapons to Ukraine. He would support Ukraine's military to defend itself. Since 2014, the United States had committed more than $2.5 billion in security assistance to Ukraine including specialized training by U.S. and U.K. forces.

But Biden drew the line on the kinds of weapons he was prepared to send. He would not go too big or too powerful. If Russia invaded and Ukraine fell in three to five days, the president did not want top-of-the-line American military technology falling into Russian hands. After the withdrawal from Afghanistan, the images of the Taliban brandishing U.S. weapons and equipment provided to the Afghan military still burned.

Former president Trump called retired Lieutenant General Kellogg, his former national security adviser, in December.

There's a lot of chatter that Putin is going to go in, Trump said. "Why would he do that?"

"If you want the truth, sir," Kellogg said, "it's because he sees weakness. He sees presidential weakness in decision-making as a result of what happened in Afghanistan."

"Fucking debacle," Trump said, referring to the Biden administration's messy withdrawal. "It was really fucked up."

"It's going to actually embolden other leaders out there," Kellogg said.

"Yeah, it was really fucked up," Trump said. "Biden's fucked us up. He's a weak leader."

"You think he'll go in?" Trump asked of Putin.

"No, he's not going to go," Kellogg said. "I don't think he has intent or the troops to do it. They're not postured right to do it. It's going to take a major effort." Kellogg was convinced the Russians were not prepared enough to invade Ukraine.

"Okay, okay," Trump said.

TWENTY-ONE

B iden was at his home in Wilmington, Delaware, on December 30 when he picked up the phone on his desk to take another swing of the bat at Putin. It was a hot 50-minute call and one of their most acrimonious exchanges. Putin was furious about the economic sanctions Biden was threatening and warned it could result in a "complete rupture" in relations between the U.S. and Russia. Putin continued to claim he had no plans to attack Ukraine and that he could move his troops on Russia's territory as he pleased.

He accused the U.S. and NATO of planning to place nuclear weapons near Russia's border. Biden assured Putin there were no such plans. It got so heated that at one point Putin raised the risk of nuclear war in a threatening way. Biden responded by reminding Putin that "it's impossible to win" a nuclear war.

"They fucked up in 2014," President Biden said to a close friend, reflecting his frustration with the Obama administration's inadequate response to Putin's previous invasion of Ukraine.

"That's why we are here. We fucked it up," Biden said. "Barack never took Putin seriously."

In 2014, Putin invaded Crimea with swift, calculated precision. "Little green men"—soldiers without any insignia identifying them as Russian—occupied Ukrainian parliament buildings by force, raised Russian flags and annexed Crimea as a so-called act of self-determination. Putin took Crimea and a section of the Donbas in less than a month with few consequences for Russia.

"You know we never should have let Putin just walk in there

and take the Donbas in 2014. We did nothing," Biden said. "We gave Putin a license to continue!"

Biden was very angry, a characteristic he avoided displaying in public.

"Well, I'm revoking his fucking license!" Biden said.

Biden's friend could hear the president's fixation on preventing Putin from doing it again. He's not going to let it go. "Ukraine is the whole ball game for his presidency."

TWENTY-TWO

In mid-January 2022, Biden sent Burns to secretly meet with Ukrainian president Zelensky.

"Convince Zelensky this is going to happen," Biden said. The intelligence now showed a sharper picture of what the Russians were going to attempt to do militarily.

Burns met with Zelensky in Kyiv.

"There is going to be a significant invasion of your country, including your capital," the CIA director said to President Zelensky. "Russian Special Forces are trying to assassinate you. They are coming for you personally.

"Russian forces will come straight across the Belarus frontier and try to take Kyiv, decapitate your regime and establish a pro-Russian government," Burns said. That was the spear of Russia's attack.

Russia plans to seize Hostomel, Burns continued, referring to the main cargo airport northwest of Kyiv, and then use it as a platform to bring in airborne forces to take control of Ukraine's capital.

From what we can see in the intelligence, this is coming in a matter of weeks, Burns said, and advised Zelensky to look closely at his personal security detail. There were also concerns of a Russian penetration of the Ukrainian services.

"Thank you for your information," Zelensky said. "But please stop going out publicly and saying this because it's hurting my economy."

Zelensky remained doubtful that Russia could be planning a full takeover of a country of 44 million people. The U.S. was focused in on the most aggressive and least likely option, Zelensky said. European leaders had told him the American forecasts were exaggerated and that Putin had insisted in private conversations with them and publicly that he wasn't invading.

But Zelensky nonetheless appeared to take seriously the CIA director's warning that an invasion was coming. Burns could see that the Ukrainian president was reluctant to go to full mobilization of his military because Putin then could seize upon that and allege Ukrainian provocation. Zelensky said Putin would claim: "Look, the Ukrainians are getting ready for war. We're just responding to them."

Burns also believed the Ukrainian intelligence services were very good and they were also keeping close tabs on the massive numbers of Russian troops on the Ukraine border.

It was a serious conversation, Burns felt, both emotionally and personally. This was devastating news for the young Ukrainian leader, who was listening but not entirely believing, facing an unimaginable political and strategic crisis.

One of the more novel sets of challenges for CIA director Burns and Director of National Intelligence Avril Haines was Putin's false flag operations—staged events that looked like ethnic Russians had been killed by Ukrainians as a pretext for conflict. They could see Putin and the people around him preparing these operations in the Donbas, in eastern Ukraine.

Burns, Haines and Sullivan debated extensively how to carefully declassify and share some of the intelligence hoping to checkmate the Russians.

In the White House, Director for Intelligence Programs Maher Bitar reviewed intel reports that Russia planned to stage an explosion in eastern Ukraine and claim Ukraine was responsible. Russia would say the Ukrainian government had killed ethnic Russians and then move into Ukraine under the false pretext of rescuing them. The Russian plot even talked about hiring actors who could play mourners at a funeral.

Russian media was also running stories about the deterioration of human rights in Ukraine and portraying Ukraine's leaders as a violent junta.

"Without getting into too much detail," Pentagon press secretary John Kirby said in a public briefing on January 14, "we do have information that indicates that Russia is already working actively to create a pretext for a potential invasion.

"We've seen this kind of thing before out of Russia," Kirby said. "When there isn't an actual crisis to suit their needs, they'll make one up."

TWENTY-THREE

On January 19, 2022, Biden declared in a rambling press conference that Putin was likely to "move in" on Ukraine.

"I'm not sure he [is] certain what he's going to do," Biden said. "My guess is he will move in."

Then came the raw, unvarnished aside from Biden.

"I think what you're going to see is that Russia will be held accountable if it invades. And it depends on what it does," Biden said. "It's one thing if it's a minor incursion and then we end up having a fight about what to do and not do, et cetera. But if they actually do what they are capable of doing with the forces amassed on the border, it is going to be a disaster for Russia.

"If there's something where there's Russian forces crossing the border, killing Ukrainian fighters, et cetera, I think that changes everything," Biden said. "But it depends on what he does, to what extent we're going to be able to get total unity on the NATO front."

That message was not on his notecards. Without seeming to know it, Biden had just totally undermined the idea that the U.S. was seriously committed to Ukraine's sovereignty. And, instead, he gave weight to the idea that, like 2014, any U.S. and allied response to a Russian invasion of Ukraine would be impeded by debate and division. The blunder echoed Biden's long history of gaffes.

President Zelensky responded in a tweet, "We want to remind the great powers that there are no minor incursions and small nations. Just as there are no minor casualties and little grief from the loss of loved ones. I say this as the President of a great power."

Was the United States changing its position on Ukraine? Biden's unscripted remarks caused confusion among allies and unease about the president's ability to articulate clear red lines to Russia.

Sullivan had phone calls with counterparts in nine NATO eastern flank countries, as well as Japan, to contain the damage and provide reassurance that the U.S. had not changed its position.

Biden was forced to clarify that if any Russian military forces moved across the border, it constituted an invasion.

"If there's a 1 percent chance, a 0.1 percent chance to still deter this," President Biden said to Blinken, "it will have been worth it." Go see if Russia has any practical security concerns we can address. Biden was still seeking a compromise.

It was a clear, sunny day in Geneva on January 21, 2022, but especially windy. Lake Geneva was a swirl of whitecaps.

"I don't know if you've looked at the lake today but there are turbulent waters," Blinken said to Russian foreign minister Lavrov. "It's our chore to see if we can't restore some calm and to see if we can avert what would ultimately be a disaster."

We are confident that you are preparing to mount an all-out invasion of Ukraine, Blinken said. You tell us you have security concerns. We are prepared to work with you on these.

Ukraine was Russia's buffer separating it from NATO, which had expanded over the last three decades to include over a dozen former Soviet and Soviet-aligned republics.

Mikhail Gorbachev, the final leader of the Soviet Union when it collapsed and was dissolved in 1991, said years later that the United States had a "dangerous winner's mentality."

The Russians, Blinken believed, legitimately worried about the deployment of nuclear or long-range offensive weapons on or near the Russian border. Blinken wanted to lower the temperature and avoid an appearance of smugness or winner's arrogance.

Like Putin, Lavrov had always had a flair for the dramatic. He was not averse to staging a public put-down or walkout on a Western counterpart. But in private, Blinken hoped Lavrov would drop the performance.

"Look, it's just us," Blinken said to Lavrov in the privacy of the room. "What is going on here? Tell me what's really going on here?"

Lavrov was silent.

"Is this practical? In other words, is this about your actual concerns about Russia's security? If so, we can talk about that. We can talk about the placement of offensive missiles. We can talk about stability mechanisms and confidence building measures that would alleviate any real security concerns that you have," Blinken said.

"We are not seeking to pose a threat to you," Blinken assured him. "NATO is not a threat to you so let's work on this if this is, you know, practical.

"But if this is theological, if this is born of the conviction that Ukraine as an independent sovereign state cannot exist, if this is predicated on the idea that Ukraine and its people belong to Mother Russia then there's nothing to talk about."

Lavrov denied any invasion was planned.

The U.S. intelligence later found that Lavrov still was not fully informed of what Putin had in store.

Blinken almost felt sorry for Lavrov. He had become a mouthpiece. It was sad someone so senior and with such longevity was not clued in, making the attempt at diplomacy pointless.

TWENTY-FOUR

In late January, Trump had started to throw around the idea of making another run for the presidency.

"You know Jack Nicklaus was pretty famous for letting people collapse and just hanging around," Trump mused to Senator Lindsey Graham over lunch at Mar-a-Lago, referring to the legendary American golfer. Trump said that should be his strategy with Biden. "When Nicklaus was behind in a tournament, he'd always say, well, what are you going to do? I'm just going to hang around and see what happens. That's how he won the Masters in '86. You know, you have two good holes and people start beginning to fall apart.

"Well," Trump said, "I'm just going to be hanging around!"

TWENTY-FIVE

◆ ◆

Along Ukraine's borders, Russian field hospitals were being visibly constructed, blood banks were transported in along with more military equipment and mobile morgues for expected dead. U.S. intelligence agencies were reporting to the White House that Putin's order to invade Ukraine could come in a matter of "weeks, days or hours."

Still mindful of the 1979 Iranian Hostage Crisis when 53 Americans were held hostage for 444 days during the Jimmy Carter presidency, Sullivan went to the podium on February 11. He had a steady, accommodating manner, treating all questions as reasonable.

"We are continuing to reduce the size of our embassy footprint in Kyiv," Sullivan said. "We encourage all American citizens who remain in Ukraine to depart immediately. Any American in Ukraine should leave as soon as possible, and in any event, in the next 24 to 48 hours.

"The president will not be putting the lives of our men and women in uniform at risk by sending them into a war zone to rescue people who could have left now but chose not to," Sullivan said. They did not want a repeat of Afghanistan.

"We are not going to war in Ukraine," Sullivan said. American forces "are not going to war with Russia."

French president Emmanuel Macron was calling Putin almost every day. He was convinced he could talk sense into the Russian leader. Macron called President Biden before and after many of his talks with Putin.

"I think it was a good conversation," Macron reported on one call to Biden. Putin gave me his word that he is not going to invade, Macron said.

"If you're having this conversation that's a good thing," Biden said. I'm very open to more conversations with Putin if you think we can dissuade him.

"Personally," Biden added, "I think he's already decided to invade."

Chairman of the Joint Chiefs General Mark Milley and Secretary of Defense Lloyd Austin were actively refuting Russia's claims that this was a military exercise. Russian troops had been massing on Ukraine's border since September 2021. "No one exercises that long," Milley said. "What kind of exercise is that?"

As Austin's motorcade drove through Poland on February 18, he placed a call to Russian defense minister Sergei Shoigu. The U.S. Secretary of Defense rolled in a pretty significant motorcade overseas. It wasn't as large as a presidential motorcade, but depending on the country could be relatively close.

"I know exactly what you're doing," Austin said to Shoigu. "I can see what you're doing with your troop buildup along the border."

"It's just an exercise," Shoigu said. "It's just a military exercise."

Austin's motorcade had reached their next destination but continued to drive in loops around town so he could finish the call.

"Well, if it's an exercise, when is it going to end?" Austin pressed. Shoigu tried to dodge the question with bluster.

"We know exactly what you're doing," Austin injected. "Don't do it."

The next day, Austin traveled to Vilnius, Lithuania, to reassure Baltic allies that the United States and NATO would support and defend them. Countries like Estonia with small militaries were extremely worried that if Ukraine fell to Russia, they were next on Putin's menu. No one expected Ukraine to last long against Russia's military.

The secretary's top advisers who traveled with him and attended many of his meetings reported a common theme: former president Trump's "Article 5 saber rattling" over four years was causing many NATO allies to question if the U.S. would actually show up when it mattered. The nervousness in the room was palpable.

"When the time comes, we'll have your back," Austin said to Estonia's Defense Minister Hanno Pevkur. "You'll open up the windows and be able to smell the jet fuel." That's how quickly the U.S. military would move in.

Austin, a towering presence at over six feet tall and 250 pounds, delivered the emphatic assurance in a cool, matter-of-fact tone. "We are going to be here," he said. "We will stand by Article Five."

"People don't make good decisions when they're nervous and skittish," Austin told his advisers afterwards. "If Putin does this, it could create the largest land war in Europe since the end of World War II." They needed calm along the eastern flank.

As a final diplomatic push for deterrence, President Biden sent Vice President Kamala Harris to Germany for the Munich Security Conference on February 19, 2022. He wanted the United States represented at the highest levels and the vice president was tradition. Biden had attended as vice president and even the Trump administration had kept the tradition going.

So Harris was up.

Biden said he needed her to convince Zelensky that they were now in the days and possibly moments before Russia invaded his country. The intelligence had crystallized. Zelensky needed to accept this was happening.

Harris was also given a recovery mission. After Biden's bruising slipup about a "minor incursion," she needed to demonstrate unified United States and NATO support for Ukraine's sovereignty.

"Not since the end of the Cold War has this forum convened under such dire circumstances," Vice President Harris said, addressing world leaders at the Hotel Bayerischer Hof in Munich. "Today, as we are well aware, the foundation of European security is under direct threat in Ukraine."

In what is widely considered the best speech of her vice presidency, Harris succeeded in showcasing U.S. commitment to Ukraine, to NATO Article 5 and to peace. Instead of warning Putin, typical of Biden's approach, she called out Russia for pleading "ignorance and innocence."

"As we have seen all along, there is a playbook of Russian aggression," she said. "We see Russia spreading disinformation, lies and propaganda.

"We will target those who are complicit and those who aid and abet this unprovoked invasion," she warned. "Make no mistake."

And she drew a sharp distinction between the Biden-Harris view of America's leadership role in the world and in NATO, and the Trump administration's isolationist America First approach.

"The theme of this conference two years ago questioned the staying power of the West," she said, "whether or not the transatlantic community was losing its cohesion, its influence, its appeal.

"So I will answer the skeptics and those seeking to test us: Today, the United States, our allies, and our partners are closer together. Today, we are clear in our purpose.

"Our strength must not be underestimated," she said. "As we have always shown, it takes a lot more strength to build something up than it takes to tear something down."

After her speech, in a private room in the Commerzbank across from the Bayerischer Hof, Vice President Harris pulled out a chair and sat down opposite Ukrainian president Zelensky. Her national security adviser Philip Gordon sat alongside her. Zelensky brought his principal adviser, Andriy Yermak, and Defense Minister Oleksii Reznikov.

Germany had Covid protocols in place. So Harris and Gordon wore masks. They did not shake hands with the Ukrainians. It disgruntled Zelensky. It felt like he was about to be reprimanded. Two sides, supposedly on the same team, facing off.

"You need to take seriously the likelihood that any day the Russians will invade your country," Harris told him forcefully.

Her manner and communication style was often criticized for being overly adversarial. It was a trait hammered almost into her DNA by her years as a prosecutor and attorney general in California.

"We just don't think they're going to invade," Zelensky pushed back. "Yes, they're threatening us, they're bullying us. That's what they do."

Harris began to read out the latest troop numbers.

"The Russians have 200,000 troops devoted to this operation, including about 40,000 in Belarus."

"There are fewer than 10,000 troops in Belarus," Defense Minister Reznikov interjected.

"That's not at all consistent with our information," Harris said.

"The Belarusians won't be supportive," Reznikov said, "they won't join in the fighting."

Harris's national security adviser Phil Gordon told him the U.S. intel was good. This was not U.S. analysis or an ambiguous assessment. This was raw data. Satellite photographs. Gordon wasn't sure who the Ukrainians thought they were fooling by denying the Russian threat.

"Look," Harris said to Zelensky, "our teams will share more specific information with you but we are telling you that your numbers are wrong. You really face a potentially imminent invasion."

Zelensky was all denial. Harris sounded more and more like a prosecutor. They went back and forth. Zelensky reiterated that he took seriously the situation on his borders.

"We do clearly understand what is going on," Zelensky said. "This is our land, and the only thing we want is to have peace, bring the peace back to our country." End the fighting in eastern Ukraine.

The psychological dynamic in play was that Zelensky did not want to signal that a full Russian invasion was going to happen because it would create a self-fulfilling prophecy of the Ukrainian economy and potentially the government collapsing.

Finally, Zelensky looked Harris directly in the eye and said, "What do you want me to do?"

The silence between them stretched awkwardly.

"What will that give you?" Zelensky said. "If I acknowledge it here in this conversation, will you impose sanctions?" Close ports to Russian ships. Give us Stinger and Javelin missiles, warplanes?

Harris said the U.S. would not impose sanctions on Russia yet. "The punishment can only come after the crime."

That seemed like a cop-out to the Ukrainians. Russia had been "committing crimes" against Ukrainians in the Donbas since 2014.

Reznikov wondered, What did the United States think Ukraine was supposed to do? Surrender? Acknowledge that they would not win if Putin launched a full invasion? Concede to more Kremlin demands? Sign more peace accords that Russia would violate?

"Start thinking about things like having a succession plan in place to run the country if you're captured or killed or cannot govern," Harris suggested. Have an escape plan so that you won't be captured or killed. Possibly mobilize more Ukrainian troops. Have a plan for continued governance.

"But you can't decide the right things to do if you're just going to pretend that this isn't happening," Harris urged him. "If they do this, they're coming to Kyiv.

"We're with you," she added, trying to soften her tone. She assured him Russia would face consequences. But as Harris looked at Zelensky, she couldn't help but wonder if the U.S. had done enough.

After the meeting Gordon turned to the vice president. "They're crazy not to have a plan to escape and go somewhere to hide," he said. Zelensky was clear he would be staying in Kyiv.

We might never see him again, Harris replied.

TWENTY-SIX

O n Monday, February 21, President Putin officially put Russia on the public path to war. In a lengthy televised Russian Security Council meeting in the Kremlin, Putin aggressively polled his top officials on the question of whether to recognize the independence of two Russian-backed separatist regions in the east of Ukraine, Donetsk and Luhansk.

The Russian leader sat alone at a desk in a vast, white-columned oval room and faced his advisers, who perched nervously in flimsy chairs at least 30 feet away from him. Putin called them one by one to a lectern to state their opinion, drumming his fingers impatiently.

Foreign Minister Lavrov, former Russian president Dmitry Medvedev, Secretary of the Security Council Nikolai Patrushev and Duma speaker Vyacheslav Volodin dutifully gave Putin the endorsements he wanted to hear.

Director of the Foreign Intelligence Service Sergei Naryshkin faltered, tripping over his prepared lines. Putin's jaw clenched. "Speak plainly," Putin ordered with unmistakable pleasure as Naryshkin squirmed.

Naryshkin tried again to find the words the president wanted. "I would support the proposal for recognition—"

"Would support or do support?" Putin snapped, now visibly irritated. "Speak plainly, Sergei."

"I support the proposal . . ." Naryshkin said with as much assertiveness as he could muster, but unable to hide his humiliation.

"Just say yes or no," Putin said icily.

"Yes. I support the proposal to admit the Donetsk and Luhansk People's Republics into the Russian Federation," Naryshkin said.

Putin laughed, shaking his head. "That's not what we're talking about. We're discussing whether to recognize their independence."

Naryshkin's hands shook as he looked almost pleadingly to Putin, who was leaning forward over the microphone on his desk, his hands clasped in front of him as if he were enjoying himself immensely.

"Yes," Naryshkin said. "I support the proposal to recognize their independence."

"You can take your seat," Putin said dismissively and leaned back comfortably in his chair.

President Biden immediately issued an executive order that blocked all economic activity in Donetsk and Luhansk. Germany announced its $11 billion Nord Stream 2 gas pipeline project with Russia would not go forward.

Russian forces took up tactical positions on the border. Russian-backed separatists in eastern Ukraine had begun to force Ukrainian civilians to leave their homes and to conscript Ukrainian men and boys into Russia's military.

"This is genius," Trump said during an interview on a conservative radio show the next day, February 22, at Mar-a-Lago, praising Putin's move to declare certain Ukrainian regions independent.

"So Putin is now saying, 'It's independent,' a large section of Ukraine. I said, 'How smart is that?' And he's going to go in and be a peacekeeper. That's the strongest peace force. We could use that on our southern border. That's the strongest peace force I've ever seen. There were more army tanks than I've ever seen. They're going to keep the peace all right. No but think of it. Here's a guy who's very savvy, I know him very well. Very, very well," Trump said gleefully.

"I knew that he always wanted Ukraine," Trump said. "I used to talk to him about it. I said, 'You can't do it. You're not gonna do it.' But I could see that he wanted it."

TWENTY-SEVEN

At 9:15 a.m. on February 23 Sullivan was holding his Ukraine meeting in his West Wing office when the door opened and CIA director Bill Burns walked in holding a piece of paper.

The CIA director had never crashed a meeting.

"Hey, Bill," Sullivan said.

Burns looked around as if to check who was in the room. He said he was on his way to the Oval Office.

"Is it happening?" Senior Director for Europe Amanda Sloat asked Burns. They were all waiting on edge for the signal that Putin had given the order for Russian forces to invade.

"It's happening," Burns said.

Before sunrise in Moscow on Thursday, February 24, Putin appeared on television. He sat alone at a desk in the Kremlin flanked by Russian flags.

"I have decided to conduct a special military operation in Ukraine," Putin said.

"Whoever tries to hinder us," Putin continued, "and even more so, to create threats to our country, to our people, should know that Russia's response will be immediate. And it will lead you to such consequences that you have never encountered in your history.

"Russia remains one of the most powerful nuclear states," he threatened.

Thunderous blasts were reported in Kyiv, the capital, and Kharkiv, the second largest city. Ukraine's Interior Ministry said Russian troops had landed in Odessa in the south and were crossing the border. The sun was not yet up.

President Zelensky raced in his motorcade through the dark streets of Kyiv passing cars packed full of people fleeing in the opposite direction. It was still dark out. He thought about the rockets flying toward his children, all of Ukraine's children and struggled to come to terms with the enormous scale of Russia's attack. All he could think was, a huge number of deaths.

Zelensky's phone rang. It was his minister of internal affairs, Denys Monastyrsky, who oversaw the country's police and border guard.

Where are the Russians coming from? Zelensky asked. What direction? The north, east or south? He wanted to know exactly what axis Putin had chosen to invade Ukraine.

"All of them," Monastyrsky said.

Bruno Kahl, the head of the BND, Germany's Foreign Intelligence Service, was in Kyiv the morning of the invasion. Up until the first Russian missiles launched, he was convinced it wasn't going to happen despite all the U.S. and British intelligence assessments.

The Poles, rivals of Germany, enjoyed telling the story of how the BND chief had to be driven out of Ukraine by special forces because once the Russians started invading, he couldn't take his plane.

In Washington, D.C., eight hours behind Moscow, it was just after 9:30 p.m. in the evening on February 23. Biden's principals gathered in the Situation Room. The president was connected by secure phone from the Residence.

Chairman Milley and Secretary of Defense Austin said Putin had mobilized 123 Russian battalion tactical groups with between 175,000 and 190,000 soldiers. Russian forces were invading along multiple axes: Belarus in the north, Russian-occupied Donbas in the east, and Crimea in the south. There were two lines of Russian forces heading directly for Kyiv to decapitate the government and install their own.

Some Pentagon assessments projected that Kyiv would fall within the first 72 to 96 hours. Other intelligence assessments projected it would take several weeks. Russia had a far superior military force in every measurable respect.

Biden authorized Austin and Milley to move U.S. ground and air forces already stationed in Europe to Estonia, Latvia, Lithuania, Poland and Romania—near the Ukraine borders—to remind Putin that the United States would defend every inch of NATO territory.

He is "pretty smart," Trump said of Putin during a Florida fundraiser that evening, assessing the invasion like a real estate deal rather than a former president.

"He's taken over a country for $2 worth of sanctions," Trump said, "really a vast, vast location, a great piece of land with a lot of people—and just walking right in."

At the presidential compound in Kyiv, Zelensky turned to what he did best—communicate. He called first British prime minister Boris Johnson, one of his strongest supporters.

"We will fight, Boris," Zelensky told him. "We are not going to give up."

Zelensky also called French president Emmanuel Macron, who had been so intensely engaged with Putin to try to personally deter him from invading.

"It's very important, Emmanuel, for you to speak with Putin," said Zelensky. "We are sure that European leaders and Biden can connect. If they call him and say stop, he will stop. He will listen."

"I want to talk to President Zelensky," Biden said to Sullivan and Jon Finer. It was now late in the evening in Washington. Biden was very concerned about Zelensky's personal safety.

"What can I do for you? How can I be of help?" Biden asked Zelensky.

"Gather the leaders of the world," Zelensky said. "Ask them to support Ukraine."

Sullivan and Finer, who were listening in, could tell Zelensky was frightened. The Ukrainian president's usual cowboy rhetoric on phone calls with Biden was gone.

"We're going to be with you," President Biden said. "You should always tell us what you need." He offered to help get Zelensky out and set up a temporary Ukrainian government in exile in Poland.

Zelensky declined. He was staying. He asked Biden to set up a no-fly zone around Ukraine. We need to close the skies, Zelensky said. Ukraine was getting hammered from the air.

Biden said no. Enforcing a no-fly zone would require U.S. or NATO planes to shoot down Russian aircraft—an impossible escalation for Biden.

"I don't know when I will be able to talk to you again," Zelensky said at the end of the call.

The comment seemed to hang in the air.

"If you ever want to talk to me, I'm here," President Biden reassured Zelensky.

A few hours later, around 11:20 a.m., Zelensky addressed his nation by video in Kyiv, saying anyone who wanted an assault rifle could get one from distribution centers that had been set up around the city. Powerful images shared through social media showed Ukrainian people picking up a gun, many for the first time. As the Russian brigades advanced toward Kyiv, Ukrainians took to the streets yelling at approaching troops to "fuck off" and leave. Others helped guide Ukraine's military to Russian targets.

At Snake Island, a tiny Ukrainian outpost on the Black Sea,

two Russian warships ordered the 13 Ukrainian border guards stationed there to surrender. One guard picked up the transmitter and responded, "Russian warship, go fuck yourself." Russia captured Snake Island, but the defiance of the Ukrainians was played on media outlets all over the world, becoming a symbol of Ukrainian resistance.

Later that day rumors circulated that Zelensky and his team had fled Ukraine. So Zelensky filmed a video of himself walking through the heart of Kyiv with his team of advisers, including his chief of staff Andriy Yermak.

"We are all here," Zelensky declared, "defending our independence, our state and it will remain so. Glory to our women defenders. Glory to Ukraine!"

Watching this, Chairman of the Joint Chiefs General Mark Milley said, "Zelensky was a master and still is a master of the airwaves."

CIA director Burns was also impressed with Zelensky's leadership. "In those first 48 to 72 hours he stayed. He took the best punch the Russians could provide. He was still standing, and I think he brought the whole country along with him."

In the early hours of the war, as predicted by U.S. intelligence, Russian forces tried to capture Hostomel airport—a big cargo airfield located less than 10 miles from Kyiv. The world's largest aircraft, the Mriya, was hangared at Hostomel.

The airport had enormous strategic value for the Russians, who planned to use it as an airbridge to land big Il-76 military transport planes packed with armored vehicles and airborne battalions to take control of Kyiv. Already the Russians had loads of Il-76 planes in the air ready to land.

The Ukrainians had made a tactical mistake in sending their most combat-ready brigades to the east. But the attack on the airport did not go as Russia planned. The Ukrainian troops encircled Russian forces inside the airport before they had a chance to bring in reinforcements. It was the first big battle of the war.

Ukrainian troops fought back with such ferocity that Russia

could not land its planes. While Russia eventually won control of the airport, the Ukrainians had inflicted so much damage to it with bombings and artillery, the Russians could not use it to resupply.

"Military theory does not account for regular dudes with track pants and hunting rifles," said General Valerii Zaluzhnyi, the so-called Iron General, the commander in chief of Ukraine's military.

In the first wave, Russian forces also seized the nuclear power plant Chernobyl, but again made fatal errors, driving tanks and armored vehicles through the "Red Forest," the most toxic area. Chernobyl employees reported the Russians said it was suicide for those who inhaled the radioactive dust.

Burns had seen in the intelligence that "the spear of Russia's invasion was going to be straight south from Belarus and aimed at Ukraine, which without a lot of traffic is a two-and-a-half-hour drive. The aim was to strike fast at Kyiv. It was to decapitate the regime."

Another surprise was the Russian helicopter pilots did not like to fly at night, the key time for American pilots. In the day they made themselves easy targets for Ukrainian fire. Ukrainian forces were also executing complex ground operations using the cover of darkness to push back the Russians.

By the fifth day of the invasion, February 28, a 40-mile convoy of 15,000 Russian troops, tanks, supply trucks, weapons and artillery was stalled in a massive traffic jam—a clear Russian tactical error.

"It wasn't rocket science what the Ukrainians did," Burns said. "They pretty methodically took out the first and last vehicles in the convoy and then they went after each of the fuel trucks. Pretty soon they were stuck."

Russia's tanks were stopped in the mud, out of fuel, and some were simply misdirected away from Kyiv after Ukrainians switched up street signs. A Ukrainian sniper killed a Russian major general who ventured out in front of the stalled vehicles.

The Russian convoy had brought food and water for only three days. Video footage of burned-out Russian tanks and vehicles also showed the soldiers had brought their parade uniforms expecting a victory celebration.

"They thought they would drive easily all the way from Belarus to Kyiv and they all were preparing for the parade," Ukrainian ambassador to the U.S. Oksana Markarova said as she watched the column from Belarus head toward her hometown Vorzel.

"The sheer incompetence of the Russian military operation became clear," Burns believed as he watched it unfold. "Part of this was because the decision-making circle was so tight that the Russian military had levels beneath the senior general officer and the defense minister who really were kind of catching up to this as they went along.

"Commanders of units didn't really understand what their goals were," Burns said. "Their logistics and their generalship were pretty screwed up."

The Russian military, unlike the U.S. military, was a very top-down-driven system. There was little initiative at the field grade of lower officer ranks. So Russian troops waited for directions from headquarters, rather than adapt and improvise.

Burns had anticipated the Russian military would make the obvious move according to military doctrine.

"We expected them to do exactly what the U.S. military would have done, which is spend the first 24 hours taking out the command-and-control system and taking out the air defense system. They didn't do that."

The CIA director consulted his intelligence analysts. Why didn't Russia do the obvious? Part of it was hubris. "They were so convinced the Ukrainians were just going to roll over. Why destroy all these systems and then have to rebuild them later on?"

The battle for Kyiv lasted less than five weeks. The Russian Ministry of Defense—not Putin—announced it was withdrawing Russian troops from the capital. At least 35,000 Russian troops had participated in the failed march on Kyiv. By NATO calculations at least 10,000 Russians had been killed.

The Ukrainians had forced the second most powerful military

in the world to retreat, shattering the image of Russia as a fiercely capable fighting force.

Over at the Pentagon, Secretary of Defense Austin was constantly assessing the battlefield in Ukraine.

"I don't think he really made the final decision [to invade] until pretty late in the game," Austin told his close advisers about Putin. "His troops were not as prepared as they should have been.

"Troops will do in combat exactly what they've been trained to do, and if they believe in their leaders, if they trust their leaders, they will go above and beyond any expectation. If they don't then it's difficult to get things done," Austin said.

When the Russians pulled back from the battle for Kyiv, they left in their wake evidence of horrific war crimes. Mass graves of hundreds of civilians, bodies mutilated by torture, and others subjected to sexual violence.

U.S. intelligence showed that Russia planned to create concentration camps in the Ukrainian cities and towns it occupied to "filter out" civilians who would not succumb to Russian rule.

Inside the National Security Council, Sullivan, Finer and their staff reflected on all that had transpired so far.

"We got one thing absolutely right which was what they were going to do, where they were going to do it and when they were going to do it," director for strategic planning on the National Security Council Alex Bick said.

"Everything else we got wrong," he said. "We underestimated the European response." For months it had felt like they were dragging their European partners along like a heavy sled up a steep hill. But after Russia invaded, the Europeans moved quickly and decisively.

"We underestimated the Ukrainians' resolve badly and we over-estimated the Russian military," Bick concluded.

"All three of those things broke in our favor," he said.

"We executed the best possible strategy we could have," Jon Finer said. "But you look at the outcome and it's hard to feel good about it. It's still a horrible war."

———◆———

TWENTY-EIGHT

S teve Bannon, the shaggy gray-haired far-right strategist and longstanding Trump adviser, had been watching what was happening between Russia and Ukraine with fervor.

"Putin ain't woke," Bannon said on his podcast, *War Room*. "This is going to be old-school original gangster.

"Ukraine," Bannon said, "is kind of a concept. It's not even a country."

As soon as Russia invaded, Bannon called for Biden to be impeached, claiming the president was more interested in protecting Ukraine's borders than the U.S. southern border. "He's getting impeached. We're impeaching him!

"Is Hunter Biden over there with his business partners? Is he sitting there with the Ukrainian flag? Where is Hunter? Is he in his art gallery? Is he with more strippers? Is he smoking more crack?" Bannon heckled.

Fox News host Tucker Carlson was also stoking the culture wars and asking Americans to rethink any criticism of Putin. He framed the Russian leader's brutal attempt at territorial conquest as a mere "border dispute" with Ukraine. He told viewers to ask themselves: "Why do I hate Putin so much? Has Putin ever called me a racist? Has he threatened to get me fired for disagreeing with him? Is he trying to snuff out Christianity?"

TWENTY-NINE

"**T**hat fucking Putin," President Biden said furiously to his advisers in the privacy of the Oval Office. He was on fire about the Russian president. "Can you imagine if we hadn't done what we've done? For Christ sakes!" he yelled.

"I mean he'd be going after Estonia, he'd be going after the Baltics. He's the most surprised human being on the face of the earth because of the opposition that he faces now. He's fighting for his survival," Biden said.

Biden was disgusted at the reports and images he was shown daily of Russia's attempt to "gobble up Ukraine."

"Putin is evil. We are dealing with the epitome of evil," Biden said with almost religious fervor.

Biden said Putin was controlled by his lust to be seen, and to be remembered in Russian history, as the leader of a great power—a global leader equal in status to Chinese president Xi Jinping and the president of the United States.

It's a "fantasy," Biden said. "We have to stop him."

Putin would not stop at Ukraine, Biden was convinced of that. The Ukraine war was now a fight for freedom and freedom loving nations everywhere.

Russia had displayed shocking ineptitude in the opening hours and days of the war, piercing the mythology that the Russian army was a formidable, super-capable fighting force.

Ukraine had fought the David and Goliath of battles and held Russia off against all of their expectations. But U.S. intel reports to Biden showed that Putin believed time and the size of Russia's army were on his side.

President Biden said he wanted to make sure Putin's invasion was a massive strategic failure for Russia. He wanted a clear, unmistakable blow to Putin.

The president called his national security experts on Russia and Ukraine to the White House Residence late one evening to workshop ideas.

Sullivan and Finer, who led the discussion, pointed out that Putin invaded, at least in part, to keep one country, Ukraine, out of NATO and to deter others from aspiring to join by showing the alliance as crumbling, weak, divided and fragile.

Suppose they added more countries to the NATO alliance, the exact opposite of what Putin wanted? It would be a huge strategic blow to Putin and a powerful public statement of NATO unity if it could be done right.

Finland and Sweden had historically maintained military nonalignment as a core tenet of their foreign policies but Russia's invasion had clearly shaken them.

Public polling in Finland and Sweden, Finer noted, showed that Russia's invasion of Ukraine had prompted new interest in joining NATO. Finland declared independence from Russia in 1917 and shares an 832-mile border with Russia. Suppose Finland joined NATO?

Before the invasion polls indicated only about 25 percent of Finland's population favored joining NATO. The new polls were recording an astonishing 76 percent of Finns in support. And Sweden for the first time had recorded 51 percent of Swedes in favor of NATO membership, up from 42 percent in January before the invasion. Shifts politicians would have to take seriously, Finer said.

For the Finns, especially, the Ukrainians' fight was hauntingly familiar. Russia invaded Finland in 1939 during World War II. Despite being vastly outnumbered, the Finns fought off Soviet occupation in what was later known as the Winter War, but lost a 10 percent chunk of their eastern province, Karelia, which still today remains part of Russia.

Biden saw an opportunity. The two Nordic countries were strong democracies with developed economies and established militaries. Finland has a wartime military strength of 280,000 personnel. Sweden's is much smaller at around 46,000 but its investment in its military grew after Putin invaded Crimea in 2014.

If Finland joined NATO, it would effectively double NATO's frontier facing Moscow and give the alliance strategic dominance in the Baltic Sea, where Sweden also had a maritime border with Russia.

"You've basically given the middle finger to Russia," Finer said.

Amanda Sloat, senior director for Europe on the National Security Council, pushed for Biden to meet with President Sauli Niinistö to get Niinistö's perspective on Putin.

"The Finnish watch Putin more closely than almost anybody else in Europe," Sloat said. "Niinistö is really a longtime observer of Russia." Niinistö had spoken to Putin on numerous occasions. "I mean, their countries have fishing disputes and other things they have to sort out," Sloat added.

Let's explore this and see what's possible, Biden said.

On March 4, ten days after Putin's invasion, President Biden met with Finnish president Niinistö in the White House to talk about Finland's path to NATO.

Niinistö said he had known Putin for a long time. He used to play hockey with him sometimes, but Putin never lost.

Anything you need from us to be able to make this any easier for you, let us know, Biden said.

Niinistö said he was worried about the gap in time between when they might announce Finland's intention to join NATO and when they were actually admitted into the alliance, gaining Article 5 protection. The gap was too long and uncertain, potentially leaving them vulnerable. Putin might take advantage of that interregnum and try to force Finland to reverse their decision. Niinistö didn't want Finland to be the next Ukraine.

Biden told Sullivan and Finer to look at options to manage risk during that period. Could they increase the pace of joint exercises with Finland and Sweden? What strong declaratory messages could they send to discourage Russia from trying anything? What security guarantees could be given?

"There's not much Russia can do," Finer said to Sullivan. "Probably 50 or 60 percent of Russian combat power and capability is pointed south in Ukraine. The last thing Russia can actually afford is another front of some kind."

Dmitry Medvedev, deputy chairman of Russia's Security Council, warned that if Sweden and Finland joined NATO, Russia would deploy nuclear weapons and hypersonic missiles to Kaliningrad—a Russian exclave sandwiched between Poland and Lithuania.

"There can be no more talk of any nuclear-free status for the Baltic. The balance must be restored," said Medvedev.

In early May, Sweden confirmed publicly that it had received security guarantees from the United States, the United Kingdom, as well as other NATO nations.

"Russia can be clear that if they direct any kind of negative activities against Sweden, which they have threatened, it would not be something that the U.S. would just allow to happen . . . without a response," Sweden's foreign minister Ann Linde said on Swedish TV after a meeting with Blinken in Washington.

NATO countries Norway, Denmark and Iceland released a joint statement that pledged to provide support in the event of Russian retaliation. "Should Finland or Sweden be victim of aggression on their territory before obtaining NATO membership, we will assist Finland and Sweden by all means necessary."

U.K. prime minister Boris Johnson was far more public with his offer of security guarantees, traveling to both Sweden and Finland to sign mutual security agreements that said if either country faced an attack or disaster, they would assist each other in a variety of ways, which might include military means.

At a press conference held at the Presidential Palace in Helsinki after the signing, Niinistö was asked about Russian retaliation if Finland joins NATO.

"If that would be the case then my response would be: You caused this. Look in the mirror," Niinistö said, directing his response at Putin, his old friend.

When Finland's president Niinistö and Prime Minister Sanna Marin announced on May 12 that Finland would officially seek to join NATO, the Kremlin immediately accused Finland of turning its territory into a new line of military confrontation with Russia.

"Russia will be forced to take retaliatory steps, both of a military-technical and other nature, in order to stop the threats to its national security," the Russian Foreign Ministry warned. "Helsinki must be aware of the responsibility and consequences of such a move."

Two days later, Niinistö called Putin and broke the news directly: Finland was joining NATO. Putin was calm, surprisingly muted in his objection.

He said it was a mistake, Niinistö reported, that Finland was not under any threat.

Like clockwork, Sweden then announced publicly its intention to join NATO, breaking its 73-year policy of military nonalignment.

On the same day, NATO launched one of its largest military exercises in the Baltic region, involving some 15,000 troops from 10 countries, eight NATO countries, and Sweden and Finland. The exercise, called "Hedgehog," took place in Estonia, 40 miles from Russia's nearest military base, and simulated a Russian attack on that nation, getting into Putin's face dramatically.

Meanwhile across Europe from the north to the Balkans, NATO exercises kicked into gear with 18,000 troops in Poland, helicopter exercises in North Macedonia, and 3,000 allied troops and 1,000 vehicles, including German Leopard 2 tanks, in Lithuania.

The message to Putin was clear.

Finland formally became a member of NATO with the Article 5 protection on April 4, 2023, adding 832 miles to Russia's border with NATO. It was a momentous transformation in Finland's foreign and security policy.

Turkey and Hungary initially blocked Sweden's accession to NATO but, on March 7, 2024, Sweden also finally became a full member.

THIRTY

O ne weekend after the invasion, Republican senator Lindsey
Graham of South Carolina was at Mar-a-Lago, to play golf
and have dinner with Trump.

"Going to Mar-a-Lago is a little bit like going to North Korea,"
Graham said. "Everybody stands up and claps every time Trump
comes in.

"So I come in behind him and I get a standing ovation!" Graham
said. He assumed it was for his comments about Putin. "I've been
saying get rid of Putin. If you have to kill him, kill him," he said.

In a March 4 interview on Fox News, Graham had declared
that Russians should assassinate President Putin. He followed it
with a post on social media: "The only way this ends is for somebody in Russia to take this guy out. You would be doing your
country—and the world—a great service," Graham said.

The comments caused a brief firestorm.

White House press secretary Jen Psaki was quick to clarify this
was "not the position of the United States government."

Kremlin press secretary Dmitry Peskov hit back by suggesting
Graham was insane. "Unfortunately, in such an extremely tense
atmosphere, there is a hysterical escalation of Russophobia. These
days, not everyone manages to maintain sobriety, I would even say
sanity, and many lose their mind."

Graham downplayed his comments to others at Mar-a-Lago.

"I don't think it's fascinating," Graham said. "I mean would
anybody doubt that they'd have been better off if the Germans had
gotten rid of Hitler?"

During dinner that evening Trump and Graham talked about the threat of Putin using nuclear weapons in Ukraine.

"We can't let him get away with that," Trump said. "We've got a bigger military. We've got deadly submarines. I would have submarines going up and down the coast of Russia saying we're watching you.

"Why can't we get involved?" Trump asked Graham. "Why do we let the planes fly?" Graham realized Trump was wondering about why the U.S. hadn't set up a no-fly zone to stop Russian planes from entering Ukraine's airspace.

Zelensky was pleading for Biden to "close the skies." Biden had repeatedly refused. He did not want a situation where U.S. or NATO forces would have to take out Russian planes. That could too quickly escalate into World War III.

"Everybody felt the Russians would roll through Ukraine in about a week and do some kind of peace deal and that'd be that," Graham said. "Well, the Ukrainians are fighting like tigers. Zelensky has become the Churchill of his time and the Russians are in a world of hurt. They actually could lose this. They could actually lose this military engagement if we could do better in the air."

The next morning, Graham played nine holes with Trump, who was now golfing five times a week. Some of the caddies came up and asked for a photo. Not with Trump, but with Graham.

"The caddies want to get rid of Putin too," Graham joked to Trump. But the former president was no longer paying attention. He was fixated on the caddies, as if suddenly realizing being tough with Putin was popular.

On March 5, during a fundraiser in New Orleans with top GOP donors, Trump suggested that the U.S. should label its F-22 planes with the Chinese flag and then "bomb the shit out of Russia.

"And then we say, China did it, we didn't do it, China did it, and then they start fighting with each other and we sit back and watch," he said almost gleefully.

The crowd laughed.

THIRTY-ONE

In Poland surrounded by huge crates of humanitarian aid for Ukraine, Defense Secretary Lloyd Austin was asked about America's goals for the war.

"We want to see Russia weakened to the degree that it can't do the kinds of things that it has done in invading Ukraine," Austin said, adding that Russia "has already lost a lot of military capability and a lot of its troops, quite frankly."

A signal that America's goalposts had shifted beyond helping Ukraine defend itself. Biden now wanted to decisively blunt Russia's ability to threaten Europe.

Two days later, on April 26, Austin convened a Ukraine Defense Contact Group meeting at Ramstein Air Base in Germany. Defense ministers from 40 countries debated what assistance, training and advice should be provided to Ukraine. What should NATO's involvement look like?

Ukraine's defense minister Oleksii Reznikov was energized by the meeting and updated Zelensky of a "tectonic philosophical shift" in NATO's approach to Ukraine. NATO membership was not a consideration, but the alliance had committed to supply Ukraine's military with NATO weapons, training and intelligence as if they were a team.

By invading Ukraine, Putin had massively accelerated precisely what he feared. Ukraine would become a highly capable, NATO-standard fighting force backed by the most powerful military alliance in the world.

THIRTY-TWO

O ne evening that spring, Biden was having dinner with a friend at the White House when Hunter Biden wandered in, pulled up a chair and sat down at the table. First Lady Jill Biden was out of town.

Interrupting the conversation, Hunter started talking about why he was the person who had the most to lose from the outcome of the midterm elections.

If Republicans won control of both the House and Senate, they would continue to try to investigate everything about him.

Hunter rambled on about his personal crisis.

President Biden leaned back in his chair, closed his eyes and sighed. It was almost a trance that continued for some time.

"None of us can really measure the toll, the burden that Hunter is on him," his friend said later.

After dinner, Biden gave his friend a tour of the White House Residence.

"I want to show you where my grandchildren come and sleep in the White House," Biden said, walking into a bedroom in the back of the Residence.

Along the bureau was a clutter of framed pictures that displayed Biden's family at different ages and walks of life, smiling, embracing. At the end was a picture of a young man dressed up in a suit and tie.

Biden picked it up and showed it to his friend.

"That's my dad," Biden said. "Quite a man."

He went into his characteristic story-telling mode. "Once when

I was young I was going out at night and my dad said to me, Joey, don't go out. I'm going to take you to New York City to a fancy restaurant. I'm going to show you how to deal with a maître d'."

The friend realized that Biden's dad most likely had no idea how to deal with a maître d', but might have thought it was important that his son learned.

The president got out his wallet and pulled out a picture.

"This is my daughter," Biden said as he started to tear up. It was a picture of Naomi Biden, who was killed in a car accident along with his first wife, Neilia Hunter Biden, in 1972. Neilia had been out shopping for a Christmas tree with their three children before the crash. Their two sons, Hunter and Beau, had survived. Biden was sworn in as a senator the next month.

It was as if Biden were in an emotional trance as he picked up and put down the photographs he had probably seen a thousand times. There was something ordinary and familiar about it, the friend thought. Biden continued to talk about the past and his family like a comforting bedtime story.

THIRTY-THREE

◆

During a windy round of golf at Bedminster, Trump's golf club just outside New York City, Senator Lindsey Graham urged Trump to run for president again. On the green with them was Jay Clayton, Trump's Securities and Exchange Commission (SEC) chairman.

"I'm going to do it," Trump told them. He didn't need to be drafted, he said, he would jump into the race whenever he wanted.

Trump added that he was "90 percent there." It was a business decision for him too, he said. He had to think about his finances, his houses. What can he do as a candidate versus not being a candidate?

"If you compare what you did as president to what they're doing you've got a good chance of winning," Graham told him. "If you ask the Republican Party, do you think Trump should run again or is it time for somebody new? It's about 60-40 right now.

"If you run again and win, then January 6 won't be your obituary," Graham said. "If you don't run, then time marches on." The next Republican nominee will try to be different from you personally: "I like Trump's policies, I just don't like Trump."

"If you run and win then it's the biggest second act in the history of American politics," Graham said. "Then you have four years to rewrite your legacy and make Trumpism a more sustainable movement. It becomes something you can pass to the next generation."

Trump's attention seemed to latch on to Graham. He liked that a lot. After a moment, Trump said, "What does that mean?"

"Second acts are hard to get in politics, Mr. President," Graham said. "If you get a second act, use it."

Graham wanted Trump to think big. Bring the country together on immigration, entitlement reform, on energy, he said.

But Trump wanted to keep going over the 2020 election result, which he still refused to accept he had lost.

"Mr. President, the 20 percent of people who want to keep talking about 2020 is not going to get you elected," Graham said.

Trump didn't buy it.

"Republicans are ready to move on from 2020 I promise you," Graham implored him. When Trump went to bed each night did he truly believe the election was stolen? Graham couldn't be sure. But it was the narrative Trump would never give up.

"They want you to run again. They thought you were a good president," Graham said. "But if they believe you can't win, they will throw you over.

"Winning is more important than anything to Republicans right now," Graham added.

From his conversations with colleagues, Graham believed he had a very accurate read on the Republican Party. "There's 50 percent of people that would follow Trump off a cliff in the Republican primary. There are 20 percent that would push him off a cliff. And 30 percent are just waiting for the wind.

"You've got to convince them that you can win, and winning means 2024 not 2020," Graham finished.

He had likely lost Trump's attention long ago.

A few days later Graham called Trump to tell him that the Israeli government had dissolved. "[Yair] Lapid is going to be the new prime minister. They're going to have an election in October and there's a 40 percent chance Bibi Netanyahu could come back," Graham said. It would be Israel's fifth election in three years. Trump was still furious that Netanyahu called Biden to congratulate him on winning the 2020 election.

"Bibi will probably try to call you to get you to endorse him,"

Graham said. "Just stay out of it. You don't need to get involved in all that."

"I gave a speech today and I only mentioned the 2020 election twice!" Trump said as if it had shown maximum restraint.

In May, Congress passed a $40 billion emergency Ukraine aid package that included $19 billion in military funding. Many Republicans, including Lindsey Graham, accused the Biden administration and the Pentagon of "slow walking" the military assistance.

Russia had lost 30,000 troops. But the Ukrainians desperately needed more weapons to hold off the seemingly endless flow of Russian soldiers.

"They're in an artillery battle and they're out-gunned 10 to one!" Graham said. "If they blink they'll get creamed.

"The way you usually win wars is they run out of people, they run out of money, they run out of weapons," Graham said. "So who's going to run out of people, money and weapons first?"

Obviously Ukraine, Graham argued.

"If we can get through the next five or six months and if the Europeans begin to actually move away from Russian gas and oil, Putin's in a world of hurt," Graham said. "Because that's the only thing that keeps him going.

"As long as we keep the weapons flowing and the economy supported, this is a war of attrition, right?"

While the aid bill was supported by a majority of House Republicans, passing 378–57, Trump lambasted Democrats for sending billions to Ukraine.

"The Democrats are sending another $40 billion to Ukraine, yet America's parents are struggling to even feed their children," Trump said, claiming that "no one is talking about" baby formula shortage in the United States.

"There's always been isolationist voices in the Republican Party," Senate Republican leader Mitch McConnell said. "It won't be a problem."

THIRTY-FOUR

In late June 2022, Secretary of State Tony Blinken sat next to German chancellor Olaf Scholz at the bar in Schloss Elmau, a beautiful, palatial resort nestled in the Bavarian Alps. They were unwinding after a full day of G7 meetings. The G7 is an informal, powerful group of the advanced democracies—the United States, France, Germany, U.K., Italy, Canada and Japan.

It was a chance to share some deeper, private worries over a drink.

It's extraordinary what you've done, Blinken said to the chancellor, in moving Germany to play such a strong leading role in defense not only of Ukraine but reorienting the country's posture in Europe. Scholz had announced that Germany would increase its defense budget by 3 percent, while the overall budget was being substantially cut.

It was a historic change from Germany's post–World War II antimilitarism, Blinken noted.

"I feel strongly about it," Scholz said. "I'm worried about it too."

"What do you mean, Chancellor?" Blinken asked.

"People are applauding this now," Scholz said. "I'm not sure how they're going to feel in a few years' time as we make good on this, when Germany is once again the leading military power in Europe. I'm not so sure people are going to like that."

The chancellor explained. "I have the weight of history on my mind so this is not easy, and it's so important that Germany—deeply embedded as a European country—retain that and people may not be so enthusiastic about this."

"I think it's admirable that you're also putting this in a historical frame," Blinken said. "Ultimately from my perspective, you're doing the right and important thing because actually the best way to uphold peace, to avoid another global conflagration, is for the countries that can play leadership roles in upholding the order to do that. And Germany under you is doing that."

But Blinken could see the decision weighed on the chancellor. Being clear-eyed about a nation's history is central to moving forward. And that was as hard for Germany as perhaps any country.

Months later, Blinken was reminded of this moment during a conversation with Germany's foreign minister Annalena Baerbock—a Green Party leader who was one of the most ardent, vocal supporters of Ukraine in Germany's parliament.

Blinken had been talking regularly with Baerbock in an effort to get Germany to provide Leopard 2 tanks to Ukraine, or at least allow third-countries to transfer the tanks.

The German-manufactured, 62-ton battle tanks had a massive turret and gun barrel. The earth literally shook when they moved. They were a fierce instrument of war, a mainstay of ground combat, and psychologically and physically a key measure of strength and combat seriousness. Opponents take notice when they move. The Leopard 2 has a range of about 300 miles and is equipped with specialized night-vision capability and a laser rangefinder that would also enable the Ukrainians to better hit moving targets.

Ukraine had been requesting tanks to help them defend against and push back on Russia's increasing artillery firepower.

Importantly, more than a dozen European countries used Leopard 2 tanks. Availability, readiness, logistics and maintenance were already in Europe. But as with all sorts of weapons, countries who buy them must seek permission from the manufacturing country to give them to another country. With Germany's go-ahead, European allies could contribute tanks, training or spare parts to Ukraine.

Baerbock told Blinken she was advocating for the provision of Leopard 2 tanks in the German government.

"But the chancellor is not enthusiastic," she said. "He said in one of our meetings, 'Can you imagine the images of German tanks sweeping over Europe? How are people going to react to that?'" A vivid reminder of German aggression in both World War I and World War II.

"Look," Blinken said, "I get it. I really do." He recounted to Baerbock the conversation he'd had previously with Scholz at that bar in the Alps.

This wasn't that Scholz didn't want to provide the tanks to Ukraine, Blinken believed. It really was about the weight and imagery of history that could not be dismissed.

"He was very, very concerned about what this would say to people about Germany," Blinken said.

What will the Americans do? Baerbock asked Blinken. Will you provide Abrams?

The U.S. M1 Abrams tanks are the heavy American-produced battle tanks that have been used by American forces in combat in the Afghanistan and Iraq wars.

"Look, I think our military sees this as apples and oranges," Blinken said, "because the tanks you have are something the Ukrainians can use right away. The Abrams is a totally different system. It's going to take a while to get Ukraine trained on it. It's tougher to maintain. So I don't think there's an equivalence between the two."

"I just don't know if we can move the chancellor on this," Baerbock said.

The Pentagon was also arguing against providing Ukraine with Abrams given the long lead times and difficult logistics.

"The Abrams tank is a very complicated piece of equipment," Undersecretary of Defense Colin Kahl told reporters in January 2023. "We should not be providing the Ukrainians systems they can't repair, they can't sustain, and that they, over the long term, can't afford, because it's not helpful."

President Zelensky joined a summit in Davos by video link and complained about the delays and overthinking. Ukraine needed tanks. Act now he said urgently. "The time the free world uses to think is used by the terrorist state to kill," he said.

Soon after, President Biden sat at the Resolute Desk in the Oval Office and reached Scholz by phone. He put the German chancellor on speakerphone so Blinken and Sullivan could hear the exchange.

After greetings and routine best wishes, Scholz turned to business.

"Are you doing the Abrams?" Scholz asked.

Biden repeated the reasoning why he didn't plan to. Ultimately, it didn't make sense. There was a long lead time, it would take a while to train the Ukrainians to use the U.S. tanks, they would be difficult to maintain and resupply, and they wouldn't be immediately useful to them on the battlefield.

"But your tanks really would be useful to them now," Biden said. "Can we get them the tanks?"

"Well, what about your tanks?" Scholz repeated.

Blinken and Sullivan listened as the two leaders went back and forth a few times.

"Joe, you know, if you're not moving on this it's really hard for me to do this," Scholz said, haunted by the image of how German tanks once again rolling across Europe could be perceived. "I don't think I can do this," he said.

"Okay," Biden said, "I hear what you're saying but let's keep talking about this. I think it's really important that we get there. I'll have our teams follow up."

Biden ended the call and looked at Sullivan and Blinken. "I think we've got a dead end here," Biden said. "A brick wall."

"Mr. President, I think there's actually a way of squaring the circle," Blinken said. "You're 100 percent right that we can't get the Ukrainians Abrams in time for them to be useful probably in this immediate counteroffensive. But if we're going to eventually do it anyway—because we've been talking about Ukraine's force of the future and they need a strong ground defense—why not say we're doing it and give the Germans cover to move forward with their tanks even if our tanks are not going to arrive for another year?

"As long as we announce it," Blinken added, "that might give Scholz what he needs." Political cover was an ally in the decision, as it was in most.

"That's a good idea," Biden said, "let's pursue it."

Blinken and the State Department tested out the proposition through back channels with the Germans.

The response was: "Okay, we'll do it. You commit to providing the Abrams in principle. We'll commit to providing Leopards on a nearer-term basis."

Later, on January 25, 2023, in the Roosevelt Room, President Biden would announce that the U.S. was sending 31 Abrams tanks to Ukraine, "the most capable tanks in the world."

"There is no offensive threat to Russia," Biden said. "If Russian troops return to Russia, where they belong, this war would be over today."

THIRTY-FIVE

◆ ◆

In late September 2022 Jake Sullivan sat alone at his desk in the West Wing of the White House thumbing through the Top Secret Sensitive Compartmented Information (SCI) which showed the extraordinary depth of U.S. intelligence penetration all over the world, particularly inside countries like Russia.

Sullivan stared at the new intelligence in front of him with dread.

The U.S. intelligence agencies were reporting new highly sensitive, credible conversations inside the Kremlin showing Russian president Vladimir Putin was seriously considering using a tactical nuclear weapon in the Russia-Ukraine War.

Putin, the agencies reported, was showing increasing signs of desperation over Russia's recent battlefield failures.

The Ukrainians, supported with large amounts of U.S. and European weaponry, had just pulled off a breathtaking counteroffensive in the northeast, breaking through Russian lines with surprising speed and pushing Russian forces out of cities and towns in the entire region of Kharkiv, situated just 35 miles from the Russian border.

U.S. intelligence reported it was a humiliating defeat for Putin.

Russian soldiers had fled in any way they could including on stolen bicycles and by disguising themselves as locals. The collapse of fortified Russian lines up to 70 kilometers (43 miles) in some places and loss of more than 1,000 square miles of territory sent shock waves through Moscow. The Ukrainians had recaptured more territory in five days than the Russian forces had taken in their entire operation.

Now with Ukrainian flags flying in Kharkiv, Ukrainian forces had pivoted to the south in an effort to liberate the city of Kherson on the west bank of the Dnipro River.

Putin had about 30,000 troops stationed in Kherson. The intelligence agencies assessed that if Russian troops were encircled by Ukrainian forces in Kherson, there was a 50 percent chance Putin would order the use of tactical nuclear weapons to avoid such a catastrophic battlefield loss.

Kherson was of enormous strategic importance for Moscow. Control of Kherson gave Russia a land bridge to the Black Sea peninsula and access to the Dnipro River's freshwater supplies, which Ukraine had blocked from flowing into Crimea after Russia had forcefully seized it in 2014.

CIA director Burns reported that the intelligence showed some of Putin's generals were finally telling him to withdraw across the river to a more defensible position.

But if Kherson fell, "it was at least conceivable that the Russian military could crack and that Putin's grip on Crimea would be threatened," Burns said.

Under Russian nuclear doctrine, a potential catastrophic battlefield loss or existential threat to Russia could permit Putin to resort to nuclear use—the first use since 1945 when American forces in World War II dropped nuclear bombs on Japan.

"The thing about Crimea," Burns reported. "In many ways that was existential for Putin because if he lost Crimea, his whole reason to be as Russian president in his eyes would be challenged."

Putin announced on September 21 that he would mobilize 300,000 Russian troops and annex four Ukrainian provinces, including Kherson—declaring them part of Russia.

"If the territorial integrity of our country is threatened, we will without doubt use all available means to protect Russia and our people—this is not a bluff," Putin warned in his address.

————————

The intel reports Sullivan read were deemed "exquisite," meaning derived from the best sources and methods. This was the most
alarming and deeply unnerving assessment of Putin's intentions
since the start of the war in February 2022.

Director of National Intelligence Avril Haines was more concerned than she had ever been about the potential for Putin to stick
his toe in the water and break the seal on nuclear weapons. There
was *enough* data coming in that suggested *enough* people within
Russia's system were talking about it, Haines reported.

Among the other troubling indicators was intelligence that
Putin had also loosened operational controls to make it easier to
order the use of a tactical nuclear weapon in the war.

President Biden ordered Sullivan, "On all channels, get on the
line with the Russians," he said. "Tell them what we will do in
response." Find language that is threatening without being directly
threatening, he said. Too strong and it might trigger exactly the
response we are trying to avoid.

Biden had seen enough unintentional mistakes and did not want
the use of any nuclear weapon, no matter how low a yield.

Total nuclear weapon deterrence had maintained great power
peace and stability since World War II. Any use would shatter the
fragile norm and could set off an unpredictable escalation ladder
that would be very difficult to control, Sullivan calculated. No matter what else happened during Biden's presidency, it would mark a
failure that would live in history as a damning legacy.

Second, Biden told Sullivan, "let's send Bill to talk to his counterpart." That was CIA director Bill Burns, who knew all the main
Russian players, especially Putin.

"We need to open up a channel," Biden said, "not on negotiating Ukraine but on the United States and Russia avoiding a
cataclysm."

The president then communicated with Putin directly. He sent
him a message to emphasize the seriousness of this and the "catastrophic consequences" if Russia were to deploy a nuclear weapon.

The message also said "I want to send someone to talk to

someone from your side in more detail about our concerns." The president named Bill Burns.

Putin responded to Biden and said he would send Naryshkin, the head of their Foreign Intelligence Service, to meet with Burns.

On September 30, Putin held a signing ceremony at the Grand Kremlin Palace in Moscow for the annexed regions and promised to protect the lands with "all the forces and means at our disposal.

"I want the Kyiv authorities and their real masters in the West to hear me so they remember this," Putin said. "People living in Luhansk and Donetsk, Kherson and Zaporizhzhia are becoming our citizens. Forever.

"The United States is the only country in the world that has twice used nuclear weapons," Putin added, "destroying the Japanese cities of Hiroshima and Nagasaki, and setting a precedent."

The following week, on October 6, Biden delivered a blunt warning during remarks at a private fundraiser at James Murdoch's home in New York. James is the younger more liberal son of Rupert Murdoch, the founder of News Corp and Fox who built a publishing empire worldwide.

"We have not faced the prospect of Armageddon since Kennedy and the Cuban Missile Crisis," Biden said. "We've got a guy I know fairly well, his name is Vladimir Putin. I spent a fair amount of time with him. He is not joking when he talks about the potential use of tactical and nuclear weapons or biological or chemical weapons.

"We have some real difficult decisions to make," Biden added. "We're trying to figure out: What is Putin's off-ramp?"

At the Pentagon on the third floor in the outer E-Ring, Secretary of Defense Lloyd Austin gazed down at the carefully tailored talking points he had directed his closest adviser Colin Kahl to prepare.

Austin was not known for eloquence or crispness at public

briefings or interviews. His uneasy public delivery had sidelined him as a public spokesman for the administration, but in private conversations he carried himself with a genuineness and seriousness that gave him particular gravitas. Austin knew President Biden was absolutely determined not to let the Ukraine War become World War III and he shared that determination.

Putin had expected his forces would have a lightning victory in Ukraine—invade, chop the head off the snake and put a new Russian head on it within days of their invasion. He had failed miserably. Austin believed that Putin's new theory of victory was to simply outlast the West's support of Ukraine.

He could see from the intelligence that Russia's army was highly demoralized, struggling to resupply, and its leadership disorganized. Russian forces were folding like a cheap suit.

Was Putin desperate enough that he would be willing to use battlefield nuclear weapons to stop a Ukrainian advance?

Kahl recalled a scene in *The Lord of the Rings* where Gandalf slams his staff into the ground and declares "You shall not pass." Was there a version of that where Putin used a dozen tactical nuclear weapons in southern Ukraine to obliterate Ukrainian forces charging toward Kherson, and ultimately Crimea?

Austin was now preparing to speak to Russia's defense minister Sergei Shoigu, a hardliner and close ally of Putin. After Russia's invasion of Ukraine in February, Austin had spoken with Shoigu only once, in May 2022. Even during the Cold War, military counterparts spoke via back channels but the Russian defense minister had been unreachable and frustratingly closed off.

Shoigu, short and grim-faced, was part of Putin's most loyal inner circle having known and worked with him for three decades. In 2012, Putin appointed Shoigu as his defense minister and Shoigu had helped plan Russia's 2014 annexation of Crimea. In his first year as defense minister, Shoigu had directed commanders to begin every day in the barracks with a rendition of the Russian anthem. Praise and adherence to Putin and Russia never slackened. Shoigu was a classic Russian apparatchik—hard-ass, dutiful and subservient.

Russian media for years was filled with photographs of Putin and Shoigu together in matching outfits hunting, fishing, dining and camping in the Siberian wilderness. It was a strange pairing.

On Friday, October 21, Austin finally got through to Shoigu.

"We know you are contemplating the use of tactical nuclear weapons in Ukraine," Austin said bluntly in his deep baritone voice. "Let me tell you a few things about that.

"First," he said, "any use of nuclear weapons on any scale against anybody would be seen by the United States and the world as a world-changing event. There is no scale of nuclear weapons that we could overlook or that the world could overlook.

"Any use of nuclear weapons anywhere would implicate the vital national interests of the United States," Austin said. "Why? Because we cannot live in a world where nuclear powers use nuclear weapons against non-nuclear powers with impunity. We can't live in that world. So you may believe that Ukraine matters more to you than us but in this circumstance this matters just as much to us as it matters to you.

"It wouldn't matter how small the nuclear weapon is," Austin said.

Shoigu just listened. Despite being heralded a general with a Soviet uniform adorned with medals, Shoigu had never served in the military before Putin appointed him as defense minister.

"If you do this," Austin said, "it would be the first use of nuclear weapons anywhere in the world in three-quarters of a century and it could set in motion events that you cannot control and we cannot control.

"Our leaders and your leaders have repeatedly said a nuclear war can never be won and should never be fought. This could put us on the path of a confrontation that would have existential implications for you and for us. Don't step on that slippery slope," Austin said.

Austin moved to his next point. "If you did this, all the restraints that we have been operating under in Ukraine would be reconsidered," he said. "We have taken care not to do certain things. There are certain things we haven't provided the Ukrainians. There are certain restrictions we've put on how they can use the stuff we've given them and we have not directly intervened in the conflict against your forces. If you did this, all of those constraints, all of those restraints we have imposed on ourself would be reconsidered."

The message of direct retaliation could not be more starkly presented.

Austin delivered his final point. "All these actors in the world that you think are your friends or who are looking aside, would all turn against Russia in this scenario—the Chinese, the Indians, the Turks, the Israelis," he said. "This would isolate Russia on the world stage to a degree you Russians cannot fully appreciate."

"I don't take kindly to being threatened," Shoigu finally responded.

"Mr. Minister," Austin said bluntly with not a hint of anger, "I am the leader of the most powerful military in the history of the world. I don't make threats."

At the Pentagon, Chairman of the Joint Chiefs General Mark Milley also had a secure phone call with his counterpart in Russia, General Valery Gerasimov.

"General Gerasimov," Milley began. "Some of your political leaders are rattling the nuclear sabre and they're talking about the use of nuclear weapons. That has a lot of people's attention so I need you to tell me: Under what conditions you would use nuclear weapons?"

Milley was blunt. He had known Gerasimov for years. In the room with Milley were people from the intelligence community listening in on the call.

"You already know under what conditions," Gerasimov said, "because you have our manuals and our doctrine." He cited a page number.

"Well, I appreciate that," Milley said. "I don't have the manual in front of me. I need you to tell me under what conditions you're going to use nuclear weapons."

He wanted to hear them from the Russian general directly.

"Okay," Gerasimov replied. "It's public by the way. You can look up the conditions." But he recited Russia's nuclear doctrine.

"If there's an attack on Russia that threatens the stability of the regime," Gerasimov said, "condition one." Milley knew that could be interpreted as a threat to the Russian government or to Putin himself.

"Second," Gerasimov said, "is if a foreign power attacks Russia with a weapon of mass destruction so that's chemical, biological or nuclear.

"Third," Gerasimov recited, "Russia reserves the right to use tactical nuclear weapons in the event of catastrophic battlefield loss.

"Those are the conditions under which we will do it," he added.

"Well, that's good," Milley said, "because none of those conditions are going to obtain so I guess you're not going to use nuclear weapons because nobody is going to attack you with a weapon of mass destruction. No one is doing any kind of regime change. And my analysis of the battlefield is I don't think you're going to be suffering a catastrophic loss like losing your entire army so . . ."

Milley was satisfied. Gerasimov had conveyed and agreed to the established conditions in Russia's nuclear doctrine. Nothing had changed there at least.

"Great," Milley said. "I'll pass what you said on to my government."

"Okay, thanks," Gerasimov replied.

At the White House, Jake Sullivan and Jon Finer were in overdrive. The key piece of the intelligence assessment was the 50 percent chance Russia would use a tactical nuclear weapon. The assessment had gone from around a 5 percent chance, to a 10 percent chance to now a coin flip. Finer felt a gut-wrenching foreboding.

While Sullivan often found a "false precision" in the intelligence, especially with regard to numbers, the 50 percent assessment could not be dismissed. Even before this intel assessment, he carried the worry that at some moment during the war Putin would resort to nuclear use.

"All the people who wave it off are fundamentally just in a way naïve," Sullivan said. After the Afghanistan withdrawal the Biden administration was hyper-focused on preparing to deal with the possibility of really bad things happening.

Back in May, only three months after the Ukraine War began, Sullivan had stood up a tiger team to analyze and prepare for low-probability, high-impact events in the war, including Russia's use of a nuclear weapon. The tiger team had produced a playbook on nuclear response options. Suddenly the playbook was no longer abstract and had to be carried out.

In the greatest secrecy, Sullivan met at the Pentagon with Austin, Chairman Mark Milley, and their teams of nuclear experts to map out and analyze the various possible nuclear scenarios. Moves. Countermoves. Military response options that would be triggered if Putin used nuclear weapons.

Austin and Milley showed Sullivan how they were gaming it out from a military perspective. Putin uses a tactical nuclear weapon. That's the first move. Second move, U.S. responds. Then the Russians take a turn. Then the U.S. and it was off to the races. It was classic war-gaming but alarmingly real.

At each of the "turns" Austin and Milley prepared for the president what his options were in escalating order of magnitude. With Sullivan they examined how each option mapped onto an expected response by Russia.

"And so it becomes a very complex algorithm of choices for the president," Sullivan said. A single nuclear detonation would trigger the highest stakes of brinkmanship possible.

Sullivan, Austin and Milley talked through each of the options with Biden in excruciating detail to get his guidance about how the president would respond. At no point was Biden supposed to make a final decision and lock himself into a response. Instead, he retained discretion—keeping the options open.

Biden had said privately that if Putin used a tactical nuclear weapon on the battlefield in Ukraine, the U.S. would not respond with nuclear weapons.

"I'm not going to have a nuclear response to battlefield use in Ukraine," Biden said to his advisers. But the reality was—and everyone in the room knew it—nuclear weapons were always a possibility once escalation began. Nuclear weapons were the silent shadow present in all their deliberations.

Response options ranged from a warning shot that didn't kill anyone to a U.S. military strike inside Russia with conventional forces, also a nightmare scenario for the president. Biden and Sullivan believed that an armed clash between U.S. and Russian forces at any level could too easily lead to World War III. It was alarmingly obvious. They were in a completely new world.

There was no "good" option. In a direct conflict between the U.S. and Russia, U.S. declaratory policy was that the U.S. would only use nuclear weapons to respond to a nuclear attack or existential threat.

The World War III escalation path would become extremely pressurized, and harder and harder to find an off-ramp if nuclear use started.

What were the signposts, the clues to what Putin would do next? How real was this threat? Biden's National Security Council and State Department had become accustomed to living in two contradictory worlds ever since U.S. intelligence had obtained Putin's invasion plan in excruciating detail, five months in advance of the invasion. It had not been clear precisely when he would invade but all the evidence indicated the invasion was coming. The national security team had lived in this world and tried to deter Putin.

In the other world, Putin's plan seemed so irrational and self-defeating that the Russian leader could not possibly go through with it.

But Putin invaded, launching a global crisis.

Now Sullivan and the president were locked into the world of uncertainty and doubt once again. Would Putin undertake another irrational and self-defeating step?

"We have to stay one step ahead of Putin," Sullivan instructed his NSC staff many times. "We have to."

He questioned them, What economic options do we have? What diplomatic options do we have? What does the U.S. do militarily? Do you take military action or not? If you do take military action, where do you take military action? Inside Ukraine? Inside Russia? Inside occupied parts of Ukraine?

But as an unpredictable aggressor, Putin had the upper hand. As the all-powerful Russian autocrat, he was the one who decided Russia's actions and red lines.

Sullivan tried to get in Putin's head, asking: "How do I, Vladimir Putin, avoid ignominious defeat?"

What was Putin planning?

"Ordering the use of tactical nuclear weapons to avert a catastrophic battlefield loss is something he is prepared to do," Sullivan believed.

"I think he is worried about using nukes, drawing us directly into the conflict," Sullivan said. "But at some level he's not going to care about what we think or do."

Making Ukraine part of Russia had become an absolute single-minded need for Putin.

For Deputy National Security Adviser Jon Finer, the notion that such a world-changing event—actually using nuclear weapons—rested on a "coin flip" was beyond imagination and the implications extended well beyond the war in Ukraine. The detonation of a single tactical nuclear weapon would destroy the world order erected after World War II, which was predicated on never again using nuclear weapons.

The Pentagon had an entire series of contingency war plans for using nuclear weapons called the 5000 series. For example

OPLAN 5027 covered plans made by the U.S. and South Korea for a response to North Korean nuclear weapons use. Thorough contingency plans existed if Russia attacked the U.S. first. Now the NSC and Pentagon were having meetings to update and synchronize contingency plans for a nuclear war in the same way, Finer realized, as his predecessors would have done during the Cold War or 1962 Cuban Missile Crisis more than half a century ago.

Finer was also tasked with running a very quiet, very small series of meetings at the deputies level and with core U.S. allies in the Euro Quad—Germany, France and the U.K.—to come up with allied contingency plans for the various scenarios.

Finer said, "As with the invasion itself, we also have to be ready for the possibility that this won't work." It was all too possible that deterring Putin from using a tactical nuclear weapon could fail.

Russia, then in 2022, had an arsenal of about 2,000 tactical nuclear weapons, 10 times the number in the U.S. arsenal. The Russian tactical nuclear weapons range in explosive power from 0.3, or a fraction of a kiloton, to 50 or more kilotons. Meaning today a nuclear weapon could take the form of a warhead small enough for one person to deploy. Or be so large to require deployment from a submarine, bomber, or intercontinental ballistic missile.

Putin's arsenal gave him an extraordinary number of options along the nuclear scale. He could unleash a single low-yield "tactical" nuclear weapon or strike with a large number.

In 1945 President Truman ordered the only use of atomic bombs to end World War II. A 15-kiloton atomic bomb dropped on Hiroshima and 21-kiloton bomb on Nagasaki.

The nuclear scenarios being practiced in tabletop exercises included Putin ordering a test nuclear detonation over the Black Sea to intimidate Ukraine into surrendering territory; or deploying a tactical nuclear weapon against a Ukrainian military base that would render the land around it uninhabitable for years because of radiation contamination.

Colin Kahl, Defense Secretary Austin's principal strategic adviser and right-hand man, was at home in his pajamas with his kids when a request came through from the Russians very early Sunday morning, October 23, for a second call between Austin and Shoigu. It was just 36 hours after Austin had issued his warning to Shoigu.

This is weird, Kahl thought. What is going on?

All the staff who write the talking points for Secretary Austin were at home. Nobody was in the office but the Russians were frantically calling.

Kahl went into a room in his house that had been turned into a SCIF—sensitive compartmented information facility for the most highly classified work—to see if any intelligence had come through overnight that might explain the urgency of the call. Nothing stood out on the intel channels.

On his cell phone Kahl noticed Russian sources on social media and Telegram—a secure messaging app—circulating an allegation that the Ukrainians were planning to use a dirty bomb.

A dirty bomb is a mix of explosives with radioactive material that spreads hazardous radiation but does not create a nuclear chain reaction or atomic blast. A dirty bomb is still extremely serious because it makes an area uninhabitable.

Reports started coming through that the Russians were also calling the defense ministers in the United Kingdom, France and Turkey.

"Holy crap," Kahl thought, "the Russians are going to fake a dirty bomb in Ukraine as a predicate for using nuclear weapons against Ukraine.

"The nightmare scenario."

This is straight out of the Russian playbook, Kahl thought. What had they seen the Russians do the entire war? Try to create false flags and the predicate for escalation. He had no confirmation. It was a hunch.

Kahl jotted down speaking points for Austin.

————

"We have all this intelligence that says the Ukrainians are thinking about using a dirty bomb," Shoigu blurted when he got on the phone to Austin. "If they do this we would consider it an act of nuclear terrorism and we'd have no alternative but to respond." Bingo, Kahl thought.

"We don't believe you," Austin said firmly. "We don't see any indications of this, and the world will see through this.

"This seems to us like you trying to establish the predicate for using nuclear weapons," Austin said, his baritone voice full of warning, "and if you do it these will be all the consequences."

Lloyd Austin, usually soft-spoken, once again powerfully conveyed the president's deterrent message: "Don't do it."

"I understand," Shoigu said. "We will share our information with you and the world."

Jake Sullivan called Andriy Yermak, Zelensky's top adviser, and told him to immediately call in the International Atomic Energy Agency (IAEA) to Ukraine's nuclear facilities. Open them up to inspection.

IAEA inspectors arrived swiftly and found no evidence of preparations to build a dirty bomb.

The White House and Pentagon mobilized every communication line, calling the Chinese, the Indians, the Israelis, the Turks—countries friendly with Russia who were also having calls with Putin. Nobody should use a nuclear weapon in Ukraine. Send the signal to Putin.

These countries did.

In under 12 hours it appeared they had blown the whistle on Russia's plot.

"Let me just say Russia would be making an incredibly serious mistake if it were to use a tactical nuclear weapon," President Biden told reporters on October 26, putting it directly on the table.

Director of National Intelligence Avril Haines updated President Biden that the intelligence community's assessment was that Chinese president Xi had the most leverage over Putin and was best placed to influence Putin's thinking on nuclear weapons.

Biden called Xi and underlined the need to deter Russia from using a nuclear weapon in Ukraine. If Putin were to break the seal on nuclear use, that would be an enormous event for the world.

President Xi agreed. He would warn Putin not to go there. Xi even did so publicly. "Nuclear wars must not be fought," President Xi said from Beijing on November 4, 2022. He called on countries to oppose nuclear use or threats to use nuclear weapons.

The other decisive factor in dissuading Putin from nuclear use was that there was no catastrophic break in Russia's forces. Ukraine moved slowly, incrementally and Russian forces withdrew safely across the Dnipro River and out of Kherson. Only then did the U.S. intelligence community revise their assessment on the nuclear threat.

Putin held on to his nuclear cards for the time being.

"It was probably the most hair-raising moment of the whole war," Kahl said.

Afterward, President Biden wanted to make sure Russia had gotten the message.

In Ankara, Turkey, CIA director Burns had a secret meeting with Russian Foreign Intelligence chief Sergei Naryshkin for four hours on November 14, 2022. It was a scene that could come out of a John le Carré spy novel.

As they sat down, Russia leaked the fact of the meeting between them, another power play.

Burns sat across from Naryshkin. They had known each other for 20 years as adversaries. Almost instantly Burns could see Naryshkin wanted to talk about "a new American peace plan to end the war."

"Listen," Burns said. "Whatever you're reading in Washington, we're not negotiating without the Ukrainians." Biden had been firm on that. "And what I'm here to talk about is the grave risk of use of nuclear weapons."

Burns laid out in detail to Naryshkin what the "catastrophic consequences" would be if Russia used a tactical nuclear weapon and broke the nuclear taboo.

"It will be Russia, not only terribly isolated and a pariah," Burns warned, "but there would also be very practical consequences in terms of the damage we'd inflict on the Russian military."

Naryshkin swore up one side and down the other that they had no intent or plan to do this. He said he was speaking for Putin.

Burns reported back to President Biden that he was confident the Russians had gotten the message.

President Biden faced a genuine catch-22.

The Russia-Ukraine War presents a fundamental conundrum for the United States and the world, President Biden said to his national security adviser.

"If we do not fully succeed in ejecting Russia from Ukraine, we will have let Putin kind of get away with something," Biden said. "If we do fully succeed in ejecting Russia from Ukraine, we face a very strong likelihood of nuclear use because Putin is not going to let himself be routed out of Ukraine without breaking the seal on tactical nuclear weapons. So we're stuck. Too much success is nukes, too little success is a kind of uncertain indefinite outcome."

The commander in chief concluded: "That's the strategic picture we're looking at and trying to navigate through right now."

By example and experience Biden was acknowledging that the world is not protected from the punishments and catastrophe of a great power war. The goal, unstated but threaded through every action and policy, was to devise a way to try to get Putin to accept modified failure with a battlefield stalemate or even better, for Putin to defeat himself.

THIRTY-SIX

Former president Trump saw the midterm elections as his opportunity to cement his political comeback. He would reward candidates who supported his rigged election claims and punish those who had not.

But the midterms were not the red wave the GOP or Trump had anticipated. Republicans narrowly took back control of the House on November 16, 2022, but Democrats held on to the Senate.

Trump was furious at the result. Many of the candidates he backed flopped. In the gubernatorial races his picks in Pennsylvania, Maryland and Michigan lost. In Arizona, his pick, Kari Lake, lost her governor's race. She claimed, baselessly, that the vote had been rigged. In the Senate race, Trump's favorite, Herschel Walker, a three-time All American and 1982 Heisman Trophy winner, lost in Georgia and Mehmet Oz lost in Pennsylvania.

Trump blamed his wife, Melania, for his decision to back Oz. "Not her best decision," he said, casting blame on everyone but himself.

Exit polls indicated that the former president was viewed favorably by just 39 percent of voters, putting him below Biden's 41 percent rating, and almost one in three voters said their vote was a message of opposition to Trump. Candidates with Trump endorsements underperformed while those without it overperformed by a whopping difference of more than seven points.

"While in certain ways yesterday's election was somewhat disappointing," Trump wrote on his social media platform, Truth Social, "from my personal standpoint it was a very big victory—219 WINS and 16 Losses in the General—Who has ever done better than that?"

But the result was generally viewed as a referendum on Trump.

"You've got a problem with moderate women," Lindsey Graham told the former president. "The people that think the earth is flat and we didn't go to the moon, you've got them. Let that go."

Trump needed to move on from re-litigating 2020 and get back to a focus on real policy issues and on making 2024 a referendum on Biden, Graham believed.

Your argument, Graham said to Trump, should be:

"When I was in charge, we had a secure border, and look what's happened. When I was in charge, you could fill up your tank without having to mortgage your house. When I was in charge, Russia and China were in a box. When I was in charge, Iran was weak. When I was in charge, the Taliban didn't have Afghanistan," Graham said. "On and on and on.

"Mr. President, it's not enough to criticize Biden, it's also you've got to say: *I can fix this.*

"Nobody gives a shit about the 2020 election," Graham said.

But Trump did.

A week later, Trump was ready to announce his third presidential campaign. He hailed the announcement the "most important speech given in the history of the United States of America" that would be "remembered FOREVER."

Republicans urged Trump to delay the announcement. Be patient. Let the GOP regroup after the midterm losses. He didn't.

"We are a nation in decline," Trump said on November 15, 2022, before a small crowd in Mar-a-Lago's lavish ballroom. "America's comeback starts right now." He described his presidency as "the golden age." But when Trump left the White House in January 2021 he had the lowest approval rating of any president.

Trump was launching his presidential campaign as civil and criminal investigations stacked up against him, including Justice Department probes into his conduct on January 6 and retention of classified documents at Mar-a-Lago after he left office.

"Anyone who truly seeks to take on this rigged and corrupt system will be faced with a storm of fire that only a few could understand," Trump said in his one-hour speech, as if the decision to run for president again was at great personal sacrifice.

Over at the White House, the reaction to Trump's announcement was mixed. The received wisdom among staff was that Trump was finished. President Biden and Vice President Harris did not share their view. Donald Trump defied convention. All the things that should be disqualifying seemed to endear him more to his followers. The Republican elite would see the writing on the wall in terms of their voter base and soon fall back in line. Harris found Trump's announcement deeply troubling.

"This is an immensely consequential election," Harris told her national security advisers, "the most consequential election probably this country has ever seen." The vice president believed that to elect Trump once was to make a great error but with a lot of unknowns. To elect Trump a second time after everything he'd done might be a "death knell for American democracy."

"The vice president and the president feel the weight of that very acutely in terms of what needs to happen," Rebecca Lissner, Harris's deputy national security adviser, said.

THIRTY-SEVEN

Jake Sullivan often described himself as "the quartermaster of the Ukrainian army." The irony was not lost on him.

His father was a hardcore pacifist, a conscientious objector in the Vietnam War who had studied for the priesthood, dropped out, and was now a Jesuit volunteer in San Francisco supporting kids who had aged out of foster care but who still needed some support.

As a child, Sullivan was not allowed to have a squirt gun or video games.

Now he was managing a war, getting U.S. lethal weapons into Ukraine—at the center of Ukraine's survival. In the White House, Army Colonel Joe Da Silva, who had served in the Afghanistan and Iraq wars, was in charge of the Ukraine weapons supply line for the National Security Council.

In November after the optimism of Ukraine's bold counteroffensive, the Ukrainians had taken up a defensive posture to try to hold their ground through the coming brutal winter months. Ukraine had a major air defense problem, Da Silva advised Sullivan, and they were running out of artillery.

Since October 2022, Russia had been bombarding Ukraine's energy grids in a targeted effort to deprive the Ukrainians of light, heat and water during the coming winter months. Temperatures would soon plummet to as low as -5 degrees Fahrenheit. Cities had been plunged into darkness, and millions of Ukrainians were without electricity.

President Biden told Zelensky they were rushing two NASAMs—National Advanced Surface-to-Air Missiles—which are sophisticated defense systems to Ukraine to help buffer the barrage of Russian missile attacks.

NASAMs are the premier air shield that are used to protect the airspace over the White House, the Capitol and the Pentagon. Each NASAM battery costs $23 million and shoots ten-foot-long missiles. Within a week of their arrival, the NASAMs proved their worth. Zelensky reported that the Russians fired ten Iranian-made Shahid drones and missiles and the NASAMs took down all ten.

To defend against Russian ballistic missiles, the U.S. sent one of the world's most advanced long-range air defense systems, the Patriot. Patriots were first used by the U.S. in the 1991 Gulf War to protect Israel and Saudi Arabia. Each Patriot battery cost $400 million plus another $690 million for 150 missiles at $4 million each, expensive but priceless on the battlefield.

The Patriots would become a game changer for the Ukrainians, routinely knocking down Russian Kinzhal hypersonic missiles, which traveled at multiples of the speed of sound. Putin had boasted publicly that the Kinzhal was "indestructible."

On December 21, President Zelensky secretly traveled to Washington to address Congress. Not even the flight crew on the U.S. military 737 C-40 that collected him in Poland had advance notice of who they would be transporting back.

In his distinctive army-green sweatshirt, Zelensky thanked "every American" and delivered a powerful plea for continued support to Ukraine. At times serious and demanding and at other times funny, Zelensky showed again his greatest weapon: his extraordinary communication skill.

"We have artillery, yes. Thank you. We have it. Is it enough? Honestly, not really," Zelensky said, inviting laughter.

He received a standing ovation.

The acute weapons issue Sullivan and Da Silva had to deal with was the sustainability of Ukraine's 155mm ammunition. Maintaining a steady supply of ammunition was vital to Ukraine's ability to stay in the fight and push Russia back.

The massive, 36-foot-long howitzer had become the mainstay of Ukraine's defense, a successful and versatile weapon on the battlefield. The howitzer, a cross between a cannon and a mortar, catapulted 155mm ammunition, which is a big bullet six inches wide and two feet long and weighing 100 pounds each. It had a range of up to 15 miles with a sustained rate of fire of 40 rounds per hour, which made it incredibly valuable for ground troops to take out enemy targets from a distance without putting themselves in harm's way. But Ukraine was churning through 155mm ammunition at an alarming pace and at risk of running out.

The 155mm shortfall would be one of the bellwethers in the war, Sullivan realized. Ukraine was the most challenging military environment for an army since World War II, Da Silva said. It was a full-on artillery war now with Ukraine and Russia bogged down in trench warfare. The front lines were barely moving.

In late January 2023, General Mark Milley provided a grim update at a Principals Committee Meeting.

"It will take Ukraine 700,000 rounds of 155mm artillery ammunition between 1 February and 1 June to both sustain the defense, execute a counteroffensive and consolidate gains," Milley said. That was a huge number.

Ukraine was burning through around 100,000 rounds a month, about 3,000 a day, and the United States did not have the stockpile to keep up.

Sullivan, Finer and Blinken scoured the globe for 155s but their biggest donors, European allies, were almost as tapped out as the United States. The war had exposed how far behind the United States and Europe were in basic weapons production and stockpiling.

"Look for countries that want to stay under the radar," Sullivan instructed Colonel Da Silva, those that might not want to donate to Ukraine but who might be willing to sell to the U.S. instead—for the U.S. to deliver to Ukraine.

When President Biden had a call scheduled with a world leader, Da Silva would consider what weapons or artillery request they could tack on to the call.

What did South Korea have? South Africa? Egypt? Cyprus? Ecuador?

The Pentagon was able to work out an agreement with South Korea that resulted in more than half a million rounds of 155 shells for Ukraine. But it was never enough to fill the growing deficit on the battlefield.

Da Silva ran a daily interagency meeting from mid-February through April 10, 2023, focused on plugging the 155 shortfall.

"What's the deficit?" Sullivan asked every day, throwing out the names of countries like a quiz show host peppering contestants in a game of Global Geography. Who haven't we tried yet? Who hasn't come through? Whose inventories have not been provably exhausted?

Pentagon officials were almost desperately urging the Ukrainians not to overly rely on artillery.

"Fire less, try to be more precise, don't run out, you have to maneuver," was the message.

Da Silva, who was coordinating with the Pentagon daily, pushed back hard.

"They are not wasting it," Da Silva said. "They are using it the best they can to achieve the tactical dynamics they need." The Russians had laid thousands upon thousands of mines in square kilometer interlocking areas. These death traps were only adding to the nightmare for the Ukrainians.

There was no "going around." Ukrainian sappers poked into the earth square foot by square foot to locate and clear the mines. "Six sappers lost their legs," a Ukrainian sapper in the 35th Brigade told CBS News. The whole process required such judicious de-mining work it began to seriously delay Ukraine's plans for a counteroffensive.

Sullivan pushed Secretary Austin and others in the Pentagon to accelerate the production of 155s. Their stockpile was limited because the U.S. had not been contemplating a future massive artillery war. U.S. production schedules had instead focused on advanced weapons like nuclear weapons, giant aircraft carriers, F-16 jets, ballistic missiles and air defenses. Sullivan was clear they needed the defense industrial base also geared toward producing a lot more 155mm rounds.

The national security adviser was spending half an hour most days on the search for 155s. It was becoming clear that if they could not find enough they would be faced with a difficult, morally complex choice: Send cluster munitions or leave Ukraine defenseless.

THIRTY-EIGHT

◆——◆

In Munich, Germany, Secretary of State Blinken stepped inside the cozy white tentlike structure his communications team had set up in his hotel suite for secure communications. Music played backward as interference.

"It can drive you crazy after a while," Blinken said of the sound. But the technicians said it masked what he was saying, making eavesdropping almost impossible.

The secretary of state put on his headset and was dialed into a top secret call with the president, Austin, Milley and Sullivan.

There is a lot of interest on the part of European partners to provide Ukraine with F-16s, the premier U.S. fighter jet, Blinken reported. He was in Germany for the Munich Security Conference and had been fielding multiple inquiries from allies about whether and when the Americans would move forward. Zelensky had been requesting them for a year.

The F-16 is an American-developed single-engine supersonic multirole fighter aircraft that would give the Ukrainians cutting-edge offensive and defensive air capabilities. Since F-16s are American technology, the U.S. requires other countries to obtain U.S. approval to provide them to third countries like Ukraine.

So far President Biden had withheld approval. His main concern was escalation that could draw NATO into war with Russia or push Putin to use a nuclear weapon.

There was no perfect measure for this, Blinken believed.

He could sense the reluctance on the other end of the phone.

"We should be focused on the counteroffensive," Austin said, "and this won't do the Ukrainians any good in the counteroffensive because we can't get them trained or provide them F-16s during that." It would take too long.

The Pentagon's position had consistently been that F-16s were not an immediate need. They would not have a near-term impact on the battlefield because the Ukrainian pilots would require specialized training to fly the planes as well as intensive English language training because the manuals, the controls, everything relating to the planes was in English.

Very legitimate logic, Blinken believed.

"Look," Blinken said, "a modern air force is going to be part of that equation so this is something that we're likely to do eventually. Why not get started?

"And there will be a long lead time," he added, "but it will answer the mail, it'll enable us to get going, you know? And it'll send a message that we're in this for the long haul."

"Tony," President Biden said, "I love you but it's not going to happen."

"What about a Cessna?" Blinken joked.

The president laughed.

Blinken was undeterred. After two decades of conversations with Biden, Blinken knew the president could adamantly say "we're not going to do that" while he was still listening, keeping an open mind.

"Why don't we start in on the training?" Blinken said. "Because there's a long lead in time on the training. And then you can make the decision on F-16s down the road."

Blinken was emulating Biden's marriage counselor approach to resolving policy debates, preferring the middle ground. It was not unusual for Biden to hedge and postpone a hard decision.

"The thing that's important to know about the president," Blinken told others later, "is that he will in a discussion, in a friendly argument he will often stake out a position that convinces you he is resolutely for something or resolutely against something.

"In fact what he's really trying to do is push the people he's talking to," Blinken said. "To people who don't know him as well they conclude, Oh, forget it, he's not doing that. I know from having spent so much time with him that he's really trying to pressure-test the idea by going at it really hard."

Let's go ahead with the training, Biden said finally.

THIRTY-NINE

G eneral Mark Milley, the chairman of the Joint Chiefs of Staff, the United States' most senior uniformed officer, had conducted a long campaign beginning early in Biden's presidency to get in to see Attorney General Merrick Garland.

Garland, very lawyerly and cautious, had taken his time thinking it over but he finally agreed and the Justice Department arranged a lunch.

It is highly unusual, if not unprecedented, for the chairman of the Joint Chiefs to personally visit the attorney general at the Justice Department. One senior Justice Department lawyer involved thought that it was the first time in American history.

General Milley thought of it as a routine part of his job as adviser to the National Security Council of which Garland was a member. He told his staff it was his responsibility to meet with all cabinet officials to "level bubbles," an infantry term for leveling all the guns on a gun line for accurate fire.

Milley, deeply convinced that Trump was a danger to the country, pressed Garland to investigate domestic threats. He was especially concerned about the far-right militia groups, many of which had attacked the Capitol on January 6, 2021, and were still threatening violence against the federal government.

"There's a large militia movement out there," Milley reported, "and there's a groundswell of anger and anxiety that unless properly dealt with could lead to the potential for violence. It's not going to get to civil war levels or any of that but it potentially could get to levels of domestic violence."

Milley was not the only one to press Garland. There were so many allegations and lines of inquiry swirling around Trump and the January 6 insurrection that an independent investigation of the former president was almost inevitable.

On November 18, 2022, Attorney General Garland announced that there would be an independent investigation of Trump.

Garland appointed Jack Smith, a former career Justice Department prosecutor, as special counsel to oversee and run the investigation of the January 6, 2021, insurrection. Encouraged by President Trump, rioters had stormed the Capitol in an effort to overturn the 2020 presidential election result. Jack Smith was also appointed to probe Trump's handling of classified documents and other presidential records kept at his Mar-a-Lago club and residence in Florida.

"Based on recent developments," Garland said, "including the former President's announcement that he is a candidate for President in the next election, and the sitting President's [Biden's] stated intention to be a candidate as well, I have concluded that it is in the public interest to appoint a special counsel."

Trump spoke for one hour and 42 minutes on March 4, 2023, at the Conservative Political Action Conference (CPAC), the large, influential conservative group. It was founded in 1974 when Ronald Reagan, then the California governor, gave the inaugural keynote speech.

"Today," Trump said, "I am your warrior. I am your justice. And for those who have been wronged and betrayed, I am your retribution."

This was an important and central theme of Trump's 2024 presidential campaign, a promise to get payback for those who felt mistreated or cast out.

Two days later, on Monday, March 6, 2023, I attended a reception at the Willard Hotel in Washington, D.C.

"We gotta talk," General Milley said as I approached him.

Milley was not in uniform but wearing a fashionable dark sports coat and plaid shirt. He had a freshly showered look and he seemed relaxed, though he stood barrel-chested with the ramrod-straight posture of an Army general.

Milley was still worried about Trump.

"No one has ever been as dangerous to this country as Donald Trump," Milley said. "Do you realize, do you see what this man is? I glimpsed it when I talked to you back—for *Peril*, but I now know it. I now know it."

Milley had shared with me his worries about Trump's mental stability and control of nuclear weapons for the book *Peril* I coauthored with Robert Costa.

Milley and I continued to talk, proving it is possible to have a very private conversation in the middle of a crowded room.

"We have got to stop him!" Milley said. "You have got to stop him!" By "you" he meant the press broadly. "He is the most dangerous person ever. I had suspicions when I talked to you about his mental decline and so forth, but now I realize he's a total fascist. He is the most dangerous person to this country."

His eyes darted around the room filled with 200 guests of the Cohen Group, a global business consulting firm headed by former defense secretary William Cohen. Cohen and former defense secretary James Mattis spoke at the reception.

"A fascist to the core!" Milley repeated to me.

I will never forget the intensity of his worry.

In June, Trump announced on social media that he was being indicted for mishandling classified documents at Mar-a-Lago, making him the first former president to face federal criminal charges. "The corrupt Biden Administration has informed my attorneys that I have been Indicted, seemingly over the Boxes Hoax," Trump said on Truth Social. "I am an INNOCENT MAN."

His former attorney general, Bill Barr, provided a frank

assessment to Fox News. "He's toast," Barr said if even half of what was alleged was proven true. "He's not a victim here. He was totally wrong that he had the right to have those documents. Those documents are among the most sensitive secrets that the country has."

President Biden was also ramping up his re-election campaign, attending several fundraisers in June 2023. Silicon Valley's tech hub was flush with important deep-pocketed cash donors. The first fundraiser hosted by Kevin Scott, the chief technology officer of Microsoft, at his home in Los Gatos on June 19, was attended by 38 guests, including some of the most serious Democratic donors in the valley. The event raised $2.7 million for Biden's re-election fund. Guests, however, said that Biden was "frighteningly awful." It was "like your 87-year-old senile grandfather" wandering around the room, saying to women guests, "your eyes are so beautiful."

Biden, who was 80, had flown in from Washington earlier that day. A donor acknowledged he had probably woken up very early but appeared tired. "He could not wait to sit down and only took two pre-arranged questions." He carried a handful of note cards with the answers printed out, but even then seemed to wander off point.

At a second much larger fundraiser that same day hosted by venture capitalist Steve Westly, the former state controller and a big Tesla investor, and his wife, Anita Yu, attendees reported an almost opposite experience with President Biden. "He was energetic," the host told others, "he wouldn't sit down for two hours." There were about 170 people at that fundraiser.

Biden's performances, particularly at fundraisers, continued to show troubling signs of decline through June.

During an event at the New York City Four Seasons, Biden could not find the word for "veteran." At a loss, he asked the small group of donors to help him find the right word for someone who had served in the military. One guest did and Biden used it—"veteran." The group was surprised and unsettled.

And after a small "meet the president" fundraiser attended by about 20 people at the home of philanthropists Susie and Michael Gelman in Chevy Chase, Maryland, on June 27, 2023, guests described their interactions with Biden as "painful."

"He never completed a sentence," said Bill Reichblum, cofounder and president of Liberties Journal Foundation, who attended with his wife and father-in-law, a former U.S. ambassador to Romania. "He would start to talk about something, jump somewhere else. He told the same story three times in exactly the same way and it meandered so much. . . . It was striking.

"Frankly, my impression was there were times," Reichblum said, "it was as though we didn't exist. He was just rambling and talking as to what came into his head." Biden seemed to Reichblum like an elderly grandparent or parent who talks and talks but "makes no sense."

Many wondered if it was just a "bad night" for Biden.

I would learn the significance of these fundraisers as early markers of Biden's decline only a year later, in June 2024.

FORTY

O n June 11, 2023, Colonel Joe Da Silva updated Sullivan on the dire state of Ukraine's ammunition stores.

"They are burning through a tremendous amount of artillery every day," Da Silva said. "It is about double what we've projected." The Ukrainians are using "upwards of 10,000" rounds of 155mm ammunition per day. Sullivan's eyes got big, "Well, when are they going to run out?"

"Potentially by the end of July," Da Silva said. Six weeks.

Da Silva looked at Sullivan grimly. They both knew an artillery war without artillery ammunition would mean the end for Ukraine.

This was Da Silva's third war. He had served 38 months in the Iraq War. He saw the flaws in the U.S. approach in Iraq and Afghanistan and felt strongly that helping Ukraine defend itself against Putin's ruthless attempt at territorial conquest was the purest cause he had ever been a part of in his 21 years in the U.S. Army.

Da Silva's 93-year-old father, a Portuguese immigrant who had been a high school janitor, was always skeptical of the U.S. wars in Afghanistan and Iraq.

"Joe," he said to his son, "I just don't know what the heck we're doing there."

But in the Ukraine War, his father said, "The Russians should not have done this and I'm glad we're helping these people."

Despite the political divisions, Da Silva felt Americans did have an innate understanding of right and wrong. Most Americans, Republicans, Democrats and independents, felt the war was a just cause.

The Pentagon confirmed that the only significant supply of 155s on earth that could fire from the howitzers were the U.S. cluster munitions.

Banned by 123 countries as inhumane and indiscriminate, cluster munitions explode in the air above a target releasing dozens or more bomblets over an area as wide as two football fields. The lethal, individual bomblets then explode into flying metal fragments. Those that don't detonate become ticking time bombs, sitting on the land, often exploding months, years or even decades later when civilians and children find or disturb them in the fields of old wars. Studies in Vietnam found that the cluster bombs caused eight times more casualties than the regular ammunition. They are one of the ugly expedients of war.

President Biden had made it clear he was deeply uncomfortable with cluster munitions. "A last resort," he said when his advisers had raised Ukraine's requests for clusters.

It was now the last resort.

The Pentagon, which had been reluctant to give Ukraine many other weapons, said the U.S. clusters (Dual-Purpose Improved Conventional Munitions) would effectively double Ukraine's kill efficiency on the battlefield. The U.S. had a large stockpile of 413,000 DPICMs with a safer 1.3 percent dud rate and a little over 800,000 clusters with a 2.35 percent dud rate.

Russia was already actively using cluster munitions in Ukraine that had an astronomically higher dud rate of 30 to 40 percent.

Opposition to clusters was framed in terms of human rights but it was difficult for Sullivan and Finer to think of a more brazen violation than if the Russians were allowed to march forward to conduct further atrocities in Ukrainian occupied territories.

More than 2,400 Ukrainian civilians were killed in Mariupol. More than 450 civilians were massacred in Bucha with clear evidence of execution: hands tied behind backs, gunshots to the head, slit throats. In Irpin, more than 290 civilians were found dead—many from indiscriminate Russian fire or execution. The missile strikes in crowded urban centers were at the busiest time of the day.

Putin was also responsible for the mass abduction of at least 6,000 Ukrainian children, taken from occupied territories like Mariupol, Kherson and Kharkiv and adopted out to Russian families.

One U.S. intelligence assessment put it starkly: If the clusters were not given, the Russian army would have a 5-to-1 or 10-to-1 advantage in the artillery rounds at their disposal—a crippling disparity. The implication was that not only would Ukraine lose the war but it would be a slaughter.

During the President's Daily Brief on June 29, all the principals were in lockstep. Austin and Milley made the recommendation to Biden: send clusters.

Austin and Milley had been in command units during the Iraq War when cluster munitions had been used by U.S. forces. They argued no better substitute existed for them on the battlefield.

Sullivan and Finer said they had received explicit assurances from allies who were signatories to the international ban on clusters that if Biden went ahead it would not cost the U.S. anything in alliance unity.

Intelligence chiefs, DNI Haines and CIA director Burns, advised that sending cluster munitions would not be considered a major escalation by the Russians. The Russians were using more dangerous clusters at a higher rate. For them to call a red line would be laughable.

I agree to the transfer, Biden said.

"How did I become the leading public advocate for the use of cluster munitions?" Sullivan remarked later to Da Silva. "I never thought in my life I'd do that. Joe Da Silva that's your fault," he said jokingly. "You know you made me do it."

Sullivan understood it was one of the messy, undesirable necessities of war forcing a difficult and far from clear-cut moral choice.

FORTY-ONE

Yevgeny Prigozhin, Putin's personal chef turned private military contractor, was publicly incensed at the incompetence and disorganization of Russia's military.

Burly, baldheaded and straight out of central casting for a Russian thug, Prigozhin had used social media during the war to challenge the Kremlin's motives for fighting in Ukraine.

"The war wasn't needed to return Russian citizens to our bosom, nor to demilitarize or de-nazify Ukraine," Prigozhin said. "The war was needed so that a bunch of animals could simply exult in glory."

He was also engaged in a brazen public feud with Russia's defense minister Shoigu, whom he accused of depriving his Wagner forces—a mix of elite mercenaries and thousands of Russian prisoners—of ammunition in Ukraine. It had turned Wagner, which was fighting for Russia, into a meat grinder.

"The scum that doesn't give us ammunition will eat their guts in hell," Prigozhin sneered.

In the months-long battle for Bakhmut, a Ukrainian city in the east, Prigozhin reported that Wagner had lost more than 20,000 men. He posted a video of himself walking in a field at night among dozens of corpses in uniform. "These are boys from Wagner who died today," Prigozhin said. "Their blood is still fresh!"

He then unleashed on Russia's defense leaders, yelling into the camera: "Shoigu, Gerasimov, where is the fucking ammunition?"

Fed up, on Friday, June 23, 2023, Prigozhin turned his forces around in Ukraine and ordered them to "march for justice" to Moscow. It was a dramatic showdown. A column of tanks slowly rolled away from Ukraine and toward Russia's capital, capturing worldwide attention. Iran played minute-by-minute coverage on their news channels and Iran's president, Ebrahim Raisi, placed a worried call to President Putin.

"Actions that split our unity are a stab in the back of our country and our people," Putin said with undisguised venom during a televised address to the nation that day.

In less than 24 hours, 125 miles from Moscow, Prigozhin announced he had struck a deal with Belarusian president Alexander Lukashenko and would stand down.

Two months later, Prigozhin was killed in a plane crash north of Moscow.

"Taking action, like killing Prigozhin, like doing the kinds of things that he's done," DNI Avril Haines reported as she watched Putin, "he feels a sense of empowerment. He's in control, he's done this, and that's part of the psychology of it."

During an economic conference in Russia in September, Putin said, "Mr. Trump says he will resolve all burning issues within several days, including the Ukrainian crisis. We cannot help but feel happy about it." He labeled the criminal cases piling up against Trump—now totaling 91 felony counts—as political persecution. "Given today's conditions, what is happening is good for us, in my opinion," Putin added, "because it shows the rottenness of the American political system, which cannot pretend to teach democracy to others."

Asked about Putin's comments in a *Meet the Press* interview with NBC journalist Kristen Welker, Trump gloated. "I like that he said that because that means what I'm saying is right.

"I would get him into a room, I would get Zelensky into a room and I would get a deal worked out," Trump said. Pressed by Welker for specifics, Trump added, "If I tell you exactly, I lose all my bargaining chips. I mean, you can't really say exactly what you're going to do. But I would say certain things to Putin. I would say certain things to Zelensky." It was not clear Trump had any concrete ideas on how to resolve the war.

"I get along with him really well," Trump said about Putin, "and that's a good thing, not a bad thing."

FORTY-TWO

◆─◆

Ron Dermer, the closest adviser to Israeli prime minister Benjamin "Bibi" Netanyahu, often called Bibi's brain, was at home in Jerusalem with his family for the start of the Jewish holiday Simchat Torah on Saturday, October 7, 2023. Around 6:30 that morning his phone started buzzing and buzzing and buzzing and buzzing. The red alert system, the sophisticated app on his phone that notified him every time a rocket launched at Israel and where it would hit, was going berserk.

He watched with growing alarm as a rapid stream of notifications flashed on his phone screen. A barrage of 3,000 rockets had launched at Israel. Hamas, the Palestinian militant group that controlled the Gaza Strip south of Israel, had started a massive surprise attack.

The Sabbath was a day of rest for Jewish people but when Dermer switched on his television and saw white pickup trucks full of Hamas gunmen driving along main roads in southern Israel, he got straight in his car and drove to Tel Aviv to meet Netanyahu.

By the time Dermer arrived at the Kirya, Israel's version of the Pentagon, and descended deep into the underground bunker, Hamas militants had begun to massacre any Israeli they could find.

"This is war," Netanyahu told Dermer. A statement that reverberated across the entire country.

Middle East NSC coordinator Brett McGurk, age 50, had been alerted by the White House Situation Room to rocket attacks in Israel just after midnight in Washington, D.C., on October 7, 2023. Israel's time zone was seven hours ahead of Washington.

McGurk didn't think too much of it. The rocket alerts were common in Israel.

Moments later, at 12:17 a.m., his phone buzzed with a text from Israeli ambassador to the U.S. Michael Herzog, a former Israel Defense Forces general: "Hamas just launched a massive rocket strike against Israel. This is war."

Next was Israel's national security adviser Tzachi Hanegbi: "What is happening is an attack against Israel, a coordinated attack!"

Then an update from Herzog: "They launched the attack by surprise, including cross-border infiltration. This is an unprovoked massive attack that cannot be unanswered. We need strong public condemnation from you and clear support."

McGurk wrote back at 1:12 a.m.: "We are with you."

He was up the rest of the night.

The initial hours of the invasion were a blur of chaos and confusion, but the fuller picture emerged in time and it was one of unthinkable horror. Hamas militants from Gaza stormed across the border into southern Israel. They smashed through barrier crossings, took down communication towers, and attacked unsuspecting Israeli military command posts. Then using pickup trucks, vans, jeeps, motorcycles and even paragliders, 3,000 Hamas militants streamed into kibbutz communities, burning homes and slaughtering entire families, including children and babies in cribs and bunk beds. Many were still in their pajamas. Others were sitting down to have breakfast. Hamas shot, beheaded, immolated, dismembered and burned Israelis alive.

Another 50 Hamas terrorists swarmed a music festival in Re'im, Israel, about three miles from the Gaza border. Jeeps and vans teeming with Hamas gunmen fired at the festivalgoers, surrounding them in the open desert with few places to hide. Gunmen picked off the young men and women as they fled or hid in trees or shrubs.

The Hamas militants also committed vicious acts of sexual violence against women, including tying them to trees and raping them. Rami Davidian, an emergency worker at the music festival, recounted later in Sheryl Sandberg's documentary *Screams Before Silence*, "I saw girls tied up with their hands behind them to every tree here. Someone murdered them, raped them and abused them here on these trees. Their legs were spread. . . . They inserted all kinds of things into their intimate organs, like wooden boards, iron rods. Over 30 girls were murdered and raped here."

Raz Cohen, another festivalgoer interviewed in the documentary, was hiding with his friend Shoham. "Shoham, who was next to me, said, 'He's stabbing her. He's slaughtering her' . . . and I didn't want to look. . . . When I looked again, she was already dead, and he was still at it. He was still raping her after he had slaughtered her."

Later, Hamas members paraded the body of a woman they had killed, Shani Louk, a 22-year-old German-Israeli national, in a pickup truck through Gaza City. She wore only underwear. The militants chanted "Allahu Akbar," meaning God is great, and spat on her body.

Deep underground in Tel Aviv, the evening of October 7, Prime Minister Bibi Netanyahu and Ron Dermer met with Israel's security and military leadership as the surprise attack in Israel's south continued to ravage communities.

Every hour reports of the horrors worsened. The death toll reports were growing by the hundreds.

Are we in control of the situation? Netanyahu demanded of his security cabinet. He had only been informed of the attack at 6:30 that morning as it unfolded. Early warning signals first went off around 3:00 a.m., but had never escalated to the level of informing the prime minister. It was a massive intelligence and military failure.

"Why didn't you wake up the prime minister?" Dermer asked. Nobody had a good answer.

Netanyahu kept a hawklike focus on the situation unfolding: Is the IDF going to the communities under attack? Has Hamas infiltrated beyond the outskirts of Gaza? Is another attack coming? What are we prepared to do? What do we need to do diplomatically?

President Biden convened a call with his national security team, including Sullivan, Blinken, Austin and Burns. They provided an update on everything they were seeing unfold in Israel.

Biden said he wanted to speak to Netanyahu as soon as possible. "There needs to be the strongest condemnation of what has happened, and of Hamas," Biden said.

On the phone later that day, Netanyahu said to Biden, "Israel will win" a war against Hamas. His focus was not on the Hamas attack but on what might still be coming.

"You need to begin messaging Hezbollah to stay out," Netanyahu said to Biden. "Hezbollah needs to get the message from the United States: Don't enter the war. Don't enter the war. Stay out of the war."

Netanyahu, who sounded shaken, was worried that Hezbollah, the powerful Iran-backed militia in Lebanon, would attack Israel from the north.

"These guys think we're weak," Netanyahu said. "And in the Middle East if you're weak, you're roadkill."

"We're with you," Biden said to Netanyahu and reassured him that there would be close coordination ongoing between U.S. and Israeli military and intelligence.

Netanyahu then called Jake Sullivan directly.

The national security adviser was in a small fishing village in the South of France about to start a short holiday with his wife, Maggie Goodlander, and a few of their good friends, when he received the alert of the Hamas attack. Now he would be heading back to Washington.

"Jake, we need you to basically threaten Hezbollah," Netanyahu implored him. "That's what we need you to do. We need you to tell them that if they mess with us, they mess with you."

Hezbollah had the largest fighting force of any non-state actor in the world with tens of thousands of soldiers and upward of 150,000 missiles and rockets.

Sullivan could tell from Netanyahu's tone, this was existential for Israel—a moment of the most acute vulnerability. Netanyahu sounded like he believed he might really lose his country. Hezbollah might come, Iran might come, everyone might come all at once to try to destroy Israel.

A cornerstone of Israel's deterrence was Israel's vaunted military and sophisticated intelligence. That notion had just been shattered.

At the White House, Brett McGurk was poring over the intelligence reporting to see if another attack was coming for Israel. He also was monitoring the reports from Israelis on the ground.

"We've got it contained. We've got them all," Israel said of the Hamas militants.

Hours later, McGurk realized they had not. "There are still a thousand Hamas guys inside Israel!"

It was a true fog of war. The scale of Hamas's brutality wasn't fully apparent until days later.

At a podium in the State Dining Room of the White House that afternoon, President Biden, flanked by Secretary Blinken, delivered a warning to Iran and its proxies, such as Hezbollah in Lebanon.

"Today, the people of Israel are under attack, orchestrated by a terrorist organization, Hamas," Biden said.

"In this moment of tragedy, I want to say to them and to the world and to terrorists everywhere that the United States stands with Israel. We will not ever fail to have their back."

Biden added, "Let me say this as clearly as I can: This is not a moment for any party hostile to Israel to exploit these attacks to seek advantage. The world is watching."

It took three days for the Israelis to get a handle on the attack.

"We were counting the dead for many, many days," Dermer said. "That number kept going up for 10 days because there were bodies all over the place."

Overall, Hamas killed more than 1,200 Israelis and dragged more than 240 hostages back across the border into underground tunnels in Gaza.

It was the deadliest attack in Jewish history since the Holocaust.

Ron Dermer racked his brain about how this attack could have happened right under their noses.

On October 6, the day before the attack, Israel's intelligence assessment was that Hamas in Gaza was deterred. Hamas was not strong enough to take on Israel.

Israel had exchanged big blows with Hamas in May 2021 after Hamas fired a rocket into Jerusalem. At the time, Israel believed they had destroyed a lot of Hamas's key capabilities. "On October 6," Dermer said, "I believed that [Hamas] got hit by a stick two years earlier." They weren't looking for a fight.

Netanyahu had also changed Israel's policy to allow Gazans to work in Israel. The number of Gazans given work permits had gradually increased to around 20,000 by October 7. The extra workers were helping Israel's economy but significantly improving Gaza's economy as well.

Hamas, Israeli intelligence assessed, now had an incentive to keep the calm so that Gazans could continue to work in Israel. Any violence would shut access down.

"The assessment that people had was that Hamas did not have an interest in going to war with Israel," Dermer said.

Hamas also had stayed out of the few "mini" fights Israel had over the last two years with Palestinian Islamic Jihad, a smaller terrorist organization in Gaza that was a direct subsidiary of Iran. Islamic Jihad fired rockets at Israel and Israel retaliated by taking out some of the militant leaders. Hamas had not engaged.

Israel's intelligence analysts interpreted that as another signal that Hamas was not looking for war. Now, after October 7, the assessment was that Hamas had remained quiet in order to prepare its surprise attack, which members of Palestinian Islamic Jihad had also participated in.

"Netanyahu knows Hamas is dedicated to our destruction," Dermer said. "He doesn't have any doubt about their will to kill us and their capabilities. It's just actually having an attack plan on this scale." The scale of the October 7 attack was the biggest surprise of all.

Months later, Israel's intelligence assessments showed that on October 6, only three Hamas leaders knew the plan for the attack on Israel the next day. Hamas concealed it from Israeli intelligence by keeping it within the smallest circle. Most of the 3,000 militants only found out they were not on another training exercise in the moments before the massive attack launched.

In another extraordinary oversight, Israel's intelligence agencies later discovered that they had been in possession of Hamas's attack plan almost a full year ahead of the October 7 attack.

"I don't know who in our hierarchy saw it or read it," Ambassador Herzog said, "but nobody believed it.

"Everybody said that Hamas is not strong enough to take on Israel. They would not dare do something like that," Herzog said. "Now we know that our intelligence managed to put its hands on the full Hamas plans about a year before the attack.

"It gave the full plan of Hamas," Herzog said, "of a massive cross-border attack with rockets, with everything—going into army bases and to all the kibbutz and the civilian-populated villages and towns close to the border. It was a very meticulous plan and they exercised it. They trained."

Israel had failed to act on the information and as a consequence, did not have enough of their forces close to the border when the invasion began. Israel's military secretary later said that even 15 minutes of warning would have made a world of difference to Israel's ability to defend against the Hamas attack on October 7.

Instead, Israel was caught by total surprise.

As the death toll was still being counted, Prime Minister Netanyahu and Israel's security cabinet began to plan a military response unlike Hamas had ever seen. Netanyahu wanted "a decisive victory over Hamas in Gaza," to eliminate Hamas's leaders and permanently dismantle their control over Gaza.

For Israel, Dermer said, "the existential threat is that if we do not wipe out an organization that did what they did to us on October 7, then that imperils the whole future of the country because all the buzzards circling around Israel are going to look and see, we can get away with it.

"It's not enough to just hit it hard," Dermer added. "It's not enough to deplete their capacity. You have to, for a country like Israel that relies on deterrence—on deterring enemies from doing these attacks—what we have to show all of the enemies in the region is that if you do this type of attack, they don't survive it."

October 7 struck an existential nerve for Israelis, Ambassador Herzog believed. He had been a combat soldier, a corporal, in the 1973 Yom Kippur War, 50 years before this Hamas attack.

"I think this war touches an existential level among Israelis the way that the 1973 war never touched," Herzog said about October 7. Back then it had been Israel's military fighting against the Egyptian and Syrian militaries. The eventual cease-fire led to the Camp David Accords with Egypt becoming the first Arab country to recognize Israel as a state.

Now Israel was fighting against a very different invading force: Hamas, a terrorist organization bent on Israel's destruction.

"If we do not remove this threat, we cannot lead normal lives," Herzog said. "Hamas has become an Iranian proxy over the last decade and if we don't defeat Hamas then we just embolden this axis."

Hamas was not thousands of miles away but, for Israelis, physically and psychologically right next door.

The scale of the October 7 Hamas attack on Israel had surprised U.S. intelligence agencies as well.

Director of National Intelligence Avril Haines scrutinized the reports. Before October 7 there were signs of mounting tensions between Israel and Hamas. The U.S. intelligence agencies had warned of an increasing potential for a more limited attack, something consistent with what Hamas had done in the past. But the massive scale of October 7 was a curveball out of the blue. "Unquestionably, a surprise," Haines reported.

What stood out to Haines in the intelligence leading up to October 7 were reports of protests by Palestinians in Gaza against Hamas. "Pretty unusual," Haines mused. There were indications of the beginning of a fraying of Hamas political support in Gaza.

U.S. intelligence had been more focused on Hezbollah, the militant organization that controlled Lebanon, north of Israel.

"In many respects, we were looking at the tensions increasing with Hezbollah during this period, even more so than with Hamas," Haines reported.

U.S. intelligence showed that Hezbollah was "in a relatively stable position, but growing." A lot of Hezbollah's elite fighters who had been sent to Syria had returned to Lebanon. Hezbollah was also stockpiling advanced conventional weapons.

"We don't see Nasrallah as being in a position where he wants to go to war with Israel in a full-out escalation," Haines said, referring to Hezbollah's leader Hassan Nasrallah. "But in the lead-up to October 7th, he was becoming more confident of his space and pushing against Israel. And Israel was pushing back."

Now, in the aftermath of the massive Hamas attack, Haines pushed the U.S. intelligence agencies into overdrive. Help Israel see what's happening on their other borders, she instructed. Hezbollah, Iran, the Houthis in Yemen, Iranian-aligned militias in Iraq and Syria were circling.

FORTY-THREE

The day after October 7, Jake Sullivan was looking for deterrence measures or symbols of deterrence in order to cool down the region. No better deterrent than the American aircraft carrier.

Sullivan called Kelly Magsamen, a civilian foreign policy adviser and chief of staff to Secretary Austin, and asked, "Don't we have a carrier strike group in the Med for Ukraine purposes?" Sullivan had almost forgotten about the carrier because it wasn't doing a lot for Ukraine. "Let's reposition the *Ford*. See what Austin thinks."

Austin agreed and directed the USS *Gerald R. Ford* Strike Group, which included the carrier, guided missile cruisers and destroyers, to move to the Eastern Mediterranean. Closer to Israel. Sullivan also sought Biden's approval.

"This is the sweet spot for us," Biden said about moving the ships. He would not have to issue a public threat or declare a red line. The messaging should be straightforward. "We shouldn't hype it. Just make the move." Biden was delighted they could generate deterrence without putting the U.S. or himself on the hook in a way that might be risky. Reward without risk.

FORTY-FOUR

◆

S ecretary of State Tony Blinken called the head of Qatar's government, Prime Minister and Foreign Minister Mohammed
bin Abdulrahman Al Thani, or MBAR as he was known in the
U.S. for short.

"There are American hostages," Blinken told MBAR urgently.
"There are hostages and there are *Americans* who are hostage. It's
a game changer for us," he said with emphasis.

Hamas had taken over 240 hostages, including 33 children and
12 Americans.

MBAR said he understood.

Qatar, a small but wealthy emirate on the Persian Gulf, played an
outsized role in the realpolitik of the Middle East. Home to some
of the world's largest natural gas reserves, Qatar had the highest
per capita income in the world and a GDP of about $250 billion
annually.

Its 43-year-old leader, Emir Sheikh Tamim bin Hamad Al
Thani, educated in Great Britain at Harrow, the elite school, and
the Royal Military Academy Sandhurst, had transformed Qatar's
relationship with the West while maintaining close ties with Iran
and financially backing controversial political-militant groups like
Hamas, which had attacked Israel so brutally. The Emir was considered one of the shrewdest politicians in the region.

The Emir had helped the U.S. evacuate its citizens from Afghanistan in 2021 when the Afghan government collapsed, prompting
President Biden to designate Qatar a "major non-NATO ally."

"We have a channel with Hamas," MBAR said on the phone with Jake Sullivan a few days later. He was the Emir's most trusted adviser. He had served as foreign minister since 2016 and in March 2023 the Emir appointed him to also serve as prime minister.

"You need to set up a cell that will work with my team," MBAR said to Sullivan, meaning a core group of Americans and Israelis dedicated to working on getting the hostages out.

Sullivan jumped at the opportunity of negotiating a channel, knowing how important the hostages were to President Biden and American policy.

He told MBAR he would set up a cell and link in the Israelis. Sullivan built his cell with CIA director Bill Burns, NSC Middle East coordinator Brett McGurk and NSC legal counselor Josh Geltzer.

Israel chose David Barnea, the head of Mossad.

Sullivan knew Emir Al Thani and Prime Minister MBAR were key to getting the hostages out safely. The Emir had hosted Hamas political leadership in the capital, Doha, for years and contributed aid in the form of hundreds of millions of dollars to Hamas in Gaza. Israeli prime minister Bibi Netanyahu had even approved of the Qatar aid on the grounds that it would contain and stabilize Hamas in Gaza.

For Netanyahu, a contained Hamas leadership in Gaza was his preference as it greatly reduced pressure on Israel to negotiate a two-state solution with the Palestinians. There was no push to recognize Hamas as a head of state. This was often referred to as "Buying Quiet" of the terrorist group Hamas. Now it was obvious Bibi's strategy was a catastrophic failure. This sounded like astonishing hypocrisy. But buying protection was a way of life for leaders in the Middle East.

———

Qatar has a channel with Hamas, Sullivan updated President Biden, outlining his idea for the cell and the plan he and MBAR had set in motion.

"What do you mean?" Biden said. "I will get the hostages out. That's my job. You can do whatever you want but I'm going to have to call the Emir and I'm going to have to call Sisi and I'm going to have to call Bibi." Biden was referring to Egypt's president Abdel Fattah el-Sisi.

"Who's responsible for getting the hostages home?" Biden underscored his point to his national security adviser. "I'm responsible."

Biden gave Sullivan the go-ahead to proceed with the cell.

"Great," Biden said. "However you want to organize it, fine. But keep in mind that I feel responsible and I feel ultimately I will have to deliver."

Hostages were the emotional spine for most leaders, especially Biden. Getting the hostages back safely would be a victory, failure to do so could permanently stain a presidency.

FORTY-FIVE

President Biden put Israeli prime minister Netanyahu on speakerphone. His senior staff gathered around the Resolute Desk in the Oval Office. It was 9:55 a.m. on October 11, 2023, four days after 3,000 Hamas terrorists from Gaza crashed through Israel's southern border and slaughtered around 1,200 Israelis.

Netanyahu was seeking unequivocal assurance from Biden that the United States would fully support Israel in a preemptive attack on Hezbollah, the massive Iranian-backed terrorist organization operating out of Southern Lebanon on Israel's northern border.

He claimed to have rock-solid intelligence that Hezbollah was about to attack Israel. Hezbollah's arsenal of more than 150,000 rockets dwarfed Hamas's cache of weapons in the south.

Netanyahu wanted to strike first with a total blitz of every Hezbollah missile site and military location.

"Do you really think you're going to be able to take all those rockets out before they just launch against your cities?" Biden said to Netanyahu. "And if they do launch against your cities in that volume do you really think you're going to have the air defenses to be able to defend them? Is this the moment for Israel to kick off that kind of situation and put its population at risk?"

Biden continued, "This is going to lead to a situation that is going to get out of control very quickly, that is going to implicate much if not most of your population, all of whom are in rocket range."

The president had intelligence that showed Hezbollah's rockets could reach every corner of Israel. Just 290 miles north-to-south and 85 miles east-to-west at its widest point, Israel is about the size of New Jersey.

"No doubt you can inflict significant damage on Hezbollah," Biden said, "but the damage they'll be about to inflict on you and your cities and among your people is great.

"Their arsenal is huge and capable of reaching virtually all major Israeli cities," Biden said.

"I just talked to my chairman of the Joint Chiefs. I just talked to all my intel people, I just talked to my military people," Biden said. "What you guys are contemplating here is not going to work."

The president added, "Hey, do we all agree we do not want this to become a broader regional war? It's going to be a disaster."

"Of course, Joe," Bibi said. "That's what we don't want. But we have no choice and this will shorten the war. This will shorten the war."

Biden knew an Israeli-Hezbollah war would likely explode into an Israel-Iran war. Hezbollah was basically a syndicate led by its secretary-general Hassan Nasrallah, a Lebanese cleric who helped end the Israeli occupation of Southern Lebanon in 2000, and the Supreme Leader of Iran, Ali Khamenei. Iran had the largest military in the Middle East.

Intercepts showed Nasrallah and Khamenei were scheming regularly. Both had an avowed commitment to the elimination of Israel as a state. Up to this point, Iran had used its proxies to target Israel but large-scale efforts to decimate Hezbollah would be impossible for Iran to ignore.

"Look," Biden said, "one of our objectives with this terrible October 7 Hamas attack is to try to contain it to Gaza and not have a broader regional war. What you're about to do is going to guarantee a regional war."

After what Hamas did I can't say there won't be a regional war, Biden said, but "I can tell you if you launch this attack there will be one. So let's kind of take our time here.

"And by the way we are not on board," Biden added.

If there were any doubt, the president repeated his point: "We, the United States, are not on board for that conflict so you should not count on our support if you preemptively launch a war against Hezbollah.

"If they attack you," Biden said, "if they attack Israel, the United States will always stand up for Israel's security.

"But if you launch a preemptive war like this we do not support it," Biden said.

U.S. intelligence agencies had been monitoring the Israel-Lebanon border closely since the devastating Hamas attack on October 7. Israel had sent troops to reinforce its defenses fearing Hezbollah might stream across the border in the north just as Hamas, the terrorist group in Gaza, had done in the south. In response to Israeli reinforcements, Hezbollah had added more troops of its own and moved some of their elite forces closer to the border. The atmosphere couldn't be tenser, with both sides staring at each other, looking for the slightest provocation.

"First, we do not read the situation the same way you do," Biden said. "We do not believe war is inevitable."

Second, Biden said, this is a moment where you cannot get pushed into war by your military.

Israeli defense minister Yoav Gallant was raring to go, advocating for the preemptive strike. Israel Defense Forces chief Herzi Halevi believed Israel had their military plan perfected and sensitive sources and methods had presented them with unique operational opportunities.

The Israeli generals feared Hamas and Hezbollah were allied and working together, that the October 7 attack was part of a larger, coordinated master plan to destroy Israel. First, Hamas would attack on October 7 to distract Israel in the south and then Hezbollah would launch devastating attacks from the north.

Before his call with Netanyahu, Biden had been briefed by his principal advisers. He asked, Have we seen any intel to support a Hezbollah attack on Israel? The unanimous answer from CIA director Bill Burns, Director of National Intelligence Avril Haines, and Chairman of the Joint Chiefs CQ Brown was no.

Biden continued to make his argument to Bibi.

There is a reason that we have elected political leaders in democracies, Biden said. We have to, yes, take the advice of the military but it's your call and don't think that just because your military is telling you, you have to go, that absolves you of the responsibility of making the decision.

Nearly 15 years earlier when Biden was President Obama's vice president he had passionately—and unsuccessfully—fought the military pressure to persuade Obama to add 30,000 additional troops to the Afghanistan War. So incensed, Biden had declared at the time "the military doesn't fuck around with me," a statement that later incurred the distrust of much of the U.S. defense establishment.

Doubt about the military and military advice was part of Biden's approach as president.

Three, Biden advised Netanyahu, "Take a breath. Let's have our teams work together and figure out what we're actually dealing with and then we can make a considered judgment that isn't just rushed into."

Finally, Biden said, you start this war, I have people all over the Middle East.

Overall, 45,000 U.S. military personnel and contractors were based in the Middle East and would instantly become targets too.

"The conditions are not set," Biden said to Netanyahu. "The theater is not set for them. So I've got to look out for my people. I have skin in the game here. I don't want you doing something that's going to put our people at risk without you and me really coming to an understanding about what this is all about."

Netanyahu said his cabinet would now convene to debate a preemptive strike on Hezbollah.

"We're going to continue discussing it," Netanyahu said. "We'll make the decision based on Israeli interests and it doesn't mean we won't go ahead."

Netanyahu and Biden had known each other for 40 years, meeting first when both were young men in Washington, Biden as a freshly elected senator and Netanyahu as the deputy chief of mission in the Israeli embassy in Washington in the 1980s. Their relationship had its ups and downs with more downs in recent years. But in his recent memoir, Netanyahu had referred to Biden 28 times with an unusual warmth and playfulness amid more than a few score-settling moments directed at other Israeli and American opponents.

Biden, Netanyahu wrote, had a frankness that he particularly appreciated. "You don't have too many friends here, buddy," he recalled Biden telling him after inviting him to the vice president's residence. "I'm the one friend you do have so call me when you need to."

Now the relationship was defined by a distrust that had festered for years. It was so deep that it could fracture the alliance at a time when trust was most needed.

Brett McGurk, the National Security Council's Middle East expert, was one of the president's top advisers and was sitting in front of the Resolute Desk. McGurk had managed intense crisis situations across four Republican and Democratic administrations— George W. Bush, Barack Obama, Donald Trump and now Biden. He was the only person in the senior ranks of the Biden administration to have clerked for one of the most conservative members of the Supreme Court, Chief Justice William Rehnquist, 20 years earlier.

He was considered a straight down the middle, nonpartisan adviser who had more experience than almost anyone other than Biden.

For McGurk, "It was a classic fog of war crisis. You could teach it in a seminar." The danger lay in the unknown—what Hezbollah was or was not about to do—and in the military momentum building after the October 7 attacks. Hearing Netanyahu's tone, less aggressive than usual, McGurk believed Netanyahu was looking for the president to help walk him and his military leadership back off the ledge.

Biden ended with a final word in the October 11 call: "Do not do this. You know me, we have known each other a long time. This is a mistake. Do not go down this road."

"I hear you," Netanyahu said. "You've been very clear. But I also want to be clear that we're going to make our own decision and while this conversation will inform it, it will not decide it."

President Biden had spent the last year and a half equipping Ukraine with billions of dollars' worth of U.S. weapons to defend against Russia's invasion. He'd made a point of insisting *no* U.S. troops would fight in Ukraine. Now, a war in the Middle East might be hours away, and this time the U.S. could be dragged in.

Dread hung in the room among the advisers. They all knew Biden had immense strategic and political influence with Netanyahu. The U.S. was Israel's largest provider of military aid. But at the same time they felt like bystanders. As close as the U.S. was to Israel, there was little that they could say or do that could ultimately stop Israel from acting in what they believed to be their vital national interest.

Secretary Blinken was reminded of one of the central truths of foreign relations. Even with the closest ally, each country ultimately makes its own decisions.

Blinken felt a sense of global vulnerability, unlike anything he'd felt in 30 years of national security work. If Israel decided to launch, it could lead to a war that would shake the entire world.

"We may just have to do it," Netanyahu finally said to Biden. "We may just have to do it."

At 10:35 a.m. Biden reconvened the principals on a secure call so they could prepare for the worst. The atmosphere was one of frightening uncertainty. Secretary Austin was rushed out of a defense ministerial meeting in Brussels so he could join the call from a small classified space, Room 17, in NATO headquarters.

Left unsaid in Biden's conversation with Netanyahu but clearly understood by the president and his national security team was the recognition that Netanyahu and his military leaders had suffered a devastating loss, personally, professionally and nationally, in the surprise Hamas attack. They had failed to keep Israel safe, failed their primary promise of "never again" to the people of Israel. And a successful preemptive strike on Hezbollah could conceivably restore a sense of strength and provide a much needed win.

Five minutes into the president's call with the principals at 10:40 a.m. word came to the Oval Office that Bibi's right-hand man, Ron Dermer, Netanyahu's top aide and alter ego, had phoned the White House Situation Room. He was requesting to talk to Jake Sullivan at once.

Pulled from the Oval Office, Sullivan took the call from Dermer, who had stepped out of the Israeli cabinet meeting.

"The direction of the debate is shifting in the direction of preemptive strike," Dermer said. Our entire military is pushing us to go. Dermer expressed extreme displeasure that President Biden had pushed Netanyahu not to attack.

Reiterating Biden's argument, Sullivan reminded Dermer that this is what civilian leadership and political leadership is actually for—to have a broader perspective than just what is the military interest of the moment.

Sullivan, whose tone is normally calm and steady, raised his voice: "What you are thinking about doing is dangerous. It's irrational." Not in your interests and not in the interests of the United States. "You'll decide what's in your interest," he said, but the risk was huge.

Sullivan continued, "We do not believe this is good for Israel and we fundamentally know it is not good for us . . . do not go ahead with it." He added, "The president was deadly serious about that."

At 11:13 a.m. Sullivan walked back to the Oval Office to quickly update Biden, Blinken and McGurk about what he had told Dermer. He headed to his office down the hall from the Oval.

Three minutes later at 11:16 a.m. Dermer called Sullivan again about Hezbollah. Sullivan hit the speakerphone so McGurk could listen. It was now almost an open line with Israel.

"Hey, we're just being transparent with you guys," Dermer said. "They've launched the attack. There are paragliders coming from the north. One of them just landed and shot up a funeral for someone who was killed in the October 7 attack. We are going to launch the attack. And I'm telling you, you've got to batten down the hatches."

Dermer said they were also getting reports of Hezbollah drones coming across the northern border, air raid sirens going off.

"I'm just telling you we have no choice," Dermer said. "We're going to launch the attack." Israel had aircraft with munitions ready to strike.

He said they were going to go in 30 minutes.

They were inches away from a major Middle East war.

"Shit," McGurk thought, "maybe Hezbollah did launch a paraglider attack." Hamas had used paragliders on October 7.

But they had no corroborating intelligence.

McGurk left Sullivan and ran to his desk in Room 326 in the Executive Office Building next to the White House. It was the same office he was in during the Republican Bush administration. He called Centcom commander Erik Kurilla.

"Hey, my J2 says there are no paragliders," Kurilla said, referring to the military's intelligence portfolio. "There is no sign of any of this. It's a phantom."

"The Israelis always do this," McGurk thought. "They claim "We got the intel! You'll see it. You'll see it. But like 50 percent of the time the so-called intel doesn't actually show up.'"

McGurk ran back to the Oval Office, borrowing a spare tie from Deputy National Security Adviser Jon Finer on the way.

While McGurk was on the phone to Kurilla, Sullivan and Blinken made a secure call from the national security adviser's office to DNI Haines, CIA director Burns, Secretary of Defense Austin and Chairman of the Joint Chiefs CQ Brown.

"Are we seeing any of this?" Sullivan asked them.

No we are not, the intelligence and military leaders said. Sullivan re-checked this assessment with Burns at 11:31 a.m. Still nothing, Burns said emphatically.

But they could see social media and mainstream media were

filled with reports of drones and sirens. Millions of Israelis were scrambling for shelter.

Sullivan called Dermer, pulling him out of Israel's cabinet meeting.

U.S. intelligence agencies are not seeing any of this, Sullivan said. "In fact, it's just not there." The social media reports were not supported at all. Israel could not make decisions based on social media. Go back into the cabinet and tell them they are false reports.

Sullivan then called Dermer's chief of staff and dictated a note to send to Dermer, who was back sitting beside Netanyahu in the cabinet meeting.

"Jake to Ron: Your information is false. You're making decisions in a fog of war. Slow down."

At the same time, McGurk received a message from Iran, strong backers of Hezbollah, through a back channel the U.S. has with the Islamic Revolutionary Guard Corps (IRGC). The communication came through a trusted Norwegian intermediary.

Iran's message was: "We're not looking for a conflict. Whatever is going on we are not looking for a conflict."

McGurk said they obviously couldn't know for sure if the Iranians were being honest, but it was a message consistent with the U.S. intel assessment.

"Let's deflate this thing," McGurk said.

The time frame for action was shrinking.

Secretary Blinken couldn't believe it. The Israelis are "30 minutes from launching a preemptive, or preventive in their minds, attack based on totally erroneous information," he said.

At 1:00 p.m. Dermer called Sullivan, who was in the Oval Office.

The Israeli cabinet has voted against taking military action in Lebanon, Dermer said.

With relief, Sullivan briefed the president. No preemptive strike.

The Israel Defense Forces came out publicly and said the

information about drones, paragliders and other attacks on the northern border was false. None of it had actually happened.

"There was an error, and we are investigating it," IDF spokesman Rear Admiral Daniel Hagari said. "The bottom line is I want to calm the public and say that at this stage, there is no major security incident in the north."

The "drones" Israelis reported seeing near the northern border turned out to be birds.

Blinken was shaken, saying to the others, "It was such a close call. The idea that this conflict could have significantly expanded on the basis of bad information." Israel could have found itself at war with Hezbollah because of some birds. It was almost unbelievable, but he had been there and witnessed it.

Later Dermer said to Sullivan, "Well, the prime minister and I were never supportive of this. It was being driven by the military, and you know, so this is a good outcome basically."

Biden remained worried. "These guys are not thinking clearly," he said to McGurk. "I've got to get there." The president wanted to fly into Israel, an active war zone, to meet Netanyahu and his war cabinet face-to-face.

Jake Sullivan believed that he, Biden and others had never experienced a day quite like this. Had Israel attacked Hezbollah first, it could have quickly escalated, plunging the Middle East into war. They had lived five hours and 12 minutes—from 7:48 a.m. that morning until 1:00 p.m.—on the brink. Moving toward and then veering away from catastrophe with breathtaking speed, hearing the certainty and seeing it fade.

That evening Jake Sullivan finally went home to his wife of eight years, Maggie Goodlander, a former Navy Intelligence officer and current senior Justice Department lawyer.

It has been the most stressful day in my entire professional life, he told her, perhaps in my entire life. He had never thought coalition management would be so fraught and full of risk. The stress was taking its toll. He was not eating enough, definitely not sleeping well.

"We did come within an inch of all-out war in the Middle East," he told his wife, "basically instigated by Israel believing Hezbollah was about to attack and they needed to go."

It was sobering and clarifying to see Israel in this fragile condition with the stakes so high. "The sense that they were—the emperor has no clothes, we're lying naked, was so palpable and profound. It was very raw. The thing that was most profoundly in their minds was, is our nation just existentially at risk right now? Is this the moment when it all comes down on us?"

During a campaign speech in West Palm Beach, Florida, later that day, Trump called Hezbollah "very smart" and Israel's national defense minister Yoav Gallant a "jerk."

"If you listen to this jerk, you would attack from the north," Trump said.

The White House, in a rare response to the former president, called Trump's statements "dangerous and unhinged."

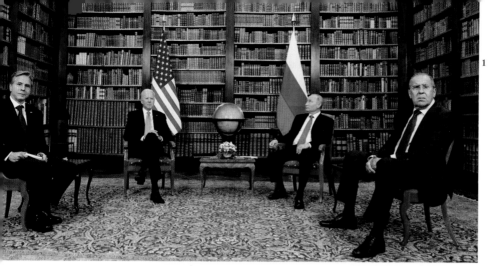

Secretary of State Tony Blinken (*left*) and President Biden (*center left*) meet with Russian President Putin (*center right*) and Foreign Minister Sergey Lavrov (*right*) on June 16, 2021, in Geneva, Switzerland. "Why did you leave Afghanistan?" Putin, the black belt judo master, asked Biden in an attempt to unbalance him. "Why did you leave?" Biden taunted back, a reference to the Soviet Union's embarrassing withdrawal from Afghanistan in 1989, after 10 years of occupation.

"I want Putin to respect our country, okay?" Trump told me in a 2016 interview. "He said very good things about me. He said, Trump is brilliant, and Trump is going to be the new leader and all that. And some of these clowns said, 'you should repudiate Putin.' I said, why would I repudiate him?" At the Helsinki Summit in 2018, Trump appeared to strongly defend Putin and wave off the conclusions of U.S. intelligence agencies that Russia had interfered in the 2016 election.

"Jake Sullivan, he's almost like a law firm," Chairman of the Joint Chiefs General Mark Milley said about Biden's national security adviser and indispensable aide. "He loads you up with these readings. You get homework all week long with Jake. And that's good and they're usually binders that are an inch or two thick."

CIA Director Bill Burns was President Biden's leading expert on Russian President Vladimir Putin. Burns had been ambassador to Moscow from 2005 to 2008 and knew Putin. Biden sent Burns to Moscow on November 2, 2021, to deliver a message to Putin: We know you plan to invade Ukraine. If you do it, this is what we will do. The CIA director carried with him a secret letter from President Biden to Putin.

Secretary of State Tony Blinken pressed Russian Foreign Minister Sergey Lavrov to choose diplomacy over war in Ukraine. "Tony," Lavrov scoffed in December 2021, "do you really think we're going to invade? Are you really serious with this stuff?" Blinken left multiple meetings convinced that Lavrov was not fully aware of the extent of Putin's war plans. He had a sliver of sympathy for how far outside Putin's confidence Lavrov was.

"Going to Mar-a-Lago is a little bit like going to North Korea," Senator Lindsey Graham, Republican of South Carolina, said. "Everybody stands up and claps every time Trump comes in." Graham, who often played golf with Trump, told the former president: "If you run and win then it's the biggest second act in the history of American politics. Then you have four years to rewrite your legacy and make Trumpism a more sustainable movement. It becomes something you can pass to the next generation."

"If you do this there are going to be enormous costs to Russia," President Biden warned Russian President Vladimir Putin during a videoconference in the Situation Room on December 7, 2021. "We're going to ensure that." Putin denied Russia had any plans to invade Ukraine. Biden left the call convinced the invasion was coming.

On February 21, 2021, President Putin aggressively polled his security council on recognizing the "independence" of two cities in the east of Ukraine, Donetsk and Luhansk. He was laying his public grounds for war. "Speak plainly," Putin ordered as his Director of the Foreign Intelligence Service Sergei Naryshkin stumbled over his prepared lines.

"Gather the leaders of the world," Ukrainian President Volodymyr Zelensky said to President Biden on the phone as Russian forces invaded. "Ask them to support Ukraine." On February 24, 2022, President Putin launched the most brazen attempt at territorial conquest since World War II. "We're going to be with you," Biden promised Zelensky. "You should always tell us what you need." As of June 2024, the U.S. had provided Ukraine about $51.2 billion in military assistance alone.

"We expected [the Russians] to do exactly what the U.S. military would have done," CIA Director Bill Burns said about Russia's invasion of Ukraine, "which is spend the first 24 hours taking out the command-and-control system and taking out the air defense system. They didn't do that." By the fifth day of the invasion, February 28, 2022, a 40-mile convoy of 15,000 Russian troops, tanks and supply trucks was stalled in a massive traffic jam.

"We know you are contemplating the use of tactical nuclear weapons in Ukraine," Defense Secretary Lloyd Austin said during a phone call with Russia's Defense Minister Sergei Shoigu, one of Putin's closest advisers, on October 21, 2022. Shoigu said he did not take kindly to being threatened.

"Mr. Minister," Austin said bluntly with not a hint of anger, "I am the leader of the most powerful military in the history of the world. I don't make threats."

Russian President Vladimir Putin shows Russian Defense Minister Sergei Shoigu mushrooms during a vacation in the Siberian wilderness. Shoigu, who helped plan Russia's 2014 annexation of Crimea and 2022 invasion of Ukraine, has been in Putin's inner circle for three decades. It was a strange and dangerous pairing. Shoigu was a classic Russian apparatchik—a hard-liner, dutiful and totally subservient to Putin.

Ukrainian soldiers wounded in a Russian cluster bomb attack as they retreated in armored personnel carriers from the front lines. Ukraine was the most challenging military environment for an army since World War II. It was a full-on artillery war with Ukraine and Russia bogged down in trench warfare. The front lines barely moved.

The howitzer, a cross between a cannon and a mortar, had become the mainstay of Ukraine's defense and relied on 155mm ammunition. On June 11, 2023, Colonel Joe Da Silva warned National Security Adviser Jake Sullivan that the Ukrainians were burning through "upwards of 10,000 rounds" of ammunition per day and at risk of running out by the end of July. The only significant supplies of 155mm left on earth that could fire from the howitzers were cluster munitions, banned by 123 countries for being inhumane and indiscriminate. President Biden gave the order to send them. Russia was already using them.

"Today, the people of Israel are under attack, orchestrated by a terrorist organization, Hamas," President Biden said from the State Dining Room on October 7, 2023, flanked by Secretary of State Tony Blinken. "In this moment of tragedy, I want to say to them and to the world and to terrorists everywhere that the United States stands with Israel. We will not ever fail to have their back," Biden said. The United States was the first nation to recognize the State of Israel, 11 minutes after its founding, 75 years ago.

Emir of Qatar Sheikh Tamim bin Hamad Al Thani, age 43, was key to getting Hamas, the militant group that attacked Israel so brutally on October 7, 2023, to release hostages. The Emir had hosted Hamas political leadership in Doha for years and given hundreds of millions of dollars in aid to Hamas in Gaza. Qatar had an open channel. "They are ready to release some of the hostages," the Emir informed Secretary of State Blinken on October 13, 2023, in Doha.

President Biden landed in Israel on October 18, 2023, 11 days after the Hamas attack that killed about 1,200 people and one week after holding Netanyahu and his cabinet back from a preemptive strike on Hezbollah in Lebanon. Biden descended the steps of the plane, aviator sunglasses dangling from his left hand, and immediately threw his arms around Bibi in a hug. A few months later, in the spring of 2024, Biden would privately refer to Netanyahu as "a bad fucking guy" and a "liar."

"How are you going to go after Hamas?" President Biden asked Israeli Prime Minister Bibi Netanyahu in a conference room that doubled as an underground bunker in Tel Aviv. We want to eliminate them, Netanyahu said. All of them. Well, Biden said, you know, we had the same approach in places like Iraq and Afghanistan and it was difficult for us to erase an ideology. Sometimes you create fighters by the way you go after them.

Secretary of State Tony Blinken urged Israeli Prime Minister Netanyahu and his cabinet to let humanitarian aid into Gaza. "Not a drop, not an ounce of anything will go into Gaza to help people," Netanyahu said. "What about if we send experts in?" he suggested. "Prime Minister," Blinken said in frustration, "you can't eat or drink an expert. People need the food and water." After an almost nine-hour negotiation, Netanyahu finally agreed to open the spigot of aid just a notch.

"Bibi, you've got no strategy. You've got no strategy," President Biden said to Israeli Prime Minister Netanyahu on April 4, 2024. "That's not true, Joe," Netanyahu said. "We are dismantling Hamas. . . . We have to clear Rafah and it's over. It'll take three weeks." Biden knew this was not true. Netanyahu at times sounded aggrieved, as if the whole world had turned against Israel, the U.N., everybody. He challenged that the humanitarian situation was that bad in Gaza where Israel's military operations had produced 39 million tons of debris. By mid-April 2024, more than 30,000 Palestinians had been killed and 80,000 homes destroyed. International aid agencies reported that half a million Palestinians were facing starvation.

A Palestinian family in their destroyed home after an Israeli air strike in Rafah, February 22, 2024.

Middle East coordinator Brett McGurk was in the Situation Room with President Biden and National Security Adviser Jake Sullivan when Iran launched 110 ballistic missiles at Israel on April 13, 2024. On a big screen, they watched the missiles, yellow streaks, move across the screen like something out of an old '80s movie or computer game. McGurk had managed intense crisis situations across four Republican and Democratic administrations— George W. Bush, Barack Obama, Donald Trump and now Biden. This was one of the most intense moments of his life.

Retired Lieutenant General Keith Kellogg was supporting Trump's 2024 campaign "100 percent." Kellogg still spoke to the former president on the phone regularly, offering advice on the wars in Ukraine and the Middle East, and even secretly meeting with Prime Minister Benjamin Netanyahu on a trip to Israel in March 2024. "Biden, Netanyahu, do not see eye to eye about virtually anything," Kellogg told Trump.

Colin Kahl, who served as Biden's national security adviser during his vice presidency (2014–2017) and then as top policy adviser to Secretary of Defense Lloyd Austin (2021–July 2023), could see that Biden's strategy with Netanyahu back then was directly translating into his approach now. "Biden was a firm believer that we should basically do big hugs, little punches. That is hug the Israelis in public and then rough them up behind the scenes," Kahl told others. "I do not believe that Biden trusts Netanyahu. I do not believe that he personally likes Netanyahu."

Director of National Intelligence Avril Haines, who oversees all U.S. intelligence agencies including the CIA, reported in 2024 that Russia had been weakened by the war in Ukraine, but that only made Putin more dangerous. "Between the United States and Russia, we have over 90 percent of the world's nuclear weapons," Haines reported. "You do not want a country that has got that kind of a stockpile of nuclear weapons to feel as if it's slipping."

"They tell me if I get convicted, it'll be even better for me in the election," Trump said on the phone to his former lawyer Tim Parlatore in the midst of his hush money trial in New York. "But Tim," Trump said, "I don't want to get convicted." On May 30, 2024, Trump was convicted of all 34 counts of falsifying business records, becoming the first former U.S. president to be a convicted felon.

"I really don't know what he said at the end of that sentence," former president Trump said after President Biden's time expired on a question about the southern border. "I don't think he knows what he said either." Biden closed his eyes during questions as if he were fighting his own internal battle to remember, to focus and complete his thought. It was sad, a shocking portrait of a struggle to revive his authority. Even before the debate was over, Democrats were in a full-blown panic about Biden's fitness to compete for a second presidential term at age 81.

"Get down! Get down!" Secret Service agents yelled to Trump as a lone gunman, Thomas Matthew Crooks, opened fire from a nearby rooftop during a rally in Butler, Pennsylvania, on Saturday, July 13. Trump slapped a hand to his right ear and dropped to his hands and knees behind the podium, blood coating his ear and dripping down his cheek. Secret Service agents surrounded the former president and moved to hustle him offstage. "Wait, wait," Trump insisted. He threw his fist into the air and mouthed, "Fight. Fight. Fight." The crowd erupted with cheers. "USA, USA, USA," they chanted.

On Sunday, July 21, 2024, President Biden announced in a letter that he would not seek re-election and endorsed Vice President Kamala Harris to replace him as the Democratic nominee. Harris entered the race with a surge of energy, Democratic support and a degree of relief behind her. She was presented as the former prosecutor pitted against a convicted felon. During a rally in the battleground state Georgia, on July 30, Harris mocked Trump's indecision on whether to debate her. "Well Donald, I do hope you'll reconsider to meet me on the debate stage," she said. "Because as the saying goes, 'If you've got something to say, say it to my face.'"

FORTY-SIX

S ecretary of State Tony Blinken touched down in Israel the morning of Thursday, October 12, and went straight to see Netanyahu. When the White House needed something from Israel there were two approaches. Either the secretary went and tried to beat it out of Bibi or the president called him. Often neither worked.

In a highly unusual move, Bibi brought Blinken straight to his war room, his inner sanctum of decision-making, the Kirya. Bibi introduced Blinken to the core of Israel's political and military leadership who were planning their military response into Gaza.

"We need three things: ammo, ammo, ammo," Bibi declared. Blinken was not surprised Bibi's first focus was ammunition.

Nauseating footage and graphic photographs from the October 7 attacks played on a screen in the backdrop. Charred human bodies, burnt babies. It was hard to look away.

"We're there with you," Blinken said to Bibi and his security cabinet. "We're there with you. We're going to support you. We have already set up channels and been talking about how to deliver things. That work is already going on," he repeated. "We're with you."

The U.S. was already supplying ammunition and interceptors to replenish Iron Dome, the Israeli air defense system that destroys rockets and artillery shells fired from distances up to 40 miles. The first transport plane carrying advanced U.S. armaments for Israel had arrived at the Nevatim Air Base in southern Israel two days earlier.

America provides Israel, the only democracy in the Middle East, with more than $3 billion in military assistance every year and the Pentagon maintains stockpiles of weapons and ammunition at about half a dozen sites around Israel. These stockpiles had already been tapped to provide 155mm military ammunition to Ukraine. More was in the pipeline for Israel, Blinken said.

Turning to the immediate question Blinken asked, "What is Israel going to do about the civilians in Gaza?"

The Gaza Strip, still controlled by Hamas, is one of the most densely populated places in the world. Bordered by Egypt, Israel and the Mediterranean Sea, Gaza's population of 2.3 million people is squashed into the isolated enclave of 18 square miles. Gaza City is even more crowded than New York City.

Blinken knew most of Bibi's close advisers in the room were different shades of Netanyahu. Gallant is a hawk, political but more flexible. IDF chief Herzi Halevi is a hawk too but he's reasonable. But how reasonable would a deeply traumatized Israeli leadership be?

Netanyahu had a response ready for Blinken's question. "Let's set up a humanitarian corridor," Bibi said. "We'll take them all into Egypt and let them go there."

Blinken was stunned. From the very beginning it was painfully clear the U.S. and Israel were not going to see this situation the same way. Just push all the Palestinians out of Gaza into Egypt? That was the plan? Blinken knew that Sisi, the Egyptian leader for nearly 10 years, would be outraged. He would not want or accept hundreds of thousands, even perhaps a million, Palestinian refugees.

Right away Blinken thought of the long history of moving Palestinians out of their land. It was the Nakba, the mass displacement of Palestinian people during the 1948 Arab-Israeli War, that was seen by Arab leaders as the great historical crime, the biggest loss in Palestinian memory. Nakba was the Arabic word for catastrophe.

"There may be concerns about that but let us talk with others," Blinken said to the Israeli leaders. He was scheduled to meet with leaders all over the Arab world in the next few days.

"There won't be a humanitarian crisis in Gaza if no civilians are there," Dermer said. "One man—Sisi—can't stand in the way."

Egypt's President Sisi was refusing to open the Rafah Crossing—the single crossing point between Egypt and the Gaza Strip—to let Palestinians into Egypt. Sisi knew Netanyahu would love Egypt to open its border, push the Palestinians out and then never let them back. After all, Israel had done it before. Following wars with Israel in 1948 and 1967 Palestinian refugees who fled to Jordan, Lebanon and Syria—and millions of their descendants—have not been able to return to their homes. Israel's stance had been: Any resettlement of Palestinian refugees must occur outside of Israel's borders. The right to return was one of the major stumbling blocks in all peace negotiations.

"Without the Egyptian crossing open, what do you do in the meantime? You need to find a way to get subsistence items in," Blinken said.

Dermer was adamant. "Israel won't support it as long as hostages are being held."

"You have to do something about food and water," Blinken said.

"We're not going to do anything right now as long as the hostages are being held," Dermer repeated, holding to what was clearly Netanyahu's bottom line.

When Bibi wasn't speaking he was either passing notes with Dermer or looking around to see how his security cabinet members—and Blinken—reacted to what was being said. There was a sense he was constantly taking the temperature of the room.

"The entire world has to be clear that Hamas is ISIS," Bibi said. The Islamic State in Iraq and Syria (ISIS) was known for genocide, ethnic cleansing, rape, murder, enslavement and other war crimes. "ISIS doesn't have a political wing. Al Qaeda doesn't have a political wing. Hamas is like ISIS.

"If you see what they did to civilians here," argued Bibi, "murdering babies, murdering women. This is brutality on the scale of ISIS and the entire world should look at it as ISIS."

"We ought to talk about that and think about it," Blinken said. "From our perspective humanitarian assistance for the Palestinians and civilian protection is a moral imperative. But even if you disagree with that, it's a strategic imperative."

October 7 was an earthquake event in the region, Blinken knew, partly because of what Israel's full-scale military response would look like. It was going to be completely destabilizing.

With Hamas still shooting rockets at Israel from across the border in Gaza, Blinken could not stay in Tel Aviv overnight so he flew 45 minutes to Amman, Jordan.

The next morning, October 13, Blinken went to meet King Abdullah II.

Abdullah, 61, had ascended the throne in 1999 and shut down the Hamas presence in Jordan—exiling Hamas officials to Qatar and closing their offices in Amman. Jordan was home to over two million Palestinian refugees.

"We told Israel not to do this," King Abdullah said. "We told them not to get close to Hamas. Hamas is the Muslim Brotherhood."

The Muslim Brotherhood is the oldest political Islamist organization in the Arab world and father to some of the most extremist terrorist groups today. Founded in Egypt, its violent offshoots have taken on different forms and ideologies, including Hamas and the Palestinian Islamic Jihad in Gaza.

"Hamas has to be defeated," King Abdullah said to Blinken. "We won't say it," he clarified, "but we support Hamas being defeated and Israel should defeat Hamas.

"They should never have been in bed with them in the first place. They should have actually dealt with the Palestinian Authority and worked with them." The Palestinian Authority was the governing body in the West Bank.

"Israel propped Hamas up for years," the King said. Tens of millions of dollars flowed to Hamas with Israel's knowledge and acquiescence based on the argument that the money improved life and helped stabilize Gaza.

It was one of the contradictions and risks of survival. An expedient but compromising.

A few hours later Blinken met with the leader of Qatar, Emir Sheikh Tamim bin Hamad Al Thani, in Doha while the Hamas political leadership was working at their political office down the street.

The Emir said to Blinken, "We explained to Hamas that no one accepts this. No one accepts what they did. You have no friends left. What do you expect us to tell the Americans and Israelis?"

The Emir invited Blinken into a lavish room with royal blue curtains and thick carpeted floors. His trusted political adviser, MBAR—Qatar's prime minister and foreign minister Mohammed bin Abdulrahman Al Thani—joined them.

Both were in long white robes and sandals, their customary dress. Blinken was in the American diplomat's uniform—a black suit and tie.

Emir Al Thani said it wasn't clear whether Hamas leaders in Doha knew about October 7 in advance.

"It's possible that Sinwar just did it on his own," the Emir said. "But it's also possible they know and don't want to let anyone know."

Yahya Sinwar, the Hamas chief in Gaza, was suspected of being the main orchestrator of the October 7 attack. Sinwar, a Palestinian, had previously been imprisoned in Israel for 22 years where he received life-saving surgery for a brain tumor. He was released in a prisoner swap in 2011 and had not been seen since October 7 but the Israelis suspected he was hiding in Hamas's network of tunnels beneath Gaza.

"Two things on behalf of the president," Blinken said to the Emir. "Right now you're dealing with Hamas for the hostages. We recognize the value of having a channel to negotiate the release of hostages," Blinken relayed, "but when this is over, it can't continue to be business as usual with Hamas. That's out."

"I understand and it won't be," the Emir said. "I don't need it anymore. I don't want to have obstacles with America. We'll keep the channel open now because you find it useful. Our relationship with America is very important."

Blinken was surprised. He had thought getting rid of the safe haven for Hamas leadership would be an area they would have to work on over time and potentially even fight over.

But the Emir seemed to be indicating without directly stating it that if you come to us at the end of this and say get rid of Hamas, we'll get rid of Hamas.

"Hamas has told us they would release some hostages," the Emir continued. "They have some, Palestinian Islamic Jihad has others."

Blinken was surprised again. This was the first indication Hamas would release hostages.

"They are ready to release some of the hostages," the Emir continued, "but they need humanitarian corridors to allow hostages to leave.

"They need two to three hours of calm to move around and get the hostages safe passage," he added. "But they're ready to do it.

"Now of course, they're probably going to want something but they showed a willingness."

Israel had begun an aggressive bombing campaign in Gaza. Wall-to-wall bombing followed by more bombing. Everywhere Blinken went there was Al Jazeera on TV or Arab media with coverage of the rising civilian death toll in Gaza and buildings reduced to rubble. Hamas was asking Israel to pause their offensive in order to move and deliver the hostages.

"I've been trying to get someone in Israel and I just can't get anyone to listen to me," MBAR said.

"I will call the Israelis immediately to work on a pause," Blinken told the Qataris. "That decision, that will be made at the political level, and I will work on it."

Heading back to his plane, Blinken was somewhat impressed. The Qataris had laid the groundwork for a hostage deal just six days after October 7. It was extraordinary.

———————

On the flight to Bahrain, Blinken called Ron Dermer in Israel.

"Hamas is ready to start talking about this," Blinken said urgently. "There are Americans hostage. There are Israelis hostage. We need to get this going."

He then called Biden and Sullivan. Hamas is prepared to release hostages. They quickly set in operation their cell with CIA director Burns taking the lead.

After stopping in Bahrain, Blinken and his exhausted staff spent the night in Riyadh, Saudi Arabia. It was their fourth country in one day.

The following morning, October 14, Blinken met with Saudi foreign minister Prince Faisal bin Farhan Al Saud, age 48.

"Bibi should have known better," the Prince said. "Everyone told them not to do this with Hamas. We told him. He should have known better anyway. But we absolutely told him not to do this.

"Hamas is Muslim Brotherhood," the Prince added.

Blinken had heard this a lot. All the Arab leaders had dealt with some version of Hamas causing trouble in their countries, Blinken realized. It's why the King of Jordan, the Emir of Qatar, the Crown Prince of Bahrain, the Saudis, Egyptians and all these leaders were so interested in this. Terrorist groups don't want to just eliminate Israel, they wanted to overthrow other leaders.

"We're concerned about the impact Israel's operations will have on all our security," the Prince said. "What comes after Hamas could be worse."

"You know Daesh," he said—their term for ISIS—"Daesh was worse than al Qaeda."

Blinken asked about Saudi support for Gaza's reconstruction after the conflict.

"We're not going to pay to clean up Bibi's mess," the Prince said. "If Israel destroys all of this, we're not paying to rebuild it."

The Saudi Prince was worried they'd invest in reconstruction only for conflict to break out again that would destroy what they had rebuilt.

How Israel responds matters, Blinken said. This was something he and President Biden had underscored publicly.

Next Blinken flew to the United Arab Emirates to meet with President Sheikh Mohammed bin Zayed Al Nahyan, known as MBZ, the head of the royal family and a former UAE Air Force general.

"Hamas must be eliminated," the 62-year-old MBZ said. "We can give Israel the space to destroy Hamas, but Israel has to give us space. Let humanitarian assistance in. Establish safe areas to make sure they are not killing civilians. Control settler violence in the West Bank."

Implicit in the request was an understanding that a pause would help placate his citizens, who were infuriated by the images of destruction in Gaza.

MBZ's clear and fair request of the Israelis—give us space to give you space—stuck with Blinken. The Arab leaders were prepared to give Israel space to do what they need to do with Hamas but Israel needed to create space for humanitarian assistance in Gaza. He stored that away in his mind for later use with Bibi.

Israel was offering backdoor financial support to Hamas, MBZ added. "We warned Israel not to do this with Hamas. They are the Muslim Brotherhood."

Unlike Saudi Arabia, the United Arab Emirates had normalized diplomatic relations with Israel under the Trump administration's Abraham Accords.

Before flying out, Secretary Blinken and his staff were given a tour of the Abrahamic Family House, a multifaith religious complex where a mosque, church and synagogue are built on a secular visitor pavilion. It represents a path to coexistence, a path for the region, the Emirati told Blinken.

Blinken flew back to Riyadh that night because Saudi prime minister Crown Prince Mohammed bin Salman, MBS, had tentatively agreed to meet.

In 2018, Jamal Khashoggi, a Saudi-born, U.S.-based journalist and dissident, was brutally murdered in the Saudi consulate in Turkey. His body was dismembered with a bone saw. The CIA later concluded that MBS ordered the assassination. Relations with the United States had been particularly tense ever since. President Biden had called Saudi Arabia a "pariah."

Blinken viewed MBS as just someone he had to deal with in the region. The Crown Prince had a stranglehold on power and he also had the only carrot—the only thing the Israelis wanted—normalization with Saudi Arabia, the biggest country in the Middle East.

The secretary and his staff checked into the Radisson Blu Hotel in the diplomatic quarter and were told to be ready for MBS to send word about a meeting either later that night or early the next morning.

It had been a grueling few days for Blinken and his staff, who would wake up wondering what country they were in. But they waited by their phones.

MBS kept them awake, still waiting until 7:00 a.m. on October 15. Blinken knew this wasn't unique to him. It happened to all kinds of people. The Saudis were night owls because evenings were cooler than days but MBS took it to extremes.

For Blinken, "MBS was nothing more than a spoiled child."

Look, MBS said to Blinken when they finally met, I just want the problems created by October 7 to go away.

Saudi Arabia and Israel had been pursuing normalization before the October 7 Hamas attack. It was part of his ambitious "Saudi Vision 2030" plan designed to reduce Saudi Arabia's dependence on oil exports and transform the country into an economy and society of the future.

I would love to get back to that vision but Gaza has to be calm, MBS said. Normalization is not dead. We obviously can't pursue it right now. They're about to launch a war. But I would love to get back there at some point.

Before returning to Israel, Blinken took a detour to Cairo to meet with president of Egypt Sisi.

Sisi threw Blinken's staff out so it was only him and the secretary. Sisi had one goal—to preserve the peace with Israel brokered by President Jimmy Carter in the 1979 Camp David Accords.

Blinken's team, which included his deputy chief of staff Tom Sullivan, counselor Derek Chollet, and State Department spokesman Matthew Miller, went to meet with Egypt's minister of foreign affairs Sameh Shoukry and intel chief Abbas Kamel. Other than Sisi himself, Kamel was the most powerful person in Egypt, effectively running half the country for Sisi.

Kamel offered the Americans assessments of how deep and extensive the Hamas tunnels were beneath Gaza. Hamas is entrenched in Gaza, he explained, it will be very difficult to eliminate them.

"Israel shouldn't just go in all at once. Sit back, wait for them to pop up and chop their heads off," Kamel said.

He wasn't joking, the Americans realized.

FORTY-SEVEN

——◆——

Blinken landed back in Tel Aviv the morning of October 16. Biden's first task: Get the Israeli government to open the spigots to let humanitarian assistance into Gaza, which had been ravaged already by Israel's bombs.

Blinken knew this would be a big ask of the Israelis. Getting food and water to civilians should not be controversial. But everything in war was a weapon to be leveraged.

The secretary joined Netanyahu, Dermer and a few other key Israeli officials at the prime minister's office in Jerusalem.

"We need you to let humanitarian assistance in," Blinken said.

Netanyahu erupted, rejecting it, completely rejecting it. "The people of Israel will not tolerate giving these Nazis aid if we have not completely destroyed Hamas," he said.

"This is aid for innocent men, women and children who will starve and who will die if they don't get aid," Blinken said. "It's the right thing to do to let this aid in but it's also in your interest.

"Since we last saw you, we've traveled around the region," Blinken added. "Met with your friends and people who are not friends, but not hostile to you. And the one thing we heard over and over is they support what you're doing. They support defeating Hamas. They can't all say it publicly right now but they support you doing that. They want to have stability. There's no love lost with any one of these countries with Hamas.

"But as one of your friends said: Israel needs to give us space to give them space," Blinken said, repeating the words Emirati president Sheikh Mohammed had said to him.

"No, absolutely not," Netanyahu said.

President Biden was planning to visit Israel in the next few days.

Blinken did not yet threaten that the president would not come. He wanted to hold that in reserve so he went one notch less. "You know the president's going to be here. We need to be able to say before he comes that you're letting humanitarian assistance in," he said.

"You know that would be a huge mistake," Netanyahu said crossly. "This country's been attacked. The president's visit should not be seen as a visit to help the Palestinians. He's here to stand with Israel. Shouldn't be a visit to help the Palestinians."

They all could see the meeting was getting nowhere. Bibi wanted to sit and negotiate but Blinken suggested regrouping and coming back later in the afternoon.

Blinken went to meet Israeli defense minister Yoav Gallant. Two days after October 7, Gallant had said, "I have ordered a complete siege of Gaza. There will be no electricity, no food, no fuel. Everything is closed. We are fighting human animals and we are acting accordingly."

"How do you assess this campaign will go?" Blinken asked, referring to their plans for a full-scale military offensive into Gaza. "What will the cost be? What will the casualties be? How long will it go?"

Gallant said, "I have a mission and I am going to fulfill it. The price is not important—not on our side, not on their side."

Blinken felt a chill to his core. Gallant was saying: It doesn't matter how many people die. I have a mission to eradicate Hamas and it doesn't matter how many Palestinians die. It doesn't matter how many Israelis die. I'm going to fulfill my mission.

Jesus, Blinken thought, that's the headspace the Israelis were in.

At 5:00 p.m. at the Kirya, the military headquarters in Tel Aviv, Blinken was given the floor to speak to Netanyahu and his security cabinet.

Blinken pushed again for allowing humanitarian assistance in. Open a point of access through the Rafah border crossing, he argued. Help us—with humanitarian assistance—to help you.

"Look," Blinken said, "you may disagree with us that it's the right thing to do. We believe that it's the right and morally imperative thing to do. But it's also profoundly in your strategic interest to do it because if you want to have any time and space to deal with Hamas, if you're not providing innocent men, women and children with what they need, that space is going to close down on you very quickly."

"Not a drop, not an ounce of anything will go into Gaza to help people," Netanyahu continued, unfazed. "This is not me," he added. "This is not even my coalition. No one in this country can accept the idea that we're going to be providing assistance to Palestinians in Gaza when they're holding these hostages and after they've slaughtered our people."

"Palestinians," Blinken said, "not Hamas. These are men, women and children who have nothing to do with October 7th.

"Again, from our perspective it's the right and morally imperative thing to do," Blinken repeated. "If you want time and space to deal with Hamas, if you are not providing for people who desperately need the assistance, that time and space will close down almost immediately. So you need to do this in order to do what you believe you need to do to protect your security and to defend yourselves."

They went back and forth for two hours.

"You know the president is going to be here in two days," Blinken said. He had seen the president's advance team at the airport in Tel Aviv that morning and the plane that carries the Beast—the president's sleek heavily armored black Cadillac—sitting on the tarmac. The trip had leaked in Israeli media but had not been announced publicly.

"I cannot make that announcement if we don't have an agreement in principle that you're going to allow assistance into Gaza," Blinken said.

All of a sudden an alarm went off signaling that Iron Dome had launched. The Israelis all stood up and the Americans followed suit, marching down a stairway together to a secure bunker. Blinken felt the tension from the meeting room break as they chatted, waiting 10 minutes or so for it to be over so they could go back upstairs. The clap of the missile could be heard as it was taken down by Iron Dome right over them.

Returning to the meeting room, Bibi said, "Okay, we agree, the security cabinet agrees but I've got to go take it to the larger cabinet."

His full cabinet was about to meet. "I have to go chair this cabinet meeting," Bibi said. "Other ministers have to be in this meeting. Come with me," he said to Blinken. "You'll set up in one room. We'll set up in another room and we'll negotiate this process."

Blinken agreed.

Around 7:00 p.m. and for the next few hours, he holed up in a small office bunker six floors belowground to hammer out the U.S. proposal with his team: counselor Derek Chollet, assistant secretary for Near East affairs Barbara Leaf, chargé d'affaires Stephanie Hallett, and his deputy and right-hand man, Tom Sullivan.

Every now and then Tom Sullivan walked out to the garage where he could get a phone signal in the underground compound and call his brother, Jake Sullivan, at the White House to update him on where they were. He wanted to know how much Blinken could threaten Biden's trip. That was the main leverage he had with the Israelis.

At one point Blinken also called Biden directly: "I want to be able to say if they don't agree to open this up then you're not going to be able to come," he said.

"Absolutely," Biden replied. "Tell them I'm not coming if they don't agree to this."

Dermer stopped into the bunker a few times to argue things out with the American team and then passed notes to Netanyahu during the cabinet meeting. Blinken would get notes back from Dermer with Bibi's handwritten edits and proposals on it. Blinken wanted the first humanitarian trucks to start moving into Gaza through the Rafah Crossing before President Biden arrived in Tel Aviv.

They continued to negotiate back and forth until 1:00 a.m. when the cabinet meeting ended.

Bibi came in.

"We don't have a deal," he said to Blinken.

They hammered it out for another hour and 15 minutes.

"Oh no, no," Bibi said. "We can't have trucks going in. We can't have trucks going in."

"What do you mean you can't have trucks going in?" Blinken asked. "How are we going to get the assistance to people?"

Dermer joked, "Maybe a cart and donkey would do it."

"No, no, no, it's this image of, you know, things going into the Palestinians," Bibi said. "We can't have that. What about if we send experts in?"

"Prime Minister," Blinken said in frustration, "you can't eat or drink an expert. People need the food and water."

Finally at 2:15 a.m., after more than nine hours of back and forth, Bibi agreed in principle to open the spigot a notch to let humanitarian assistance into Gaza.

Bibi said he was under a lot of pressure not to let this aid in. They could announce their intention to work out an agreement but Bibi said he wanted the assistance to start going in *after* Biden's visit so it looked like the president made him do it. Bibi said that would give him the political coverage and leverage he urgently needed with Israel's cabinet and the Israeli public.

FORTY-EIGHT

◆

In Washington, D.C., Brett McGurk, the National Security Council's Middle East coordinator, was in full operational mode preparing for President Biden's trip to Tel Aviv that night, October 17.

"I've got to get out there and see these guys," Biden had urged McGurk after they had narrowly avoided Israel sparking a wider war with Hezbollah on October 11.

"These guys are not thinking clearly," Biden said. The president wanted to meet with Bibi and Israel's war cabinet in person.

But a presidential trip into a war zone was no small feat and McGurk had been practically living out of his office for the past week trying to arrange it.

McGurk bumped into one of the White House operational staff members in the West Wing who said, "Hey, I need your passport."

"Shit," McGurk said and drove home to get it.

Just as he made it back to the White House, reports started coming through that Israel's Defense Forces had struck a hospital in Gaza and killed 500 people. McGurk was directed to go to the Treaty Room, the president's private study in the Residence.

Secretary Blinken, now in Jordan, was having dinner with King Abdullah in the King's "man cave"—a handsome room in his home with a bar set up, but no alcohol—when word came that the hospital had been bombed. Everyone was blaming Israel.

Blinken returned to his hotel and was dialed into the call with the president, who had Sullivan, Jon Finer, an out-of-breath McGurk, and other staff with him on the line.

What should they do? Should they cancel the trip? Biden asked.

From the media reports it appeared Israel had committed a terrible atrocity, bombing a hospital.

President Sisi of Egypt, whom Biden was scheduled to meet on the Middle East part of his trip, had just canceled his meetings with him. So had Palestinian National Authority leader Mahmoud Abbas. Blinken added King Abdullah to the list.

King Abdullah says the president can't come to Jordan, Blinken said. There was a sense among the Arab leaders that the whole region could come apart.

"Well," Biden asked, "what happened? Did Israel strike?"

None of his advisers could answer. No one knew.

Blinken said they were getting new information all the time. He was talking to the Israelis, the Pentagon, the intelligence community to try to figure out what happened. The question they couldn't yet answer: Whose strike was it?

"It may not be the Israelis despite what's being initially reported," Blinken said, "but we just don't know. It's not clear when we will know."

The president called King Abdullah of Jordan.

"Joe," Abdullah said. "It's just too hot. I want you to come but they're so mad," he said, referring to the raw anger among his people. "This is a tragedy. You can't come now."

Biden then called Bibi.

"It wasn't us, Joe!" Bibi said defiantly. "This is a Hamas rocket. It hit the hospital. It wasn't us, I'm telling you. I'll prove it. I've got the intel."

It was classic, McGurk thought. The Israelis always claimed they had the intel. "Do they really?" Many times they didn't.

"You've got to come!" Bibi insisted.

"Okay, okay," Biden said. "I'm going to talk to my team."

"Should I go?" Biden asked.

Normally presidential trips are carefully teed up with a clear to-do list along with a show of choreographed announcements and accomplishments designed for maximum public relations impact. When Biden visited the Middle East a year earlier, for example, Saudi Arabia had announced that they were opening their skies to Israeli flights for the first time in history.

Now Biden would be flying into complete uncertainty in a time of war. And with no real guarantee that Bibi and his war cabinet would let humanitarian aid into Gaza—the publicly stated goal of Biden's trip. It could expose the president to a public failure.

They debated, engaging in the common intellectual competition among presidential assistants to prove their skepticism and their ability to see the advantages and downsides.

Maybe you should put the trip off a few days? You don't know what you're going into. You don't know what's going to happen. We don't know where the region's going to be tomorrow. The Israelis say they didn't strike this hospital but who knows?

"I think you can't cancel now," Blinken argued. "Israel is saying they didn't do it and if you canceled now it looks like we don't believe them. We're publicly calling them liars if you cancel the trip."

Biden agreed. "I need to be there so we're going ahead," he said.

On the flight over Biden received the U.S. intelligence report: It is definitely Palestinian Islamic Jihad that launched the rocket, which malfunctioned and landed in the parking lot of the hospital and blew up. Even so, most of the Arab media continued to blame Israel. The damage was done.

The president worked on his speech for hours on the way to Israel. He wanted it to speak not only to his convictions about Israel but also to be a reminder not to repeat the mistakes the U.S. had made after 9/11.

Biden said to McGurk, "I've made wartime decisions. There's no harder decision. Nothing is black-and-white. You have to be thoughtful. You have to be deliberate and you have to constantly be asking whether the path you're on is leading to your objectives."

McGurk labeled it "The Biden test." Ultimately, common sense.

Biden said he wanted to embrace Israel, "not Bibi," in this hour of their need. But, he added to McGurk, I also have to speak "some hard truths."

Biden could be much more indignant and profane in private than he appeared in public. One Saturday afternoon during his first year as president, Biden had called a friend from the Oval Office. "I have spent almost five hours going back and forth, back and forth on the phone with two of the biggest fucking assholes in the world—Bibi Netanyahu and Mahmoud Abbas," he said, referring to the prime minister of Israel and the Palestinian leader. "Two of the biggest fucking assholes in the world," Biden repeated with emphasis.

When Air Force One landed at Ben Gurion Airport the morning of October 18, Netanyahu was waiting for Biden on the tarmac.

Biden descended the steps of the plane, aviator sunglasses dangling from his left hand, and immediately threw his arms around Bibi in a hug. A slightly bewildered Netanyahu patted Biden on the back.

As their motorcades drove through the streets of Tel Aviv, Israelis lined the streets. Expressions were fearful. Some waved American flags. It was eerie.

Bibi addressed Biden and the press at 11:40 a.m. "Mr. President, for the people of Israel there is only one thing better than having a true friend like you standing with Israel and that is having you standing in Israel. Your visit here is the first visit of an American president in Israel in a time of war."

"Look, folks," Biden said, "I wanted to be here today for a simple reason. I wanted the people of Israel, the people of the world to know where the United States stands.

"We have to also bear in mind that Hamas does not represent all the Palestinian people and has brought them only suffering."

Netanyahu brought Biden, Sullivan, Blinken and McGurk to an underground conference room that doubled as a bunker in the five-star Kempinski Hotel on Tel Aviv Promenade to meet with his war cabinet.

"How are you going to go after Hamas?" Biden asked Bibi. "What do you mean eliminating Hamas? What does that look like?

"Are you just going to go after the leadership or are you trying to erase every fighter from Gaza?"

We want to eliminate them, Bibi said. All of them.

Well, Biden said, you know, we had the same approach in places like Iraq and Afghanistan and it was difficult for us to erase an ideology. Sometimes you create fighters by the way you go after them.

Opposition leader Benny Gantz said they understood "how" they responded mattered, using the American-coined phrase.

Defense Minister Yoav Gallant, a retired military general, outlined Israel's plan. There's going to be a siege on Gaza, he said. Israel will smash three military divisions into Gaza right away. Israel will not let anything into Gaza, no aid or assistance, until the hostages come out. Not a single Tylenol pill. That was their policy.

Biden replied, "We don't agree with that. We will not support that. You've got to open up the gates and let trucks in with humanitarian aid.

"You have to," Biden said.

Bibi reluctantly agreed or appeared to, and the Israeli war cabinet eventually acquiesced, moving them from the elusive "in principle" agreement Blinken had received from Bibi two days prior to action.

In the bunker, Biden told the group about the first time he met Golda Meir, Israel's first woman prime minister, in 1973. Netanyahu and Dermer had heard the story too many times.

"It's always the same story," Dermer said.

"Mr. President, I have a Golda story too," Dermer said.

"You didn't meet her," Biden replied. Dermer would have been too young.

"No. It's not that Golda," Dermer said. "I have five children. My youngest daughter is named Golda. On the third day of this war, my wife came over to me while I was getting dressed for work and she whispered in my ear where she was going to hide our daughter Golda, if what happened in some of those communities outside of Gaza happens in our neighborhood in Jerusalem."

Dermer's wife, Rhoda Pagano, had been terrified that Hamas

would come back. She wanted to make sure that when Dermer came home, if she had been slaughtered, he would know where to find their daughter.

Around the room, the other Israelis nodded in agreement. The fear and anxiety was shared. In the few days after the Hamas attack, everybody seemed to be afraid there would be an invasion in their neighborhood next.

"The sense of real insecurity," Dermer said. "The trauma of October 7 is really that. These terrorists are going to flood into the country, flood over the border, or flood into the community and just massacre people again.

"Little children are now afraid to answer the door when there's a knock," he said, "because they don't know what's on the other side. They know what happened on October 7th and they're afraid.

"Their lives will never be the same," Dermer said. "Israel on the 8th of October is not the same as it was on the 7th of October and it never will be."

Biden listened.

"Mr. President," Dermer said, "Jews did not come to this country to hide. We will fall in battle, we have and unfortunately we will. We can suffer terror attacks, we have and unfortunately we will. But we will not hide in this country. Jews did not come here to hide.

"The promise of this country, Mr. President, is not only that Jews returned to our ancestral homeland," Dermer said, "it is that we had the ability to defend ourselves and, in a fundamental way, the promise of Israel was broken on October 7.

"And I see our job in the war cabinet as restoring that promise," Dermer said. "That means utterly defeating Hamas and those who did what they did to us on October 7."

An hour later, at 5:00 p.m., Biden delivered the 16-minute speech he had personally drafted on the flight to Israel.

Dermer, who had shared his personal trauma, believed that Biden had heard him.

"I know the recent terrorist assault on the people of this nation has left a deep, deep wound," Biden said.

"It has brought to the surface painful memories and scars left by a millennia of antisemitism and the genocide of the Jewish people. The world watched then, it knew, and the world did nothing. We will not stand by and do nothing again."

The U.S. had been Israel's closest ally since its creation. "Seventy-five years ago, just 11 minutes after its founding, President Harry S. Truman and the United States of America became the first nation to recognize Israel," Biden recalled.

For a country the size of Israel, October 7 "was like 15 9/11s," Biden said.

"But I caution this: While you feel that rage, don't be consumed by it. After 9/11, we were enraged in the United States. And while we sought justice and got justice, we also made mistakes."

President Biden had pushed the Israelis to agree to open the Egypt-Gaza border for the delivery of humanitarian aid on the condition that it was not diverted by Hamas for its own use.

On the flight home Biden called Egyptian president Sisi and implored him to open the Rafah Crossing to let humanitarian aid trucks through to Gaza.

"Okay, I've got Netanyahu on board, I need you to do your part," Biden said to Sisi. "I need you to open that gate. Let those trucks in."

Egypt's president had so far been firmly opposed to opening the Rafah Crossing. He would not have a surge of Palestinian refugees onto his border or into Egypt. Sisi said he believed that if he let refugees in, the refugees would never leave and could become an agitating force in Egypt. What if there were Hamas among them and they started shooting across the border into Israel? Then they could pull Egypt into war. Sisi's answer had consistently been: No way.

Sullivan knew Sisi's resolve was deeply rooted. "If Sisi goes to sleep at night and thinks he has one job, one, it's don't allow Palestinians across the border. Period. No refugee camp in Sinai.

"He will fire upon refugees before letting any into Egypt," Sullivan believed.

But on the phone now Biden was clear he was asking Sisi to open the Rafah Crossing to let humanitarian trucks into Gaza.

Sisi finally agreed. "I'll do it, Mr. President, but it's going to take me a couple of days because the road's not in good condition," he said. He would allow 20 humanitarian trucks through to begin with.

When Biden hung up he was satisfied. He believed his trip had been a success. They had opened the spigot to getting humanitarian aid, however little, into Gaza.

"The bottom line is Sisi deserves a lot of credit," Biden said to reporters on the plane.

And, ultimately, Sisi did exactly what he said Egypt would do. They opened up the crossing. They fixed the roads and 20 aid trucks started passing slowly through on Saturday, October 21, three days after Biden's trip to Israel.

But it was a trickle of desperately needed food, water and medical supplies to the two million Palestinian civilians in Gaza, the first in the 14 days since the October 7 attack. The humanitarian conditions were getting worse in Gaza by the day.

Before October 7, because of a 16-year blockade by Israel, 95 percent of Palestinians living in Gaza already did not have access to clean water and 80 percent relied on humanitarian aid for food.

FORTY-NINE

On November 30, Sullivan and Secretary of Defense Lloyd Austin spoke for 45 minutes on a secure call about how to respond to the increasing attacks from the Houthis in the Red Sea.

The Houthis, another Iranian-backed violent militia group who controlled the quasi-nation-state Yemen, at the southern end of the Arabian Peninsula, had been regularly attacking commercial shipping in the 1,200-mile-long inland Red Sea. The Houthis were part of the so-called Axis of Resistance, an Iran-led political and military coalition of the most radical groups, including Hamas and Hezbollah. In the White House they called the axis a "multiheaded monster." Iran had armed the Houthis to the teeth. The Houthis claimed they were acting in defense of Gaza.

Austin wanted to think and work through the pressing questions: How to deter, how to manage, how to avoid escalation?

Austin was "the star pick" of Biden's cabinet, "the best cabinet member," as far as Sullivan was concerned. Biden trusted Austin. His colleagues trusted him. The military revered him. And Sullivan was constantly learning from him.

"Jake, we own the clock," Austin had told Sullivan numerous times the past two years and repeated again now. "We own the clock." The president could decide whether to use force and when, or not to use force.

Another Austin lesson had occurred in the aftermath of the U.S. nuclear submarine deal with the Australians. Australia initially had agreed to purchase the submarines from France, but withdrew in favor of a deal with the United States. The French were furious.

"We are all taking incoming from our French counterparts and genuflecting and apologizing," Sullivan recalled.

"Austin's French counterpart calls him up and gives him a 22-minute diatribe of American perfidy. When he finished, Austin replied, 'Acknowledged, next topic.'" Sullivan decided to adopt that approach next time someone yelled at him.

On another occasion, Sullivan asked Chairman Milley and Austin to come to the White House to go over a Defense Department budget issue. Sullivan knew they sensed he planned to overrule them on this one. Austin sat down and looked at Sullivan calmly. "It's your meeting, dude," Austin said.

Sullivan was immediately on defense. "We got what we wanted," Sullivan said, "but I also felt extra bad about it."

Secretary Austin was one of the few who could manage Israeli Defense Minister Yoav Gallant. They had spoken regularly since the Hamas attack on Israel.

Often these calls involved Austin holding Gallant's feet to the fire about civilian casualties. Gallant's usual excuse or defense mechanism was to harken back to October 7.

"Remember what Hamas did to us," Gallant said on one such call. "The horror . . ."

"Yo, yo!" Austin said, cutting him off. "This is Lloyd you're talking to. Just give it to me straight. I know what happened. I got it. I got it. I got what happened. But what I'm asking you about is how you guys are responding." Why did you decide to take the military action the way you did?

FIFTY

———————•—————————

"**I**srael *must* do more to protect innocent civilians," Vice President Harris said at a press event on the sidelines of the COP28 Climate Change Conference in Dubai on December 2, 2023.

Biden had made a point of including Harris on almost all of his calls with Netanyahu, now more than a dozen, which they referred to privately as "The Bibi calls." Before and after the calls, the president and vice president briefed with Blinken, Austin and Sullivan.

While Biden had kept a tight lid on his criticism of Israel's handling of Gaza in public, Harris was direct.

"Too many innocent Palestinians have been killed. Frankly, the scale of civilian suffering, and the images and videos coming from Gaza are devastating," Harris said. "It is truly heartbreaking."

She also had a pointed warning for Netanyahu: "Under no circumstances will the United States permit the forced relocation of Palestinians from Gaza or the West Bank, the besiegement of Gaza, or the redrawing of the borders of Gaza," she said.

In the midst of the climate summit, Harris met with the leaders of Egypt, Jordan and the UAE and held phone calls with others, including the Emir of Qatar. She almost had to jog to make her speech on climate change. Trying to manage a war was a nonstop diplomatic push; ending one was even more difficult.

King Abdullah of Jordan said he had no love lost for Hamas but Israel needed to do better on civilian casualties and finish its military operation. Jordan has a large Palestinian population and he was feeling the heat from angry protests and unrest on his streets. The longer this war went on the more unsettled the entire region became.

On the plane, she sent a report to the president. It said the Arab leaders were supportive of planning for the day after the conflict ended if it involved Palestinian leadership in Gaza and a pathway to a Palestinian state. The quiet, almost unspoken shared view of Arab leaders was that a prerequisite to any of it realistically happening was different leadership in both Israel and Gaza.

Netanyahu was on a war path. He was not looking for a peace deal with the Palestinians.

Blinken was also in Dubai for talks with Arab foreign ministers about day after planning. Many Arab countries did not want to be seen engaging in these discussions as it could make them appear acquiescent to or complicit in Netanyahu's ongoing military operations in Gaza.

"Look," Blinken said to Egyptian foreign minister Sameh Shoukry and Jordan's foreign minister Ayman Safadi, "one way or another this is going to be over and we need to be ready for it. Because there are big questions about what happens in terms of security in Gaza, what happens in terms of governance, what happens in terms of humanitarian assistance and development and we need to get going on that now."

Shoukry and Safadi disagreed. Unless and until there was a clear plan for the "day after the day after"—by which they meant the creation of an independent Palestinian state—they would not talk about the "day after" in Gaza.

Virtually all the Arab foreign ministers were in agreement: There can't be an effective day after unless there's a political plan to deal with Hamas in Gaza. Israel was only demonstrating they had a military plan. Israel was not going to kill every Hamas person and was not going to kill the idea of Hamas. So, they argued, there has to be a political plan for leadership and security in Gaza.

They were convinced that Israel couldn't effectively defeat Hamas—the idea of Hamas, the ideology—absent a real political horizon for the Palestinians.

It was a version of the message Harris received: When this planning is realistic, we'll come to the table.

Blinken told them he agreed with their analysis and would also work on the pathway to a Palestinian state. It was wishful thinking.

Blinken met alone with President Sisi in Egypt to discuss the security situation in Gaza after Israel had completed its military operations.

"I'm prepared to put troops on the ground," Sisi said. "But we need the United States with us. I can bring other Arabs along. I want you to take that back to President Biden."

Blinken did.

"Okay, let's flesh this out," Biden said. "We're not going to put American boots on the ground in Gaza but we can look at how we can support a mission by Arab countries and others."

Blinken, Sullivan, Austin, and Joint Chiefs chairman CQ Brown drafted a plan. The idea they came up with was to support an Arab-led force with a headquarters run by the United States with a U.S. military command probably in Egypt where the U.S. could assist with command and control.

"Hamas is an idea, and you cannot destroy an idea," Blinken later pressed Israel's war cabinet during yet another trip to Tel Aviv.

"Tony," Dermer said, "Nazism is an idea and the Nazis in Charlottesville had picket torches that they got from Bed Bath & Beyond, but they don't have a state called Germany anymore!"

Dermer was referring to when white supremacists, carrying flaming torches and chanting "Jews will not replace us" and the Nazi slogan "Blood and Soil," had marched onto the Charlottesville campus of the University of Virginia the weekend of August 12, 2017.

"It's one thing to have a bad idea," Dermer said. "It's another thing to have a bad idea in control of territory!

"Our goal," Dermer argued, "is to remove the territorial control that Hamas has over Gaza. We have to dismantle this army."

Blinken tried to bring the discussion back to "day after" planning. What would Gaza look like when they had dismantled Hamas? Who would lead?

"We should have a Palestinian state? Really?" Dermer said. "So what are we going to do? Turn October 7 into Palestinian Independence Day? You're going to give a great reward for terrorism by giving them a state? Giving the Palestinians a state after the worst terror attack in Israel's history and the worst attack on Jews since the Holocaust?

"That makes total sense," Dermer said sarcastically.

Blinken could see the conversation was going nowhere.

FIFTY-ONE

Middle East coordinator Brett McGurk had been holding daily morning calls with Qatari prime minister MBAR about the 252 hostages held by Hamas in Gaza.

"Brett," MBAR said on one call, "the way to de-escalate this and buy some time is a hostage deal."

"For us to really push the Israelis on a hostage deal," McGurk said, "prove to us that this can work." He suggested they start with a test run. Negotiate the safe return of an American-Israeli mother, Judith Raanan, and her daughter, Natalie, who were being held by Hamas, and then go for something bigger.

MBAR was confident Qatar could get Hamas in Gaza to deliver. McGurk remained skeptical. He updated Sullivan and Biden daily on their progress in the negotiations and floated the idea of the pilot plan.

"Let's try it," Biden said.

A Red Cross team entered Gaza on October 20 and a U.S. embassy team was at the Israeli border ready to meet the two Americans.

In Washington, McGurk was on edge as he tracked Judith and Natalie as they moved through Gaza, worried that at the last second Hamas might decide to blow up their vehicle as it approached the border. Israel had agreed to a fragile six-hour cease-fire.

McGurk's phone rang. It was Stephanie Hallett, the U.S. chargé d'affaires, who was on the border in Israel.

"They're here," she said with relief. "They look healthy."

McGurk grabbed Sullivan from his office and they went straight to the Oval.

President Biden called Judith and Natalie.

"Hey," Biden said to Judith Ranaan, "I've been working on getting you guys out. I'm just so blessed to hear from you. We're going to make sure you get everything you need."

Judith, overcome by emotion and exhaustion, was at a loss for words. "Thank you, thank you, thank you," she repeated.

Biden turned to McGurk after the call. "Keep going," he said. "Keep this going."

Qatar had delivered. CIA director Burns began working intensely with Director of Mossad David Barnea to hammer out the contours of another much bigger hostage deal from the Israeli side. McGurk coordinated with MBAR and Egypt's intel chief, Abbas Kamel, who had the channels with Hamas in Gaza.

Now that there was a real possibility of securing the release of a large number of hostages, Biden pushed Netanyahu to agree to a longer pause in fighting. The pause was the only realistic path to getting hostages out safely. But in Netanyahu's view it would also give Hamas time to regroup and reorganize.

Netanyahu wanted to know how many hostages would come out.

Hamas, at first, guaranteed 10. Netanyahu wanted far more. He requested the release of all women and children being held by Hamas and for Hamas to provide proof of life of the hostages it held. Biden said he supported the request.

Hamas came back and said it could guarantee the release of 50 hostages. In exchange, Hamas said, Israel would release 150 imprisoned or detained Palestinian women and teenagers. Hamas refused to provide identifying information for the hostages.

President Biden called the Emir of Qatar.

"Enough is enough," Biden said. "We need the names or clear identifying information for who's in the 50." Age, gender, nationality. "Without that there's no basis to move ahead."

Hamas produced the identifying criteria for the 50 hostages.

McGurk, in Israel, watched as Netanyahu pounded the table in his war cabinet meeting on November 14 and declared: "I'll never accept. Never accept these terms."

"Bibi always wants to squeeze every ounce of blood from the stone," McGurk thought.

"They're going to cave!" Netanyahu shouted and banged the table once more.

Coming out of the meeting Netanyahu grabbed McGurk's arm. "We need this deal," Netanyahu said.

So much of politics was performance, McGurk realized.

Netanyahu called Biden the same day to confirm that he agreed to the deal.

MBAR passed the final text to Hamas five days later on November 19. "This is the final offer," he told them. They would have to wait a few days for the reply. Hamas political leadership in Qatar had to pass the text by hand through a complicated network to Hamas leader Yahya Sinwar, who was deep in the tunnels beneath Gaza.

Three days later on the morning of November 21, Qatar received word that Sinwar approved.

Hamas released 50 of the 252 hostages, among them three Americans, in four phases starting November 24. For every additional 10 hostages Hamas released beyond the initial 50, Netanyahu would extend the cease-fire an extra day. On November 30, 105 hostages had been safely returned, including two Americans.

Sullivan met with the remaining American-Israeli hostage families in the White House that day. Some of the families came in person, others attended online.

"It was brutal," Sullivan told his wife, Maggie Goodlander, that night. Hamas was still holding six Israeli-Americans hostage.

Sullivan kept checking his phone. "The pause ends at midnight tonight our time," he said. Unless Hamas presented a new list of names for the release of at least 10 more hostages.

"We are actively waiting to hear if they will produce a list or not," Sullivan said. "If not, then tomorrow we'll see bombs drop."

Sullivan glanced at his phone again.

The real sticking point for tomorrow's list, Sullivan said, was that the women who were still held by Hamas were in their 20s and 30s.

"The Israelis fear that part of the reason Hamas does not want to part with them is because they were raped," Sullivan said. "Or still are." The other factor was that Hamas believed all the Israeli women in their 20s and 30s were IDF. It made them more valuable, in Hamas's view, to getting concessions from Israel.

The next day, Hamas shot rockets at Israel and Israeli jets launched a barrage of rockets at 200 targets in Gaza.

War resumed.

FIFTY-TWO

Christmas Day, December 25, 2023, Brett McGurk was at his home, a row house in Southeast Washington, with his family. By 9:00 a.m. his young daughter had opened all of her presents, and he was sitting down with a cup of coffee when the White House Situation Room duty officer called.

"We had an attack on Erbil Air Base in northern Iraq. Three American servicemembers have been wounded by shrapnel from an Iranian drone from an Iraqi militia group," the duty officer said, "one critically."

In the 11 weeks since October 7, U.S. forces had been attacked at least 100 times in Iraq and Syria, mostly involving rockets and drones. But this was the first serious U.S. casualty.

The National Security Council staff and the Central Command General Staff working on this holiday were gathering facts fast on what happened so they could provide options to the president. McGurk drove to the White House.

President Biden, who was at Camp David—the presidential retreat in Maryland—for Christmas, convened a call with his national security team, Secretary Austin and Chairman of the Joint Chiefs General CQ Brown. The military leaders briefed him on his strike options. He could target the Iranian-backed militia group responsible and Iran's Revolutionary Guard facilities, particularly in Iraq where the attacks emanated from. Biden could also strike so-called persona targets, the four individuals responsible for planning the attack. Using very specific signals intelligence and overhead satellite imagery, Austin and his team at the Pentagon were tracking the precise locations of the four individuals.

Biden quizzed his advisers on the risks of each option. Their response needed to be carefully calibrated. He ordered them to strike first at the sites and then progress to the persona targets once the strongest opportunity to take the individuals out presented itself.

That night, at about 4:45 a.m., the U.S. military conducted discreet air strikes against three sites used by Iranian-backed militia groups to launch unmanned aerial drone attacks. U.S. Central Command said the air strikes likely killed a number of militants but there were no civilian casualties.

"The strikes were taken to deter future attacks and were conducted in a manner designed to limit the risk of escalation and minimize civilian casualties," the president said in a letter to Speaker of the House Mike Johnson. "The United States stands ready to take further action, as necessary and appropriate, to address further threats or attacks."

About two weeks later, Biden ordered strikes on the persona targets. After two were hit, the attacks on U.S. forces in Iraq and Syria paused. So Biden paused. His message to the militia leaders was clear: We have pinpointed your location, if you attack again, we will kill you.

But the violent threat was not mitigated.

On Saturday, December 30, the Houthis shot two antiship ballistic missiles toward a large commercial container ship named the *Maersk Hangzhou*. U.S. naval forces on the USS *Gravely* shot down the missiles before they hit. The next day, New Year's Eve, Yemeni forces in fast boats attempted to sink the same container ship.

U.S. naval helicopters launched from the *Eisenhower* and the *Gravely* and fired at the fast boats, which fired back. The U.S. sank three of the four small boats, killing the crews. The fourth boat fled.

President Biden was in St. Croix in the U.S. Virgin Islands for his annual New Year's vacation with the first lady. Jake Sullivan and his wife, Maggie Goodlander, had traveled with them. They had planned for a relaxing New Year's weekend on the beachfront.

The morning of New Year's Day, however, President Biden was on another secure call with Secretary Austin, General CQ Brown, Jake Sullivan, Brett McGurk and others to discuss whether Biden should conduct direct strikes into Yemen against the Houthis.

Austin and CQ Brown said the military would need preparation time for a strike of that nature so Biden did not authorize immediate strikes but wanted to make sure they did the planning.

"What happens if we hit those targets?" Biden asked, peppering his advisers with questions. "What's the collateral damage? How might the Houthis react? Are we ready for their counter-reaction? Are our people protected? Do we have enough missile defense? Do you have the resources you need?"

The president made it clear he did not want to use military force in a way that would generate second- or third-order consequences. The region was already a classic tinderbox which could catch fire and spread instantly.

Get everything set up and ready to go, Biden said.

He also directed them to coordinate with their allies to provide a strong condemnation and warning to the Houthis against further attacks. A joint statement signed by 13 countries was released two days later.

Through January, the Houthi attacks continued. Biden told McGurk he wanted to try diplomacy with the Iranians in addition to the threats and use of force. The Middle East had to be managed carefully. Biden wanted to be active, but not too active as was his style. He was anxious to tamp down the Wild West feel of the Middle East.

Biden had three clear messages for the Iranians. "We're not looking for a massive Middle East conflict here, we want to contain this conflict to Gaza and we're not looking for a war with Iran," Biden told McGurk.

"But, but," Biden said, "and a big but, we will protect our people and we will protect our interests."

He told McGurk to warn the Iranians: "You either stop this or else."

McGurk flew to Muscat, the capital of Oman. The U.S. did not communicate directly with the Iranians but used intermediaries, like the Omanis. It was a grueling flight of more than 7,000 miles.

"You have to get a handle on the Houthis which are firing these missiles at ships," McGurk said in a message passed via the Omanis to Ali Bagheri Kani, Iran's deputy foreign minister and chief nuclear negotiator.

The setup always felt strange to McGurk. He could see the Iranians on the other side of the room and they could see him. But they did not talk to one another directly. The Omanis passed the messages back and forth. It was, however, the best in-person communication option the U.S. had to get a message to the Supreme Leader of Iran.

"We can't control them," the Iranian representatives replied. McGurk heard this answer a lot from them. He knew Iran had totally shut off, at least temporarily, the attacks on U.S. forces in Iraq. So they could turn it off in the Red Sea, McGurk believed. He relayed Biden's warning.

"If you can't stop the Houthis, we're going to directly target them," McGurk said. "And we could directly target you because we hold you responsible."

Iran would not give McGurk a commitment.

President Biden ordered air and naval strikes against the Houthis that night. They hit Houthi missile and drone launch sites, weapons storage areas and radars with precision-guided bombs. A Navy submarine fired a Tomahawk cruise missile. Five U.S. allies—Britain, the Netherlands, Australia, Canada and Bahrain—joined the response. The Houthis came back with a warning: "The U.S. and U.K. must be prepared to pay a heavy price."

McGurk believed it showed the careful, intentional way Biden was using military force.

A week later, the administration and the U.K. announced a package of sanctions against four key Houthi leaders. Limiting the sanctions to individuals was intended to minimize harm to Yemen's population of 32 million, who already were ravaged by famine and war.

Biden wanted to increase the pressure and escalate the threats but only so much. One of his basic foreign policy tenets was still "great powers don't bluff." So there would be no bluffing. He was determined to avoid a wider regional war.

On Sunday, January 28, the Iran-backed militia groups operating in Syria and Iraq launched an unmanned aerial drone attack on U.S. forces stationed at a remote desert outpost, Tower 22, in northeast Jordan near the Syria border. Three American servicemembers were killed and more than 30 had injuries ranging from cuts to serious brain trauma.

"Today, America's heart is heavy," Biden said in a statement that condemned the "despicable and wholly unjust attack." He vowed to hold "all those responsible to account at a time and in a manner of our choosing."

On Friday, February 2, the U.S. Central Command forces struck 85 targets across seven sites, three in Iraq and four in Syria linked to Iran's Revolutionary Guard Corps and militia groups. Biden did not strike inside Iran.

House Speaker Mike Johnson criticized Biden's response. "The tragic deaths of three U.S. troops in Jordan, perpetrated by Iran-backed militias, demanded a clear and forceful response," he said. "Unfortunately, the administration waited for a week and telegraphed to the world, including Iran, the nature of our response. The public handwringing and excessive signaling undercuts our ability to put a decisive end to the barrage of attacks endured over the past few months.

"Now is the time for President Biden to wake up to the reality that his policy of placating Iran has failed," Johnson said. "To promote peace, America must project strength."

FIFTY-THREE

O n January 8, Blinken and his top advisers crossed the desert in an SUV to meet with Crown Prince Mohammed bin Salman (MBS) at his royal winter camp in the ancient oasis city Al-Ula in Saudi Arabia. MBS, the 38-year-old all-powerful leader who oversaw a country with one-fifth of the world's oil reserves, was there on a retreat. He had been hosting American congressmen over the weekend.

Blinken entered the cavernous tent, lavishly decorated with colorful rugs and floor cushions. A feast of local cuisine awaited them, including baby camel burgers, lamb and chicken.

Before October 7, Biden, Sullivan and Blinken had been working with the Saudis for months to settle the relationship between the U.S. and Saudi Arabia, seriously damaged by the murder of journalist Khashoggi.

Another potentially globe-shaking project was a proposal for normalization, as it was called. It would mean full diplomatic, economic and strategic ties between Israel and Saudi Arabia. Should this be achieved it could change the balance of power in the Middle East. Diplomatic relations between the two Middle East powerhouses could further isolate the threat from Iran, which had the biggest military in the region.

After the trauma of October 7, however, and Israel's military campaign and relentless bombing of Gaza, it was hard to know whether the Saudis were willing or even able to move forward with normalization. The Saudi population was roiling with anger at the devastating humanitarian crisis in Gaza.

Sitting on floor cushions, Blinken asked MBS directly, "Do you want to pursue normalization and what is required in order to actually do it?"

Normalization between the two Middle East superpowers would be a turning point for the region, securing Blinken's place in diplomatic history on the scale of Henry Kissinger.

"Not only do I want to pursue it, but I want to pursue it with urgency," MBS said. "I think we need to try to get this done in the next few months because then you will be into your election season. It's going to be hard for you to do anything then."

It was a surprising strategic understanding of American priorities and politics.

MBS added, "Who knows what comes after the election. So this is the moment and I'm prepared to do it."

The U.S. was also getting closer and closer to finalizing its own agreements with the Saudis on defense cooperation, on civil nuclear power so the Saudis could build up their nuclear power industry, and an economic plan.

"If we conclude our agreements," Blinken added, "what do you need from Israel in order to actually do the normalization?"

"I need two things," MBS said. "I need quiet in Gaza and I need a clear political pathway for the Palestinians, for a state."

"Your Royal Highness, the word in Israel is that when it comes to the Palestinian state you don't really mean it and that you don't really want it. You pay lip service to it. So just tell me," Blinken said, "what is the answer?"

The Saudi royal family had a lengthy history of being disappointed by Palestinian leadership.

"Do I want it?" MBS said and tapped his heart. "It doesn't matter that much. Do I need it? Absolutely."

He continued, "And I need it for two reasons. One, I have 70 percent of my population that's younger than I am.

"Before October 7 they paid no attention to Palestine and the Israeli-Palestinian conflict. Since October 7 that's all they are focused on," MBS said. "And I have other countries in the Arab world, in the Muslim world that care deeply and I will not betray my people."

Millions of Muslims from around the world travel to Saudi Arabia for the annual Hajj, a pilgrimage to Mecca, the birthplace of the Prophet Muhammad.

Blinken knew MBS viewed himself as the leader of the Muslim world writ large, the Arab world.

"I will not betray my young people or the Arab or Muslim world," MBS said.

"Can I tell that to Bibi?" Blinken asked. He would be traveling to Israel next.

"Yes," MBS said.

"In those words?"

"Yes, in those words."

In Israel on January 9, Blinken sat alone with Prime Minister Netanyahu in his small, stark office with white walls and a wood floor. They sat almost knee-to-knee. Bibi on a chair, Blinken on a couch. Netanyahu had been filmed and photographed in this office many times.

He looked tired and worn. Blinken, also tired, lost no time in hammering home the inadequacies of humanitarian aid going into Gaza. Netanyahu argued back that they had taken steps. Bibi being Bibi, Blinken thought with frustration.

Israel had taken a few small steps on humanitarian assistance but it was all grudging, pulling teeth.

The Kerem Shalom border crossing in southern Israel was finally open. Israel had agreed to guarantee a minimum daily supply of fuel to Gaza. They reluctantly agreed that flour the Turks had sent, which was sitting at Ashdod Port, an Israeli cargo port south of Tel Aviv, could enter Gaza. And agreed that a U.S. shipment of flour could also go in. But they agreed only in principle.

"It's not going as fast or as effectively as it needs to be," Blinken said. He confronted Netanyahu about the toll to civilians. Israel was now conducting military operations in Khan Yunis, Gaza's second largest city.

"When is that going to be done? When are operations going to be over?" Blinken asked. "Because this is getting to a very difficult place."

Bibi was defensive.

"Look, I need to tell you what I heard from MBS, from the Crown Prince," Blinken added, switching topics. Netanyahu visibly perked up and leaned in.

"He wants to pursue normalization," Blinken said, "wants to pursue it urgently but he needs two things. He needs quiet in Gaza and he needs a Palestinian pathway."

Bibi was animated. "I want to do this," he said immediately. "What do you think he means by quiet in Gaza?"

"Well, I can tell you what he told me was: No Israeli boots on the ground," Blinken said. "I said well that may be a pretty high bar to reach."

"We're going to work on this," Bibi said, seemingly unfazed. Then he paused again. "Palestinian pathway. What does that mean?" Bibi, for his entire political career, had been adamantly opposed to an independent Palestinian state.

"It's got to be credible. It's got to be irreversible. It's got to be something that people can really believe and buy into," Blinken said. "We understand that there have to be some conditions particularly to make you confident about your security. But it's got to be a clear and irreversible pathway."

Bibi said, "Well, look, I think we can work something. We can work something. We'll need creative wordsmithing on it."

"No, no, no, you missed the point," Blinken said. "It can't—not creative wordsmithing. It's got to be real. If it's creative wordsmithing there is not a person on this planet who will not believe that you will find a way to weasel out of whatever words you put down on a piece of paper. That will not do it."

"No, no, we'll work on it," Bibi said.

Netanyahu then brought Blinken into his security cabinet meeting where the Israelis were laying out their next phase of military plans.

"It's clear that this is not going to be over anytime soon," Blinken thought with alarm as he surveyed the preparations.

At the end of the meeting as they stood up to leave, Blinken grabbed Netanyahu's arm and said, "You got one more minute?"

"Yeah, of course," Bibi said.

"What you told me in your office about wanting to pursue normalization and what's required and what we just heard, that doesn't line up," Blinken said. "It can't work."

"Let me work on it," Bibi repeated.

Blinken called Biden on the plane home. "Mr. President, look, I heard a lot of interesting things on this trip," Blinken said, updating him on the tragic situation in Gaza and his new list of concerns, as well as his conversations with MBS and Netanyahu.

"Okay, let's get together as soon as we can when you get back," Biden said.

FIFTY-FOUR

Sullivan and Blinken drove to the 125-acre Camp David and had lunch with Biden on January 14. It was just the three of them sitting around a table. There was snow on the ground. A beautiful day but cold.

Blinken relayed in detail his conversation with MBS about pursuing a normalization agreement between Israel and Saudi Arabia and Netanyahu's reaction.

"Look, my sense is this," Blinken said of his talk with Bibi. "Right now the prime minister's legacy is October 7 and that's not a legacy that he wants. Now maybe he thinks he can get some quote unquote victory over Hamas but that's I think very elusive and ephemeral. But if he actually could produce normalization with Saudi Arabia . . ."

It would define Netanyahu's legacy. Netanyahu had long argued that making peace with his other neighbors in the Middle East was the path to security for Israel.

"It's the holy grail or the golden ring," Blinken said. "It's what Israel has wanted from day one, which is normal relations with its neighbors."

"Oh, come on, there's no way he can do what's necessary now, right?" Biden pressed Blinken. "There's no way that can happen."

Biden's bullshit detector was blinking red.

Polls in Israel since October 7 showed 65 percent of Israelis opposed a two-state solution, a complete reversal from 2012 when polls indicated 61 percent of Israelis supported it.

"Sir, you're right that it's unlikely but it's not impossible. Bibi is being tugged in different directions on this but there's part of him that clearly would like to do this," Blinken said. "More than would like, wants to do this."

"Okay, let's pursue the normalization piece," Biden said. "Let's see if we can conclude our own agreements with the Saudis and bring this to a point where it becomes a real decision for Netanyahu, not just a hypothetical.

"Maybe that will prove to be leverage," Biden added. He said he was still skeptical Israel and Netanyahu could do what they needed to do to move forward with the deal but was willing to test the proposition.

Sullivan and Blinken agreed.

They had the added challenge of getting part of the U.S. treaty with the Saudis through Congress. The first agreement, the defense cooperation agreement, was short of NATO Article 5 protection but similar to the defense agreements the U.S. had with Japan, Australia and South Korea. It promised if Saudi Arabia were attacked, the U.S. would come to its defense.

Blinken remembered early on in the administration, Biden had told him, "Every administration has its Middle East crisis." When fighting broke out for 11 days in Gaza in 2021, Blinken had gone to Biden and said, we checked the box.

Biden had just laughed and told him, "Famous last words, right?"

Blinken was back in Israel three weeks later when he placed a worried call to President Biden. Israel's war cabinet had just given a briefing on their plans to enter Rafah, in southern Gaza where remaining Hamas battalions were hiding among civilians.

There were somewhere around 1.4 million people in Rafah, most of them living in squalid conditions in makeshift tents with open sewers, and pushed there by Israel's military operations in northern Gaza. Where would they go?

"The Israelis don't have any plan that we can see for what to do about those civilians," Blinken said. "It's a recipe for disaster. We need to demand a plan." He spoke so quickly, his words falling over one another, it was clear Blinken was worried and shaken.

Blinken added, "Look, personally I can't be part of supporting something like that absent a plan."

"Tell the Israelis that we need to see a plan," Biden said. "Let's talk more about this when you get back," Biden reassured Blinken.

Biden called Netanyahu on February 11, their first phone call in three weeks due to simmering disagreements. Biden had played down his frustrations with Netanyahu on a number of occasions with journalists. In December he shared an inscription from an old photograph of him and Netanyahu: "Bibi, I love you, but I don't agree with a damn thing you have to say."

"It's about the same today," Biden had noted.

Now he said publicly that he told Netanyahu he needed a clear, credible, implementable plan to protect civilians in the absence of which the U.S. could not support an operation in Rafah.

On February 14, Valentine's Day, Blinken had lunch alone with the president in his small private dining room off the Oval Office.

Rafah could be a civilian catastrophe. "Mr. President, as we discussed, there is no plan that the Israelis have to get civilians out of harm's way in Rafah," Blinken said. There was nowhere for the people to go.

The Israelis had told Blinken they would send the civilians to Al Mawasi, a beach area on the coast. "But it's already saturated. There are already 250,000 people there and there is almost no sufficient humanitarian support for them.

"It doesn't add up," Blinken said. "There's no place to put them, much less care for them."

He continued, "But even if the Israelis do come up with a plan to move people out of harm's way, there are 1.4 million people in Rafah. They're not going to move all of them.

"We think as many as half a million will remain in Rafah," Blinken said.

Biden agreed. From everything he knew of Israel's military operations, they would do terrible harm to civilians.

"If you extrapolate from what we've seen it probably adds up to more than a thousand children being killed and women and others," Blinken told the president. "We can't be part of that."

It's such a tightrope to walk for me and for the United States, Biden said with frustration. His patience with Netanyahu was wearing thin.

There were four remaining Hamas battalions the Israelis said they wanted to destroy.

Biden said the Israeli Defense Force was "overrated."

"Look," Blinken added, "even if they somehow succeed in eliminating these remaining battalions, by our estimate there are going to remain north of 10,000 armed Hamas who have not been killed or injured such that they were off the battlefield."

In addition, the IDF told Blinken they estimated there were about 130,000 card-carrying members of Hamas. Not militarized. Not engaged in terrorism but they could jump in. Then there were those, particularly young people, who had been radicalized by what's happened over the last few months, people whose relatives and community members had been killed by Israel's military operations.

"Basically the Israelis are going to inherit an insurgency that will bleed them for a long time," Blinken said.

"Look," Biden said, "you know I've committed my entire career to Israel's security." This trajectory was damaging Israel's security. "We can't countenance the civilian harm that's being done. We have to try to move them off this.

"I'm prepared to draw a clear line," Biden added. "Let's say we draw the line at Rafah." But Biden did not trust Netanyahu. What if they do it anyway? What then?

Blinken said, "There are three broadly speaking categories of things that we can look at. One is public separation. Two is something at the United Nations." The U.S. had so far resisted calls for a cease-fire at the U.N. that weren't attached to getting hostages out but they could amend that position. "Three, suspending some military assistance to Israel for Gaza."

Biden was clear: "I will not cut off or suspend defensive assistance to Israel, Iron Dome, anything to defend itself. It has to
preserve its deterrent against Iran and Hezbollah."

The president believed that if U.S. support for Israel appeared
wobbly, Iran and its proxies, particularly Hezbollah in the north,
could take it as the signal to escalate the conflict in Gaza by opening up another front in the war.

The once solid public support for Israel's military operations in
Gaza had been cratering in the United States. Daily news reports
showed devastating images of Palestinian children wounded and
killed, families searching for food and water, tent encampments
and cities reduced to rubble in Gaza.

Biden's continued military aid to Israel, despite the growing civilian death toll in Gaza and lack of humanitarian aid getting in,
was roiling Democrats, labor unions and university campuses in
the United States.

"But I agree," Biden told Blinken, "we need to look at whether
we could and should pause assistance that goes directly for use in
Gaza if they don't get this right."

A diffuse wave of student-led protests over the worsening humanitarian situation in Gaza had sprung up at colleges across the
country. The more college administrators cracked down on the
pro-Palestinian demonstrations and tent encampments, the more
the protests grew, attracting participation from faculty and members of the public. At Columbia University, the school called in the
police to clear a major student protest for the first time since the
Vietnam War. About 100 were arrested.

Some Republicans described the college protests as "hotbeds
of antisemitism." Mostly they were a mixed bag of messages, predominantly aimed at bringing about an end to Israel's military operations in Gaza.

Biden called Netanyahu on February 15.

"We already said we were not going to support an operation

absent a plan to get the civilians out of harm's way and care for civilians," Biden said.

"We don't see how you can do that. It doesn't add up. We don't know where you'll take people, never mind how you'll care for them," Biden continued. "Even if you could, we don't see how you don't do something that does terrible damage to the civilians who remain in Rafah.

"And," Biden said, "it doesn't lead anywhere because you're going to have a long-term problem on your hands."

Meanwhile, Blinken and McGurk had been pushing the Israelis on a cease-fire. They had a dilemma. "We saw the quickest way to short-circuit what was happening in Gaza was the hostages for cease-fire agreement," Blinken said. "If we got that agreement, we'd get at least a six-week cease-fire with the prospect of extending it."

Instead of going guns blazing into Rafah, Israel could work with the Egyptians to control the border so that nothing could get in to resupply Hamas—suffocating Hamas of resources.

Blinken delivered President Biden's message to Bibi, "We're not going to support you on a major operation into Rafah," he said.

You're heading to a place where either Hamas is going to be left in Gaza running it, which the U.S. agreed was unacceptable; Israel will have to stay and inherit an insurgency; or there will be nothing left just anarchy, Blinken said.

"Well, you're right," Bibi said. "We'll have our hands full for decades."

"That can't possibly be good for Israel," Blinken said. What the Arabs kept telling Blinken, and Blinken believed they were right, was that there had to be a political answer to Hamas—specifically Palestinian leadership.

"It needs to be, in our judgment, Palestinians and the Palestinian Authority," Blinken told Bibi.

"We believe that's where you need to get. Maybe it can't be done in one fell swoop," Blinken added. "The Egyptians, the Emiratis have expressed real interest in being part of a security force that would transition to Palestinian authority. We'd be training up Palestinian authority."

Netanyahu liked the idea of the Arabs going in. He was not keen on the Palestinian Authority to say the least.

"Look," said Blinken, "your place in the world is in peril. You might not realize it until it's too late. But you're losing support from your remaining supporters and the countries that have been the most supportive of Israel besides the United States—Germany and the United Kingdom—I can tell you from my conversations with their foreign ministers that it's right at the edge of the table and it's about to fall off. You may not be able to see it but you need to know it," Blinken said angrily.

Netanyahu still did not move off the idea of a military operation into Rafah.

It was obvious Blinken had no influence.

So he called Biden. "Let me get on the phone with Bibi on this," the president said.

"I have ideas for dealing with Rafah in a different way," Biden told Bibi. "Dealing with your main problem—Hamas—in a different way and you need to hear them because we're not—we can't support a major military operation there," Biden said. "And we still haven't seen a plan to get people out of harm's way."

Netanyahu agreed to send Israeli representatives to Washington but he pulled the plug after the U.S. abstained from a U.N. Security Council resolution on a cease-fire.

Bibi viewed it as a betrayal.

"He is a handful," Blinken said about Netanyahu. "But as much as it's tempting to blame everything on Bibi or blame everything on Smotrich or Ben-Gvir, the extremists in his cabinet, the hard reality is most of what's coming from Israel these days is a reflection of the overwhelming majority of its people."

In a remote prison camp known as "Polar Wolf" in the Arctic Circle, Putin's opposition leader and vocal critic, Alexei Navalny, age 47, was pronounced dead on February 16, 2024. The cause was unclear.

"Make no mistake, Putin is responsible for Navalny's death," President Biden declared. "What has happened to Navalny is yet more proof of Putin's brutality."

It was a vivid warning to opposition figures inside Russia.

FIFTY-FIVE

Retired Lieutenant General Keith Kellogg picked up the phone on Sunday, March 10, 2024. It was Trump checking in after Super Tuesday. Kellogg still prided himself on being one of only five senior advisers who had lasted through Trump's entire presidency.

"Just get ready when we start campaigning hard," Trump said. He was in good spirits. "Get ready to go!"

Super Tuesday's results had been expected. It was now all but assured that the November 2024 election would be a Biden-Trump rematch. Trump had won 2,231 delegates and only 1,215 were needed to guarantee him the Republican nomination.

Kellogg told everyone that he was supporting Trump's 2024 campaign "100 percent." For him, it was a binary choice between Biden's policies and Trump's policies.

"The southern border, that's number one," Kellogg said. "I think we've got a broken military, which is number two. Then you look at the regional conflicts, Europe with Russia. You look at the Middle East and you look at the Far East.

"I fall really, really hard on the side of Donald J. Trump," Kellogg said. "And I'm just very, very nervous about the current policies of Joe Biden.

"Trump's policies are good and the fact is I know the guy," Kellogg said. "And Joe, for all of his experience, Joe Biden's experience in national security, he just doesn't get it."

Kellogg regularly argued that Trump was a different kind of person out of the spotlight. He could listen and actually wanted to hear every voice in the room.

"When the door was closed in the Oval Office," Kellogg said, "we'd sit there, and the term I'd use is a BOGSAT which is a bunch of guys sitting at a table bullshitting."

During one heated National Security Council meeting in the Situation Room about Afghanistan, Kellogg recalled how Trump paused and went around the table to ask everyone's opinion.

"Okay, what do you think?" Trump asked the woman two seats down from Kellogg.

"Mr. President, I'm the notetaker."

"Oh, no," Trump said, "if you're in this room, you're talking."

So the notetaker weighed in briefly.

Trump appeared to enjoy putting his advisers in the hot seat. "He would tell me up front, this is what I'm thinking about and then you would need to push back on it or support him," Kellogg said.

"And I saw a lot of people fold under pressure," he added. "I mean absolutely fold.

"There were other times when I actually sat there and said, you know, I really want the popcorn concession on this one because this is just an absolute knock-down drag-out. It was fun to watch."

As president, Trump's decisions were often made in an instant. "It wasn't a come back tomorrow, come back a week from Tuesday, come back three weeks from now," Kellogg said.

When Trump had decided to move the U.S. embassy in Israel from Tel Aviv to Jerusalem in 2018, he was told in the Situation Room that a Third Intifada was going to start because of it.

"Well, we'll take that risk," Trump said with a shrug and ordered the move, creating a firestorm in the press but no Third Intifada in Israel.

It was Trump's demeaning and aggressive language that would be a problem for some voters, Kellogg believed. For instance, Trump had repeatedly called Republican rival Nikki Haley a "birdbrain" and his campaign had left a bird cage with birdseed outside her hotel room.

He's much different now, Kellogg reassured others. "His mind's in a good place." He could see the possibility of a second term within reach and was ready for a contest.

Trump's cabinet selection process and decision-making would also be significantly different this time, Kellogg believed.

"There's no book out there that says: Presidents for Dummies," Kellogg said. "You learn on the job and you figure out okay, this is the way it's going to go."

Referring to 2017, Kellogg added, "Last time, he didn't come out of the gate fast.

"We were not prepared for governance because everybody was new," Kellogg said.

Now Trump and Biden both had four years in the White House and knew what was possible as president.

"This will be the longest general campaign this nation's ever seen," Kellogg said, but he believed Trump was ready for a long political fight in 2024.

On the phone with Trump now in March, they jumped through topics. "From apples to oranges to apricots in about 45 seconds," Kellogg said. They landed on Israel.

Kellogg had just returned from Tel Aviv. He updated Trump on his meetings with Netanyahu's right-hand adviser, Ron Dermer, and Defense Minister Yoav Gallant. Kellogg had also secretly met with Netanyahu.

What was Bibi's state of mind? Trump asked Kellogg.

"Netanyahu is a wartime leader," Kellogg said. "This is a guy who came out of special operations and the Israel military." He understands war.

Netanyahu had served in the Sayeret Matkal, an elite Special Forces unit of the Israeli army that conducted clandestine reconnaissance missions. He later fought in the 1973 Yom Kippur War and was promoted to the rank of captain in the IDF Reserves.

Kellogg said he believed that Biden was too critical of Netanyahu in public. "Biden, Netanyahu, do not see eye to eye about virtually anything," Kellogg added. "I understand in our administration when you were president that there were times you had some quips with Netanyahu whilst you were doing the Abraham Accords. But he was closer to you than he is to Biden.

"If people think there's a two-state solution now they're wrong," Kellogg said. "It will not happen in the near term and it won't happen because of the animosity now within the Jewish population."

He told Trump about his visit to some of the kibbutzim attacked on October 7. He had met with an Israeli woman who said she would never again trust Palestinian people because she had recognized some of the attackers who came across the border on October 7. They had worked in her kibbutz, she claimed.

In the five months since October 7, no Palestinians had been let back into Israel to work.

Israelis look at this in almost biblical terms, Kellogg said, as a fight for survival.

"Unless you understand that, you don't understand what's happening in Israel. And this administration does not understand that," he said referring to Biden.

Kellogg also criticized Biden for pushing Israel to call a cease-fire.

"They're not going to go along with a cease-fire," Kellogg scoffed on the phone to Trump about the Israelis. Dermer had told him as much in their separate one-and-a-half-hour meeting. "They're going to go into Rafah, they're going to finish the battalions.

"They're going to eradicate Hamas," Kellogg said. "And I mean *eradicate* Hamas—all the leadership of Hamas."

Kellogg said Biden was not being supportive enough of Netanyahu. "You cannot have humanitarian assistance be your primary thought," Kellogg said. "Your primary thought should be eradicating Hamas as a fighting unit."

Trump was quiet on the other end of the line. He'd criticized Netanyahu's handling of Hamas and the images of Israel's military operations in Gaza.

"I think Israel made a very big mistake," Trump had said during an interview with Israeli media at Mar-a-Lago. "I wanted to call and say don't do it. These photos and shots. I mean, moving shots of bombs being dropped into buildings in Gaza. And I said, Oh, that's a terrible portrait. It's a very bad picture for the world. . . . I think Israel wanted to show that it's tough, but sometimes you shouldn't be doing that."

Kellogg said he would write up an after-action report with his main conclusions: One, we need to support the state of Israel and the administration of Bibi Netanyahu. Two, understand a two-state solution is not going to happen. It's just not. Three, Israel will have a cease-fire but it will be a short-term cease-fire to try to get the hostages out. Four, this is a war. Some of the scenes you see will not be pretty. Just accept that. Five, this is resolved by the U.S. and Saudis.

"The Middle East is broken," Kellogg said. "It's fractured and you're going to have to bring it back in balance. You can do it because of your ability to talk to people."

Kellogg mailed Trump a hard copy of his four-page action report. He knew it was too long for Trump.

"When you're with Donald J. Trump that's a long memo," Kellogg said. "You need to try to keep it one page."

Former Trump cabinet members were making the rounds to various embassies in Washington saying that a new Trump administration would be friendly and accommodating to their countries.

Former Trump national security adviser Robert O'Brien and former CIA director and secretary of state Mike Pompeo had visited South Korean ambassador to the U.S. Hyundong Cho.

The line they pushed was that Trump would be more reasonable and more predictable this second time round.

They advocated the "essential" nature of Trump's relationship with each country. For instance, that Trump realized the relationship between South Korea and the United States was instrumental to mutual security and the two nations would be shouldering many burdens together.

Ambassador Cho said, "O'Brien is probably on the short list to be the next secretary of state if Trump is elected."

Koji Tomita, the Japanese ambassador to the United States, thought Trump courted former Japanese leaders by playing golf with one and in "a very clever way" sharing information about Japan's vast investments.

"Japan has been the largest foreign investor here in the U.S. for the past several years," Tomita said.

Of course, that rang a bell with Trump.

The former Trump senior officials were carefully bonding and planting seeds. They were building a new network out of the old one.

FIFTY-SIX

"Hey, let's call Trump," Republican senator Lindsey Graham said to Crown Prince Mohammed bin Salman in Saudi Arabia during a visit in March. Graham, who had traveled to the Middle East five times since October 7, was trying to keep the negotiations for a normalization deal between Israel and Saudi Arabia alive—an incredibly ambitious, almost unreachable goal.

MBS, the powerful 38-year-old who effectively ruled the oil-rich kingdom, had one of his aides bring over a bag containing about 50 burner phones. He rummaged through it and pulled out one labeled "TRUMP 45."

"Hey, I'm here with Lindsey," MBS said moments later to Trump with a laugh. "How are you doing?"

The Crown Prince then put the cell phone on speaker so Graham could also hear Trump's side of the conversation.

"Lindsey's great," Trump said to MBS. "He was your worst problem. He tried to get me to overthrow you!"

Laughter erupted on both sides of the call.

"Yeah," Graham said into the phone. "You were right [about MBS], I was wrong." Graham's relationship with MBS had soured after the horrific killing and dismemberment of journalist and *Washington Post* contributor Jamal Khashoggi in 2018. The CIA had concluded that MBS ordered the assassination. Back then Graham had referred to the Crown Prince as a "homicidal maniac" and warned of a "bipartisan tsunami" against Saudi Arabia. "Nothing happens in Saudi Arabia without MBS knowing it," Graham said on *Fox & Friends* in October 2018. "I'm not going back to Saudi Arabia as long as this guy's in charge. This guy is a wrecking ball."

Now Graham considered himself to be pretty good friends with the Crown Prince.

On one of his earlier trips to Saudi Arabia, Graham had asked MBS to get Jake Sullivan on the phone during their meeting so that Graham could brief them both on a conversation with Netanyahu. The Crown Prince had pulled out a burner phone, this time labeled: JAKE SULLIVAN.

"Hey, I'm here with Lindsey," MBS said on the phone with Sullivan.

"Where with Lindsey?" Sullivan asked MBS, his voice full of surprise. "I'm in Saudi Arabia," MBS said. "He [Lindsey] just got back from Israel."

After they hung up, this time with Trump, Senator Graham pressed MBS on talks of a Saudi normalization treaty with Israel.

"If you want to recognize Israel, you've got to do it on Biden's watch," Graham said. "There's no way you're going to get Democrats to vote for a defense agreement to go to war with Saudi Arabia introduced by Donald Trump."

The carrot the U.S. continued to dangle in front of MBS was the prospect of a serious bilateral defense cooperation agreement with the United States. It would mean that if Saudi Arabia was attacked, the U.S. would come to its defense.

"It's a big fucking deal," Graham reminded MBS. "It's an insurance policy against Iran. It's a checkmate against Iran."

MBS pointed to the anger on his streets at the situation in Gaza. He could not possibly sign the treaty with Israel unless there was some commitment to march toward a Palestinian state over the arc of time. But after October 7, Graham knew that Netanyahu and Israeli society had only hardened more firmly against the idea of a two-state solution.

MBS said he still wanted to enrich the uranium in Saudi Arabia to diversify his energy sector to include nuclear power.

"Well, that's going to be hard to do because people are afraid you'll create a bomb," Graham said.

"I don't need uranium to make a bomb," MBS said. "I'll just buy one from Pakistan."

Pakistan was one of the nine countries with nuclear weapons.

———

Months before the Hamas attack on October 7, Graham had up-dated President Biden in the Oval Office about his talks with the Saudis and Israelis. Sullivan and Blinken had attended.

"Mr. President, here's what I told MBS," Graham said. "I told him I think that normalizing with Israel is possible. I would sup-port it on your watch, Mr. President.

"I'm trying to help Blinken and Sullivan," Graham added. "I'm telling MBS if you recognize Israel, I'll get you 45 votes for the defense agreement you need from the United States from Republi-cans. Trump's not going to get in your way.

"Democrats *wouldn't* vote for it if Trump introduced it because they hate Bibi and they hate Trump," Graham said. "Republicans *would* vote for the defense agreement with Saudi Arabia if Israel encouraged us to. We can get 45 Republican votes," Graham said. "You have to get the rest from your caucus."

"I can do that," Biden said.

"Listen," Graham pushed, "this guy's willing to do it because he gets under our nuclear umbrella and he doesn't have to worry about building a bunch of bombs."

"Do you think you can deliver?" Biden had asked Graham.

"I can deliver," Graham said. "Can you deliver?"

"I can deliver," the president replied.

"Mr. President, the Abraham Accords made this possible," Gra-ham added, referring to the Trump administration's Middle East bilateral agreements between Israel and the UAE and Israel and Bahrain. "Trump will get his fair share of the credit. But you're not going to get a treaty through the Senate unless it's on your watch. It's going to take a Democratic president to convince Democrats to vote to go to war for Saudi Arabia."

"Let's do it," Biden said confidently.

Back in the Middle East in the early fall of 2023, Graham had called President Biden. Once close friends, Biden and Graham had worked various deals together. As vice president, Biden told President

Obama, "Lindsey Graham has the best instincts in the Senate." Obama agreed. But along came Trump and Graham's support of Republican attacks on Hunter Biden had ended the friendship.

"We're good to go," Graham said to Biden on the phone. They were on the "five yard line" of the defense agreement and working on hashing out the precise language of the civil nuclear deal.

Israeli prime minister Netanyahu "lit up like a Christmas tree" during our meeting, Graham told Biden. "This thing is on the verge of being done."

They had scheduled a quiet negotiation between Netanyahu and a Saudi ambassador in Tel Aviv in November 2023. It would be a historic moment.

But along came October 7. The Hamas attack and Israel's military operations in Gaza had set back all real prospects of a historic peace treaty.

"Only way you can do this is to get a cease-fire," Graham said to Blinken and Sullivan after his latest meeting with MBS in March 2024. "And during that cease-fire close this deal."

FIFTY-SEVEN

T he Israeli ambassador to the U.S. Michael Herzog, a former IDF general, pulled Brett McGurk aside during a White House meeting the afternoon of Monday, April 1.

"We just did a strike and took out IRGC commander Mohammad Reza Zahedi in Damascus, Syria," Herzog said, along with six other members of the Iranian Revolutionary Guard Corps (IRGC).

"You did what?" McGurk said. "Have you really thought through the consequences?"

Mohammad Reza Zahedi, age 63, had been a general, the highest-ranked Iranian commander in the IRGC Quds Force, a U.S.-designated terrorist organization, and a founder of the IRGC going back 45 years to the 1979 Iranian Revolution. Zahedi was also a personal friend of Iran's Supreme Leader Khamenei. Killing him was a strike at the core of Iran.

Israel had just driven a stick into a hornet's nest.

McGurk, Sullivan and Finer looked at each other. There were mixed feelings. On one hand, the Americans could understand the targets. The IRGC existed to run these proxies, like Hezbollah, who were focused on destroying Israel.

Ambassador Herzog argued it was a legitimate act of self-defense. But the White House advisers wondered if the Israelis had considered how Iran might respond.

McGurk knew from years of experience that Israel thought they were very good at managing the escalation ladder. The Israeli Defense Forces had taken calculated shots for some time, which they called their "freedom of action," and which the

United States supported. But this, McGurk believed, was a major miscalculation.

The U.S. had received no advance warning from Israel, which perhaps was a good thing, but the strike had immense implications.

The precision strike had been carried out by two U.S.-made, Israeli-operated F-35s.

At around 6:00 p.m., Iran sent a message via Swiss intermediaries that said Iran will respond against Israel but also holds the U.S. responsible for the attack. Iran claimed in the note that Israel could not have conducted the attack without U.S. approval.

Immediately, U.S. forces, which had already sustained more than 150 attacks from Iran-backed militias, went on alert again.

At 8:00 p.m., Sullivan and McGurk sent a response to the Iranians that underscored the U.S. had *no* prior knowledge of the attack, *did not* approve it and *did not* participate in it. The U.S. is prepared to respond to any attacks against our personnel and facilities, the message warned. "We do not seek a war with Iran." The U.S. wanted no part and had no part in it.

At 9:00 p.m. John Kirby, now National Security Council spokesman, reiterated the message publicly. "Let me make it clear," Kirby said from the White House podium. "We had nothing to do with the strike in Damascus. We weren't involved in any way."

The tension ate away at McGurk. It was clear from the intelligence and public statements that Iran considered Israel's strike a huge blow.

McGurk's real fear was Hezbollah might take this as an opportunity to enter the war with a large-scale attack on Israel, which the United States had been trying for years to prevent.

Suddenly the region was ablaze with hot, dangerous uncertainty again. The question lingered: How and when would Iran respond?

Three days later on Thursday, April 4, Biden spoke to Netanyahu in a secure call for 30 minutes. Blinken and McGurk listened in.

"We are seeing the Iranians preparing to do something big,"

Biden said. "Look, Bibi, we have our differences. I want you to know that when it comes to your defense—Israel's core defense against Iran—I, Joe Biden, I've got your back and you don't need to question that. Okay?"

We're going to help you defend against whatever Iran is going to do. "I'm not with you on attacking Iran. I'm just not. We're not going to do that," Biden said.

The conversation then turned to the situation in Gaza.

"What's your strategy, man?" Biden asked.

"We have to go into Rafah," Bibi said flatly.

"Bibi, you've got no strategy. You've got *no* strategy," Biden said.

"That's not true, Joe," Netanyahu replied. "We are dismantling Hamas. We've taken out 75 percent of their battalions. We have to go after the next 25 percent. That's what we're doing now.

"And Joe," Netanyahu said, "it's only going to take three weeks. Trust me, it's not going to take long! This is the end of the war. We have to clear Rafah and it's over. It'll take three weeks.

"I'll put a time limit on it, Joe," Netanyahu said. "Three weeks."

"No," Biden said. "It'll take months." They had heard this before. The Israelis had, for example, said their operation in Khan Younis would take three weeks. It had taken nearly five months.

Netanyahu at times sounded aggrieved, as if the whole world had turned against Israel, the U.N., everybody. He challenged and questioned whether the humanitarian situation was that bad in Gaza.

Biden read out a list of actions Israel needed to take in terms of humanitarian assistance. His tone was no longer diplomatic.

"You need to flood the zone. There needs to be a surge in assistance," Biden said. "It needs to be sustained and you need to have a process in place so that the humanitarian workers can do their job safely."

Biden's asks of Israel were specific, down to the number of trucks that Israel needed to let into Gaza and the crossings that needed to be opened.

We want the Ashdod Port open for the direct delivery of assistance into Gaza, Biden said. Open the Erez Crossing so that aid can reach northern Gaza and deliveries from Jordan can go directly into Gaza.

"We want to see 350 trucks a day, including 100 trucks a day to the north," Biden said. Before the October 7 attack, about 500 trucks had been crossing the border into Gaza to bring food and medicine. Inside Israel there were protests blocking roads for trucks going into Gaza, showing opposition was not isolated to Netanyahu. Inside Gaza there were alarming indications of famine.

You need a deconfliction cell to make sure the humanitarians are in the room with the IDF and your command units to make sure that something like World Central Kitchen can't happen again, Biden said. He was referring to the Israeli drone strike that had mistakenly hit a World Central Kitchen aid convey, killing seven international aid workers, including an American. The convoy had just unloaded more than 100 tons of food shipped to the Gaza Strip.

"If you don't do that and we don't see results then you've lost me," Biden said, "I'm out."

This was an unusually categorical statement for Biden.

The president then turned to the hostage deal. The U.S. believed there were about 70 or so Israeli hostages still being held by Hamas in the web of underground tunnels beneath Gaza.

McGurk, who had managed the U.S. side of the hostage negotiations with CIA director Bill Burns, believed there would have been a cease-fire months ago if Hamas had agreed to release more hostages.

On multiple occasions, McGurk had seen hostage exchange offers approved by the Hamas political leadership in Doha and Egypt. But when those Hamas representatives sent it through their network and into the tunnels to Yahya Sinwar, the leader of Hamas in Gaza, it came back with: "We reject this offer."

This is what drove the Israelis completely crazy. Israel had put a *full* cease-fire on the table in exchange for the release of women, elderly and wounded hostages. And Sinwar rejected it.

Now Biden pushed Netanyahu to make the most forward-leaning offer to Hamas yet. Burns had advised Biden that this deal had a pretty good chance of working because it gave Hamas what they wanted.

The offer was: Hamas releases 40 hostages. Israel releases 900 Palestinian prisoners, including 100 with life sentences.

McGurk thought it was an astonishing offer and not an easy thing by any stretch of the imagination for Netanyahu to agree to do. Israel considered the 100 with life sentences to be "terrorists," many who had killed Israelis.

"It's worth paying a big price to get the hostages out," Biden told Netanyahu. They both knew that otherwise the hostages would very likely die in the tunnels.

Netanyahu said they would make the offer.

After the call, the Israeli government released a four-page list of steps that they were going to take in response to what Biden said they needed to do on the humanitarian side.

Blinken was pleased but also frustrated. "These four pages are almost verbatim the things that the president in his conversations with Bibi had been telling them to do going back to December," he said. "Had they actually done them in December we might be in a different place."

The next day, April 5, Sinwar responded through intermediaries: No.

Sinwar had spent years in Israeli prison, learned Hebrew and devoted his life to destroying Israel. A total ideologue, he was believed to be hiding out in underground living quarters beneath Gaza surrounded by hostages for protection. The Israeli military had found some of his furnished suites deep in the tunnels with comfortable sleeping quarters and showers. On one occasion IDF soldiers found his handwriting on a chalkboard shortly before he fled.

U.S. intelligence and other direct observations showed there was an extraordinary labyrinth of hundreds of miles and multiple levels of tunnels in Gaza. Sinwar had categorically rejected leaving the tunnels and appeared to be living in his underground kingdom without a care in the world for what was happening to Gazans above him, willing to sacrifice every last Palestinian for his cause, according to the intelligence.

"It's hard to negotiate with someone with a death wish," Burns said about Sinwar.

Israeli and U.S. intelligence analysts also concluded that Sinwar thought the war was going his way. Israel was becoming increasingly less popular and isolated. Sinwar had rejected Israel's offers of a cease-fire in exchange for hostages. So Israel now argued they "had to go into Rafah," believing the only way to get the hostages out was a combination of negotiations and military pressure.

The leader of the United Arab Emirates Sheikh Mohammed bin Zayed Al Nahyan, MBZ, had told McGurk, "The Israelis have to learn something that we know in the Arab world. Take time with your revenge. Be patient. It's a better approach.

"To go in and smash up Rafah is not serving the interest of the Israelis when in fact you could kill Sinwar," MBZ said.

Take your time, he advised.

The Israelis were determined to kill Sinwar, who was already projecting himself as a martyr.

Meanwhile, in Tehran on April 5, thousands of Iranians gathered for the funerals of Commander Zahedi and the other six IRGC members killed in Israel's strike. "Martyrs on the road to Jerusalem" was written on the trucks that transported the coffins. People at the funeral held placards that read: "Death to Israel" and "Death to America." Iran's Supreme Leader Khamenei had vowed that Israel would pay.

Amir Ali Hajizadeh, the senior Iranian missile commander, was pushing for a big missile attack on Israel. U.S. intelligence indicated that the Supreme Leader, who was usually pragmatic because he was not looking to get into a major war, was so furious about the assassination of Zahedi, his friend, in Damascus that he was not putting the brakes on Hajizadeh.

On April 9, Iran sent another message through the Swiss intermediary. Iran said it had "no intention of targeting the U.S." but threatened U.S. bases in West Asia if the U.S. challenged Iran's response against Israel.

That night new information showed Iran was preparing a historically unprecedented attack on Israel using a variety of missile and drones, including ballistic missiles.

At 10:00 a.m., April 10, Sullivan called the principals together. Secretary of Defense Austin, Chairman of the Joint Chiefs CQ Brown and Centcom commander General Erik Kurilla briefed them on the defense preparations. The principals agreed the moment called for direct engagement with Iran's chief of defense Mohammad Bagheri. Direct engagements with Iran were extremely rare. CQ Brown sent a letter to Bagheri urging restraint and warning that the scale of their planned attack could cause an escalation into an all-out Middle East war.

General Kurilla and military coordination officers flew to Israel to help prepare the defense. Secretary Austin moved the USS *Eisenhower* to the northern Red Sea, closer to Israel. He sent the *Arleigh Burke* and *Carney*, two missile destroyers, as well as fighter planes. France, the U.K., Saudi Arabia and Jordan agreed to help with Israel's defense.

FIFTY-EIGHT

On Saturday, April 13, at 3:00 p.m. Eastern Standard Time, Iran launched Operation True Promise beginning with a swarm of 150 UAVs, which would take seven hours to reach Israel. Iran then launched 30 cruise missiles, which would take about three to four hours. Then 110 ballistic missiles were in the air, which only take 12 minutes to reach their target.

The drones, cruise missiles and ballistic missiles were all designed to reach Israel at the same time.

The Saudi chief of defense notified Kurilla that the U.S. couldn't go into Saudi airspace yet because he didn't have the approval of the Crown Prince and his brother. McGurk sent a message to the Crown Prince: "The attack is underway. We need access to your airspace. Please instruct your Chief of Defense." MBS gave the order and opened the airspace for U.S. F-15 jets.

President Biden returned from Wilmington and was in the Situation Room at the White House at 5:15 p.m. with Jake Sullivan, Jon Finer, Brett McGurk, Phil Gordon and others when the first missiles launched. General Kurilla, who was positioned in Oman, was projected on a screen to narrate in real time what they were seeing. Vice President Harris, who was traveling domestically that day, also called in.

U.S. surveillance systems can detect any ballistic missile launched anywhere in the world. The missiles go into outer space and then re-enter the earth's atmosphere, traveling at 15,000 miles per hour.

"Mr. President," Kurilla said, "we have confirmation of 30 ballistic missiles." They were in the air.

The missiles appeared on a screen in the Situation Room as

yellow streaks. It was like looking at something out of an old '80s movie or computer war game. Biden watched as the yellow streaks moved toward Israel. From intel and reporting, they knew Iran's missiles were good.

"Mr. President, we can probably defeat 30 missiles," Secretary Austin said.

About three minutes later 30 more Iranian missiles launched. Minutes after that, 30 more. Soon it was 110 ballistic missiles flying toward Israel. A mind-blowing number. Far more than they expected.

Biden was very quiet, silent as he watched the missiles from his chair at the head of the table.

McGurk was watching President Biden very closely. Steve Hadley, national security adviser to President George W. Bush, had told him in situations like this keep your eye on the president to see if you can get a read on what he might be thinking.

Never in history, McGurk realized, had any country tried to defeat 110 ballistic missiles. Even if only 30 missiles hit their target, Israel would have to respond in a very decisive way and the result would almost inevitably be a major Middle East war.

Then the integrated defenses kicked in.

"What are you seeing?" Biden asked Kurilla, who talked through the defense operations.

They had set up kill baskets for the UAVs as they came in.

U.S. military coordinators in Israel were leading the ballistic missile defense: You take down those, we'll take down these, the Brits have those, the Saudis have these. It was an extraordinary integrated defense operation.

A lot of history was made as they watched. This was the first time Iran had ever directly attacked Israel and the first time the U.S. military had ever directly defended Israel. Saudi Arabia and Jordan had come to Israel's defense. It was unprecedented. A major power move against Iran.

Then the bad news. "We've confirmed four impacts in Israel,"

General Kurilla reported, meaning four missiles had struck Israel. Tension in the room heightened. They didn't know what had been hit or how many more would get through the defenses.

When Iran announced the end of its military operation, the U.S. and its partners had intercepted and shot down almost all of Iran's missiles and drones, nearly 300 in total, proving for the moment the enormous power in collective defensive capability. A lot of Iran's missiles failed. One seven-year-old girl was badly wounded but the damage to Israel was unbelievably small. No deaths, no major damage to Israel.

But Biden knew Netanyahu. Israel would respond and it risked bringing them right back to the brink of war with Iran. Biden said his instinct was to tell Bibi, look, let it end here. You started this by taking out some IRGC guys. They responded and we avoided major casualties. They didn't hurt you. Let it end here. Biden looked up at Vice President Harris on the screen.

"What's your view?"

"That's right," Harris said. "Tell Bibi to take the win."

Biden and Netanyahu spoke on the phone at 9:00 p.m. It was 4:00 a.m. in Israel.

"Let's take time to think through the next move," Biden said, "because in my view you won. You just took out the entire leadership of the IRGC in the Levant. They just launched everything at you. And we just defeated it with a coalition of Saudi Arabia, Jordan, France and the U.K. Just extraordinary. You don't need to make another move. Do nothing."

"We were just attacked by 100 ballistic missiles," Netanyahu said. "I live in the Middle East. You cannot let this stand. We have to respond."

"Take the win," Biden advised. He reiterated that the United States would not participate in any Israeli offensive action against Iran. "We're not going to be part of an offense," Biden said.

Netanyahu said, "I want to be clear: We will make our decisions ourselves. The State of Israel will do whatever is necessary to defend itself."

After the call with Bibi ended, Biden said to his advisers and cabinet officers in the Situation Room, "I know he's going to do something but the way I limit it is tell him to do nothing."

Israel's cabinet debated how to respond. They were considering a range of options, including strikes outside of Tehran. Some of the hardliners in the cabinet like Israel's finance minister Bezalel Smotrich argued that this was the moment to take out Iran's nuclear facilities. This was rejected.

On April 18, Israel's defense minister Gallant notified Sullivan that Israel would take "a small precision retaliatory response." He said that Israel would not publicly confirm the strike to give Iran the chance to save face and de-escalate.

Later that day Israel sent a back-channel message to Iran that said, "We are going to respond but we consider our response to be the end."

U.S. intelligence showed Iran fueled about 30 of their missiles, potentially to launch after Israel attacked. The U.S. military again postured to defend Israel.

At 8:00 p.m. on April 18, Israel struck the air defense system outside Isfahan, the city where Iran's main nuclear facilities are located.

Israeli pilots launched sophisticated missiles from airplanes that Iranian air defenses did not detect.

It was Israel's way of saying to Iran: We can hit you with pinpoint accuracy whenever we want. So let's stop this.

Brett McGurk was in his office watching the missiles, little yellow streaks, cross the trajectory of his screen in real time.

The calibrated strike caused a small explosion. Social media took over. Someone posted they had just heard an explosion in Isfahan. What was that?

Television coverage in the U.S. suggested major war was

breaking out. Reporters bombarded the White House with questions. What was happening? Sullivan and Finer directed the National Security Council and White House press teams to stay quiet. If a U.S. official said Israel had just retaliated against Iran, it would become a bigger story and Iran might feel compelled to respond.

In Iran, the message released through official channels was: Nothing to see here. Nothing happened. Iran said a quadcopter—a small drone that anyone could buy on Amazon—had exploded and done no damage.

Iran reopened their airspace to civilian planes. McGurk was relieved. It was a signal they were not going to respond.

It was over. They had again averted a Middle East war.

FIFTY-NINE

◆ ◆

In the spring of 2024, CIA director Bill Burns made his 10th visit to Ukraine. The CIA provides massive intelligence assistance to Ukraine, but he also believed that Ukraine had grown an impressive intelligence service.

Burns met secretly with President Zelensky and later reported, "He's aged and he's tired because there's an awful lot of strain on him too. But he hasn't lost his resilience either. He still strikes me as tough as he was at the beginning of the war."

"We're running out of air defense munitions," President Zelensky said warily, "artillery munitions as well." He was deeply worried about the U.S. Congress where the question of continued aid to Ukraine was stuck in a bitter partisan battle he could not impact or understand.

Burns had arrived in Ukraine three days after a grim battle was lost. Avdiivka, a Ukrainian city in the east, had held out almost the entire war but the lack of ammunition had forced Ukrainian troops to retreat. The loss signaled to Ukrainians and the West that Russia was now gaining the decisive upper hand in the war.

Burns spoke with the Ukrainian Special Forces commander.

"We fought as long and as hard as we could. We ran out of ammunition and they just kept coming."

Burns returned to Washington and engaged in endless conversations with members of Congress, especially House Republicans who were opposed to Ukraine funding. "There's going to be more Avdiivkas unless we come through. It's not an issue of courage and tenacity of Ukrainians. It's the running out of ammunition." That was how wars are lost. "It's not any more complicated than that."

He could see Ukraine running out of ammunition by the end of

April 2024. Throughout the war, the certainty that Uncle Sam had their backs was a source of hope in the trenches. As U.S. support waned so did the morale of Ukrainian soldiers on the front lines.

Burns was convinced if Russia won the war, it would have huge implications not just for Ukraine, not just in Europe but for the entire world.

China was a huge factor, Burns believed. Xi Jinping was watching.

"It's about Xi Jinping's view of the world," Burns said. "He was actually quite sober in the first year of the war in Ukraine. He didn't expect the Ukrainians were going to fight back as hard as they did, that we're going to support them in the way the president did, that our intelligence turned out to be as reliable as it was. So it's getting him to pause a little bit about Taiwan scenarios."

If we're seen to be walking away from the Ukrainians, it's the surest way to stoke Xi's ambition and his confidence and everything else, Burns believed. "So there's a lot at stake in this right now too."

Then he made perhaps his most important point: "If you want to deter Xi, then show we're capable of staying in Ukraine, a war of territorial conquest."

During his confirmation hearings before the Senate in 2021, Burns said, "An adversarial, predatory Chinese leadership poses our biggest geopolitical test."

In his 2019 memoir of his 32 years as a diplomat, *The Back Channel*, Burns wrote it was all about "maneuvering in the gray area between peace and war."

As CIA director he had lived in that gray area to avoid war. But war had come.

SIXTY

P resident Biden faced another war much closer to home, the one at the United States–Mexico border.

"Demonic" is the word Ali Mayorkas privately and angrily used through gritted teeth to describe the Republican attacks on his leadership of the Department of Homeland Security, which oversees the roughly 2,000-mile southwest border of the United States.

As homeland security secretary, at times described as the second toughest job in Washington after the presidency, the 5-foot-8, 64-year-old bald Cuban immigrant was contending with a cascading crisis at the border.

As the 2024 election grew nearer, the border was a visible high-impact political target. News channels showed thousands of migrants piling into caravans, walking along dusty roads across Mexico, and families crossing the Rio Grande on makeshift rafts or climbing through border fencing without much hindrance.

In 2022 and 2023 the number of migrants apprehended at the southern border each year has exceeded two million, a record outpouring of migrants predominantly from Central America. Migrant crossings in a single month had risen from 75,316 in January 2021, which was already a problem when Biden took office, to 249,785 in December 2023.

From his first days as president, Biden revoked Trump's hardline immigration policies, promising instead to transform the U.S. immigration system with a gentler, more humanitarian approach. Biden appointed his vice president, Kamala Harris, to address the "root causes of migration in Central America's northern triangle," a portfolio Biden had responsibility for during his vice presidency.

Some called it an opportunity for Harris, others saw it as Biden handing off a poisoned chalice to his vice president.

Many of Trump's "zero tolerance" policies had been viewed as cruel, including his policy of separating children from their parents at the border, expelling more than 13,000 unaccompanied children, and his ban on Muslims from certain countries entering the United States. Trump's largely unsuccessful effort to build a wall along the border had also been widely assessed as ineffective.

Biden's approach focused on creating legal pathways for people to come to the United States and to citizenship. But as migrants started streaming across the border by the hundreds of thousands, sentiment in the United States quickly started to change and ignited a political firestorm.

Republicans blamed Biden for replacing Trump's DO NOT COME message with a WELCOME TO AMERICA sign. The word "invasion" now appeared in 27 Republican television ads ahead of the November 2024 election.

Biden blamed Republicans for the lack of funding to improve border controls. "Congressional Republicans have refused to consider my comprehensive plan. And they rejected my recent request for an additional $3.5 billion to secure the border and funds for 2,000 asylum personnel and 100 new Immigration judges," he said on January 5, 2023.

And in 2024, Biden blamed Trump for killing his attempt at a bipartisan border deal, which had included the strictest border measures to date. But Trump had opposed the bill as a "gift" to Democrats and Republican Speaker Mike Johnson called that plan "dead on arrival."

"I'm told my predecessor called members in Congress and demanded they block the bill," Biden said in his State of the Union address on March 7, 2024. "He feels it would be a political win for me." Republicans booed in response and ridiculed Biden's "open-border policy" as "weak." The bipartisan bill, negotiated as part of a trade-off with Republicans to get a Ukraine aid supplemental bill approved, would have funded 1,500 more Immigration and Customs personnel and 100 more Immigration judges to help with the backlog of around three million cases.

There had been more than six million illegal crossings at the southern border since Biden took office, one of the greatest levels of human displacement in world history.

Records showed that once someone was in the United States for over a year they were unlikely to be removed.

Trump referred to the people coming across the southern border as "prisoners, murderers, drug dealers, mental patients and terrorists, the worst they have.

"In some cases they're not people, in my opinion," Trump said during a rally in Ohio in March 2024. "These are animals, OK, and we have to stop it."

Biden condemned Trump's rhetoric during his State of the Union. "I will not demonize immigrants saying they 'poison the blood of our country,'" Biden declared. "I will not separate families. I will not ban people from America because of their faith."

But nearly 80 percent of Americans and 73 percent of Democrats said they disapproved of the Biden administration's handling of the large number of migrants at the U.S.-Mexico border. America, home to more immigrants than any other country, was intensely divided on what immigration should look like today.

New York mayor Eric Adams, a Democrat, had repeatedly criticized Biden for the flood of migrants to New York City, which had a record-high homelessness problem and was now also trying to house more than 42,000 migrants.

"The president and the White House have failed New York City on this issue," Adams said. "Allow people to work, which I believe that's one of the Number 1 things we can do."

Sensational video footage also showed the new range of nationalities arriving at the border. Historically migration to the southern border was primarily a regional phenomenon, involving people from Mexico and Central America. Now due in part to a rise in transcontinental human smuggling networks, people were also coming from places much farther away, including China and India.

The reasons for this massive migration influx at the border were numerous. Employment opportunities in the United States were skyrocketing. In Biden's first year 6.7 million jobs were added. No other president since World War II had such job growth in their first or any year in office. Some studies found a strong correlation between the number of job openings in the U.S. and the number of border arrests.

U.S. polls indicated that American voters believed the major pull factors for migrants were good economic opportunities, Biden's more welcoming approach and the threat of violence in migrants' home countries.

Global and regional forces were also contributing, including a rise in authoritarian regimes and gang violence, worsening economic conditions in some countries, greater climate change pressures, including food and water shortages and forced displacement from natural disasters. The rise of social media also showed people how to make the crossing.

"Fundamentally, our system is not equipped to deal with migration as it exists now," Homeland Security Secretary Mayorkas said on NBC News. "We have a system that was last modified in 1996." Congress had not been able to pass comprehensive immigration laws in decades due to political gridlock.

The Republican-led House Committee on Homeland Security had singled out Mayorkas as the villain and voted to impeach him by a single vote 214–213 on Tuesday, February 13, 2024. He was charged with "high crimes and misdemeanors" for "willfully and systematically" refusing to enforce existing immigration laws and a breach of public trust by lying to Congress and saying the border was secure.

He was only the second cabinet officer in U.S. history to be impeached.

An angry House Republican report accompanying the homeland

secretary's impeachment concluded that Mayorkas "has emboldened cartels, criminals and America's enemies."

The House Democrats released a 29-page rebuttal saying: "In
a process akin to throwing spaghetti at the wall and seeing what
sticks, Committee Republicans have cooked up vague, unprecedented grounds to impeach Secretary Mayorkas. The MAGA-led
impeachment is a baseless sham, and the few rational Republicans
left in Congress know that—even if they refuse to admit it."

But spaghetti on the wall can move American politics. It is not
naturally there. And it is ugly.

On January 3, 2024, House Speaker Mike Johnson led 64 Republicans to the southern border port of entry Eagle Pass, Texas,
with maximum hoopla.

"It's been an eye-opener," Johnson said at a news conference
there. "One thing is absolutely clear: America is at a breaking point
with record levels of illegal immigration." He said Biden should reinstate former president Trump's "Remain in Mexico" policy and
restart border wall construction and other provisions to stop illegal
border crossings, which were up 25 percent just in the last month.

Republicans had Biden over a barrel that he had, in part, created for himself by revoking Trump's policies and not replacing
them with an effective, more humanitarian alternative. They had
their spaghetti on the wall for display.

"The system is broken," Mayorkas said. He believed much of
the Republican effort was driven by contempt for immigrants, adding "Hate is its own ammunition."

The Democrat-controlled Senate permanently tabled the impeachment charges against Mayorkas. But the political war over the
border was deadlocked. Biden contended he needed new funding
and legislation, while Speaker Johnson and Republicans said the illegal border crossings could be dramatically cut by presidential and
executive branch action, especially by restoring Trump's policies.

It was inevitable that Trump would weigh in. "As the leader
of our party there is zero chance I will support this horrible open
borders betrayal of America," Trump said to his supporters at a

campaign rally in Las Vegas. "I'll fight it all the way. A lot of the senators are trying to say, respectfully, they're blaming it on me. I say, that's OK. Please blame it on me. Please."

Trump was out of the presidency but his shadow not only lingered over Biden, but absolutely controlled Republicans.

The average American might not fully understand that Trump had influence but Congress did. Trump waved his little finger and the party bowed and obeyed.

The only good day for the Biden White House on immigration was when there was absolutely no immigration news—none, zero. And that was not often.

SIXTY-ONE

"You are at a pivot point in the Ukrainian struggle," I said to President Andrzej Duda of Poland, in a bright, sunlit room of the Polish consulate in New York on April 17, 2024.

I wanted to see whether the populist right-wing president felt vulnerable sharing a 330-mile border with Ukraine. Should Russia take Ukraine, what might it mean for Poland?

Duda, age 52, with short-cropped hair and rimless glasses, has a powerful and expressive confidence. His eyes flash and his hands punctuate each phrase. Duda's nine-year presidency had spanned three American administrations—Obama, Trump and Biden. The Polish leader prided himself on having good relations with all of them, but he was particularly close with Trump.

"My biggest political dream is to make sure that Russia does not win in Ukraine," he said. "This is absolutely the most important thing for the security of my country, Poland, of our part of the world, but also, I believe, for the security of the whole world.

"Ukraine is our neighbor and it is of fundamental importance to us that Ukraine remains a sovereign independent state that does not succumb to Russia," Duda said. "We know what Russian occupation means, we know what Russian terror stands for and we know that Ukrainians *have* to be helped." He leaned forward and tapped the desk in front of him with his index finger for emphasis.

Poland also shares part of its northern border with Kaliningrad, a Russian province, and part of its northeastern border with Belarus. Russia stored nuclear weapons in both places. Did Duda believe his country could be next if Russia took control of Ukraine?

For the 26 months since Russia's invasion of Ukraine, Polish people had lived with war on their doorstep. "You might not feel it in the United States the same way," Duda said.

Polish families brought millions of Ukrainian refugees into their homes and communities. Poland had world leaders flying in and out of their airports and taking the 12-hour train ride to Kyiv. They hosted embassies that could no longer operate in Ukraine as well as weapons facilities to enable huge quantities of military equipment and humanitarian aid, mostly from the United States, through their border to the Ukrainians.

Duda asked me to think about 1939.

During World War II, Hitler and Stalin had made a pact to attack and occupy Poland. Poland was attacked first by Germany on September 1, 1939, and then by Russia on September 17. "We did not get any help," Duda said. Polish people remember that. The Allied powers did not come to aid Poland in 1939.

"We joined NATO in 1999 and for 17 years there were no NATO forces in Poland," Duda added. "That's when I said, okay, good so we are in NATO but there is no NATO in Poland?" His expression was incredulous.

During the Obama administration American troops were stationed in Poland for the first time on a rotational basis but not permanently. The policy was continued by Trump and then Biden.

In early February 2022, just before Russia's invasion, President Biden had sent 1,700 elite U.S. troops to Poland. Another 3,000 U.S. troops from the 82nd Airborne Division later deployed to Europe, including hundreds positioned in Poland in Rzeszów, close to the border with Ukraine, as well as Romania and Germany to bolster the eastern flank. Biden sent Vice President Harris to Warsaw in early March 2022, mere weeks after Putin's invasion, to further signal that the U.S. would not tolerate Russian aggression against NATO eastern flank allies.

Duda said Biden "has 100 percent credibility in relation to the commitments that he made vis-à-vis my country.

"We were not yet attacked and the Americans already sent their troops," he said. In a phone call, Biden had personally reassured Duda that the U.S. had Poland's back.

"We will always protect Poland," Biden told Duda.

"It was of huge importance to me emotionally, personally," Duda said.

A month earlier, on March 11, President Duda published an op-ed in *The Washington Post* that called on NATO countries to raise their defense spending from 2 percent to 3 percent of their GDP.

Poland was now spending 4 percent of its GDP on defense, more than $27 billion annually. The U.S. spent 3.49 percent or $860 billion in 2023. Many NATO members, however, were not meeting the 2 percent target, including France, Spain and Canada.

At a campaign rally in South Carolina in February, former president Trump, a frequent critic of NATO, said he would let Russia attack allies that did not pay their dues.

Trump said a president—who he did not identify—once asked him, "Well, sir, if we don't pay and we're attacked by Russia, will you protect us?"

Trump replied, "No, I would not protect you. In fact, I would encourage them to do whatever the hell they want." His audience cheered.

Duda took a more diplomatic tone in the *Post*. "The Russian Federation has switched its economy to war mode. It is allocating close to 30 percent of its annual budget to arm itself." Because of the growing threats today, Duda argued, the time has come for members to spend more.

Notably, most of the NATO members with the largest defense spending were those on the eastern flank, closest to the war, including Poland, Estonia, Lithuania, Finland, Romania, Hungary and Latvia.

"Russia cannot win this war," Duda said. "This is the most important thing.

"We are dealing with brutal Russian imperialism which is

killing people," he said. "And now these imperial teeth are red with the blood of Georgians, with the blood of Ukrainians." He was referring to Russia's 2008 invasion of Georgia, and the 2014 and 2022 invasions of Ukraine.

"We need to support Ukraine all the time with military technology," Duda said. He believed Russia could not win against the modern weapons in the U.S. and NATO arsenals, but those weapons needed to actually get to Ukrainians on the frontlines.

Ukraine was facing potentially catastrophic ammunition and weapons shortages. The massive $60.8 billion Ukraine aid package had been stalled in the U.S. Congress for almost six months. The Russians were gaining new ground.

Trump was calling leaders "suckers" for sending aid to Ukraine. He vetoed every attempt at an aid package, claiming support for Ukraine was a waste of taxpayer dollars, that Ukraine was corrupt and that Russian victory was inevitable. President Biden was irate that he had to get the package to pass through Mar-a-Lago before it could get through Congress.

President Duda said the Ukrainians desperately needed long-range ammunition and aircraft to be able to repel Russia. The Russians had far more troops at their disposal.

"Ukraine wins whenever it can keep Russians at a distance," he explained. "If there are direct clashes then such direct clashes are usually won unfortunately by the Russians because to Russians, it is not important that 10 Ukrainian soldiers died and 100 Russian soldiers died. For them, it is important that they can win." Russia saw its troops as expendable.

"These are not children from Moscow, from St. Petersburg," Duda said. "These are not families from Russian elites. These people come from distant parts of Siberia, from some distant parts of Russia who are called by Russia and they are sent to die. Their lives do not cost much to Russia."

I asked Duda if he had spoken to President Putin since the war started in February 2022.

"No," he said.

"Why not?"

"You cannot talk to people who murder others and who behave like bandits."

The Polish president had traveled to Ukraine four times to offer support to President Zelensky in Kyiv, including on February 23, 2022, just hours before Russia attacked.

"Never until the end of my life will I forget the moment when we said goodbye to each other," Duda said. "When he told me that we might never see each other again and I told him that we will do absolutely everything to make sure that they survive.

"We as Poland, but also we as NATO, we as the free world, will not leave Ukraine alone," Duda said and pounded the table.

That evening, April 17, former president Trump hosted President Duda for a two-and-a-half-hour steak dinner at Trump's apartment in Trump Tower, a lavish penthouse awash in 24-carat gold that looks out over Central Park and Manhattan. The former American president was staying in New York City while he attended his criminal trial about the cover-up of hush money payments to a porn star.

Duda's impassioned argument to Trump about the importance of continued U.S. support in Ukraine was the same I had heard earlier that day, according to aides.

One aide said, You could not hear the Polish president's "save my country" arguments and not be moved and emotionally gripped by his description of the Russian threat—not just to Ukraine, but to Poland, to Europe, and democracies everywhere.

Trump had asked Duda a lot of questions. What was Russia's intention with Ukraine? If Russia took Ukraine, was wider war likely?

"We are next," Duda told Trump.

———

Over the next several days Trump stayed unusually quiet on criticizing aid to Ukraine and this time did not fire up his base with the
America First arguments.

After the dinner with Duda, Trump said on his social media
site Truth Social: "Ukrainian Survival and Strength should be
much more important to Europe than to us, but it is also important to us!"

Ukraine aid was, for at least a single moment, "important."

President Duda had invited then-President Trump to speak in Warsaw on July 6, 2017, before the monument to the Warsaw Uprising.
Former Polish president Lech Walesa, who led the Solidarity labor
movement that put Poland on the path to freedom from Soviet rule,
attended.

"We have to remember that our defense," Trump said, "is not
just a commitment of money, it is a commitment of will.

"The fundamental question of our time is whether the West has
the will to survive. Poland is in our heart. Just as Poland could not
be broken, I declare today for the world to hear that the West will
never, ever be broken."

The crowd chanted: "Donald Trump! Donald Trump!"

"The best speech of his presidency," Senator Lindsey Graham
said. "Very much like Ronald Reagan."

President Biden, together with Republican Senate Minority Leader
Mitch McConnell of Kentucky and Democrat Senate Majority
Leader Chuck Schumer of New York, had for months been intensely engaged with House Republican Speaker Mike Johnson on
the Ukraine aid package.

Johnson was trying to convince Trump to let the bill through.
Strong national security had traditionally been the spine of the Republican Party, including the belief that America's national security was bound to global security. But the isolationist America First

view, which Trump championed, had driven a wedge between Republicans in Congress. Johnson knew that if Trump gave the green light, Republican resistance in Congress would evaporate.

Biden directed his team to "Lay off targeted attacks against Johnson as much as possible and broadly urge Republicans to act. Stay in close touch with Speaker Johnson."

Biden also called in Director of National Intelligence Avril Haines, CIA director Bill Burns and National Security Adviser Jake Sullivan to secretly brief the House Speaker on the Ukraine intelligence picture and the national security risks of inaction. They provided Johnson with detailed examples of the consequences for Ukraine, Europe and the free world if Ukraine lost the war and Putin marched on.

"If Ukraine does not get aid, it will lose the war with Russia," Sullivan told Johnson. That was the bottom line. President Biden also met with House and Senate leadership to personally push the same message.

Meanwhile, Lindsey Graham, Republican of South Carolina, was also pushing Trump on the Ukraine aid bill to at the very least agree to "leave it alone."

Graham wanted more support for Ukraine, but had himself blocked versions of this Ukraine aid package in the Senate. In April, he pitched to Trump the idea of having part of the aid be in the form of a forgivable loan to Ukraine.

"Mr. President," Graham said, "Ukraine's a good investment. Maybe they can pay us back but you'll never regret helping them.

"You know the last guy that did this wound up getting the world in a big war," Graham said, reminding Trump of Hitler in World War II.

"Putin's not going to stop. He'll go to Moldova. He'll keep going. He's getting stronger not weaker," Graham said. "Mr. President, this guy will not stop. If he gets rewarded for this you can expect more of it. And Taiwan will go as sure as I'm sitting here."

Trump said he believed that. "Weakness breeds aggression."

The former president told Graham he was "okay with a loan" and "okay with" Speaker Johnson working on a bill that turned some of the aid into a forgivable, no-interest loan.

After multiple conversations with Trump, Johnson told his close aides that it was clear to him that the former president did not see value in funding Ukraine. Trump ultimately changed his tune after Johnson convinced him that the aid package was important to keep unity among the House GOP conference and Trump. "It's beneficial for all," Johnson argued. Trump saw the benefit to himself and lifted his veto.

On Saturday, April 21, the U.S. House of Representatives voted overwhelmingly 312 to 112 to provide an unprecedented $60.8 billion in aid to Ukraine as part of a $95.3 billion foreign aid bill. Of the $60.8 billion aid to Ukraine, $10 billion took the form of a forgivable loan.

As the House voted, Republican Senate Minority Leader Mitch McConnell, age 82, said in a television interview, "it is one of the biggest days in the time that I've been here." McConnell had been in the Senate for 39 years.

"At least on this episode, I think we turned the tables on the isolationists," McConnell said, referring to the America First wing of his party.

The bill then passed the Senate in a 79–18 vote on April 23. "Tonight, a bipartisan majority in the Senate joined the House to answer history's call at this critical inflection point," President Biden said.

Biden signed the bill the next day. "In the next few hours we're going to begin sending in equipment to Ukraine, for air defense munitions, for artillery, for rocket systems and armored vehicles," Biden said. Zelensky confirmed on social media that the package also contained much needed longer-range ATACMS missiles.

If it wasn't already too late for Ukraine, it appeared this could be a turning point.

SIXTY-TWO

◆ ◆

The Israelis were still planning a large-scale military operation in Rafah. Biden warned Netanyahu to carefully consider Israel's next move.

"What happened the last two weeks is a game changer," Biden said in a private, secure phone call. "We just helped defend you with Saudi Arabia, Jordan and a Western alliance. What you do next will determine whether you nurture this alliance or whether you just fritter it away."

The Saudis had just seen a U.S. military alliance take down 100 ballistic missiles. They are eager to get back to talking about a deal with Israel.

If Israel charged into Rafah, Netanyahu risked all the progress already made.

"You're going to see the whole thing reverse," Biden told Netanyahu. "There's a risk of a break with us. Saudi Arabia won't touch it. There's a risk of a break with Egypt."

For weeks, Jake Sullivan had been pressing the same message with Ron Dermer and Israeli national security adviser Tzachi Hanegbi. "Going into Rafah will be a bloody mess," Sullivan said on one video call.

"We've got to go into Rafah," Dermer insisted. "It will only take three weeks."

"Bullshit," Sullivan said, always skeptical and disbelieving of Israel's optimistic projections.

Sullivan urged Dermer and Hanegbi to slow down, focus on fixing the humanitarian situation and getting a hostage deal. Work with Egypt to control the border with Rafah, go after the

Hamas leaders like Sinwar, and put off a ground offensive into Rafah.

We'll think about it, Dermer said.

CIA director Bill Burns and Brett McGurk were pushing Qatar's foreign minister MBAR for proof of life of one of the four Israeli-American hostages still held by Hamas.

On April 22, Hamas sent a video to the White House of Hersh Goldberg-Polin, a 24-year-old who had been at the music festival with friends during the October 7 Hamas attack. He had tried to hide but someone from Hamas threw a grenade at him. Hersh picked it up to throw it back and it had blown off part of his left arm.

McGurk watched the video of Goldberg-Polin, a rare, emotional glimpse of life in the tunnels. The young man was seated in a chair against a white wall. "Hello, Mom and Dad. I'm here in Gaza almost 200 days. I love you and I am thinking about you every day. I want you to know that I'm okay, I'm alive, but it's not easy here. I think about you every day and I want to return home as fast as I can. I'm thinking about you now before the holiday. I hope, I hope, I hope and I know that you're doing everything you guys can to bring me home as fast as possible. I miss you and I want to see you soon. Love you."

Hamas later publicly posted the video. MBAR said this was a sign there was still a chance to get the hostages out.

Two days later, on April 24, President Biden hosted Abigail Edan, a four-year-old girl who was held hostage by Hamas for 50 days.

Hamas militants had entered her family's home on October 7 and shot and killed her mother and father in front of her. Her older siblings, aged six and 10, had locked themselves inside a cupboard upstairs and hid for 14 hours. Abigail's father had been shot while shielding Abigail, who crawled out from under his body and went to a neighbor's house. Later that day Hamas took her hostage with that family of five.

Now Abigail crawled around the Resolute Desk, playing with her sister and brother in the Oval Office. The three children were now living with their aunt and uncle in Tel Aviv. Biden gave the family a tour.

Out on the White House lawn, Brett McGurk was pushing the four-year-old Abigail on a swing.

SIXTY-THREE

"I think it is very hard to argue that he has not been weak-ened," Director of National Intelligence Avril Haines re-ported about Russia's president Putin in May 2024. "That does not make him less dangerous."

Haines, age 54, the first woman to serve as America's top spy overseeing all U.S. intelligence agencies, warned that no one should be complacent about Russia.

"Hundreds of billions of dollars spent in this war," Haines said, "more casualties than we've seen since World War II, over 300,000."

"We've set back their ground forces by years," Haines said. The Ukrainian forces "through sheer blood and guts," backed by the U.S. and European countries, had forced Putin to place Russia's economy on a war footing and redouble investment in their defense industry.

"It's incredible to our military analysts what he's willing to lose in terms of people and equipment on the front lines for what he gains in territory."

Before Russia's invasion, Putin had argued for a long time that overspending on defense was one of the great mistakes of the Soviet Union. It had destroyed Russia's economy.

"Now he's basically making that same move," Haines said with bewilderment. "It is pretty extraordinary to watch.

"And while they're managing better than we thought with respect to sanctions," Haines noted, "there are critical fractures in their economy."

According to Daleep Singh, deputy national security adviser for international economics, who was the architect of many of the sanctions against Russia, the real squeeze was still to come. "Nose-bleed inflation and interest rates will inevitably choke off Russia's growth," Singh said. "Less capital, less technology and less talent implies a smaller, weaker, less productive Russian economy for a generation to come."

Putin was also having to source weapons and munitions from other countries, like China, North Korea and Iran, to resupply his front lines.

"They're trying to reconstitute," Haines said, "a lot of what we do is tracking all of that, trying to identify key opportunities to block."

This was the shadow war of economics, technology and intelligence, where the United States could directly confront and weaken Russia with far less risk of catastrophic miscalculation.

And yet, it was not without peril.

"Between the United States and Russia, we have over 90 percent of the world's nuclear weapons," Haines said. "You do not want a country that has got that kind of a stockpile of nuclear weapons to feel as if it's slipping.

"As you push states that have stockpiles to the brink, you raise the risk that they end up using it," Haines said.

This was at the core of the dilemma President Biden and his principals faced in the Ukraine War. The more mistakes Russia made, the more Putin overreached. The more the war cost Russia's economy, its military, the more Putin appeared willing to sacrifice.

President Biden had told his advisers: "Never put a man in a corner where his only way out is through you. You've got to give him another way out."

But Putin had climbed so far up the tree in pursuit of his vision to be the modern czar, the savior of Russia as a great power, it was very difficult to see how he could climb down.

"He can be weaker and at the same time even more dangerous as a result of the fact he has less to lose," Haines warned.

Putin's autobiography, *First Person*, dictated to three Russian journalists in 2000, is an authoritative look inside the Russian president's mind. "I think that there are always a lot of mistakes made in war," Putin told the journalists. "That's inevitable. But when you are fighting, if you keep thinking that everybody around you is always making mistakes, you'll never win. You have to take a pragmatic attitude. And you have to keep thinking of victory.

"A dog senses when somebody is afraid of it, and bites. The same applies here. If you become jittery, they will think that they are stronger. Only one thing works in such circumstances—to go on the offensive. You must hit first, and hit so hard that your opponent will not rise to his feet."

SIXTY-FOUR

"T hey tell me if I get convicted, it'll be even better for me in the election," Trump said on the phone to his former lawyer Tim Parlatore in the midst of his hush money trial in New York.

"But Tim," Trump said, "I don't want to get convicted."

Trump had been criminally charged with 34 counts of falsifying business records to conceal a hush money payment to adult-film star Stormy Daniels ahead of the 2016 presidential election. The trial had begun on April 15, 2024.

Parlatore, who had represented Trump for over a year on the Justice Department's January 6 and Mar-a-Lago documents investigations, believed Trump's campaign was now driving decision-making in the Manhattan courtroom. It was one of the reasons he had quit being Trump's attorney back in May 2023. Parlatore had no problems with Trump.

"The reason I left him was because he surrounds himself with the wrong people," Parlatore said, those who cared more about the 24/7 news cycle than the best interests of their client.

Trump's comment grated at Parlatore. This trial was a case in point, he thought.

"Hush money payments to Stormy Daniels in and of itself is not illegal," Parlatore explained to Trump. "It's unseemly but it's not illegal.

"Your problem here is that Michael Cohen doesn't know how to run an invoice," Parlatore said. "There's no law that says how specific the line items on an invoice should be as long as they are sufficient for you to understand what you're paying for."

Michael Cohen was Trump's former fixer and a key witness against Trump in the trial.

"Let me tell you how a real lawyer would have invoiced you," Parlatore said.

"I could have written on it: $130,000 expense reimbursement, $20,000 expense reimbursement, $30,000 fee, and your entire invoice would have been $180,000. Nobody could have claimed it was a false business record and you wouldn't be going through any of this.

"There's no business falsification with that," Parlatore said. "That's an accurate invoice."

"Are you fucking kidding me?" Trump said furiously. "I could have paid $180,000 instead of $420,000?"

Yes, Mr. President, Parlatore said. "I can put fees and expenses on the same invoice and the way that my accountant handles that is the fees are considered income, the expense reimbursements are not."

"Holy shit," Trump said.

On May 30, 2024, Trump was convicted by a unanimous jury in Manhattan of all 34 counts of falsification of business records, becoming the first former U.S. president to be a convicted felon.

Trump and his campaign immediately attacked the trial, Judge Merchan, President Biden and Democrats.

"This was a rigged, disgraceful trial," Trump declared after leaving the courtroom. "The real verdict is going to be November 5 by the people."

Parlatore waved off the rhetoric. He had firsthand experience with New York State Judge Juan Merchan and thought he did an excellent job presiding over Trump's trial.

The former president's problem was not the legal system, Parlatore believed, it was poor decisions during lawyer selection.

"It's more politically advantageous to say, Oh, this is all Alvin Bragg and the DNC and, you know, this is Biden and all that kind of stuff, than to look inward and say, I got convicted because I hired the wrong lawyers," Parlatore said. Alvin Bragg was the New York district attorney who prosecuted the case against Trump.

Parlatore pointed to Todd Blanche, Trump's lawyer in the criminal case, who following the verdict said publicly that they had "expected" a conviction. "It's clear to me he had no plan to win," Parlatore said.

In the 24 hours after the verdict, Trump's conviction raised more than $50 million for his presidential campaign.

"I'm a very innocent man," Trump said in a statement, "and, it's okay, I'm fighting for our country. I'm fighting for our Constitution. Our whole country is being rigged right now."

SIXTY-FIVE

"They're trying to destroy a presidency," Hunter Biden said in a December 2023 interview about Republican efforts to obsessively go after him, retelling and re-hyping his struggle with alcohol and crack-cocaine addiction. "They're trying to kill me knowing it will be a pain greater than my father could be able to handle."

According to one of President Biden's closest associates the Republican attacks on Hunter were "eating the president alive with anguish." He called to check in with Hunter almost every day.

"Hey, son. How you doing, buddy?" President Biden asked him on one such call. "Are you hanging in there? Are you doing okay?"

Hunter Biden, 54, was at the center of two high-visibility criminal trials over the summer and fall of 2024. Hunter had pleaded not guilty to criminal charges of lying about his drug use when he purchased and possessed a firearm, a violation of federal law. His trial began in Delaware in June. A second trial involving tax charges was scheduled for September, a month before the election.

The bond between Hunter and his father was real and lasting, another close associate said. The president had lost his first wife and daughter to a car accident, and later lost his elder son, Beau, to a brain tumor. The Republicans' relentless public campaign against Hunter was often having a more profound impact on the president than political and policy issues.

"I think Joe's biggest worry and I would say Jill's biggest worry isn't just the criminal indictments or the laptop ridiculousness or the hearings from the oversight committee, I think it's trying to make sure that [Hunter's] mental health and his physical health stays to a point where he can actually move forward in his life when this is all over.

"Hunter feels like he is trapped," the friend said of Hunter's struggle to escape his past, like there was no path back to a stable life. "He's literally fucked. And I think he sort of knows it."

President Biden privately voiced fury at his attorney general, Merrick Garland, who had appointed a special counsel to investigate Hunter. "Should never have picked Garland," President Biden told an associate. But his inner circle had pushed hard for Garland's appointment.

President Biden had pledged publicly to keep his hands off the Justice Department's investigation of Hunter. On occasion, he checked in with Hunter's lawyer, Abbe Lowell, and thanked him for representing his son.

"Let me talk to Abbe," Biden said to Hunter, taking his phone to speak to Lowell in December 2022. "I love what you are doing. Keep doing it. Keep doing it."

Tensions were rife between the White House lawyers and Hunter's legal team. The White House lawyers wanted Hunter to stay quiet and keep his head down publicly. Let the adjudication happen in court.

"His dad's communications team want Hunter just to go away," an associate said.

Hunter was focused on "surviving."

"Right now he is absolutely committed to not only never again falling to his addictions, but he wants a normal life and I think that's why he's fighting so hard," the associate said about the trials.

In his memoir, *Beautiful Things,* Hunter recounts the story of his addiction with crack cocaine—the highs and lows, the chaos, temptation and depravity.

"Cooking crack took practice but it wasn't rocket science," Hunter said in chapter seven, entitled "Cracked."

"I experienced what's called a 'bell ringer'—crack's holy grail. The sensation is one of utter, almost otherworldly well-being.

"I chased that high, on and off, for the next three years," he said, 2017 to 2020.

Hunter and his wife, Melissa Cohen, had a young son, Beau

Biden Jr., who they called "Beauie" for short, named after Hunter's late brother, Beau.

President Biden, guilt-ridden over the constant years-long Republican attacks on Hunter, told his close associate, "That's all on me. None of this would be happening to Hunter if I weren't president.

"This is never going to fucking go away," Biden complained.

Hunter was convicted on all three federal felony gun charges on June 11, 2024.

President Biden said, "I will accept the outcome of this case and will continue to respect the judicial process as Hunter considers an appeal," setting himself apart from Trump.

"Jill and I will always be there for Hunter and the rest of our family with love and support. Nothing will ever change that."

SIXTY-SIX

◆ ◆

Secrets always exist. And often the secrets have immense weight especially in human relations. What do the main characters really think of each other? What is going on behind the scenes that others might not notice nor imagine? What might be the driving forces that are not articulated or visible?

President Biden's frustrations and distrust of Israeli prime minister Netanyahu had been building for years and in the spring of 2024 finally erupted.

"That son of a bitch, Bibi Netanyahu, he's a bad guy. He's a bad fucking guy!" President Biden declared privately to one of his closest associates. "A bad fucking guy!

"He doesn't give a shit about Hamas. He gives a shit only about himself."

The president was preoccupied with bitterness and distrust of Netanyahu, who he said had been lying to him regularly.

Netanyahu was destroying the entire region of Gaza, pounding one of the most densely populated places on earth with an estimated 45,000 bombs. Almost half, 47 percent, of Gaza's population of 2.2 million were children under the age of 18. Hundreds of the bombs dropped on Gaza had been the massive 2,000-pounders. The carnage resembled some of the worst bombing during World War II.

Netanyahu was continuing to say he was going to kill every last member of Hamas.

Biden had told him that was impossible, threatening both privately and publicly to withhold offensive U.S. weapons shipments to Israel.

Netanyahu promised Biden that Israel would change strategy and pursue Hamas with more carefully targeted and sophisticated operations. They would replicate the more systematic and patient year-long hunt to eliminate the Black September Palestinian militants who killed 11 Israeli Olympic team members in Munich 1972.

No more battalions going in firing rockets and artillery without strategy, no more dropping huge bombs on urban areas. But Netanyahu continued to issue precisely those orders.

Before October 7, Netanyahu's political leadership was in tatters. He faced criminal charges of fraud and bribery that had been delayed multiple times, and he was widely criticized for pushing legal and judicial reforms that weakened the independence of Israel's judiciary. Netanyahu was close to being ousted as prime minister.

But after the large-scale October 7 Hamas attack on his watch, Netanyahu pushed aside questions of Israel's catastrophic intelligence and security failures and resurrected himself as a strong wartime leader. Israel had rallied around their prime minister. Ongoing war shielded Netanyahu.

President Biden told a friend that Netanyahu was now working hard to save himself politically and stay out of jail.

Biden was amazed that Bibi's leadership had lasted.

"Why hasn't there been an internal revolt?" Biden said. "A strong internal revolt about just voting Bibi out of office somehow, someway! Just get him out of there!"

President Biden complained bitterly that Netanyahu had spent no time on a plan for Gaza and the region after the war ends. He knew this because of multiple secure calls with Netanyahu and several meetings Blinken had reported back on over the last six months.

The White House would issue brief readouts of the Biden-Netanyahu phone calls to the media suggesting they were fruitful, cordial and productive.

"I think he is somebody that believes that he is, first of all, the savior for Israel," DNI Avril Haines said about Netanyahu. "Secondly, he does not want to lose his legacy on what he's done thus far and does not want to be remembered as the prime minister for October 7.

"His politics are definitely, in my view, factoring into his decision-making at this point," Haines reported.

Biden had pushed Netanyahu in the immediate aftermath of October 7 not to conduct a ground invasion into Gaza. Israel plowed ahead anyway. Biden pressured Netanyahu to allow sustained humanitarian aid into Gaza, but Israel's military blitz made delivering the aid almost impossible.

The humanitarian catastrophe continued to escalate in Gaza.

Secretary of State Blinken had been working almost 24/7 for months. He was exhausted, emotionally and physically drained by Netanyahu's dealings and maneuvering.

Biden warned Netanyahu not to conduct a military offensive into Rafah. Netanyahu delayed, debated, produced a plan to move civilians out of harm's way. But, ultimately, Netanyahu sent Israel's military in.

"He's a fucking liar," Biden said privately of Netanyahu. "Eighteen out of 19 people who work for him are fucking liars."

Biden believed if he were to firmly and publicly break with Netanyahu, it would risk Israel's security—something he was not prepared to do after October 7. Iran and Hezbollah were watching.

Netanyahu expanded Israel's military assault, and in late May was forced to apologize after a ground attack in the south near the heavily populated Rafah Crossing killed dozens of civilians in tent camps. He called it a "tragic accident." U.S.-made munitions were used by Israel in the deadly strike. Israel had designated the area as a safe zone. By the end of May 2024, at least 35,000 people had been killed in Gaza.

Benny Gantz, a key official in the war cabinet and Netanyahu's top political rival, resigned from Israel's emergency government on June 9, leaving the prime minister more dependent on far-right members of his coalition.

"Unfortunately, Mr. Netanyahu is preventing us from achieving true victory, which is the justification for the painful ongoing crisis," Gantz said. He called on Netanyahu to set a date for Israel's elections. Polling showed that Gantz would beat Netanyahu.

The October 7 Hamas attack on Israel was "the most colossal intelligence and operational failure in the history of the state of Israel," Sullivan said. "Israeli intelligence should have known about it. Even if they didn't know about it before it happened, they should have stopped it. It was not the Wehrmacht," he added, referring to the German armed forces. "It was a couple thousand guys in tennis shoes coming across open land." The war in Gaza had done very little to rebuild the reputation of the Israeli Defense Forces.

In June, Israel's military rescued four more hostages held by Hamas in Gaza, but killed at least 274 Palestinians in the rescue operation. Hundreds more were wounded. Israel blamed Hamas for surrounding the hostages with civilians in Nuseirat, a densely populated refugee camp.

President Biden had successfully deterred wider Middle East war, for now, but failed to rein in Israel's government to prevent a humanitarian catastrophe in Gaza. He would not alter U.S. policy toward Israel and continued to provide billions of dollars in military aid to Netanyahu.

Biden was walking a rapidly fraying tightrope with Israel.

SIXTY-SEVEN

◆ ◆

In the political war for the presidency, violence was also a top concern for many Americans in the lead-up to the 2024 election.

"If there's a terrorist attack on the homeland, game, set, match for Biden," Senator Lindsey Graham told others with worry. Trump wins.

"That's a real vulnerability. We all remember 9/11. Biden has got problems at the border. He's got a world that's very fragile that can spill over and hurt us here at home."

Trump was using the southern border crisis as the centerpiece of his fear campaign. "A lot of people coming in from Iran, a lot of people coming from China, a lot of people coming from Russia. It's interesting," Trump said at a rally in South Carolina on February 10, 2024. "They're almost all men, 18 to 25. That means fighting age. That's fighting age. So they have something planned and we're not going to stand for it. They are destroying our country, this group of fascists," Trump said referring to the Biden administration. "They're destroying our country."

"Trump is becoming more erratic," Graham observed. "These court cases. I think they would rattle anybody."

Trump's language was becoming more violent and aggressive, pledging payback against those investigating and prosecuting him like Alvin Bragg and Jack Smith, and former officials who spoke out against him.

It was shaping up to be one of the most perilous, unpredictable runs to an election in American history.

"Biden has lost control of his fate," Graham said. "His fate is sort of in the hands of fate. A single event could change the election.

"It's the strangest election cycle I've ever seen," Graham added. "But what I'm telling people. You're worried about November, I'm worried about tomorrow morning. I'm worried about getting hit."

◆ ◆

SIXTY-EIGHT

"You're Number One on our target list," a man sneered, putting his face several inches from former Chairman of the Joint Chiefs General Mark Milley, at a public event in the spring of 2024.

"I don't have time for this," Milley replied and walked away.

This was not the first threat he had received nor would it be the last. Milley had retired as chairman of the Joint Chiefs at the end of September 2023. Media coverage had recognized Milley's efforts to protect the constitutional order of the United States during Trump's final year in office.

Incensed by the coverage, former president Trump cited a backchannel phone call Milley had made to General Li Zuocheng, his Chinese counterpart, two days after the January 6 insurrection at the Capitol. I reported on this call in my book *Peril*, with Robert Costa.

"Things may look unsteady," Milley said, reassuring General Li that the U.S. was stable and not collapsing. "We are 100 percent steady. Everything's fine."

Milley also testified under oath to Congress that the call was to assure the Chinese, "We are not going to attack you." And reinforce stability in a moment of extraordinary instability in the United States.

But Trump referred to Milley's call as "an act so egregious that, in times gone by, the punishment would have been DEATH! A war between China and the United States could have been the result of this treasonous act."

———

Since retiring, Milley had received a nonstop barrage of death threats that he, at least in part, attributed to Trump's repeated, aggressive attempts to discredit him.

"He is inciting people to violence with violent rhetoric," Milley told his wife. "But he does it in such a way it's through the power of suggestion, which is exactly what he did on the 6th of January."

As a former chairman, Milley was provided round-the-clock government security for two years. But he had taken additional precautions at significant personal expense installing bullet-proof glass and blast-proof curtains at his home.

"I will order them back to active duty and then I will court-martial them!" Trump yelled in the Oval Office back in 2020, the last year of his presidency.

Then–Chairman of the Joint Chiefs Mark Milley and Secretary of Defense Mark Esper had been in the Oval Office and looked at President Trump in shock.

Two retired four-star military officers were making searing personal criticisms of Trump in the press. Trump was outraged.

"So disloyal!" he shouted.

The first retired officer making the comments was Navy Admiral William McRaven, who was the U.S. Special Operations commander who oversaw the raid that killed Al Qaeda leader Osama bin Laden a decade earlier. In an op-ed in *The Washington Post* in February 2020, McRaven said:

"As Americans, we should be frightened—deeply afraid for the future of the nation. When good men and women can't speak the truth, when facts are inconvenient, when integrity and character no longer matter, when presidential ego and self-preservation are more important than national security—then there is nothing left to stop the triumph of evil."

In an earlier piece published in *The New York Times,* McRaven said: "It is time for a new person in the Oval Office—Republican,

Democrat, independent—the sooner, the better. The fate of our Republic depends on it."

The second high-profile Trump critic was retired General Stanley McChrystal, who had commanded U.S. and NATO forces in Afghanistan a decade earlier. McChrystal had recently appeared on CNN and called Trump "immoral" and "dishonest."

Trump was furious.

Here were four-star ghosts from the distant past who had served under both Republican and Democrat presidents, re-emerging to hammer Trump.

Trump never liked to leave criticism unanswered. He wanted payback.

As commander in chief, Trump had extraordinary power over retired commissioned officers. It was within his authority to recall them to active duty and court-martial them. But it had only been done a few times in American history and for very serious crimes. For instance, when a retired two-star was charged in 2017 with six counts of raping a minor while on active duty in the 1980s.

Milley and Esper advised Trump not to pursue that route. Taking such aggressive action against distinguished officers would backfire on him. McRaven and McChrystal, by tradition and by law, had a right to voice their opinion. Recalling them would be historically unprecedented and only draw attention to their comments about Trump.

The president didn't want to hear it.

"Mr. President," Milley said, "I'm the senior military officer responsible for the good order and discipline of general officers and I'll take care of this."

Trump's head whipped round. "You really will?" he asked skeptically.

"Absolutely," Milley assured him.

"Okay, you take care of it," President Trump said.

Milley then personally called McRaven and McChrystal and warned them what Trump was talking about doing. It was time for them to step off the public stage.

"Dial it back," Milley said. If Trump actually used his authority to recall them to duty, there was little Milley could do.

In June 2024, Milley was concerned that if re-elected Trump could try again, this time to recall him and other retired commissioned officers to court-martial them for disloyalty.

"He is a walking, talking advertisement of what he's going to try to do," Milley warned former colleagues. "He's saying it and it's not just him, it's the people around him."

"We're gonna hold him accountable," Steve Bannon, the outspoken Trump loyalist and former chief strategist, said about Milley on his podcast, *War Room*. Bannon, who had been convicted of contempt of Congress for defying subpoenas from the House January 6th Committee, was about to begin a four-month prison sentence.

During his final year as president, Trump had also been eager on several occasions to use the military against American people, including in the summer of 2020 to quash Black Lives Matter protests.

"Can't you just shoot them?" President Trump asked Defense Secretary Esper on June 1, 2020, about the protesters in Washington, D.C. "Just shoot them in the legs or something?"

"We're going to send in the troops," Trump told me fervently during a phone interview on June 3, 2020. Trump appeared disinterested in engaging with the substance of the protests—the brutal murder of a Black man by a police officer. He was preoccupied with the idea that the protesters were making him and his administration look weak.

In another interview with Trump in June 2020, I said, "We share one thing in common. We're white, privileged—my father was a lawyer and a judge in Illinois. And we know what your Dad did.

"Do you have any sense that that privilege has isolated and put you in a cave, to a certain extent," I asked him, "as it put me—and I think lots of white, privileged people—in a cave? And that we have to work our way out of it to understand the anger and the pain, particularly, Black people feel in this country?"

"No," Trump answered sharply. "You really drank the Kool-Aid, didn't you? Just listen to you. Wow. No, I don't feel that at all."

"You don't?" I asked.

"I've done more for the Black community than any president in history with the possible exception of Lincoln," he declared.

Milley and Esper only narrowly dissuaded Trump from ordering 10,000 active-duty troops into the nation's capital that summer.

Esper explained to Trump the challenges involved, the logistics of getting elite forces to deploy to Washington. It would take time. It was not a simple order.

"I want you to be in charge of this, General," Trump said, turning instead to Milley.

Milley threw his hands up in a "don't shoot" manner. "I'm an adviser, Mr. President. I don't command troops," he said.

Enraged, Trump stood up and yelled that no one would help him.

"We look weak," Trump shouted at them. "You are losers! You are all fucking losers!"

"We seemed on the verge of crossing a dark red line," Esper wrote in his memoir, A Sacred Oath. "We had walked up to these thresholds in the past, but never one this important, and never with such rage.

"What would happen, I wondered, if we were all gone?" He was referring to the officials in Trump's cabinet who had repeatedly pulled Trump back from foolish or dangerous decisions, including using the American military against American citizens.

For Milley and Esper, Trump's final year in office had demanded a full-time effort to keep the U.S. military out of domestic law enforcement matters.

On the campaign trail in 2024, Trump and his advisers were already promoting the ways he might use military force within the United States if re-elected.

For instance, Trump's proposed solution to the immigration crisis was to carry out "the largest domestic deportation operation in American history."

"If I thought things were getting out of control, I would have no problem using the military," Trump said during an interview with *Time* magazine in April 2024. "We have to have law and order in our country.

"These aren't civilians. These are people that aren't legally in our country. This is an invasion of our country.

"You have to do what you have to do," he said.

Trump's speechwriter and immigration policy adviser, Stephen Miller, had talked about building large camps to hold migrants as they waited for deportation.

"Use the military to round up, put in camps, and deport more than 11 million undocumented immigrants," said Tom Homan, Trump's former acting head of Immigration and Customs Enforcement.

The violent language was a reminder of the internment camps set up for Japanese Americans during World War II, known as "relocation centers."

Esper warned that President Trump had also brought the United States to "the brink" of war many times.

"The president or some of his top White House aides proposed to take some type of military action in or against other nations on multiple occasions during the nearly eighteen months I served as secretary of defense," Esper said in his memoir.

President Biden has had one secretary of defense—Lloyd Austin. Trump went through five by the time he departed the White House in January 2021.

Former secretary of defense James Mattis had been so worried that Trump would have a nuclear war with North Korea during his watch that he had slept in gym clothes. Ready in an emergency to join a secure call, a National Event Conference, to deal with the threat. If North Korea launched an ICBM, Trump had delegated the authority to the secretary of defense to shoot down a missile that threatened the United States.

"If he shoots, he shoots," Trump told me during an interview about North Korean leader Kim Jong Un.

This cavalier attitude about nuclear weapons and impulsive, combative diplomacy terrified Trump's national security advisers.

Mattis privately went to the National Cathedral in Washington to pray and prepare himself for the possibility of having to use nuclear weapons against North Korea to defend the United States.

Based on my reporting, Trump's language and conduct has at times presented risks to national security—both during his presidency and afterward. Many of Trump's former top cabinet officers and aides have said publicly that Trump should not be president again and should not even be on the ballot.

Those include: former vice president Mike Pence; former secretary of defense Mark Esper; former chairman of the Joint Chiefs General Mark Milley; former national security adviser John Bolton; former secretary of defense James Mattis; former director of national intelligence Dan Coats; former chief of staff John Kelly; former chief of staff Mick Mulvaney; and former secretary of state Rex Tillerson.

SIXTY-NINE

By June 2024, the biggest risk to President Biden's legacy, and for the country, was his decision to continue running for another term at age 81. If he won in November and served the four years, he would leave the White House at age 86. Biden was already showing signs of decline. During the workday he could be a commanding president. Outside of that, especially in the evening, he was increasingly muddled.

"He's exhausted half the time," one of the president's friends who kept in touch with Biden told me in late December 2023. "That's obvious in his voice."

Biden's isolation wasn't helping, the friend said. "The isolation of the office itself, he doesn't have the opportunity to talk to people who he's been with in the Senate and in politics for 40 years. They no longer get to see him as much."

Historians and presidents themselves have written extensively about the loneliness of the presidency. The concentration of power and responsibility on the president's shoulders is so great that no aide, cabinet or family member can truly share in the entire experience.

One of Biden's closest associates received a call from Vice President Kamala Harris in 2023.

"Madame Vice President, how are you?"

"I'm fine," the vice president said. "I'm calling to ask you—to really beg you actually—could you please talk to the president more than you talk to him? Your president really loves you. You should talk to him more often than you do."

The Biden associate was candid with the vice president. Look, one of the biggest reasons that Biden calls me, the associate said, is I provide him a level of comfort to the point where he can swear freely about "what a fucking asshole Joe Manchin is." Manchin is the conservative West Virginia Democratic turned Independent senator who had caused Biden problems on important legislation.

The vice president laughed. "That might be the only reason that he still really is comfortable with me to a point," Harris said, "because he knows that I'm the only person around who knows how to properly pronounce the word *motherfucker*."

Former special counsel Robert Hur, who investigated whether Biden mishandled classified documents after his vice presidency, released a public report of his findings in February 2024. Hur labeled Biden "a sympathetic, well-meaning, elderly man with a poor memory." He noted that Biden had "significant" memory problems during five hours of interviews conducted over two days, on October 8 and 9, in the midst of the Israel crisis.

A transcript of Biden's interview with Hur showed that Biden asked:

"When did I announce for president?"

"When did I stop being vice president?"

"In 2009, am I still vice president?"

A sympathetic reading of the full transcript paints a picture of Biden's uncertainty as more reasonable.

Twice Biden struggled to recall the words for "fax machine."

"You see where there's a printer and there's a—what do you call it, the machine that . . ." Biden said. The White House counsel prompted "fax machine" in both instances.

Hur listed among his reasons for not pursuing prosecution that, "it would be difficult to convince a jury that they should convict him—by then a former president well into his eighties—of a serious felony that requires a mental state of willfulness."

Biden was furious.

"I'm well-meaning and I'm an elderly man and I know what the hell I'm doing!" he declared to reporters after the Justice

Department released the Hur report. During the same evening news conference at the White House on February 8, 2024, Biden was asked about the humanitarian situation in Gaza and mistakenly referred to President Sisi of Egypt as the "president of Mexico," mere moments after defending his memory as "fine."

In late February, Dr. Kevin O'Connor of Walter Reed National Military Medical Center, who had been Biden's primary care physician since 2009, examined Biden with a neurologist, two orthopedists and a physical therapist. He concluded that Biden was "fit for duty."

Dr. O'Connor noted in his public report that Biden had "significant spinal arthritis, mild post-fracture foot arthritis and a mild sensory peripheral neuropathy of the feet," that contributed to the rigid way he walked. Biden had sustained small fractures in his foot while playing with his German shepherd back in November 2020.

The president also had discomfort in his left hip, which his doctor said was certainly contributing to his stiffened gait. Biden was undergoing physical therapy. He continued to exercise and stretch four to five times a week.

Dr. O'Connor also said: "An extremely detailed neurologic exam was again reassuring in that there were no findings which would be consistent with any cerebellar or other central neurological disorder, such as stroke, multiple sclerosis, Parkinson's or ascending lateral sclerosis. The exam did again support a mild peripheral neuropathy in both feet. He did not demonstrate any motor weakness, but a subtle difference in heat/cold sensation could be elicited."

But just watching Biden on television caused other experienced doctors to say that the president could be showing early symptoms of Parkinson's disease, which develops slowly over several years. The lack of facial expressions, weak voice and slow, mechanical gestures *can be* early indicators.

President Biden's State of the Union address in March 2024, widely considered one of the most forceful speeches of his time in public office, momentarily dampened speculation about his age and cognitive ability. He parried with Republican hecklers, including Representative Marjorie Taylor Greene, over immigration and called on former president Trump to stop blocking the bipartisan immigration bill. "If my predecessor is watching, instead of playing politics and pressuring members of Congress to block the bill, join me in telling the Congress to pass it," Biden said. "We can do it together." Republican representative James Lankford had mouthed "he's right."

Watching Biden's other interviews and press conferences with professional TV anchors and without a teleprompter, however, could be like experiencing a painful dental extraction as he labored through tediously drawn out points. The weakness in his voice made him appear especially old.

At a Silicon Valley fundraiser on May 10, 2024, attended by about 30 people, guests complained privately afterward that it was "weird" that Biden used a teleprompter at such a small event.

A Hollywood studios CEO went to see President Biden and offered him some frank advice.

"You're fucking up your campaign," the CEO said to the president. "Every time you get out and walk, people think 'old.' Don't put yourself in a position where you're filmed walking."

The president could hardly avoid walking in front of cameras. But the White House attempted to distract from his stiff gait by surrounding him with aides on his walks across the lawn to Marine One.

Other visible adjustments were made to accommodate his age. Biden often wore tennis shoes that provide better, safer traction and had taken to using the shorter run of stairs at the back of Air Force One to reduce the risk of falls. These are reasonable precautions that might be taken for any 81-year-old.

Some, however, were unusual. The Biden campaign would often provide a list of suggested and approved questions to interviewers. White House aides sometimes held the microphone when a reporter had a rare opportunity to ask Biden a question, pulling it away if a line of questioning was too aggressive or included a follow-up.

During a meeting with Biden's chief of staff Jeff Zients, donors asked about Biden's preparations for the presidential debate with Trump scheduled for June 27. "He has the debate coming up. Can you get him some rest? Some sleep?" a donor asked.

"Biden is driving the schedule," Zients told them. "He's the one who wants to do everything, not the staff. They try but he's hard to control."

Up until early June 2024, Biden's age was discussed among his cabinet and senior advisers as more of an optics problem than a capability one. Biden battles a lifelong stammer and was renowned for gaffes at public press events. His advisers insisted that their experience with the president was different to how he appeared at public events.

Colin Kahl knew Biden's thinking on foreign policy, having served as Biden's national security adviser for two and a half years during his vice presidency (2014–2017) and then as top policy adviser to Secretary of Defense Austin (2021–July 2023). Kahl had watched Biden for nearly a decade and interacted with him regularly up until the summer of 2023.

Several times Biden had told Kahl and others, "My problem is not that I say what I mean. It's that I say *everything* I mean."

"There's this sense that he's being protected by staff," Kahl said in early June 2024. It "has created an impression, which has obviously been more accentuated by Republicans, that he is essentially old, out of it, and he's kind of wheeled out on a stage by his staff. And really, he doesn't run the government.

"Yes, he's older," Kahl said. "Yes, he gets tired more often."

But Kahl found Biden was different behind the scenes. "He's not diminished mentally and he knows a lot about the world. And whether one likes his foreign policy or dislikes his foreign policy, it's *his* policy. One hundred percent. Whether it's Afghanistan, Ukraine or Gaza. It's not Jake Sullivan's policy. It's not Tony Blinken's policy. It's not Lloyd Austin's policy. It's Joe Biden's policy.

"He's pushed his team. He's challenged his team. He can be convinced and nudged," Kahl said, "but at the core, like it or not, these are his policies that he has reasoned through based on 40 or 50 years of experience."

"He's alert," former chairman of the Joint Chiefs Mark Milley said of Biden's engagement in meetings during his tenure, which ended September 30, 2023. "Jake Sullivan, he's almost like a law firm. He loads you up with these readings. You get homework all week long with Jake. And that's good and they're usually binders that are an inch or two thick.

"Every meeting I went to with President Biden, without fail, he had obviously done his homework. He had done the readings. It was obvious he did the readings. And then he would have little notes or his laptop would be open and he would have a very coherent, vigorous back-and-forth discussion. That was invariable. He was always like that.

"In all the meetings I was with him, which was quite a few," Milley said, "never once did I see him doze, close his eyes as if he was sleeping. And I've seen people half his age in meetings doze off because some of the material is not particularly scintillating.

"He was always engaged with rigorous questions back and forth and he was always a good listener. He didn't cut people off, he wasn't doing any of that kind of stuff and he was listening to what you had to say.

"He may not agree with what you had to say but he's listening," Milley added. "He may not decide what we recommended, but he always listened.

"I never saw him go off the handle."

National Security Adviser Jake Sullivan told others he saw a physical difference between the Biden he worked for as vice president and Biden now. "But it's hard for me to really gauge the difference because I've just kind of seen it as a continuum."

"I have never ever in my entire life felt the urge to secretly record anything," Maggie Goodlander, a former Navy intelligence officer and senior Justice Department official, told Sullivan, her husband, after overhearing a phone call he was on with President Biden and Secretary of State Blinken on November 4, 2023.

"The thought has never occurred to me," she added. But Goodlander believed if people "heard Joe Biden in action" it would be very difficult for any person of "good faith or reason" to question whether he was acting as commander in chief.

It was her birthday and Goodlander had told Sullivan she wanted to "listen to Joe Biden talk."

She asked Sullivan, Why is watching Biden on television so harrowing when in settings like these he appears the exact opposite?

"I don't know," Sullivan said. "I don't have an explanation for it."

Polling indicated that 80 percent of Americans and 73 percent of all registered voters believed Biden was too old to be effective.

"People aren't really focused on what Joe Biden has done," Kahl said. "They have feelings that prices are too high. And they blame him because he's the president. They have feelings that the world is chaotic and so they're not evaluating him on the merits."

The next U.S. president would have to deal with new dangers, including a growing unity and interdependence among adversaries.

"The axis of upheaval," Kahl called it. "Russia, China, Iran and North Korea are increasingly connected with one another, largely driven by two things."

The sanctions on three of the four—Russia, Iran and North Korea—were driving them to rely more on China. They were also figuring out ways to connect themselves economically to make themselves less vulnerable to sanctions and the U.S. financial system.

"We don't know what a wounded post-Ukraine Russia will do," Kahl said. Putin was using the war in Ukraine to fundamentally reshape Russian society into a much more nationalistic, militaristic dictatorship.

"I think he has told himself that Russia has weathered the worst of it," Kahl said of Putin, "and that ultimately, Russia took the best punch from the West and has emerged fine."

But the reality was far from fine.

U.S. intelligence estimated that since the February 2022 invasion, Russia had lost 87 percent of its prewar army. Around 315,000 Russian personnel had been killed or injured in the Ukraine War.

"His army has been so mauled," Kahl said. If the war ended tomorrow, Russia would occupy 18 percent of Ukraine. "That will trap 100,000 or 200,000 Russian troops in Ukraine for a long, long time, occupying that part of the country."

Biden had succeeded in ways few understood, Kahl said.

"He didn't slash defense. Defense continued to be extraordinarily robust. Democrats are putting $800 billion plus on defense every year.

"And then a major investment in our allies. Everything that has been put into NATO in the lead-up and the aftermath of Ukraine."

A hallmark of Biden's presidency was his focus on alliance building. He reinforced old bonds, making seven trips to the United Kingdom, strengthened new bonds with old adversaries like Vietnam, and doubled down on U.S. allies and partners in the Indo-Pacific.

Biden visited two active war zones, secretly traveling to Poland and taking the overnight train to Kyiv to visit Zelensky on the

one-year anniversary of the Ukraine War. And, as rockets continued to launch at Israel from Gaza, he landed in Tel Aviv 11 days
after the Hamas attack on Israel.

A review of the empirical evidence suggests that Biden's age was
clearly impacting his ability to perform coherently at some public
events from the summer of 2023. By early June 2024 he appeared
to have taken a turn for the worse.

SEVENTY

O n June 27, just over four months out from election day, President Biden shuffled stiffly across the presidential debate stage at CNN's studios in Atlanta, Georgia. Biden, already the oldest serving president in American history, appeared pale, tired and weak, almost the ghost of a man. His stumbling, incoherent performance would go down in history as perhaps one of the worst public showings of a sitting U.S. president. It triggered a crisis for his political survival.

Former president Trump, only three years younger than Biden, provided a direct contrast to Biden onstage. Trump moved with the lumbering heaviness of a retired football player to his podium where he lifted his head high, calm and self-satisfied.

The two presidential candidates did not shake hands.

Asked routine questions on the economy, foreign policy, the environment and immigration, Biden struggled to find words and form a clear sentence. His voice was a weak rasp, barely audible. Asked about the national debt, Biden said:

"We have a thousand trillionaires in America—I mean, billionaires in America. And what's happening? They're in a situation where they, in fact, pay 8.2 percent in taxes. If they just paid 24 percent or 25 percent either one of those numbers—they'd raised $500 million—billion dollars, I should say, in a 10-year period. We'd be able to right—wipe out his debt . . . making sure that we're able to make every single solitary person eligible for what I've been able to do with COVID, excuse me, with . . . dealing with everything we have to do with . . . Look, if we finally beat . . . Medicare."

The thoughts were jumbled, confused.

It was sad, a shocking portrait of a struggle to revive his authority.

There was no sense of presidential command. Biden closed his eyes during questions as if he were fighting his own internal battle to remember, to focus and complete a simple train of thought. When Trump was speaking, Biden's mouth often hung agape, his eyes wide and glassy.

Trump's arguments were his characteristic mixture of outrageous exaggerations, falsehoods and lies. He attacked but came across as lively and more commanding. Biden failed to push back and debate him. Trump's facial expressions showcased the former president in his element.

"I really don't know what he said at the end of that sentence," Trump said after Biden's time expired on a question about the southern border. "I don't think he knows what he said either."

Even before the debate was over, Democrats were in a full-blown panic.

There was a visible collapse of public trust in Biden's ability to lead the country, especially another four years. Democratic leadership and donors began to call on Biden to step aside. And a pressure campaign was launched by many of his closest political allies, including Nancy Pelosi.

At first Biden shrugged off the debate as a "bad night." In a two-page letter to "fellow Democrats," the president announced he was "firmly committed to staying in this race, to running this race to the end, and to beating Donald Trump."

But his advisers knew that one fumble, even a fraction as bad, and his campaign could sink, along with the Democratic Party's election prospects. This was not just about the presidency. A red Republican wave in the House and Senate would give Trump enormous power.

Biden and Blinken retreated for lunch to the small private dining room off the Oval Office on July 4, just a week after the utter disaster of the debate that had been watched by 51 million people and unleashed a tsunami of calls for Biden to step down.

Blinken felt an immense sense of responsibility. Not only had he worked closely with Biden over the last 22 years, he also deeply admired and loved the man. He knew Biden understood that whatever Blinken was about to say was without any agenda other than what was good for Biden and good for the country.

Still, Blinken had always been the subordinate, even now as secretary of state, and he needed to transcend that, to rigorously explore every reason for Biden to stay or to drop out.

This was crunch time to get it all out between them.

"I don't want to see your legacy jeopardized," Blinken said. And he offered his theory. "Anyone who is written about gets one sentence. That's the legacy." A single sentence.

"If this decision leads you to staying in and winning re-election, great. If it leads to you staying in and losing re-election, that's the sentence."

It was the stark reality. Harsh but true.

"The real question," Blinken said, "do you really want to be doing this another four years?"

Biden said he felt fully capable of doing the job now. Blinken believed that was true. This idea that the staff was hiding Biden's cognitive decline was ridiculous. He'd seen Biden's ability to work through the toughest issues with skill every day. But the president was only going to get older and more frail.

The campaign narrative has taken a sharp turn and it might be impossible to reverse it, Blinken said. "In so far as the story remains about you and your capacity," Blinken continued, "that's going to make it harder to succeed in November because this has to get back to Trump or alternatively there has to be such a strong affirmative agenda that carries the day. But as long as this question is the predominate question, it's hard."

Blinken knew Hunter's struggles had derailed Biden emotionally much, much more than any outsider or the public realized. Another of Biden's close friends called this "the real war," the battle that affected Biden more than Ukraine, more than Israel. The guilt was overwhelming. If he were not president, "my beautiful boy," "my little boy" would not be under the crushing scrutiny of all the investigations, he'd say. Biden was heartbroken.

Hunter's problems haunted Biden, taken him off "an even keel, preoccupied him and taken a lot out of him."

Blinken had two young children and would even choke up at times thinking about "Hunter in the abyss and his father trying desperately to pull him out of it, to reel him in." Biden wanted to protect Hunter but had failed.

This decision will be your legacy. What is your thinking? How are you seeing things? Blinken asked.

Biden said his main concern was beating Trump. He had done it once. Who could win? He did not think Kamala Harris, at least at that moment, would have a better shot of beating Trump than he did. He didn't see any other candidate who might. He asked Blinken what he thought.

"You have an extraordinary legacy," Blinken said, listing Biden's greatest accomplishments. Defeating Trump in 2020. Getting the country through Covid with the best economic rebound of any country. "A legislative record second to none going back at least to LBJ and arguably to FDR." Repairing and re-energizing our international relationships. You've done exactly what you set out to do.

"I've seen this up close for a long time." Your judgment, the ability to work through the issues is very strong and sound.

"Can you see yourself doing it for another four years? You've got to answer that question. And that's different than saying I'm doing the job at the moment. And that's what I'm concerned about."

He could see that Biden definitely had a question in his own mind about where he might be in two to four years.

Now the immediate question was the campaign. "Look, the challenge is you're going to have to do this every day for the next three months," Blinken said.

"People are always going to be looking at this through the prism. That's hard. As long as the conversation is focused on you and your ability to do this that makes things very hard because the conversation really needs to be focused on Trump."

Blinken could see that Biden, who'd chased the presidency all his life, was leaning in the direction of staying in the race.

There was a "Lion in Winter" quality to Biden. An aging leader convinced he was still vital and able to lead, unsure anyone else could assume the mantle as well as he could at a perilous time.

But Biden also seemed to have an open mind on the question.

At the end of their conversation Blinken believed that the president would launch a full examination of the options. One of Biden's famous processes: full discussion, airing everyone's view especially those of Mike Donilon and Steve Ricchetti.

Biden's performance at the NATO summit in Washington, July 9–11, did little to dispel the questions swirling around his fitness to continue. While the president showed his command of his foreign policy during a NATO press conference, an unfortunate slipup introducing Ukrainian president Zelensky as "President Putin" stole the night.

It took less than a month for the next political earthquake.

SEVENTY-ONE

S everal minutes into President Trump's speech at a rally in Butler, Pennsylvania, on Saturday, July 13, a lone gunman, Thomas Matthew Crooks, age 20, opened fire from a nearby rooftop. Trump slapped his right hand to his ear.

"Get down! Get down!" Secret Service agents yelled. Trump dropped to his hands and knees behind the podium. Blood coated his ear and streamed down his cheek. Secret Service agents surrounded the former president and moved to hustle him off-stage.

"Wait, wait," Trump insisted. He threw his fist into the air and mouthed to the crowd: "Fight. Fight. Fight."

The crowd erupted with cheers and chants: "USA. USA. USA."

One spectator, Corey Comperatore, a former fire chief, was shot and killed while shielding his family from Crooks's bullets. Two other spectators were injured in the shooting.

Trump was released from the hospital that evening. He had been planning to play golf at his club in Bedminster, New Jersey, with Lindsey Graham the next morning, Sunday, so he called him.

"Hey, you play tomorrow," Trump said. "I don't think I can play."

"What are you talking about?" Graham said with surprise. He couldn't believe the president was even thinking about golf. "Listen, don't worry about the golf round. I've had a lot of people cancel on me," Graham laughed, lifting the mood, "but none like this."

Trump said he was going to spend the next day with his youngest son, Barron, now 18. "Barron's pretty rattled," he said. "Barron and Melania."

Graham said he would see Trump later on Sunday. They were flying to Milwaukee for the Republican convention.

On the plane, Trump had a large white square bandage over his ear and appeared in good spirits. He was telling the whole story, turning his head to look at the chart of immigration numbers, hearing a whizzing sound, something hitting him hard in the ear. The blood.

"It bothered him that somebody got killed," Graham believed.

Trump's advisers started talking campaign strategy.

"There's no way Biden's going to stay on the ticket," Graham said. "There's no way." Everyone else on the plane disagreed. Biden would stick it out and Democrats would stick with him.

Trump was quiet. Everyone looked to him.

He said he didn't know.

Those close to the former president could see the attempted assassination had shaken him. A bullet had come half an inch from taking his life. Was he changed? Trump and his advisers were rewriting his speech for the Republican convention to send a more "unifying message."

After 10:30 p.m. on July 19 Trump walked out onstage with a white bandage over his ear sending kisses to the crowd. His speech began with a soothing message.

"The discord and division in our society must be healed," Trump said. "As Americans, we are bound together by a single fate and a shared destiny. We rise together. Or we fall apart. I am running to be president for all of America, not half of America because there is no victory in winning for half of America." Strong unification poetry.

But it didn't last. After 20 minutes, Trump fell back into his cage-fighter rhetoric for the remainder of his 90-minute speech.

"This will be the most important election in the history of our country," Trump declared. "War is now raging in Europe and the Middle East, a growing specter of conflict hangs over Taiwan, Korea, the Philippines, and all of Asia, and our planet is teetering on the edge of World War III.

"The weapons are no longer army tanks going back and forth,

shooting at each other. These weapons are obliteration. . . . It's time for a change. This administration can't come close to solving the problems. We're dealing with very tough, very fierce people.

"If you took the 10 worst presidents in the history of the United States. Think of it. The 10 worst. Added them up, they will not have done the damage that Biden has done. The damage that he's done to this country is unthinkable. It's unthinkable."

Two days later, another earthquake shook up the race. On Sunday, July 21, President Biden, isolating in Rehoboth with Covid, announced he was dropping out of the race for re-election. He endorsed Vice President Kamala Harris to replace him as the Democratic nominee. Biden would remain president until the 2025 Inauguration.

President Biden spoke to Harris that Sunday morning, giving her only hours to prepare to enter the race.

American politics can move fast when the truth surfaces so clearly. Unlike Trump, Biden showed that he could accept the hard truths, and despite his personal ambition see what was in the public interest. He was too old to run this election race through.

It was unclear when the summer of political earthquakes might stop.

"I'm incredibly proud of what you've done," Blinken told Biden. "I can't think of many other people in your position who would do what you've done." Giving up presidential power in these circumstances, it was almost Shakespearean. "I think this is the right thing for you, for your legacy and for the future of the country."

Blinken later told a friend he believed the most significant move Biden made that day was his immediate endorsement of Harris. "It avoided crazy infighting in the party. It got everyone unified behind her. It had his imprimatur on it.

"And, I think it probably harkens back to the way Biden felt he didn't get that from President Obama back in 2016," Blinken said. "He was disappointed. He felt that, you know, as his vice president that's the normal and natural order." Harris was next in line.

SEVENTY-TWO

C IA director Bill Burns was prone to what he called regular "interrupted sleep." He worried about the Middle East exploding into region-wide conflict, about Russian plots, and about the elevated risk of a terrorist attack in the United States before the November election.

The intelligence in July 2024 showed that one of the most active and powerful terrorist groups currently operating worldwide, ISIS-K, was planning attacks inside the United States.

"We can see them doing external plotting," Director Burns reported. "A good bit of it is directed at Europe. Some of it, however, is directed at the United States."

Planned violent attacks linked to ISIS-K have already been quietly thwarted this year in Germany, Sweden and elsewhere—showing the growing reach and danger of this Islamic State terrorist group with roots in Southwest and Central Asia.

"The threat stream is picked up and it's really troubling," Burns said.

ISIS-K was responsible for the March 22 massacre at a Moscow concert hall that killed more than 130 people and injured hundreds more. The CIA covertly intercepted ISIS-K plans and warned Russia ahead of the attack. The U.S. embassy in Moscow released a public security alert on March 7 warning that the U.S. was "monitoring reports that extremists have imminent plans to target large gatherings in Moscow, to include concerts." The CIA even named Crocus City Hall as a potential target. Russian president Vladimir Putin dismissed the warnings. It was the deadliest terrorist attack in Europe in two decades. Putin tried to shift blame to Ukraine.

U.S. intelligence capabilities could be extraordinary. CIA director Burns was aware that at times he could see what was coming for Russia much more clearly than Putin could. The CIA, for example, was able to see the Prigozhin mutiny "at least a couple of weeks" before the Wagner chief ordered his ragtag mutineers to march on Moscow.

A month after the Moscow terror attack, U.S. Immigration and Customs Enforcement arrested eight people from Tajikistan in New York, Philadelphia and Los Angeles, after the CIA working closely with the FBI identified links with ISIS-K. The eight individuals had entered the U.S. at the southern border and sought asylum.

U.S. intelligence agencies are also concerned about threats from the Sahel region of West Africa where extremist affiliates of Al Qaeda and ISIS are plotting terrorist attacks. Recent coups in Burkina Faso, Mali and Niger forced the U.S. military out, impeding intelligence collection in the region. The CIA is now operating without the level or kind of capabilities they had before the coups.

Burns worried about other gaps in their vision, including the danger of radicalized individuals, the "lone wolf attackers," who could appear suddenly with little warning and detonate explosives or begin shooting.

The threats to the United States, including Americans abroad, were not limited to terrorist groups. Countries like Iran were already demonstrating what Burns described as an increased "risk appetite" since the October 7, 2023, Hamas attack on Israel.

The Israel-Gaza war was still a highly "combustible situation" that could explode into a full-blown Middle East war at any moment, Burns regularly warned. The biggest risk was a second front erupting across Israel's northern border with Lebanon. A third front could also open in the West Bank.

"One of the most surprising things to me," Burns noted, "in the last nine months is that the West Bank has not blown."

Or, a fourth front could open with Iran. The Iranian massive ballistic missile strike on Israel demonstrated the Supreme Leader's and Iranian regime's new risk appetite.

"It's the scale of the [Iranian] response that I think causes a certain amount of interrupted sleep," he said.

Going back to last year, Director of the FBI Christopher Wray testified before the Senate Homeland Security Committee in October that Tehran was continuing to plot against "current or former" U.S. government officials after the assassination of Iranian military leader Qasem Soleimani in January 2020 during the Trump presidency. The Secret Service was alerted by the Biden administration to an unspecified threat to Donald Trump before his July 13 campaign rally. Iran rejected any involvement in the attempted assassination of the former president.

National Security Adviser Jake Sullivan was also in a constant state of worry about threats to the homeland. "Something that definitely keeps me awake at night is essentially the convergence of artificial intelligence and advanced weaponry. What it will mean for our nation state adversaries and their ability to do harm and what it will mean for bands of terrorists," Sullivan said. "The artificial intelligence revolution has incredible opportunity associated with it, but man, profound, *profound* risk."

U.S. intelligence agencies were also closely monitoring to see if Russia launched a second Cosmos 2576 satellite, its newest space weapon, but this time with a nuclear payload. Even if Putin's intention was to use it as a last resort, "that would scare the crap out of all of us," Burns said.

On a trip to China in June, Burns briefed his Chinese counterparts. "This would be indiscriminate," Burns warned them. "So everybody's satellites on low earth orbit would be destroyed whether it's Chinese, Russians, ours, Europeans. . . . It could do, theoretically, considerable damage to everybody's GPS systems."

Burns didn't believe the threat to be of high probability but it was the kind of thing he worried about when the phone rang late at night.

In a long classified report to President Biden on his discussions in China, Burns noted "the increasingly strong defense partnership between Russia and North Korea unsettled the Chinese to some extent because it emboldened Kim Jong Un." The Chinese were concerned it could make North Korea's leader more reckless, especially if Kim felt he was not receiving enough attention. Kim's missile program had grown substantially but he still depended on sourcing materials from outside North Korea. That gave the CIA opportunities to covertly disrupt that trade.

On the other hand, North Korea's nuclear program was now largely indigenous and no longer depended on outside support or technology. Kim did not yet have the capability to efficiently and accurately deploy a nuclear weapon on an intercontinental ballistic missile (ICBM) to reach the U.S. but he was getting closer. It had been a focus for Kim in recent years. That's part of the risk with the Russia–North Korea defense partnership, Burns assessed, the flow of weapons supplies and capabilities could flow both ways.

The CIA director was concerned with how close Kim was getting to that kind of capability. "Logically and rationally he wouldn't do it," Burns reported, meaning launch an ICBM with a nuclear load at the U.S. "He would be deterred from doing it. But just having that capacity to do it is really troubling."

Burns described the danger as "unplanned inadvertent escalation."

It was an extremely dangerous time for the United States and global stability, Burns believed. All the warning systems were blinking red.

SEVENTY-THREE

◆ ◆

"The week after an assassination attempt and people are already forgetting about it," Jason Miller, Trump's top aide and communications director, fumed on July 25. Miller was one of Trump's most loyal, MAGA-championing aides and a veteran of the former president's 2016 and 2020 campaigns. In the days after the shooting Trump was being treated almost as a messiah by his supporters, giving his funding and polls a huge boost.

But Biden dropping out had shifted headlines and attention to the Vice President. Some of the media, which Miller believed were part of a vast left-wing liberal conspiracy, had placed a crown on her head.

"Democrats basically sent him off to the political crematorium," Miller said of Biden. "This is not nice! They just pushed this guy out and it's almost like his golden parachute is six months more as leader of the free world," he said.

"How's he going to do anything about the economy, border or anything, even internationally? You can't focus on international affairs when everyone knows that you're out in six months. Why do you think Netanyahu and all these people, or Zelensky, want to meet and see President Trump? They know Biden's not going to be around. How do you accomplish anything on the foreign affairs side when you've undercut yourself?"

Actually Biden had just freed himself up to potentially accomplish more in six months by handing off the presidential campaign to his vice president and her running mate, Governor Tim Walz of Minnesota, and focusing on governing.

Mission One for the Trump campaign was to define Kamala Harris. Acerbic direct fire was the style. "Move quick to define

Harris as an incompetent and radically liberal individual," Miller said. "The president hit that about 10 times in his speech last night."

At a rally in Charlotte, North Carolina, on July 24, Trump declared, "Now we have a new victim to defeat, lying Kamala Harris," also calling her a "radical left lunatic," "the most incompetent and far-left vice president in American history," and "the ultra-liberal driving force behind every single Biden catastrophe."

"We're not so big on the art of subtlety in Trump World," Miller said.

But was there a strategy?

"Most voters," Miller explained, "see [Harris] as being unserious, unprepared, and in our words incompetent." The Trump campaign strategy is to present him as the contrast: If you're upset with anything—the economy, the border, crime in the streets, global chaos—vote for Trump. "Let's go back to me."

Everything they had prepared to attack Biden, they would throw at Harris in equal measure.

"Keep in mind," Miller said, "she was the one who was going to get to the root causes of illegal migration in the Northern Triangle. That didn't work. She was going to go and make sure Putin didn't invade Ukraine. That didn't work. So it's not like Kamala Harris brings this giant heft to the foreign affairs equation.

"I don't think she's ready for prime time," Miller added. "If you're not ready to go. If you're not ready to punch back or lay out a vision, you're going to get gobbled up real quick. I don't think Harris is ready for prime time. This is tough.

"This race is going to be a dogfight all the way to the end," he said.

At a National Association of Black Journalists convention, former president Trump echoed his conviction that he was the best president for Black people in America since Abraham Lincoln. Trump claimed that Kamala Harris had "all of a sudden" adopted a Black identity, drawing shocked gasps from the audience.

"I've known her a long time, indirectly, not directly very much," Trump said, "and she was always of Indian heritage, and she was only promoting Indian heritage. I didn't know she was Black until a number of years ago when she happened to turn Black, and now she wants to be known as Black. So I don't know, is she Indian, or is she Black?"

Harris's late mother was from India and her father is from Jamaica. She was an alumna of Howard University in Washington, one of the most prominent HBCUs—historically Black colleges and universities—and she was a member of one of the nation's oldest, historically Black sororities—Alpha Kappa Alpha.

"I respect either one," Trump continued, "but she obviously doesn't. Because she was Indian all the way, and then all of a sudden, she made a turn, and she went—she became a Black person. And I think somebody should look into that, too."

Trump was hit by a wave of Democrat and Republican criticism after the interview. He wrote on Truth Social: "The questions were Rude and Nasty, often in the form of a statement, but we CRUSHED IT!"

The vice president barely gave Trump's words any airtime. "It was the same old show—the divisiveness and the disrespect," Harris said in a speech that night. "The American people deserve better."

SEVENTY-FOUR

Israeli Prime Minister Bibi Netanyahu knew as he followed Kamala Harris through the large wooden doors into the vice president's ceremonial office on July 25 that he was meeting not just with the Democratic nominee for president but, at least for the moment, with the likely next president.

In the elegant old world room in the Executive Office Building that overlooks the West Wing, the vice president, her senior staff and White House Middle East Coordinator Brett McGurk sat across from Netanyahu, Ron Dermer and Israeli ambassador Mike Herzog. On one side of the room was President Teddy Roosevelt's original desk. The same one used by Nixon during Watergate and where he hid a tape recorder. The desk contains a secret drawer signed by every vice president. Biden's is a particularly large, messy scrawl.

Harris welcomed the Israelis by reiterating her "lifelong support for the state of Israel" and her "ironclad commitment to Israel's security."

"This should be understood always in our conversations," Harris assured Netanyahu. As a little girl, Harris said she had carried blue boxes collecting money to plant trees in Israel. She noted that her husband, Doug Emhoff, who is Jewish, had been leading the administration's efforts to combat anti-Semitism.

But what's happening in Gaza, Harris continued, the Palestinian suffering and how it is perceived outwardly is very harmful to Israel. "Don't take for granted that Americans, particularly younger Americans, the latest generation will be as supportive of Israel as my generation and those before," Harris warned. The ongoing war and humanitarian situation in Gaza is creating and growing anti-Israel sentiment. "Today the public receives visual information," Harris said. "They see photos from Gaza and it impacts their thinking."

The Israelis felt her tone was more observational, not critical. It wasn't an "in your eye criticism," Ambassador Herzog said. The vice president was saying "these are the briefings and reports that I am getting."

"I'm disturbed by the humanitarian situation in Gaza," Harris continued, looking at Netanyahu. "It's unconscionable. People are starving. Sanitation conditions are intolerable. 4,000 people per toilet in western Gaza."

Netanyahu acknowledged the sanitation problem. "I've given orders to deal with that," he said. He denied that Palestinians in Gaza were starving.

"There is no starvation in Gaza and definitely there is no policy of starving people," Netanyahu said. "The amount of food that goes into Gaza, including calories per person meets the criteria. But not all the food that goes in reaches its destination because Hamas puts its hands on humanitarian assistance. Hamas loots the food. Hamas . . .

"Okay, we can discuss the details but the perception out there still exists," Harris said.

"Israel bought with its own money tents for people in Gaza," Netanyahu added.

Harris turned to issues related to the West Bank—referring to the Palestinian territory on the west bank of the River Jordan annexed and occupied by Israel since 1967. Between two and three million Palestinians live in the West Bank as well as around 400,000 Israeli Jews who are in settlements and outposts.

"It's a ticking time bomb," Harris said. "Some of Israel's settlements are expanding significantly. Land is being allocated for settlement use. You just legalized five illegal outposts. Settler violence is rising."

Phil Gordon, the vice president's national security adviser, noticed that Netanyahu didn't really deny the accusations.

"The settlements have not been expanding," Netanyahu said

dismissively. "They've been building up, not out. People are attacking Jews in the West Bank. That should be the main focus."

"We have a different picture than you have," Israeli ambassador Mike Herzog added. "Iran is trying to foment unrest and terror activities in the West Bank. They're smuggling weapons on a big scale and inside Israel."

"I am committed to getting the hostages out and a ceasefire," Netanyahu said, shifting the conversation back to the war in Gaza. "But we can't give Hamas a victory. If Hamas remains in power in Gaza, it's a victory to Hamas. It's a defeat to Israel. No Israeli government, right or left, will accept that. No one. It's not only me.

"We want a deal that will release the hostages and we are willing to pay with a ceasefire for a period of time to achieve this," Netanyahu said. "Your administration is saying we want a ceasefire, implicitly an end to the war, that along the way releases the hostages." That is not acceptable to Israelis.

Harris reiterated Biden's policy position. No one wanted Hamas in power. "Giving the Palestinians a political horizon and ultimately a state is what our administration thinks is the right thing to do," she said. "It's in our mutual interest not to undermine the Palestinian Authority," Harris said, "and to start working on governance and security and day after plans."

"Well, we can't do those things now," Netanyahu said, "because it would look like we were rewarding those who attacked us."

"It is challenging for Israel," Netanyahu added. He believed there were still 30 live hostages, including some Israeli-Americans. He wanted veto power over which Hamas prisoners were swapped for hostages and was insisting on the maximum number of live hostages be released by Hamas in this deal.

"I get it, these are important issues," Harris said, "but don't make the perfect the enemy of the good. If you hold out for perfect resolution on every single possible issue, including all of these, the hostages are going to be dead and the situation will be even worse."

Netanyahu reiterated that he wanted a deal. "No one should accuse me of not wanting a deal."

The meeting ended cordially and on good terms after about 40 minutes. Harris did not stray from Biden's policy.

"The meeting itself was not tense. It was okay. It was fine," said Ambassador Herzog. "Not everything was agreed upon, but it was managed in a way that we had the dialogue, we listened to each other. We responded. It was a routine policy discussion. Nothing to write home about."

At a press briefing that evening the vice president forcefully criticized Israel's treatment of civilians in Gaza and called for a ceasefire.

"We cannot look away in the face of these tragedies," Harris said. "We cannot allow ourselves to become numb to the suffering. And I will not be silent."

It was a real blast.

To the Israelis it was a complete switch. "She wants to be tough in public," Herzog said. "But she wasn't as tough privately."

When Netanyahu saw her public statement, he was furious.

"He was upset," the Israeli ambassador said, "and for good reason. If the perception out there is that there's daylight between Israel and the United States, it could have a negative impact on the hostage deal, on Hamas thinking.

"Hamas believes that time is on their side. They believe there's daylight between Israel and the United States, and that ultimately the U.S. and the international community will stop Israel and end the war in Gaza." The only thing that impacts Hamas, Herzog said, "is our military pressure on the ground, the fact that we seized the Egypt-Gaza border and denied [Hamas] a significant source of income from smuggling."

The Biden warning to Netanyahu after October 7 was being proven true: It's very difficult to eliminate an ideology. Hamas was popping back up in regions of Gaza that Israel had demolished and reported to have cleared. It could be an endless cycle of violence.

In a separate 90-minute Oval Office meeting with the Israeli prime minister the same day, President Biden took the opposite approach to Harris. He did not criticize Netanyahu in front of reporters. "We've got a lot to talk about," Biden said simply and Netanyahu thanked Biden for his long support of Israel.

"Mr. President, we've known each other for 40 years, and you've known every Israeli prime minister for 50 years, from Golda Meir," Netanyahu said before the reporters.

Biden smiled. "By the way, that first meeting with Prime Minister Golda Meir. . . she had an assistant sitting next to me, a guy named Rabin." Yitzhak Rabin had later become prime minister of Israel. "That's how far back it goes," Biden said. "I was only 12 then," he joked.

"President Biden is still very much involved and he definitely still calls the shots," Ambassador Herzog said. "No doubt about it."

"Until now, I didn't feel that Vice President Harris had any impact on our issues. She was in the room, but she never had an impact. Maybe now, because she's running for president, then she is a bit more involved, certainly in the public face of it," Herzog said. "She more than Biden, you know, tuned closer to, let's say the more progressive line of criticizing Israel over the humanitarian situation or human suffering and so on. It's not that Biden didn't deal with it or care about it or mention it, but, you know, it's ultimately how you frame things, where you put your emphasis."

Palestinian health authorities were reporting that Israel's ground and air campaign in Gaza had killed more than 39,000 people, mostly civilians, and driven most of the enclave's 2.3 million people from their homes.

The Harris approach was diplomatic in private and forceful in public. And it clearly had an impact on the Israelis.

SEVENTY-FIVE

$\mathbf{I}$n early 2024, a Trump aide loitered outside the former president's office at Mar-a-Lago.

Trump had sent the aide out of the room so he could have what he said was a private phone call with Russian president Vladimir Putin. According to Trump's aide, there have been multiple phone calls between Trump and Putin, maybe as many as seven in the period since Trump left the White House in 2021.

When I asked Trump's top campaign aide, Jason Miller, in July if he knew about phone calls between former president Trump and Putin, Miller's answer was: "Um, ah, not that, ah, not that I'm aware of."

Is Trump able to talk to Putin now?

"I'm sure they'd know how to get in touch with each other," Miller said.

Are they talking about how to stop the Ukraine War?

"Well, I mean President Trump has said he's going to get it stopped and I think he can. I think he can get it stopped before he even takes office," Miller said. Trump was also saying this publicly at rallies.

The Logan Act makes it illegal for private citizens to negotiate disputes without the clear authorization of the sitting U.S. government.

"But the person who is going to decide that is Putin," I said to Miller. Isn't it?

"No," Miller said, "I think the person who's going to decide that is President Trump because he knows the pressure points for both Putin and Zelensky to get it done.

"I have not heard that they're talking so I'd push back on that," Miller added. "But again, they know each other from the four years in the presidency. I would push back on that," he repeated about the phone calls, "and just be very careful that we're not saying they're in communication or anything beforehand."

"For the purpose of ending a war?"

"But that's not going to happen, ultimately, not going to happen until President Trump wins on November 5th and it's clear that he's coming in," Miller said. "After November 5th, I think President Trump will be able to have it solved or largely solved by the time he gets sworn in."

It did not add up. Trump was saying publicly that he could have the war fixed before he took office with a phone call?

"To each," Miller said. "I think he could. He knows the pressure points. He knows what is going to motivate both sides and I think he can do that with one phone call each," meaning to Putin and Zelensky.

Any effort by Trump to communicate with Putin before being sworn in as president on January 20, 2025, would be another earthquake. The aide closest to Trump, however, lays out how Trump could and seemingly plans to try.

Trump continued to meet with other world leaders and the next day, Friday, July 26, Israeli prime minister Netanyahu visited him at Mar-a-Lago.

DNI Avril Haines, who oversees all 16 U.S. intelligence agencies, including the National Security Agency, carefully hedged on the question of seven contacts between Trump and Putin.

"I would not purport to be aware of all contacts with Putin," Haines reported. "I wouldn't purport to speak to what President Trump may or may not have done."

During my interviews with then-President Trump in 2020, he boasted about his affinity for strongmen like Russian president Putin and China's president Xi, and gave me his "love letters" with North Korean leader Kim Jong Un.

Trump's relationship with Putin was also an area that had stumped Dan Coats, Trump's director of national intelligence for two and a half years, 2017–2019.

"It's still a mystery to me how he deals with Putin and what he says to Putin," Coats said in May 2024. "It's an enigma and it hasn't been broken yet."

Coats worked in Trump's national security inner circle at the top of the central nervous system of the American espionage establishment and its most vital secrets. He had a front-row seat to Trump's words and actions.

"His reaching out and never saying anything bad about Putin, and saying positive things about Putin. For me," Coats said, "it's scary.

"Is it blackmail?" Coats had wondered. He was never able to figure it out. But there was something there, he was sure.

"Putin manipulates," CIA director Burns said. "He's professionally trained to do that." He was widely regarded among world leaders as a master manipulator.

Before the 2016 election Putin made a comment about Trump in Russian that was interpreted in English as saying he thought Trump was "brilliant."

"The actual Russian word was colorful, which is not exactly the same kind of compliment," Burns clarified.

"There are parts of Trumpism that appeal to Putin," Burns had told colleagues. "Certainly, on Ukraine, he has to read him as being far more likely to bail on Zelensky and the Ukrainians. So from that point of view it's attractive." It was more complicated to judge Putin's view on the unpredictability and erratic nature of Trump's leadership, which neither Putin nor Xi were attracted to.

"But Putin's got a plan," the CIA director said, "just as he did when [Trump] was in office, at playing Trump."

On May 23, Trump declared that Putin will free *Wall Street Journal* reporter Evan Gershkovich, who was being held in Russian prison, if Trump was elected president in November.

Trump wrote on Truth Social: "Evan Gershkovich, the Reporter from The Wall Street Journal, who is being held by Russia, will be released almost immediately after the Election, but definitely before I assume Office. He will be HOME, SAFE, AND WITH HIS FAMILY.

"Vladimir Putin, President of Russia, will do that for me, but not for anyone else, and WE WILL BE PAYING NOTHING!"

Trump did not provide a reason for why Putin might do this.

Kremlin spokesman Dmitry Peskov was asked about Trump's claim and said that Putin had "naturally not had contacts with Donald Trump."

After months of quiet negotiations led by President Biden and Sullivan and involving at least seven countries, Evan Gershkovich was released from Russian prison on August 1, along with Americans Paul Whelan and Alsu Kurmasheva. Their release was part of the largest prisoner swap since the Cold War that saw 24 people freed.

During the presidential debate, former president Trump argued that President Putin "never would have invaded Ukraine" if Trump had still been in the Oval Office. "I'll tell you what happened, [Biden] was so bad with Afghanistan," Trump said, "it was such a horrible embarrassment, most embarrassing moment in the history of our country, that when Putin watched that and he saw the incompetence. . . . When Putin saw that, he said, you know what? I think we're going to go in and maybe take my—this was his dream. I talked to him about it, his dream. The difference is he never would have invaded Ukraine. Never."

———

Having written three books on Trump's presidency and conducted more than eight hours of interviews with him, it is clear he will say and do anything that he believes is in his interest.

Fear, my first book on Trump, revealed "a nervous breakdown" of his presidency in which senior officials removed documents from his desk so that Trump would not sign actions that would trigger a major economic or national security crisis.

White House chief of staff John F. Kelly, a retired Marine four-star general, was quoted in the book saying about then-President Trump, "He's an idiot. It's pointless to try to convince him of anything. He's gone off the rails. We're in Crazytown."

Gary Cohn, Trump's top economic adviser, referred to Trump as "a professional liar."

John Dowd, Trump's personal lawyer in the Mueller investigation of Russian interference in the 2016 election, told Trump he was so untruthful that if he testified in person he would wind up in "an orange jumpsuit" and was "a fucking liar."

Maggie Haberman of *The New York Times* wrote that my book *Fear* "depicts the Trump White House as a byzantine, treacherous, often out-of-control operation," and that the book "unsettled the administration and the president in part because it was clear that the author has spoken with many current and former officials."

Senator Lindsey Graham assured then-President Trump that I had not put words in Trump's mouth nor anyone else's. And to my complete surprise, Trump agreed to be interviewed for my second book on his presidency, *Rage*.

"I wish I met with you for the last book," President Trump said, seated in a burgundy chair behind the Resolute Desk on December 5, 2019. "But we'll make it up, we'll make it up."

Trump had props set out on the desk in front of him. There was a stack of judicial appointment orders in the center of the desk. Then on one side there was a binder of letters Trump had exchanged with North Korean president Kim Jong Un. And on the other side were large photos of Trump standing next to Kim shaking his hand and smiling.

Trump's war was the coronavirus pandemic and his performance revealed his character. These interviews showed a man with no fidelity to the truth, fixated on re-election and unequipped to deal with a genuine crisis.

Trump was warned by his national security advisers that the virus was deadly and a major threat to the country but he never developed a plan to respond. He did not know how to use his extraordinary executive power to prioritize saving American lives. Through defiant pronouncements, he downplayed and deflected any responsibility for handling it. There was no compassion. No courage.

"Oh, I have a plan, Bob," Trump said about the coronavirus in April 2020. "I mean, you know it is what it is."

During national crises, people look to their president for leadership.

"This is war," Trump told me.

I asked Trump if he had sat down to get a tutorial with Dr. Anthony Fauci, the nation's top infectious disease expert. Was Fauci his Eisenhower?

"There's not a lot of time for that, Bob. This is a busy White House," Trump said.

By the summer of 2020, about 140,000 people had died in the United States from the virus and eventually the death toll would exceed 1.1 million.

"You will see the plan, Bob. I've got 106 days," Trump told me in July 2020. In 106 days was the coming presidential election.

His lack of action on the coronavirus almost certainly cost him the 2020 election, according to his own pollsters.

I once asked Trump, "What's the job of the president?" He said, "To protect the people."

It's a good answer, but Trump failed to do it.

Donald Trump is not only the wrong man for the presidency, he is unfit to lead the country. Trump was far worse than Richard Nixon, the provably criminal president. As I have pointed out, Trump governed by fear and rage. And indifference to the public and national interest.

Trump was the most reckless and impulsive president in American history and is demonstrating the very same character as a presidential candidate in 2024.

SEVENTY-SIX

Regional blood pressure in the Middle East spiked again at the end of July. "Bibi, what the fuck?" Biden yelled into the phone at Netanyahu. Israel had taken out Hezbollah's top military commander Fuad Shukr in a strike on a densely populated suburb of Beirut that also killed at least three civilians and injured 74 others. Israel held Shukr responsible for a rocket attack on the Golan Heights that had killed 12 Israeli children on a soccer field three days earlier.

"Hezbollah crossed the red line," Israel's Defense Minister Gallant said in a social media statement after the strike in Lebanon.

"It's one thing if you'd gotten him near the border," Biden said to Netanyahu. "But in Beirut!"

Less than 12 hours later, Israel assassinated Hamas senior leader Ismail Haniyeh, while he was in Tehran for the inauguration of Iranian president, Masaud Pezeshkian. Haniyeh was photographed clasping hands with Pezeshkian hours before he was killed. Israel had apparently planted a bomb in the room of the guest house where Haniyeh was staying months earlier.

Supreme Leader Khamenei ordered Iran to strike Israel in retaliation.

"You know the perception of Israel around the world increasingly is that you're a rogue state, a rogue actor," Biden yelled at Netanyahu.

"This is Haniyeh," Netanyahu said, "one of the leading terrorists. A terrible guy. We saw an opportunity and took it."

Haniyeh, who lived in Qatar, had also been a key negotiator and decision-maker for Hamas in the ceasefire negotiations.

"The harder you hit, the more successful you're going to be in the negotiation," Netanyahu said.

The Israeli attacks in Beirut and Tehran effectively upended months of grueling back-channel negotiations for a ceasefire deal.

"How can mediation succeed when one party assassinated the negotiator on the other side?" Qatar's foreign minister and prime minister, MBAR, who had been working on the negotiations posted on social media.

"He's right," Blinken said to Biden. Israel had poked another stick directly into not one, but two raging hornets nests.

"We face not only Hamas in Gaza, we face Iran and the whole Iranian axis, all the Iranian proxies," Israeli ambassador Mike Herzog said privately, defending Israel's actions. "Everybody is firing at us, firing at Israel."

"Houthis are firing. Hezbollah has been firing on a daily basis since October 8. Shiite militias in Iraq and Syria," Herzog said. "Iran itself. The massive missile attack and they may attack us again. Iran is trying to open a front in the West Bank. They're trying to foment unrest in Jordan and ultimately topple the regime there as well.

"They are on all fronts facing us," Herzog said. "Israelis will tell you we're fighting the Iranian axis on seven fronts. I would add an international front for the state of Israel. Anti-Semites, people who de-legitimize Israel, people who don't recognize our right to exist. And we see it on campuses, in social media, in the International Criminal Court or International Court of Justice, and with the libel that we are using starvation as a weapon, which is blood libel, I can tell you that. I was in uniform for many years in the IDF.

"It feels existential to Israelis because it's *on all the fronts*. It's become very trendy to, you know, to pick on Israel," Herzog said.

"Some people when they smell blood they hover over you."

Through the first two weeks of August, Sullivan, Austin and Blinken were working overtime to try to manage potential retaliation against Israel.

"The president has unfortunately gained quite a bit of muscle memory for how we deal with spikes," Sullivan said, referring to the threats on October 11 and April 13 that brought the region to the brink of all-out war. "We're moving U.S. assets into place, messaging the Iranians, indirectly messaging Hezbollah, coordinating with the Israelis and then trying to get everyone to focus on the fact that the only way out of this is the ceasefire."

Secretary Austin directed multiple force posture moves to bolster U.S. readiness to defend Israel. He positioned two U.S. carrier strike groups in the region, increased the presence of cruisers and destroyers, and deployed an additional fighter squadron to the Middle East to assist Israel's air defense. Now they were standing by to see what Iran decided to do.

"We could see a significant attack on Israel in the coming days," Sullivan said in mid-August. "That is a distinct possibility.

"The only way out of this is the ceasefire," Sullivan concluded.

SEVENTY-SEVEN

I n *The Commanders*, my book reporting on the First Gulf War of 1991, I wrote: "The decision to go to war is one that defines a nation, both to the world and, perhaps more importantly, to itself. There is no more serious business for a national government, no more accurate measure of national leadership."

This book, *War,* presents the efforts and decisions to try to prevent war, and where war came, to avoid escalation.

Now as much as ever, I think that war decisions define national leaders. U.S. military fatalities in Vietnam were 52,880. Vietnam was a giant event for Biden's generation, my generation. Biden never fought in and never protested the war. As a practical matter he said repeatedly as a senator, it was just "lousy policy."

He was not infused with war or antiwar sentiment. As senator, Biden said that his objections to the Vietnam War were not moral but practical. There were massive fatalities and it just didn't work.

As vice president in 2009, Biden made an intense, but unsuccessful, effort to talk President Obama out of sending 30,000 additional American troops to Afghanistan. His main argument to Obama was that Afghanistan would resemble the past when the U.S. was "locked into Vietnam." Keeping the United States and American troops from fighting unnecessary war became a bedrock for Biden.

By the time Biden became president in 2021, he firmly believed that unless the United States was attacked, sending U.S. troops to solve foreign policy problems had not served the interest of the United States. From Vietnam through Afghanistan and Iraq the troop bandage had failed.

One of the most important days for President Biden's presidency was December 8, 2021—months before Russia invaded Ukraine—when he sat in the Oval Office alone with Jake Sullivan and said, "I'm not sending U.S. troops to Ukraine." He then announced it publicly.

"That is not on the table," he said as he walked across the White House lawn to Marine One, setting the direction of a new foreign policy.

When the war came and Russia invaded, Biden stuck to his word. The U.S. provided massive intelligence support and billions of dollars in military assistance to Ukraine. He provided moral support and condemned Russia's invasion. He deployed more U.S. forces to Europe and continued to pledge Article 5 protection to NATO allies if any were attacked. He mobilized NATO—the strongest military alliance in the world—to back Ukraine without sending troops into Ukraine.

"The United States and our allies will emerge from this stronger, more united, more determined and more purposeful," Biden said in February 2022. "And Putin's aggression against Ukraine will end up costing Russia dearly—economically and strategically. We will make sure of that. Putin will be a pariah on the international stage."

"Joe Biden is the first president in the 21st century who can say I don't have American soldiers in war," Sullivan said. "Yes, there are wars. We're not fighting them.

"Biden felt his ability to really support Ukraine fully, have their back with weapons and consequential levels of support, rested on his ability to reassure the American people that they were not going to get their country dragged into that war," Sullivan said. "The president has essentially created the necessary permission structure for sustained American support to Ukraine.

"Would there be a war in Ukraine today if Trump were president? I would say probably not. Why? There'd be no war because Putin would be in Kyiv," Sullivan said. "Trump would have waved him right in. Because when it comes to these dictators, Trump's basic view: I let them do what they want."

"The hard decisions are always when you have to put troops into harm's way," Secretary of Defense Lloyd Austin said. "I always measure eight times before I cut. I understand the complexities. I understand the capabilities. But it's always hard to make a decision to send troops into combat."

"What drives Biden is he wants to be effective," Austin said. "And he wants to have the best outcomes. And if he had to put troops in combat, he would do it. But if it's not necessary to do that, if you can achieve the goal another way, then I think he's skillful enough to be able to do it another way, and courageous enough."

Biden was focused on finding the best way to achieve an outcome, Austin believed. "He'll do what needs to be done. You don't always have to put troops in combat to be successful and he's demonstrated that."

When Hamas attacked Israel on October 7, 2023, in one of the most shocking and cruel acts of terrorism, the United States provided massive assistance. Ships and aircraft carriers were moved, intelligence resources mobilized, but no U.S. troops set foot in Gaza.

The U.S. military shot down ballistic missiles and drones launched at Israel by Iran in April 2024. They successfully defended Israel with a coalition of forces from the U.K., France, Saudi Arabia and Jordan. No U.S. forces engaged directly with Iran. These decisions were rooted in Biden's experience.

Biden solidified an American foreign policy that kept U.S. ground troops out of war. And, at least for the time being, the world did not slide into a great power war.

"I think it deserves to be said, even if it may not be true tomorrow, it's true today," National Security Adviser Jake Sullivan said. "The president has kept the homeland safe. We're not doing a victory lap on that point. But what is the job of the commander in chief? It's to keep the homeland safe and the president has done that."

EPILOGUE

Reporting for this book on President Biden has been a radically different experience for me. Many of the news-breaking scenes in my prior books are stories of failures, mismanagement, dishonesty and the corruption of executive power, most regularly demonstrated in my books on Presidents Nixon and Trump.

Often I have said, only half-jokingly, that when I wake up in the morning my first thought is: "What are the bastards hiding?" My experience is the hidden is often significant, even monumental.

War, this book on Biden, however, gave me what was often a real-time, inside-the-room look at genuine good faith efforts by the president and his core national security team to wield the levers of executive power responsibly and in the national interest. At the center of good governance, as evidenced in this book, is teamwork.

The legacy of the Biden presidency will be the core national security team that he built and kept in place for nearly four years. They brought decades of experience as well as basic human decency. *War* shows the traditional and novel ways Biden and his core team pursued an intelligence-driven foreign policy to warn the world that war was coming in Ukraine, to supply Ukraine with the weapons they need to defend themselves against Russia, and to try to tamp down escalations in the Israel-Gaza war.

This team included National Security Adviser Jake Sullivan and his deputy, Jon Finer, CIA director Bill Burns and Director of National Intelligence Avril Haines, Secretary of State Tony Blinken, Secretary of Defense Lloyd Austin, and former Chairman of the Joint Chiefs Mark Milley.

As this book shows, there were failures and mistakes. The

full story is, of course, not yet known. But based on the evidence available now, I believe President Biden and this team will be largely studied in history as an example of steady and purposeful leadership.

Note to Readers

All interviews for this book were conducted under the journalist ground rule of "deep background." This means that all the information could be used but I would not say who provided it.

The book is drawn from hundreds of hours of interviews with firsthand participants and witnesses to these events. Nearly all allowed me to record our interviews. When I have attributed exact quotations, thoughts or conclusions to the participants, that information comes from the person, a colleague with direct knowledge, or from government or personal documents, calendars, diaries, emails, meeting notes, transcripts and other records.

President Biden and former president Trump declined to be interviewed for this book.

Acknowledgments

The war that I haven't written about is the war to get this book finished at a time of so many political earthquakes. Jonathan Karp, the CEO of Simon & Schuster, was a force of wisdom and stability, expanding my thinking and helping redirect the reporting and constant rewriting over this massive two-and-a-half-year venture.

I am extremely lucky to have Jon as my editor-in-chief. I have never known such a seasoned, brilliant editor who directs and probes on everything from the smallest word choices to the larger questions of pacing, tone and public interest. He stuck by me with complete trust through the highest velocity of political change from the Trump assassination attempt to Biden dropping out and the unprecedented rise of Vice President Kamala Harris.

Karp's response constantly was deal with it, pushing me for more reporting, more sources. Reframe. Rewrite. He follows all the news and has the refined, sophisticated understanding of the best full-time political consultants I know. He used to be the boy wonder but is now the rock-solid elder statesman of book publishing. I owe him so much. He is always a phone call away, reachable even when on a remote road trip.

My wife, Elsa, a former reporter at *The Washington Post* and staff writer at *The New Yorker*, has devoted much of the last two years to help me with this book, and honestly much of her life to working with me on 20 of my 23 books. *War* would not have been possible without her. She read hundreds of transcripts of my interviews. She pushed me constantly to go back over details. Talk to this person again. These are the questions that still need answering. Move this scene. It connects to this other scene, don't you see it? Blessed with a natural instinct for what is important, she routinely provides me with email blasts of the latest from the internet, asking, "Did you see this?" Knowing I'm looking for a summary, she will send me an email with a more direct instruction: "Read this all the way to the end."

Her news instincts are second to none. She edits sections not once but multiple times. Elsa's handwritten suggestions often exceed the typed words on a page. And frequently are more discerning. She has endless reserves of patience.

Elsa is also reading serious books all the time. She reads more than anyone I have ever known. If I suggest dinner, she often says, "I'm in the middle of this chapter." Maybe it's Netanyahu's memoir. Maybe it's Colm Tóibín. That means no dinner until she finishes in maybe five or 10 minutes. Or more if it's a long chapter. No compromise. I have wondered at times if she was reading and there was a fire in the house she might want to finish the chapter before calling 911.

Elsa is a disciple of Henry James, who said: "Three things in human life are important. The first is to be kind. The second it to be kind. And the third is to be kind."

So kind. So tough. But so loving. We have been together since 1980—44 years ago. She is the backbone of our life together and all of my work.

My family is in my thoughts daily, at times hourly. It brings me so much joy as a father to see the intelligence, drive and passion they bring to all they do. My daughter Diana is studying in California for her PhD in clinical psychology. And my daughter Tali runs The Trace, an organization based in New York that investigates gun violence. Her husband, Gabe Roth, and my grandchildren Zadie and Theo are also constantly amazing me. Thank you to Rosa Criollo for her tireless energy and generosity of spirit while caring for all of us.

Copy editor extraordinaire Fred Chase came to Washington from his home in Texas and took up residence in my house for 10 days working from 5:30 a.m. to read the manuscript many times and apply his skills with language and knowledge of the world often to each paragraph. Fred is a unique authentic force with a "sniffer" that works full-time sensing error and imprecision.

Robert B. Barnett, lawyer and counselor, is the King of Washington publishing. Our friendship spans 35 years. As I say about him, always wise, always devoted, and always available. I often have to get in line but he never leaves business and consultation unfinished. His email question is frequently, "Are you callable?"

Julia Prosser, the Simon & Schuster publicity director, is the absolute master at finding creative ways to get the content of my books out into the world, on television, radio, podcasts, social media. When she is laying out a plan to promote and publicize a book, she thinks BIG and takes all the operational strategy out of my hands. Whew!

I am hugely grateful to Kimberly Goldstein, who oversaw each step of the editorial and production process and worked intensely with the team at S&S and my assistant Claire McMullen, to ensure this book successfully made it to the printer on the shortest timeline I've ever seen.

I wrote about my assistant Claire McMullen at the beginning of this book, but my appreciation is worth repeating. She carried an enormous workload. There would be no book without Claire. A universe of thanks to her.

I have worked at *The Washington Post* since 1971, a full 53 years. My title is associate editor—an act of generosity by the *Post* leadership as I do very little associating and editing anymore. I love *The Washington Post*, the modern embodiment of the First Amendment. My frequent point of contact is national editor Phil Rucker, a remarkable journalist and human being. His depth of knowledge about Washington politics is staggering.

We are so fortunate to have Matt Murray, a man of vast experience and journalistic IQ, as the executive editor. Managing editor Matea Gold, Rucker, and a strong team of editors and reporters are building a new golden era for *Washington Post* journalism.

Sincere thanks to *The Washington Post* photography department.

Deputy director Robert Miller and photo editor Troy Witcher spent hours working with my assistant Claire to find the right photos to bring this book's main characters and themes to life. Also, thanks to Jennifer Rockwood and Kaitlyn Dolan on the operational side.

Special thanks and deepest appreciation for Robert Costa. He and I coauthored the book *Peril* in 2021. Costa is now the chief election and campaign correspondent for CBS News. No one else covers the political news with such depth and sophistication. He also makes news. His August 2024 interview with President Biden drew worldwide attention when Biden told Costa he was worried about American democracy and he did not expect a peaceful transfer of power after the upcoming presidential election if Trump lost. Think about that. The sitting president warning that democracy may be broken by this election.

Finally, my thanks to the other executives and experts at S&S who were unflagging in their support and expertise: U.S. lawyer Elisa Rivlin for keeping me out of trouble; executive editors Priscilla Painton and Jonathan Jao for using their weekends to provide precise and thoughtful review; associate publisher Irene Kheradi; Stephen Bedford on marketing; Maria Mendez on editorial; and Amanda Mulholland on managing editorial.

To the indexers, the ever reliable Richard Shrout and talented Pilar Wyman; proofreaders Debbie Friedman, Gregory Lauzon and Rob Sternitzky; audio producers Karen Pearlman and Elisa Shokoff; art director Jackie Seow; book designer Paul Dippolito; map designer David Lindroth; production manager Beth Maglione; production editor Lisa Healy; and for the ebook, Mikaela Bielawski.

Writing a book is all about teamwork. I'm fortunate to have so many kind and talented people working with me.

Source Notes

The information in this book comes primarily from my deep background interviews with firsthand participants and witnesses, or from contemporaneous meeting notes and documents. Additional and supplemental source notes follow, which include recommendations for further reading on subjects covered in my reporting.

PROLOGUE

2. *The Trump interview*: Bob Woodward and Carl Bernstein, Transcript of Interview with Donald J. Trump at Trump Tower, 1989.
2. *"We sat at a table and we talked"*: Bob Woodward, *The Trump Tapes: Bob Woodward's Twenty Interviews with President Donald Trump* (New York: Simon & Schuster, 2022), p. 46.

ONE

11. *"Where is the president?"*: Bob Woodward and Robert Costa, *Peril* (New York: Simon & Schuster, 2021), pp. 244–258.
12. *It took President Trump*: Final Report of the Select Committee to Investigate the January 6th Attack on the United States Capitol, House Report 117-663, December 22, 2022, p. 577.
12. *At Trump's "Save America" rally*: Aaron Blake, "What Trump Said Before His Supporters Stormed The Capitol, Annotated," *The Washington Post*, January 11, 2021.
12. *The House Select Committee*: Final Report of the Select Committee to Investigate the January 6th Attack on the United States Capitol, House Report 117-663, December 22, 2022, p. 100.
13. *Garrett Miller, a Trump supporter*: Ibid, p. 3.
13. *"You need to call Joe Biden"*: Bob Woodward and Robert Costa, *Peril* (New York: Simon & Schuster, 2021), p. 288.
14. *But on his last night in the Oval*: Chris Whipple, *The Fight of His Life* (New York: Simon & Schuster, 2023), p. 53.

14   *"I'm done," Trump said*: Jonathan Karl, *Tired of Winning* (Dutton, 2023), p. 41.

14   *"You cannot do that"*: Ibid.

14   *"This isn't their Republican Party anymore"*: Dominick Mastrangelo, "Trump supporters in DC 'should send a message' to GOP 'this isn't' their party anymore," *The Hill*, January 6, 2021.

16   *President Trump, in a dark suit*: Bob Woodward and Robert Costa, *Peril* (New York: Simon & Schuster, 2021), pp. 301–305.

TWO

19   *It was April 2021*: Isabelle Khurshudyan, David L. Stern, Loveday Morris, and John Hudson, "On Ukraine's Doorstep, Russia Boosts Military and Sends Message of Regional Clout to Biden," *The Washington Post*, April 10, 2021.

20   *Russia and Ukraine had been fighting in the Donbas*: Jeffrey Gettleman, "The 'Wild Field' Where Putin Sowed the Seeds of War," *The New York Times*, September 17, 2022; International Crisis Group, "Conflict in Ukraine's Donbas: A Visual Explainer," Crisisgroup.org.

21   *Biden had also upped*: "Transcript: ABC News' George Stephanopoulos Interviews President Joe Biden," ABC News, March 16, 2021.

21   *The Kremlin had called*: Sarah Rainsford, "Putin on Biden: Russian President Reacts to US Leader's Criticism," BBC News, March 18, 2021.

22   *A transcript of the call*: "Telephone Conversation with President Zelensky of Ukraine," July 25, 2019, transcript, declassified September 24, 2019, Whitehouse.gov.

22   *He was later acquitted*: Seung Min Kim, "In Historic Vote, Trump Acquitted of Impeachment Charges," *The Washington Post*, February 5, 2020.

24   *Now on April 13, 2021*: "Readout of President Joseph R. Biden, Jr. Call with President Vladimir Putin of Russia," Briefing Room, April 13, 2021, Whitehouse.gov; "Telephone Conversation with US President Joseph Biden," The Kremlin, April 13, 2021, en.kremlin.ru.

24   *He then described to Putin*: "Fact Sheet: Imposing Costs for Harmful Foreign Activities by the Russian Government," Briefing Room, April 15, 2021, Whitehouse.gov.

25   *Biden had later claimed*: Evan Osnos, "The Biden Agenda," *The New Yorker*, July 20, 2014.

25   *Russia had more than 4,400*: Hans M. Kristensen and Matt Korda, "Russian Nuclear Weapons, 2021," *Bulletin of the Atomic Scientists* 77, no. 2 (March 18, 2021): 90–108.

25   *"Okay," Putin finally replied*: "Statement by White House Press Secretary Jen Psaki on the Meeting Between President Joe Biden and President Vladimir Putin of Russia," Briefing Room, May 25, 2021, Whitehouse.gov.

25   *In 2007 during a bilateral meeting*: George Packer, "The Quiet German," *The New Yorker*, November 24, 2014; "Vladimir Putin: I Didn't Mean to Scare Angela Merkel with My Dog," CNN, January 12, 2016.

26   *"It doesn't eat journalists"*: Ibid.

26   *In 2018, a week before*: "Grand Jury Indicts 12 Russian Intelligence Officers

for Hacking Offences Related to the 2016 Election," Office of Public Affairs, Department of Justice, July 13, 2018, Justice.gov.

26 *In a joint press conference*: "Transcript: Trump and Putin's Joint Press Conference," NPR, July 16, 2018.

26 *After returning to the U.S.*: @realDonaldTrump, "As I said today and many times before, 'I have GREAT confidence in MY intelligence people.' However, I also recognize that in order to build a brighter future, we cannot exclusively focus on the past—as the world's two largest nuclear powers, we must get along! #HELSINKI2018," 3:40 p.m., July 16, 2018, Twitter.com.

26 *"I want Putin to respect our country, okay?"*: Bob Woodward, *The Trump Tapes: Bob Woodward's Twenty Interviews with President Donald Trump* (New York: Simon & Schuster, 2022), p. 35.

THREE

28 *No adviser felt*: Dr. Fiona Hill, *Mr. Putin: Operative in the Kremlin* (Washington, D.C.: Brookings Institution Press, 2015); Dr. Fiona Hill, *There Is Nothing for You Here: Finding Opportunity in the 21st Century* (Boston: Mariner Books, 2021).

28 *Backstage in Helsinki*: Martin Pengelly, "Trump 'Would've Lost Mind Completely' if Putin Admitted Interference, Fiona Hill Says," *The Guardian*, February 24, 2024.

28 *She said*: "Full Transcript of Testimony of Fiona Hill, Former Top Russia Adviser to the White House," *The Washington Post*, November 8, 2019; John Cassidy, "The Extraordinary Impeachment Testimony of Fiona Hill," *The New Yorker*, November 21, 2019.

28 *Trump idolized Putin*: "Fiona Hill Reflects on Impeachment Testimony, Trump Presidency and Opportunity in America," PBS, October 8, 2021.

30 *Russian troops continued*: Anton Troianovski, "'A Threat from the Russian State': Ukrainians Alarmed as Troops Mass on Their Doorstep," *The New York Times*, April 20, 2021.

FOUR

31 *Putin gave his annual*: Vladimir Putin, Presidential Address to the Federal Assembly, April 21, 2021, en.kremlin.ru.

31 *Former Russian opposition leader*: Anton Troianovski, "As Evidence Mounts That Navalny Was Poisoned by State, Russians Just Sigh," *The New York Times*, December 23, 2020.

31 *On foreign policy*: Vladimir Putin, Presidential Address to the Federal Assembly, April 21, 2021, en.kremlin.ru.

32 *The next day*: Vladimir Isachenkov, "Russia Orders Troop Pullback but Keeps Weapons Near Ukraine," Associated Press, April 22, 2022; Matthew Funaiole, "Unpacking the Russian Troop Buildup Along Ukraine's Border," Center for Strategic and International Studies, April 22, 2021, cisis.org.

32 *By mid-May*: Helene Cooper and Julian E. Barnes, "80,000 Russian Troops

Remain at Ukraine Border as U.S. and NATO Hold Exercises," *The New York Times*, May 5, 2021.

32 *"What is happening"*: Dmytro Kuleba, "Withdrawal of Troops Without Withdrawal of Troops," television interview, DW Ukraine, May 17, 2021.

32 *NATO's Special Operations adviser*: Cooper and Barnes, "80,000 Russian Troops Remain at Ukraine Border as U.S. and NATO Hold Exercises."

FIVE

For public information on Putin's handling of the coronavirus: Alexey Kovalev, "The Pandemic Is Beating Putin," *The New York Times*, December 8, 2021; David E. Sanger and Anton Troianovski, "U.S. Intelligence Weighs Putin's Two Years of Extreme Pandemic Isolation as a Factor in His Wartime Mind-set," *The New York Times*, March 5, 2022.

SIX

34 *President Biden and President Putin*: Isabella Kwai, "An 18th-Century Villa Was Again a Stage for History," *The New York Times*, June 16, 2021; "In Photos: Biden Meets with Putin," CNN, June 16, 2021.

34 *Putin had been 45 minutes late*: Antonia Noori Farzan, "How Biden's Meeting with Putin Differed from Trump's," *The Washington Post*, June 16, 2021.

34 *Secretary of State*: Ibid.

34 *Top of Biden's agenda*: Isabella Khurshudyan and Loveday Morris, "Ransomware's Suspected Russian Roots Point to a Long Détente Between the Kremlin and Hackers," *The Washington Post*, June 12, 2021; "Biden and Putin Agree to Resume Nuclear Talks, Return Ambassadors to Posts," CNBC, June 16, 2021.

34 *"Why did you leave Afghanistan?"*: Franklin Foer, *The Last Politician: Inside Joe Biden's White House and the Struggle for America's Future* (New York: Penguin, 2023), p. 135.

35 *"Why did you leave?"*: Ibid.

35 *Presidents Putin and Biden*: "Watch: Putin Holds News Conference After Meeting with Biden," Associated Press, June 16, 2021, pbs.org; "News Conference Following Russia-US Talks," Transcript: June 16, 2021, en.kremlin.ru.

36 *NATO had conducted*: C. Todd Lopez, "Defender Europe 21 Exercises Multinational Interoperability, Readiness, Transparency," U.S. Department of Defense News, May 3, 2021, Defense.gov.

36 *Putin took another jab*: "News Conference following Russia-US talks," Transcript: June 16, 2021, en.kremlin.ru.

36 *"Leo Tolstoy said once"*: "News Conference Following Russia-US Talks," Transcript: June 16, 2021, en.kremlin.ru.; Eric Lutz, "Putin, After Spending the Day with Joe Biden: 'There Is No Happiness in Life,'" *Vanity Fair*, June 16, 2021.

37 *Biden followed*: "Remarks by President Biden in Press Conference," Hôtel du Parc des Eaux-Vives, Geneva, Switzerland, June 16, 2021, Whitehouse.gov.

38 *On Fox News*: "Transcript: Hannity on Biden-Putin Summit, Trump's Reaction," Fox News, June 16, 2021.

SEVEN

39 *Polls showed*: "53% of Republicans View Trump as True U.S. President-Reuters/Ipsos," Reuters, May 24, 2021.

39 *During my interview*: Bob Woodward, *The Trump Tapes: Bob Woodward's Twenty Interviews with President Donald Trump* (New York: Simon & Schuster, 2022), p. 33.

39 *"I wouldn't be surprised"*: Philip Bump, "The Obvious Goal of the Arizona Recount: Injecting More Doubt into the 2020 Results," *The Washington Post*, May 3, 2021.

39 *But more than 60 court cases*: "In More than 60 Cases, Judges Looked at the Allegations That Trump Was Making and Determined They Were Without Any Merit," PolitiFact, The Poynter Institute, January 8, 2021, politifact.com/factchecks.

40 *Prominent Republican election lawyer*: Final Report of the Select Committee to Investigate the January 6th Attack on the United States Capitol, House Report 117-663, December 22, 2022, p. 19.

41 *But Trump would not*: Philip Bump, "As on Jan. 6, Trump Won't Accept the Reality of His Loss," *The Washington Post*, June 3, 2021.

41 *In June 2021*: Quinn Scanian and Madison Burinsky, "Trump Was Privately Enthralled by Baseless Theory He Could Be Reinstated as President: New Book," ABC News, November 12, 2023; Jonathan Karl, *Tired of Winning: Donald Trump and the End of the Grand Old Party* (New York: Dutton, 2023).

41 *Trump phoned*: Joe Walsh, "GOP Rep. Mo Brooks Claims Trump Asked Him to Reinstate Trump Presidency," *Forbes*, March 23, 2022.

EIGHT

42 *In a starkly personal*: Vladimir Putin, "On the Historical Unity of Russians and Ukrainians," July 12, 2021, en.kremlin.ru. To read more about the history of Russia and Ukraine, see: Serhii Plokhy, *The Russo-Ukrainian War: The Return of History* (New York: Norton, 2023); Michael Kimmage, "Born in the Bloodlands," *Foreign Affairs*, August 22, 2023.

44 *Putin called Ukraine's leaders*: Gal Beckerman, "How Zelensky Gave the World a Jewish Hero," *The Atlantic*, February 27, 2022; Anton Troianovski, "Why Vladimir Putin Invokes Nazis to Justify His Invasion of Ukraine," *The New York Times*, March 17, 2022.

NINE

46 *"Listen to me, boss"*: Barack Obama, *A Promised Land* (New York: Crown, 2020), pp. 318–19.

46 *Also hanging over Biden*: "Agreement for Bringing Peace to Afghanistan Be-
    tween the Islamic Emirate of Afghanistan Which Is Not Recognized by the
    United States as a State and Is Known as the Taliban and the United States of
    America," U.S. Department of State, February 29, 2020.

47 *The options presented to Biden*: For more on this, see Bob Woodward and
    Robert Costa, *Peril* (New York: Simon & Schuster, 2021), pp. 334–40, 376–
    91.

47 *President Biden had given*: "Remarks by President Biden on the Way Forward
    in Afghanistan," Treaty Room, April 14, 2021, Whitehouse.gov.

48 *In an unusual public display*: Anna Gearan, Karen DeYoung, and Tyler Page,
    "Biden Tells Americans 'We Cannot Continue the Cycle' in Afghanistan as He
    Announces Troop Withdrawal," *The Washington Post*, April 14, 2021.

49 *Former president George W. Bush*: Kylie Atwood, "Bush Calls Afghanistan
    Withdrawal a Mistake, Says Consequences Will Be 'Unbelievably Bad,'"
    CNN, July 14, 2021, cnn.com.

49 *"All the troops"*: "Donald Trump, Wellington, Ohio, Rally Speech Transcript:
    First Rally Since Leaving Office," rev.com.

49 *Despite more than 50*: Michael D. Shear et al., "Miscue After Miscue, U.S.
    Exit Plan Unravels," *The New York Times*, August 21, 2021; Jonathan Swan
    and Zachary Basu, "Scoop: Milley's Blunt Private Blame for the State De-
    partment," *Axios*, September 29, 2021; Mark Mazzetti, Julian E. Barnes, and
    Adam Goldman, "Intelligence Warned of Afghan Military Collapse, Despite
    Biden's Assurances," *The New York Times*, August 17, 2021.

49 *On July 6*: Kathy Gannon, "U.S. Left Afghan Airfield at Night, Didn't Tell
    Commander," Associated Press, July 6, 2021; Oren Liebermann and Michael
    Conte, "Top Generals Who Oversaw U.S. Withdrawal from Afghanistan Slam
    State Department for Delaying Emergency Evacuation," CNN, March 19,
    2024.

50 *On July 23*: "Excerpts of Call Between Joe Biden and Ashraf Ghani July 23,"
    Reuters, August 31, 2021.

50 *In an about-face*: Andrew Stanton, "Trump Calls on Biden to 'Resign in Dis-
    grace' After 'Tragic Mess in Afghanistan,'" *Newsweek*, August 15, 2021.

51 *President Biden blamed*: "Remarks by President Biden on Afghanistan," East
    Room, White House, August 16, 2021, Whitehouse.gov.

51 *Ten days later*: Ruby Mellen, "Two Weeks of Chaos: A Timeline of the Pullout
    of Afghanistan," *The Washington Post*, August 15, 2022.

51 *On August 29*: Ibid.

51 *His speech, which hailed*: "Remarks by President Biden on the End of the
    War in Afghanistan," State Dining Room, White House, August 31, 2021,
    Whitehouse.gov.

52 *Biden shifted blame*: The Wall Street Journal Editorial Board, "A Dishonest
    Afghanistan Accounting," *The Wall Street Journal*, August 31, 2021; Jona-
    than Swan and Hans Nichols, "Scoop: Leaked Document Reveals Biden's Af-
    ghan Failures," *Axios*, February 1, 2022.

52 *"The national security adviser"*: Joseph Choi, "Ex-Obama Adviser Argues
    Biden Should Fire Sullivan over Afghanistan," *The Hill*, August 16, 2021.

TEN

55 *The parade*: "Live: Ukraine Celebrates 30 Years of Independence Amid Tensions with Russia," *Euronews*, August 24, 2021.

55 *An emotional*: "President Took Part in the Festive Parade of Troops on the Occasion of the 30th Anniversary of Ukraine's Independence," President of Ukraine, August 24, 2021, president.gov.ua.

56 *His family were*: Andrew Hammond, Historian and Curator, International Spy Museum, interview with British Defense Attaché, USA, Rear Admiral Tim Woods, *SpyCast*, Episode 612, November 21, 2023, thecyberwire.com /podcast.

ELEVEN

57 *Putin's ultimate intentions remained*: "Putin's Road to War," *Frontline* (Episode 18), PBS, March 15 and April 18, 2022.

57 *Russian forces swiftly annexed Crimea*: Serhii Plokhy, *The Russo-Ukrainian War: The Return of History* (New York: Norton, 2023), pp. 118–134; Wojciech Kononczuk, "Russia's Real Aims in Crimea," Carnegie Endowment for International Peace, March 13, 2014.

57 *Tony Blinken*: Kylie Atwood, "Blinken Becomes Biden's Top Diplomat After a Friendship Forged over Decades," CNN, January 26, 2021.

58 *Less than two weeks*: "A Memorandum on the Delegation of Authority Under Section 506(a)(1) of The Foreign Assistance Act of 1961," The White House, August 27, 2021; "Joint Statement on the U.S.-Ukraine Strategic Partnership," Briefing Room, September 1, 2021, Whitehouse.gov.

59 *In a brief notification to Congress*: Eric Tucker, "US Commits $60 Million in Aid to Ukraine Before WH Visit," Associated Press, August 31, 2021.

TWELVE

60 *On September 1*: "Remarks by President Biden and President Zelensky of Ukraine Before Bilateral Meeting," Briefing Room, September 1, 2021, Whitehouse.gov.

60 *Zelensky won a crushing*: "Ukraine Election: Comedian Zelensky Wins Presidency by Landslide," BBC, April 22, 2019.

60 *In the TV show*: Ashley Fetters Maloy, "What Zelensky's TV Show, 'Servant of the People,' Reveals About Him, and Ukraine," *The Washington Post*, March 22, 2022; James Poniewozik, "Volodymyr Zelensky Is Playing the Role of His Life," *The New York Times*, June 22, 2023.

60 *In a dark*: David L. Stern and Anton Troianovski, "He Played Ukraine's President on TV. Now He Has Taken Office as the Real One," *The Washington Post*, May 20, 2019.

60 *"Dear Ukrainians,"*: "Volodymyr Zelenskyy's Inaugural Address," President of Ukraine, May 20, 2019.

61 *During a July 25, 2019, call*: "Full Document: Trump's Call with the Ukrainian President," *The New York Times*, October 30, 2019.

62 *When I interviewed Trump*: Bob Woodward, *The Trump Tapes: Bob Woodward's Twenty Interviews with President Donald Trump* (New York: Simon & Schuster, 2022), p. 136.

62 *Zelensky later told*: Simon Schuster, *The Showman: Inside the Invasion That Shook the World and Made a Leader of Volodymyr Zelensky* (New York: William Morrow, 2024), pp. 138–39.

62 *"I would never want Ukraine"*: Ibid., p. 139.

62 *"When we're giving"*: Woodward, *The Trump Tapes*, p. 157.

63 *When Zelensky visited*: Ashley Parker and Anne Gearan, "Biden Backs Lasting Support for Ukraine as Both Nations Move on from the Trump-Era Obsession with Kyiv," *The Washington Post*, September 1, 2021.

63 *When Burns was U.S. ambassador*: William J. Burns, *The Back Channel* (New York: Random House, 2019), pp. 232–33.

THIRTEEN

65 *Putin's invasion of Crimea in 2014 had hardened*: Steven Pifer, "How Ukraine Views Russia and the West," *Brookings*, October 18, 2017, brookings.edu.

65 *Prior to 2014*: Olga Onuch and Javier Pérez Sandoval, "A Majority of Ukrainians Support Joining NATO. Does This Matter?," *The Washington Post*, February 4, 2022; Pifer, "How Ukraine Views Russia and the West"; "Ukraine's President Signs Amendment on NATO, EU Membership," Associated Press, February 19, 2019.

66 *Avril Haines*: Erin Banco, Garrett M. Graff, Lara Seligman, Nahal Toosi, and Alexander Ward, " 'Something Was Badly Wrong': When Washington Realized Russia Was Actually Invading Ukraine," *Politico*, February 24, 2023; Avril Haines, "A Conference on Today's Competitive Geopolitical Landscape—In Honor of Robert Jervis," February 17, 2023, odni.gov.

67 *Putin had long lamented*: President Vladimir Putin, "Annual Address to the Federal Assembly of the Russian Federation," The Kremlin, April 25, 2005, en.kremlin.ru.

69 *Sullivan kept in*: See Fred Kagan, Institute for the Study of War, understandingwar.org.

70 *Hanging over the intelligence*: Yaroslav Trofimov and Jeremy Page, "In Leaving Afghanistan, U.S. Reshuffles Global Power Relations, *The Wall Street Journal*, September 1, 2021.

FOURTEEN

72 *On the sidelines*: "Remarks by President Biden in Press Conference: Rome, Italy," Briefing, Lu Nuvola, October 31, 2021, Whitehouse.gov.

FIFTEEN

75 *President Biden decided to send*: Julian E. Barnes and Pranshu Verma, "William Burns, a Career Diplomat, Is Biden's Choice to Head the C.I.A.," *The New York Times*, January 11, 2021; Nahal Toosi, "The Putinologist: CIA Chief's Long History with Putin Gives Him Special Insight," *Politico*, May 30, 2022; Robert Draper, "William Burns, a C.I.A. Spymaster with Unusual Powers," *The New York Times*, May 9, 2023.

75 *The CIA director was acutely*: See William J. Burns, "A World Transformed and the Role of Intelligence," Ditchley Annual Lecture, July 1, 2023, cia.gov.

75 *Burns first went*: See also Natasha Bertrand, Jim Sciutoo, and Kylie Atwood, "CIA Director Dispatched to Moscow to Warn Russia over Troop Buildup Near Ukraine," CNN, November 5, 2021; William J. Burns, "The Global Threat Landscape," Georgetown University, February 2, 2023.

77 *Removal from the Swift system*: For more on Swift: Christian Perez, "Future of Global Commerce?," "Removing Russian Banks from the SWIFT System Is Accelerating a Global Economic Realignment," *Foreign Policy*, March 8, 2022.

79 *Burns believed*: Erin Banco, Garrett M. Graff, Lara Seligman, Nahal Toosi, and Alexander Ward, " 'Something Was Badly Wrong': When Washington Realized Russia Was Actually Invading Ukraine," *Politico*, February 24, 2023.

81 *Austin, age 71*: Joe Biden, "Why I Chose Lloyd Austin as Secretary of Defense," *The Atlantic*, December 8, 2020.

82 *Just like Zelensky*: Simon Shuster, *The Showman* (New York: William Morrow, 2024), p. 211.

SIXTEEN

84 *Vice President Kamala Harris traveled to Paris*: Sarah Kolinovsky, "Harris Heads to Paris to Soothe Tensions With French After 'Submarine Snub,' ABC News, November 8, 2021; "France Deplores 'Stab In The Back' By U.S., Australia over Subs Contract," France24, September 16, 2021.

85 *When Harris delivered her address*: Chris Whipple, *The Fight of His Life* (New York: Simon & Schuster, 2023), p. 213.

SEVENTEEN

86 *Blinken flew to Stockholm*: "Secretary Antony J. Blinken at a Press Availability at the Organization for Security and Cooperation in Europe (OSCE)," Stockholm, Sweden, December 2, 2021, State.gov; "Secretary Blinken: Remarks to the First Session of the OSCE Ministerial Council Meeting," December 2, 2021, Osce.usmission.gov.

86 *Lavrov*: "Who is Sergei Lavrov, Russia's Foreign Minister?," Reuters, November 14, 2022.

86 *"The OSCE is"*: "Statement by Mr. Sergey Lavrov, Minister of Foreign Affairs of the Russian Federation at the 28th Meeting of the OSCE Ministerial Council," Stockholm, December 2, 2021, Osce.org.

87   *"The fall of"*: Ibid.

87   *The Minsk agreements*: "What Are the Minsk Agreements on the Ukraine Conflict?," Reuters, December 6, 2021; Marie Dumoulin, "Ukraine, Russia and the Minsk Agreements: A Post-Mortem," European Council on Foreign Relations, February 19, 2024, Ecrf.eu.

87   *"The decision"*: Ibid.

88   *"The seizure by force"*: "Secretary Antony J. Blinken at OSCE, Session 1 Remarks," Stockholm, Sweden, December 2, 2021, State.gov.

EIGHTEEN

93   *Letting someone in*: "PDNSA Jon Finer's Remarks at the 2023 Intelligence and National Security Summit," transcript, July 14, 2023.

94   *Initially the intelligence*: Massimo Calabresi, "Inside the White House Program to Share America's Secrets," *Time*, February 29, 2024.

94   *The next step*: See also Julian Barnes and Helene Cooper, "U.S. Battles Putin by Disclosing His Next Possible Moves," *The New York Times*, February 12, 2022.

94   *The Washington Post*: Shane Harris and Paul Sonne, "Russia Planning Massive Military Offensive Against Ukraine Involving 175,000 Troops, U.S. Intelligence Warns," *The Washington Post*, December 3, 2021. Other examples of intelligence downgrades:

- Natasha Bertrand and Jeremy Herb, "First on CNN: US Intelligence Indicates Russia Preparing Operation to Justify Invasion of Ukraine," CNN, January 14, 2022;
- Katie Bo Lillis, Natasha Bertrand, and Kylie Atwood, "How the Biden Administration Is Aggressively Releasing Intelligence in an Attempt to Deter Russia," CNN, February 11, 2022;
- Secretary Antony J. Blinken on Russia's Threat to Peace and Security at the U.N. Security Council," U.S. Department of State, February 17, 2022;
- Bill Chappell, "The U.S. Warns That Russia Has a 'Kill List' of Ukrainians to Be Detained or Killed," NPR, February 21, 2022;
- Aamer Madhani, Josh Boak, and Matthew Lee, "U.S. Warns Chinese on Support for Russia in Ukraine War," Associated Press, March 14, 2022;
- Aamer Madhani and Josh Boak, "U.S. Official: Russia Seeking Military Aid from China," *Military Times*, March 14, 2022;
- Eric Schmitt, "More Russian Mercenaries Deploying to Ukraine to Take on Greater Role in War," *The New York Times*, March 25, 2022;
- Steve Holland and Michelle Nichols, "Exclusive—Photos Show Russian Attacks on Ukraine Grain Storage—U.S. Official," Reuters, April 1, 2022;
- Shane Harris, "U.S. Intelligence Document Shows Russian Naval Blockade of Ukraine," *The Washington Post*, May 24, 2022;
- Natasha Bertrand, "U.S. Assesses Russia Now in Possession of Iranian Drones, Sources Say," CNN, August 30, 2022.

94   *Putin continued*: Mark Trevelyan, "Putin Says Russia Has 'Nowhere to Retreat' over Ukraine," Reuters, December 22, 2021.

NINETEEN

96 *"If you do this"*: Paul Sonne, Ashley Parker, and Isabelle Khurshudyan, "Biden Threatens Putin with Economic Sanctions if He Further Invades Ukraine," *The Washington Post*, December 7, 2021; Ben Gittleson, Molly Nagle, and Sarah Kolinovsky, "Biden Confronts Putin over Ukraine in High-Stakes Meeting," ABC News, December 7, 2021.

96 *He demanded security guarantees*: Patrick Reevell, "Russia Makes Sweeping Demands for Security Guarantees from US Amid Ukraine Tensions," ABC News, December 17, 2021; Hibai Arbide Aza and Miguel Gonzalez, "US Offered Disarmament Measures to Russia in Exchange for De-escalation of Military Threat in Ukraine," *El País*, February 2, 2022.

97 *During an interview*: Bob Woodward, *The Trump Tapes* (New York: Simon & Schuster, 2022), pp. 172–73.

98 *President Obama had*: Robert Burns, Aamer Madhani, and Hope Yen, "AP Fact Check: Trump Distorts Obama-Biden Aid to Ukraine," Associated Press, March 27, 2022.

TWENTY

101 *"That is not on the table"*: John Wagner and Ashley Parker, "Biden Says U.S. Ground Troops 'Not on the Table' for Ukraine," *The Washington Post*, December 8, 2021.

101 *Fred Kagan*: Institute for the Study of War, understandingwar.org.

102 *Biden, however*: Amy Mackinnon and Jack Detsch, "Ukraine's Military Has Come a Long Way Since 2014," *Foreign Policy*, December 23, 2021.

TWENTY-ONE

103 *Biden was at his home*: David Smith, "Biden and Putin Exchange Warnings During Phone Call Amid Rising Ukraine Tensions," *The Guardian*, December 30, 2021.

103 *Putin was furious*: David E. Sanger and Andrew E. Kramer, "Putin Warns Biden of 'Complete Rupture' of U.S.-Russia Relationship over Ukraine," *The New York Times*, December 30, 2021.

103 *In 2014, Putin invaded Crimea*: Steven Pifer, "Watch Out for Little Green Men," *Brookings*, July 7, 2014, brookings.edu.

TWENTY-TWO

105 *In mid-January 2022*: Erin Banco, Garrett M. Graff, Lara Seligman, Nahal Toosi, and Alexander Ward, " 'Something Was Badly Wrong': When Washington Realized Russia Was Actually Invading Ukraine," *Politico*, February 24, 2023.

105 *Zelensky remained doubtful*: Simon Shuster, *The Showman* (New York: William Morrow, 2024), p. 11.

106 *One of the more*: Margaret Brennan, "New Details About Russian 'False Flag' Plan Prompts U.S. to Prepare for Worst in Ukraine," CBS News, February 12, 2022.

107 *"Without getting into"*: "Pentagon Press Secretary John Kirby Holds Briefing on Russia's Activities in Ukraine," PBS, January 14, 2022.

TWENTY-THREE

108 *On January 19*: Paul Sonne, "Biden Predicts Putin Will 'Move In' to Ukraine Because 'He Has to Do Something,'" *The Washington Post*, January 20, 2022.

108 *"I think what"*: "Remarks by President Biden in Press Conference," Briefing Room, January 19, 2022, Whitehouse.gov.

108 *President Zelensky responded*: @ZelenskyyUa, 9:29 a.m. January 20, 2022, Twitter.com.

109 *Biden was then forced*: Asma Khalid, "How Biden Is Trying to Clean Up His Comments About Russia and Ukraine," NPR, January 20, 2022.

110 *The U.S. intelligence*: For public reporting: Max Seddon, Christopher Miller, and Felicia Schwartz, "How Putin Blundered into Ukraine—Then Doubled Down," *Financial Times*, February 23, 2023.

TWENTY-FOUR

See also Bob Woodward, *The Trump Tapes: Bob Woodward's Twenty Interviews with President Donald Trump* (New York: Simon & Schuster Audio, 2022), p. 16.

TWENTY-FIVE

112 *Still mindful of the 1979*: "Press Briefing by Press Secretary Jen Psaki and National Security Adviser Jake Sullivan," James S. Brady Press Briefing Room, February 11, 2022, Whitehouse.gov.

112 *French president Emmanuel Macron*: "Putin Gave No Indication in Macron Call He's Preparing Invasion," Reuters, February 12, 2022; "Ukraine Crisis: Macron Says Putin Pledges No New Ukraine Escalation," BBC News, February 8, 2022.

113 *"No one exercises that long"*: Erin Banco, Garrett M. Graff, Lara Seligman, Nahal Toosi, and Alexander Ward, "'Something Was Badly Wrong': When Washington Realized Russia Was Actually Invading Ukraine," *Politico*, February 24, 2023.

114 *"Not since the end of the Cold War"*: "Remarks by Vice President Harris at the Munich Security Conference," Hotel Bayerischer Hof, February 18, 2022, Whitehouse.gov.

115 *It disgruntled Zelensky*: Simon Shuster, *The Showman* (New York: William Morrow, 2024), pp. 219–220.

116 *"What will that give you?"*: Ibid., p. 221.

116 *Harris said the U.S.*: Ibid.

TWENTY-SIX

118 *On Monday, February 21:* "The President Held a Meeting of the Russian Federation Security Council at the Kremlin," The Kremlin, February 21, 2022, en.kremlin.ru.

118 *Naryshkin tried again:* See also Shaun Walker, "Putin's Absurd, Angry Spectacle Will Be a Turning Point in His Long Reign," *The Guardian*, February 21, 2022.

119 *President Biden immediately:* "Fact Sheet: Executive Order to Impose Costs for President Putin's Action to Recognize So-Called Donetsk and Luhansk People's Republics," February 21, 2022, Whitehouse.gov.

119 *"This is genius":* "Full Interview: President Trump with C&B from Mar-a-Lago," *Clay & Buck*, February 22, 2022, clayandbuck.com; Joseph Gedeon, "Trump Calls Putin 'Genius' and 'Savvy' for Ukraine Invasion," *Politico*, February 23, 2022.

TWENTY-SEVEN

120 *Before sunrise:* "Special Report: Russia's War on Ukraine, One Year On," CNN, February 23, 2023, edition.cnn.com/interactive.

120 *"I have decided":* Andrew Osborn and Polina Nikolskaya, "Russia's Putin Authorizes 'Special Military Operation' Against Ukraine," Reuters, February 24, 2022.

121 *President Zelensky raced:* Isabelle Khurshudyan, "An Interview with Ukrainian President Volodymyr Zelensky," *The Washington Post*, August 23, 2022.

121 *Zelensky's phone rang:* Simon Shuster, *The Showman* (New York: William Morrow, 2024), p. 7.

121 *"All of them":* Ibid.

121 *In Washington, D.C.:* See also Erin Banco, Garrett M. Graff, Lara Seligman, Nahal Toosi, and Alexander Ward, " 'Something Was Badly Wrong': When Washington Realized Russia Was Actually Invading Ukraine," *Politico*, February 24, 2023.

122 *He is "pretty smart":* Andrew Restuccia, "Trump Calls Putin's Invasion of Ukraine Smart, Blames Biden for Not Doing Enough," *The Wall Street Journal*, February 24, 2022.

122 *"We will fight, Boris":* Shuster, *The Showman*, pp. 16–17.

122 *"It's very important, Emmanuel":* Ibid., p. 18.

123 *"I don't know when":* See also Banco et al., " 'Something Was Badly Wrong': When Washington Realized Russia Was Actually Invading Ukraine."

123 *"If you ever want":* Ibid.

123 *A few hours later:* "Full Transcript of Zelensky's Emotional Appeal to Russians," Reuters, February 23, 2022.

123 *At Snake Island:* "Special Report: Russia's War on Ukraine, One Year On," CNN.

124 *Later that day*: Valerie Hopkins, "In Video, a Defiant Zelensky Says, 'We Are Here,'" *The New York Times*, February 25, 2022.

124 *Watching this*: Banco et al., "'Something Was Badly Wrong': When Washington Realized Russia Was Actually Invading Ukraine."

124 *In the early hours*: Paul Sonne, Isabelle Khurshudyan, Serhiy Morgunov, and Kostiantyn Khudov, "Battle for Kyiv: Ukrainian Valor, Russian Blunders Combined to Save the Capital," *The Washington Post*, August 24, 2022.

124 *The airport had*: "Ukrainian Soldier on the Battle That 'Changed the Course of the War,' and What He Fears Russia Will Do Next," CBS, April 7, 2022.

124 *Ukrainian troops fought back*: Liam Collins, Michael Kofman, and John Spencer, "The Battle of Hostomel Airport: A Key Moment in Russia's Defeat in Kyiv," *War on the Rocks*, August 10, 2023, Warontherocks.com.

125 *"Military theory does"*: Simon Shuster, "2022 Person of The Year: Volodymyr Zelensky," *Time*, December 7, 2022.

125 *In the first wave*: "Unprotected Russian Soldiers Disturbed Radioactive Dust in Chernobyl's 'Red Forest,' Workers Say," Reuters, March 29, 2022.

125 *By the fifth day*: Nicole Werbeck, "Satellite Images Show 40-Mile-Long Russian Military Convoy Nearing Kyiv," NPR, February 28, 2022; Luke McGee, "Here's What We Know About the 40-Mile-Long Russian Convoy Outside Ukraine's Capital," CNN, March 3, 2022.

126 *The battle for Kyiv*: Paul Sonne, Isabelle Khurshudyan, Serhiy Morgunov, and Kostiantyn Khudov, "Battle for Kyiv: Ukrainian Valor, Russian Blunders Combined to Save the Capital," *The Washington Post*, August 24, 2022; Michael Schwirtz et al., "Putin's War," *New York Times*, December 16, 2022, nytimes.com/interactive.

127 *When the Russians*: Adam Shreck, "As Russians Retreat from Outskirts of Kyiv, Ukrainians Document Atrocities," Associated Press, April 6, 2022; Yousur Al-Hlou et al., "Caught on Camera, Traced by Phone: The Russian Military Unit That Killed Dozens in Bucha," *The New York Times*, December 22, 2022; Simon Shuster, "A Visit to the Crime Scene Russian Troops Left Behind at a Summer Camp in Bucha," *Time*, April 13, 2022.

TWENTY-EIGHT

129 *"Putin ain't woke"*: Steve Bannon, *War Room*, February 23, 2022; Jackson Richman, "Steve Bannon and Erik Prince Praise Putin and Russia for LGBTQ Intolerance: 'Putin Ain't Woke,'" *Mediaite*, February 24, 2022.

129 *As soon as Russia*: Dan Spinelli, "Putin Invaded Ukraine, and Steve Bannon Says That's a Good Reason to Impeach Biden," *Mother Jones*, February 25, 2022.

129 *"Is Hunter Biden"*: Ibid.

129 *Fox News host*: Tucker Carlson, "Americans Have Been Trained to Hate Putin, and Will Suffer Because of It," Fox News, February 23, 2022.

TWENTY-NINE

130 *Russia had displayed*: David Vergun, "Russia's Grand Strategy for Ukraine Takeover Unmet, DOD Official," U.S. Department of Defense News, June 14, 2022, Defense.gov; Seth G. Jones, "Russia's Ill-Fated Invasion of Ukraine: Lessons in Modern Warfare," Center for Strategic & International Studies, June 1, 2022, Csis.org.

131 *Before the invasion polls*: "Support for NATO Membership Soars to 76 percent," Yie Poll, May 9, 2022; Stine Jacobsen and Johan Ahlander, "Russian Invasion of Ukraine Forces Swedes to Rethink NATO Membership," Reuters, March 4, 2022.

132 *Biden saw an opportunity*: Jonathan Masters, "How NATO Will Change if Finland and Sweden Become Members," Council on Foreign Relations, June 29, 2022, Cfr.org.

132 *"The Finnish watch Putin"*: Jason Horowitz, "He Knows Putin Well. And He Fears for Ukraine," *The New York Times*, February 13, 2022.

132 *On March 4*: Colleen Long and Aamer Madhani, "Finnish Leader Meets Biden, Weighs NATO as War Deepens," Associated Press, March 4, 2022.

133 *"There can be"*: Emily Rauhala and Adela Suliman, "Russia Threatens to Move Nukes to Baltic Region if Finland, Sweden Join NATO," *The Washington Post*, April 14, 2022.

133 *"Russia can be"*: "Sweden Says It Received U.S. Security Assurances if It Hands in NATO Application," Reuters, May 4, 2022.

133 *NATO countries*: "Statement by Denmark, Iceland and Norway on Finland and Sweden's Decisions to Apply for NATO Membership," Ministry of Foreign Affairs, May 18, 2022.

133 *U.K. prime minister*: "Prime Minister Signs New Assurances to Bolster European Security," U.K. Government, May 11, 2022, gov.uk.

134 *"Russia will be"*: "Russia Threatens to Retaliate over Membership Move," BBC, May 12, 2022.

134 *Like clockwork*: "Remarks by President Biden, President Niinistö of Finland, and Prime Minister Andersson of Sweden After Trilateral Meeting," May 19, 2022.

134 *On the same day*: "Long-Planned NATO Exercises Across Europe Get Underway," North Atlantic Treaty Organization, May 13, 2022.

135 *Finland formally became*: "NATO Secretary General: We Will Welcome Finland as the 31st Member of Our Alliance," North Atlantic Treaty Organization, April 4, 2023, Nato.intl.

135 *Turkey and Hungary*: Krisztina Than and Niklas Pollard, "Sweden Clears Final Hurdle to Join NATO as Hungary Approves Accession," Reuters, February 26, 2024.

THIRTY

136 *In a March 4 interview*: "Lindsey Graham Calls for Russians to Assassinate Putin," *The Wall Street Journal*, March 4, 2022.

136 *White House press*: Mary Clare Jalonick, "White House Disavows Graham's Call for Putin Assassination," Associated Press, March 4, 2022.

136 *Kremlin press secretary*: Rebecca Shabad, "Sen. Lindsey Graham Defends Calling for Russians to Assassinate Putin," NBC News, March 4, 2022.

137 *On March 5*: Josh Dawsey, "Trump Muses on War with Russia and Praises Kim Jong Un," *The Washington Post*, March 6, 2022.

THIRTY-ONE

139 *"We want to see Russia weakened"*: "Secretary Antony J. Blinken and Secretary Lloyd Austin Remarks to Traveling Press," U.S. Department of State, April 25, 2022.

139 *Two days later*: "Austin Meets with Nations to Intensify Support for Ukraine," U.S. Department of Defense, April 26, 2022.

139 *Ukraine's defense minister*: Simon Shuster, *The Showman* (New York: William Morrow, 2024), p. 242.

THIRTY-TWO

140 *Hunter*: See also Hunter Biden, *Beautiful Things* (New York: Gallery Books, 2021); Bob Woodward and Robert Costa, *Peril* (New York: Simon & Schuster, 2021), pp. 36–38.

THIRTY-THREE

143 *A few days later*: Patrick Kingsley and Isabel Kershner, "Israel's Government Collapses, Setting Up 5th Election in 3 Years," *The New York Times*, June 20, 2022.

143 *Trump was still*: Andrew Carey and Amir Tal, "Trump Accuses Netanyahu of Disloyalty for Congratulating Biden After 2020 Win: 'F**k him,'" CNN, December 11, 2021.

144 *In May, Congress*: Patricia Zengerle, "After Delay, U.S. Senate Overwhelmingly Approves $40 Billion in Ukraine Aid," Reuters, May 19, 2022.

144 *Russia had lost*: See also Valerie Hopkins, "Tending Russia's Dead as They Pile Up in Ukraine," *The New York Times*, May 29, 2022.

144 *"The Democrats are sending"*: Lisa Mascaro, "GOP Splinters Over $40 Billion Supplemental Funding For Ukraine," PBS News, May 16, 2022.

144 *"There's always been isolationist voices"*: Ibid.

THIRTY-FOUR

145 *It's extraordinary what you've done*: "Coalition Government, CDU Agree Military Spending Hike," DW, May 30, 2022; Peter Hille and Nina Werkhäuser, "The German Military's New Shopping List," DW, June 3, 2022.

146 *The German-manufactured*: "Leopard 2 Main Battle Tank, Germany," *Army Technology*, April 24, 2024, Army-technology.com; Jack Piccone, "Everything

You Need to Know About the Leopard 2 Battle Tank," *SlashGear*, January 20, 2024.

146 *Ukraine had been requesting*: Lara Seligman, Paul Mcleary, and Erin Banco, " 'These Are Not Rental Cars': As Ukraine Pleads for Tanks, the West Holds Back," *Politico*, September 22, 2022.

147 *"The Abrams tank is a very"*: David Martin and Eleanor Watson, "U.S. Poised to Send Tanks to Ukraine," CBS, January 25, 2023.

148 *President Zelensky joined*: Matthew Mpoke Bigg, " 'Tragedies Are Outpacing Life': In a Video Address at Davos, Zelensky Mourns the Dead and Pleads for Help," *The New York Times*, January 18, 2023.

149 *Later, on January 25, 2023*: "Remarks by President Biden on Continued Support for Ukraine," Briefing Room, January 25, 2023, Whitehouse.gov.

THIRTY-FIVE

150 *The Ukrainians, supported*: Huw Dylan, David V. Gioe, and Joe Littell, "The Kherson Ruse: Ukraine and the Art of Military Deception," Modern War Institute, October 12, 2022; Julian Barnes, Eric Schmitt, and Helene Cooper, "The Critical Moment Behind Ukraine's Rapid Advance," *The New York Times*, September 13, 2022.

151 *Under Russian nuclear doctrine*: "Basic Principles of State Policy of the Russian Federation on Nuclear Deterrence," June 2, 2020, No. 355.

151 *Putin announced*: "Read Putin's National Address on a Partial Military Mobilization," *The Washington Post*, September 21, 2022.

153 *On September 30*: Joshua Berlinger, Anna Chernova, and Tim Lister, "Putin Announces Annexation of Ukrainian Regions in Defiance of International Law," CNN, September 30, 2022.

153 *The following week*: "Remarks by President Biden at Democratic Senatorial Campaign Committee Reception," New York, October 6, 2022; David Sanger and James McKinley Jr., "Biden Warned of a Nuclear Armageddon. How Likely Is a Nuclear Conflict with Russia?," *The New York Times*, October 9, 2022.

154 *Austin was now*: Alex Horton, "U.S., Russian Defense Chiefs Hold First Talks in Months," *The Washington Post*, October 21, 2022; "Senior Military Official Holds a Background Briefing," October 24, 2022, Defense.gov.

154 *Shoigu, short and grim-faced*: Sophia Ankel and Tom Porter, "How Sergei Shoigu, Putin's Embattled One-Time Bestie, Rose to the Top of Russia's Military and Survived the Wagner Rebellion That Called for His Head," *Business Insider*, June 26, 2023.

155 *On Friday, October 21*: "Readout of Secretary of Defense Lloyd J. Austin III's Phone Call with Russian Minister of Defense Sergey Shoygu," Defense Release, October 21, 2022; Horton, "U.S., Russian Defense Chiefs Hold First Talks in Months."

155 *Shoigu just listened*: Andrei Soldatov and Irina Borogan, "The Man Behind Putin's Military," *Foreign Affairs*, February 26, 2022.

160 *What was Putin planning?*: Eric Schlosser, "What if Russia Uses Nuclear Weapons in Ukraine?," *The Atlantic*, June 20, 2022.

161 *Russia, then in 2022*: Guy Faulconbridge, "Analysis: What Is Russia's Policy on Tactical Nuclear Weapons?," Reuters, October 17, 2022; Karoun Demirjian, "Here Are the Nuclear Weapons Russia Has in Its Arsenal," *The Washington Post*, October 6, 2022.

162 *Reports started coming*: See also "Joint Statement by Foreign Ministers of France, the United Kingdom and the United States—Ukraine," October 24, 2022.

163 *Lloyd Austin, usually soft-spoken*: See also "Russia's Shoigu Holds Second Call with U.S. Defense Secretary in Three Days," Reuters, October 23, 2022.

163 *IAEA inspectors arrived*: "IAEA Says No Sign of 'Dirty Bomb' Work at Ukrainian Sites; Kyiv Hails Report," Reuters, November 3, 2022.

163 *"Let me just say"*: David Sanger, "Biden Says Russian Use of a Nuclear Weapon Would Be a 'Serious Mistake,'" *The New York Times*, October 25, 2022.

164 *President Xi agreed*: Maroosha Muzaffar, "Nuclear Weapons Must Not Be Used Over Ukraine, China's President Says in Clear Response to Russia," *The Independent*, November 5, 2022.

164 *The other decisive*: Peter Beaumont, Luke Harding, Pjotr Sauer, and Isobel Koshiw, "Ukraine Troops Enter Center of Kherson as Russians Retreat in Chaos," *The Guardian*, November 11, 2022; Steve Rosenberg, "Putin Can't Escape Fallout from Russian Retreat in Ukraine," BBC, November 11, 2022.

164 *As they sat down*: "CIA Chief William Burns Meets with Russian Spy Boss Sergey Naryshkin," Al Jazeera, November 14, 2022.

THIRTY-SIX

166 *Trump blamed his wife*: Bess Levin, "Report: Donald Trump Is Blaming Everyone but Himself for the Midterms. And, Yes, That Includes Melania," *Vanity Fair*, November 9, 2022.

166 *Exit polls indicated*: Chris Cillizza, "Donald Trump Said the Trumpiest Thing Possible About the Election," CNN, November 9, 2022.

166 *"While in certain ways"*: Caroline Vakil, "Trump: Midterms 'Somewhat Disappointing' but Still 'Very Big Victory,'" *The Hill*, November 11, 2022.

167 *"We are a nation in decline"*: "Former President Trump Announces 2020 Presidential Bid," November 15, 2022, rev.com.

168 *"Anyone who truly seeks"*: Ibid.

THIRTY-SEVEN

169 *Now he was managing a war*: "Fact Sheet: One Year of Supporting Ukraine," February 21, 2023, Whitehouse.gov.; "U.S. Security Assistance to Ukraine," Congressional Research Service, February 27, 2023, Crsreports.congress.gov.

169 *Since October, Russia*: Max Hunder and Jonathan Landay, "Russia Launches Biggest Air Strikes Since Start of Ukraine War," Reuters, October 11, 2022.

170 *NASAMs are the premier*: Chris Gordon, "NASAMS Arrive in Ukraine in US Bid to Bolster Air Defense," *Air & Space Forces Magazine*, November 7, 2022.

170 *To defend against*: "PATRIOT Air and Missile Defense System for Ukraine," Congressional Research Service, January 18, 2023, Crsreports.congress.gov.

170 *"We have artillery, yes"*: Kevin Liptak and Maegan Vazquez, "Zelensky Delivers Impassioned Plea for More Help Fighting Russia on the 'Frontline of Tyranny,'" CNN, December 21, 2022.

170 *The sustainability of Ukraine's 155mm*: John Ismay and Thomas Gibbons-Neff, "Artillery Is Breaking in Ukraine. It's Becoming a Problem for the Pentagon," *The New York Times*, November 25, 2022.

172 *"Six sappers lost"*: Charlie D'Agata, Agnes Reau, and Tucker Reals, "Meet Ukraine's 'Sappers,' Working to Clear Ground Retaken from Russian Troops Who 'Mine Everything,'" *CBS Mornings*, July 18, 2023.

THIRTY-EIGHT

176 *Let's go ahead*: See also David Sanger, Jim Tankersley, Michael Crowley, and Eric Schmitt, "In a Sharp Reversal, Biden Opens a Path for Ukraine to Get Fighter Jets," *The New York Times*, May 19, 2023.

THIRTY-NINE

178 *On November 18, 2022*: Devlin Barrett and Perry Stein, "Garland Names Special Counsel for Trump Mar-a-Lago, 2020 Election Probes," *The Washington Post*, November 18, 2022.

178 *"Based on recent"*: Ibid.

178 *"Today," Trump said*: "Former President Trump: 'I Am Your Justice . . . I Am Your Retribution,'" C-SPAN, March 4, 2023.

179 *In June, Trump*: Carrie Johnson, "Trump Indicted In Case of Alleged Mishandling of Government Secrets," NPR, June 8, 2023.

179 *His former attorney general*: Anders Hagstrom, "Bill Barr Says Trump's Indictment is 'Very Damning' If 'Even Half Of It Is True," Fox News, June 11, 2023.

180 *President Biden was*: Ken Bredemeier, "Biden Embarking on Late June Fundraising Effort," *VOA News*, June 19, 2023.

FORTY

183 *Banned by 123 countries*: See Victoria Kim, Gaya Gupta, and John Ismay, "Here's What Cluster Munitions Do and Why They Are So Controversial," *The New York Times*, July 6, 2023.

183 *President Biden had*: See also Aaron Blake, "Biden's Complicated History on Cluster Munitions," *The Washington Post*, July 7, 2023; David Smith and Luke Harding, "Joe Biden Defends 'Difficult Decision' to Send Cluster Munitions to Ukraine," *The Guardian*, July 8, 2023.

183 *Russia was already*: "Cluster Munitions Use in Russia-Ukraine War," Human Rights Watch, May 29, 2023.

183 *More than 2,400*: See also Mstyslav Chernov, *20 Days in Mariupol*, Associated Press/PBS *Frontline*, 2023; Katharina Krebs, "At Least 290 Civilian Bodies Found in Irpin Since Russian Withdrawal, Mayor Says," May 3, 2022;

"Commission of Inquiry Finds Further Evidence of War Crimes in Ukraine," *U.N. News*, October 20, 2023; Masha Gessen, "The Prosecution of Russian War Crimes in Ukraine," *The New Yorker*, August 1, 2022.

184 *Putin was also responsible*: Deborah Amos, "Russia Deports Thousands of Ukrainian Children. Investigators Say That's a War Crime," NPR, February 14, 2023; Yousur Al-Hlou and Masha Froliak, "46 Children Were Taken from Ukraine. Many Are Up for Adoption in Russia," *The New York Times*, June 2, 2024; "Situation in Ukraine: ICC Judges Issue Arrest Warrants Against Vladimir Vladimirovich Putin and Maria Alekseyevna Lvova-Belova," Press Release, March 17, 2023.

184 *I agree to the transfer*: See also Mike Stone, Trevor Hunnicutt, and Simon Lewis, "Tortured Path to U.S. Decision to Send Ukraine Cluster Munitions," Reuters, July 10, 2023; John Hudson and Anastacia Galouchka, "How Ukraine Is Exploiting Biden's Cluster Bomb Gamble," *The Washington Post*, August 21, 2023.

FORTY-ONE

185 *Yevgeny Prigozhin*: Jim Heintz, "Russian Mercenary Boss Yevgeny Prigozhin Challenged the Kremlin in a Brief Mutiny," Associated Press, August 27, 2023.

185 *In the months-long battle*: Christian Esch, Christina Hebel, and Alexander Chernyshev, "Yevgeny Prigozhin's Meat Grinder: A Moment of Truth for Russia's Wagner Group in Bakhmut," May 17, 2023, *Der Spiegel*, Spiegal.de /international.

185 *Fed up*: Lazaro Gamio, Marco Hernandez, and Josh Holder, "How a Rebellion in Russia Unfolded over 36 Hours," *The New York Times*, June 24, 2023.

186 *"Actions that split"*: Ibid.

186 *Two months later*: See also Simon Sebag-Montefiore, "What Prigozhin's Death Reveals About Putin's Power in Russia," *Time*, August 24, 2023.

186 *During an economic conference*: Paul Sonne and Michael C. Bender, "Putin, Citing Trump 'Persecution,' Wades Back Into U.S. Politics," *The New York Times*, September 12, 2023.

186 *Asked about Putin's comments*: Phil McCausland, "Trump Says He's Pleased By Putin's Praise: 'I Like That He Said That,'" NBC News, September 15, 2023, nbcnews.com.

FORTY-TWO

188 *Ron Dermer*: Mark Landler, "Viewed Warily by Democrats, a Netanyahu Ally Is a Key Conduit to U.S." *The New York Times*, November 7, 2023.

189 *The initial hours of the invasion*: See "Maps and Videos Show How the Deadly Surprise Attack on Israel Unfolded," *The Washington Post*, October 8, 2023; Andrés Martínez, "Here's a Timeline of Saturday's Attacks and Israel's Retaliation," *The New York Times*, October 8, 2023.

189 *Another 50 Hamas terrorists*: Eliza Mackintosh et al., "How a Rave Celebrating Life Turned into a Frenzied Massacre," CNN, October 14, 2023, cnn.com.

190 *The Hamas militants*: Bret Stephens, "Sheryl Sandberg Screams Back at the Silence," *The New York Times*, April 30, 2024; Jeffrey Gettleman, Anat Schwartz, and Adam Sella, "'Screams Without Words': How Hamas Weaponized Sexual Violence on October 7," *The New York Times*, December 28, 2023; Lucy Williamson, "Hamas Raped and Mutilated Women on 7 October, BBC Hears," BBC, December 5, 2023.

190 *Raz Cohen, another*: *Screams Before Silence*: Anat Stalinsky/Sheryl Sandberg, YouTube, 2024, screamsbeforesilence.com.

192 *At a podium in the*: "Remarks by President Biden on the Terrorist Attacks in Israel," Briefing, State Dining Room, October 7, 2023, Whitehouse.gov.

193 *Netanyahu had also changed*: See also "Israel Sends Hundreds of Gazan Laborers Held Since Oct. 7 Back into Strip," *The Times of Israel*, November 3, 2023.

194 *In another extraordinary oversight*: Ronen Bergman and Adam Goldman, "Israel Knew Hamas's Attack Plan More Than a Year Ago," *The New York Times*, November 30, 2023.

195 *October 7 struck*: See also "Israeli-Palestinian Conflict Timeline," Council on Foreign Relations, November 13, 2023, education.cfr.org.

FORTY-THREE

198 *The day after October 7*: "U.S. Moves Carrier Strike Group to Eastern Mediterranean," CENTCOM Press Release, October 8, 2023.

FORTY-FOUR

199 *Qatar, a small but wealthy*: Joel Simon, "How Qatar Became the World's Go-To Hostage Negotiator," *The New Yorker*, November 16, 2023.

199 *The Emir had helped*: Aya Batrawy, "Freeing Hostages, Hosting Hamas: Qatar's Influence in Israel-Gaza War, Explained," NPR, November 2, 2023.

200 *Sullivan built his cell*: Michael D. Shear, "Political Pressures on Biden Helped Drive 'Secret Cell' of Aides in Hostage Talks," *The New York Times*, November 21, 2023.

200 *The Emir had hosted*: Nima Elbagir et al., "Qatar Sent Millions to Gaza for Years—With Israel's Backing. Here's What We Know About the Controversial Deal," CNN, December 12, 2023; Batrawy, "Freeing Hostages, Hosting Hamas: Qatar's Influence in Israel-Gaza War, Explained."

200 *For Netanyahu, a contained Hamas*: Mark Mazzetti and Ronen Bergman, "Buying Quiet: Inside the Israeli Plan That Propped Up Hamas," *The New York Times*, December 10, 2023.

FORTY-FIVE

202 *Hezbollah, the massive Iranian-backed terrorist organization*: See also Nicholas Casey and Euan Ward, "What Is Hezbollah, the Group That Poses a Threat to Israel from the North?," *The New York Times*, October 19, 2023;

Kali Robinson, "What Is Hezbollah?," Council on Foreign Relations, October 14, 2023; Rund Abdeifatah et al., "A History of Hezbollah," NPR, March 28, 2024.

205 *Nearly 15 years earlier*: Bob Woodward, *Obama's Wars* (New York: Simon & Schuster, 2010); Bob Woodward and Robert Costa, *Peril* (New York: Simon & Schuster, 2021).

206 *But in his recent memoir*: Benjamin Netanyahu, *Bibi* (New York: Threshold Editions, 2022).

206 *Biden, Netanyahu wrote*: Ibid., p. 428.

207 *President Biden had spent the last year*: John Wagner and Ashley Parker, "Biden Says U.S. Ground Troops 'Not on the Table' for Ukraine," *The Washington Post*, December 8, 2021; Zachary Wolf, "Here's What Biden Has Said About Sending U.S. Troops to Ukraine," CNN, February 24, 2022.

208 *Ron Dermer, Netanyahu's top aide and alter ego*: Allison Hoffman, "Bibi's Brain: Meet Ron Dermer, Israel's New Ambassador to the U.S.," *Tablet*, September 20, 2011.

210 *The Israel Defense Forces came out publicly*: Emanuel Fabian and Amy Spiro, "90 Minute Panic over Mass Drone Invasion in Northern Israel Proves to Be False Alarm," *The Times of Israel*, October 11, 2023.

211 *"There was an error"*: Ibid.

212 *During a campaign speech*: Soo Rin Kim, Lalee Ibssa, Kendall Ross, Mary Bruce, and Adam Carlson, "Trump Criticized for Calling Hezbollah 'Very Smart' as He Talked of Potential Risk to Israel," ABC News, October 12, 2023.

212 *The White House*: Isaac Arnsdorf, "Trump Faults Netanyahu, Calls Hezbollah 'Very Smart' Amid Israel War," *The Washington Post*, October 12, 2023.

FORTY-SIX

213 *The U.S. was already supplying*: Jim Garamone, "U.S. Flowing Military Supplies to Israel, as Country Battles Hamas Terrorists," U.S. Department of Defense News, October 10, 2023.

213 *America provides Israel*: Oren Liebermann and Natasha Bertrand, "U.S. Eyes Weapons Stockpiles as Concern Grows About Supporting Both Ukraine and Israel's Wars," CNN, October 11, 2023; Eric Schmitt, Adam Entous, Ronen Bergman, John Ismay, and Thomas Gibbons-Neff, "Pentagon Sends U.S. Arms Stored in Israel to Ukraine," *The New York Times*, January 17, 2023.

214 *The Gaza Strip*: Jiachuan Wu, Joe Murphy, and Nigel Chiwaya, "The Gaza Strip's Density Visualized," NBC News, October 10, 2023.

216 *The next morning, October 13*: For photos see Humeyra Pamuk, "U.S. Secretary of State Blinken Meets Jordanian King in Amman," Reuters, October 13, 2023.

216 *The Muslim Brotherhood*: Other violent offshoots of the Muslim Brotherhood include the Islamic Resistance Movement dedicated to the elimination of Israel; Hezbollah, the Shia Islamist militant group in Lebanon; Al Qaeda, the Islamist militant organization led by Sunni jihadists responsible for the 9/11

attacks on the United States; and the Islamic State in Iraq and Syria known as ISIS or Daesh.

FORTY-SEVEN

223 *President Biden was planning*: See also Yasmeen Abutaleb, Tyler Pager, and John Hudson, "Biden to Travel to Israel on Wednesday," *The Washington Post*, October 16, 2023.

227 *Finally at 2:15 a.m.*: See also, Vera Bergengruen, "For Antony Blinken, the War in Gaza Is a Test of U.S. Power," *Time*, January 11, 2024.

FORTY-EIGHT

228 *From the media reports*: Julian Borger, "Hundreds Feared Dead After Blast at Gaza Hospital as Biden Set to Fly In," *The Guardian*, October 17, 2023.

231 *When Air Force One landed*: Franklin Foer, "Inside Biden's 'Hug Bibi' Strategy," *The Atlantic*, October 17, 2023; David Leonhardt and Ian Prasad Philbrick, "Biden's Trip to Israel," *The New York Times*, October 17, 2023.

231 *Bibi addressed Biden*: "Remarks by President Biden and Prime Minister Netanyahu of Israel Before Bilateral Meeting, Tel Aviv, Israel," The White House, October 18, 2023, Whitehouse.gov.

231 *"Look, folks," Biden said*: Ibid.

231 *Netanyahu brought*: "President Biden and Prime Minister Netanyahu Meet with Israeli War Cabinet," C-SPAN, October 18, 2023; Isabel Kershner, "To Fight Hamas, Israel's Leaders Stopped Fighting One Another. For Now," *The New York Times*, December 14, 2023.

233 *An hour later*: "Remarks by President Biden on the October 7th Terrorist Attacks and the Resilience of the State of Israel and its People," Tel Aviv, Israel, October 18, 2023, Whitehouse.gov.

235 *When Biden hung up*: See also Tamara Keith, "Biden Says His Tel Aviv Trip Was a Gamble. Tonight, He Has Another High-Stakes Moment," NPR, October 19, 2023.

235 *And, ultimately, Sisi*: Nidal Al-Mughrabi and Aidan Lewis, "First Aid Convoy Enters Gaza Strip from Egypt," Reuters, October 21, 2023.

235 *Before October 7*: Christina Bouri and Diana Roy, "Analysis: How Bad Is the Humanitarian Crisis in Gaza Amid the Israel-Hamas War?," PBS, November 19, 2023; "Israel: Unlawful Gaza Blockade Deadly for Children," Human Rights Watch, October 18, 2023.

FORTY-NINE

236 *The Houthis, another*: Luis Matinez, "U.S. Navy Destroyer in Red Sea Shoots Down Cruise Missiles Potentially Headed Toward Israel: Pentagon," ABC, October 20, 2023; Matina Stevis-Gridneff and Aaron Boxerman, "Yemen's Houthis Hijack a Ship in the Red Sea," *The New York Times*, November 19, 2023.

FIFTY

238 *"Israel* must *do more"*: Remarks by Vice President Harris on the Conflict Between Israel and Hamas," Dubai, December 2, 2023, Whitehouse.gov.

238 *On December 2, 2023*: Humeyra Pamuk, "Blinken Pushes Arab States to Discuss the Future of Gaza," Reuters, December 1, 2023.

238 *"Too many innocent Palestinians"*: See also TOI staff, "VP Harris: Suffering in Gaza 'Devastating'; Israel Must Do More To Protect Civilians," *The Times 238 Israel*, December 3, 2023.

238 *She also had*: See also Nandita Bose and Steve Holland, "US VP Harris Urges Israel to Protect Gaza Civilians," Reuters, December 2, 2023.

240 *Dermer was referring*: Meg Wagner, " 'Blood and Soil': Protesters Chant Nazi Slogan in Charlottesville," CNN, August 12, 2017.

FIFTY-ONE

243 *President Biden called*: See also David Nakamura, "Biden Hails Freed U.S. Hostages as Family Awaits Reunion," *The Washington Post*, October 21, 2023.

244 *Hamas released 50*: For public reporting: Alexander Ward, "How a Secret Cell Got Hamas to Release 50 Hostages," *Politico*, November 21, 2023; Aaron Poris, Miriam David-Hay, "Freed from Hell: Timeline of Hostage Releases During the Israel-Hamas War," *The Jerusalem Post*, December 3, 2023.

FIFTY-TWO

246 *In the 11 weeks since*: Meghann Myers, "U.S. Troops in Iraq and Syria Have Faced over 100 Attacks Since October," *Military Times*, December 21, 2023.

247 *That night, at about 4:45 a.m.*: "Biden Orders Strike on Iranian-Aligned Group After 3 U.S. Troops Injured in Iraq," NPR, December 25, 2023.

247 *"The strikes were taken"*: "Letter to the Speaker of the House and President Pro Tempore of the Senate Consistent with the War Powers Resolution (Public Law 93-148)," Briefing Room, January 12, 2024, Whitehouse.gov.

247 *On Saturday, December 30*: "U.S. Says It Shot Down 2 Missiles Launched from Houthi-Controlled Areas," Reuters, December 30, 2023.

247 *President Biden was in*: Lisa Friedman, "Biden Begins Weeklong Vacation in Caribbean to Ring in the New Year," *The New York Times*, December 27, 2023.

248 *Through January*: Christian Edwards, "Who Are the Houthis and Why Are They Attacking Ships in the Red Sea?," CNN, February 4, 2024; Agnes Chang, Pablo Robles, and Keith Bradsher, "How Houthi Attacks Have Upended Global Shipping," *The New York Times*, January 21, 2023.

249 *McGurk flew to Muscat*: Farnaz Fassihi and Eric Schmitt, "Iran and U.S. Held Secret Talks on Proxy Attacks and Cease-Fire," *The New York Times*, March 15, 2024.

249 *President Biden ordered air and naval*: Joseph Clark, "U.S., Partners' Forces Strike Houthi Military Targets in Yemen," U.S. Department of Defense News,

January 12, 2024, Defense.gov; "Statement from President Joe Biden on Coalition Strikes in Houthi-Controlled Areas of Yemen," Briefing Room, January 11, 2024, Whitehouse.gov.

250   *On Sunday, January 28*: Eric Schmitt, "3 American Soldiers Killed in Drone Strike in Jordan, U.S. Says," *The New York Times*, January 28, 2024.

250   *"Today, America's heart is heavy"*: "Statement from President Joe Biden on Attack on U.S. Service Members in Northeastern Jordan Near the Syria Border," Briefing Room, January 28, 2024, Whitehouse.gov.

250   *On Friday, February 2*: "U.S. Strikes Over 85 Targets at 7 Sites in Iraq and Syria Against Iran's Forces and Proxies," *The New York Times*, February 2, 2024.

250   *House Speaker Mike Johnson criticized*: @SpeakerJohnson, "My statement regarding the U.S. strikes in Syria and Iraq," 6:34 p.m., February 2, 2024, Twitter.com.

FIFTY-THREE

251   *On January 8*: Nick Allen, "Antony Blinken Meets MBS in Lavish Desert Tent and Says Saudi Crown Prince Is Determined to Keep Gaza Conflict from Spreading as Fears Grow of a Wider Middle East War," *Daily Mail*, Dailymail.co.uk.

252   *The U.S. was also getting closer*: Stephen Kalin and Michael Gordon, "U.S. to Offer Landmark Defense Treaty to Saudi Arabia in Effort to Spur Israel Normalization Deal," *The Wall Street Journal*, June 9, 2024.

FIFTY-FOUR

256   *Polls in Israel since October 7*: Benedict Vigers, "Life in Israel After Oct. 7 in 5 Charts," Gallup, December 22, 2023, Gallup.com.

258   *In December he shared*: Kevin Liptak and MJ Lee, "Biden Growing More Frustrated with Netanyahu as Gaza Campaign Rages On," CNN, February 12, 2024.

258   *Now he said publicly*: Andrea Shalal, "Biden Urged Israel's Netanyahu to Protect Civilians in Rafah—White House," Reuters, February 11, 2024.

260   *At Columbia University*: Anna Oakes, Claudia Gohn, "Inside the Columbia University Student Encampment—And the Crackdown," *Rolling Stone*, May 1, 2024.

260   *Some Republicans described*: Jacey Fortin, "Campus Protests: Republicans Accuse University Leaders of 'Giving In' to Antisemitism," *The New York Times*, May 23, 2024.

260   *Biden called Netanyahu*: "Readout of President Biden's Call with Prime Minister Netanyahu of Israel," February 15, 2024.

263   *In a remote prison camp*: Anna Chernova, Christian Edwards, and David Shortell, "Jailed Russian Opposition Figure Alexey Navalny Dies, Prison Services Say," CNN, February 16, 2024.

263   *"Make no mistake"*: "Remarks by President Biden on the Reported Death of Aleksey Navalny," Briefing Room, February 16, 2024, Whitehouse.gov.

FIFTY-FIVE

265 *It was Trump's demeaning*: Amanda Tugade, "Birdcages and 'New Blood': Tensions Between Nikki Haley, Donald Trump Boil Over After Republican Debate," October 1, 2023.

266 *Kellogg had just returned*: Lt. Gen. (Ret.) Keith Kellogg, "After Action Report: My Visit to Israel," America First Policy Institute, March 15, 2024.

268 *"I think Israel made a very big mistake"*: Omer Lachmanovitch and Ariel Kahana, "Trump to Israel Hayom: Only a Fool Would Have Not Acted Like Israel on Oct. 7," *Israel Hayom*, March 25, 2024.

FIFTY-SIX

270 *Graham's relationship with MBS*: Niels Lesniewski, "Lindsey Graham Wants to 'Sanction the Hell Out of Saudi Arabia' Until Crown Prince Is Ousted," Roll Call, October 16, 2018; Mariana Alfaro, "Lindsey Graham Meets with Saudi Crown Prince, Reversing Past Criticism," *The Washington Post*, April 11, 2023.

FIFTY-SEVEN

275 *At 9:00 p.m. John Kirby*: Jonathan Landay and Idrees Ali, "No U.S. Involvement in Strike on Iran's Damascus Mission, White House Says," Reuters, April 2, 2024.

275 *Three days later*: "Readout of President Joe Biden's Call with Prime Minister Netanyahu of Israel," The White House, April 4, 2024, Whitehouse.gov.

277 *He was referring to the Israeli drone strike*: Adam Rasgon and Aaron Boxerman, "What We Know About the Israeli Strike That Killed 7 Aid Workers in Gaza," *The New York Times*, April 2, 2024.

278 *After the call*: "Statement from National Security Council Spokesperson Adrienne Watson on Steps Announced by Israel to Increase Aid Flow to Gaza," The White House, April 4, 2024, Whitehouse.gov.

278 *Sinwar had spent years*: Neri Zilber, "'Dead Man Walking': How Yahya Sinwar Deceived Israel for Decades," *The Financial Times*, November 5, 2023; Jo Becker and Adam Sella, "The Hamas Chief and the Israeli Who Saved His Life," *The New York Times*, May 26, 2024.

279 *U.S. intelligence and other*: Marco Hernandez and Josh Holder, "The Tunnels of Gaza," *The New York Times*, November 10, 2023.

279 *Meanwhile, in Tehran on April 5*: "Vowing Revenge, Iran Pays Homage to IRGC Generals Killed in Strike Blamed on Israel, *The Times of Israel*, April 5, 2024.

FIFTY-EIGHT

283 *When Iran announced*: Joseph Federman and Jon Gambrell, "Iran Fires Drones and Ballistic Missiles at Israel in Massive Retaliatory Attack," PBS,

April 13, 2024; Madiha Afzal et al., "The Impact of Iran's Attack on Israel," *Brookings*, April 15, 2024, brookings.edu.

284 *Television coverage in the U.S.*: Kathleen Magramo, Elizabeth Wolfe, and Aditi Sangal, "Iran Targeted in Aerial Attack," CNN, April 18, 2024; Courtney Kube, Mosheh Gains, and Dan De Luce, "Israel Carries Out Limited Strikes on Iran, with the Extent of Damage Unclear," NBC News, April 19, 2024.

FIFTY-NINE

285 *In the spring*: Adam Entous and Michael Schwirtz, "The Spy War: How the C.I.A. Secretly Helps Ukraine Fight Putin," *The New York Times*, February 25, 2024.

285 *Burns had arrived*: Carlotta Gall, Marc Santora, and Constant Méheut, "Avdiivka, Longtime Stronghold for Ukraine, Falls to Russians," *The New York Times*, February 17, 2024; Julian E. Barnes, "Biden Administration Blames Congress for Fall of Ukrainian City," *The New York Times*, February 17, 2024.

286 *During his confirmation hearings*: "Statement for the Record Senate Select Committee on Intelligence, Director of CIA Nominee William J. Burns," February 24, 2021, Intelligence.senate.gov.

286 *In his 2019 memoir*: William J. Burns, *The Back Channel* (New York: Random House, 2019), p. 431.

SIXTY

287 *In 2022 and 2023*: "CBP Releases December 2023 Monthly Update," U.S. Customs and Border Protection, January 26, 2024.

288 *From his first days as president*: Michael D. Shear, Hamed Aleaziz, and Zolan Kanno-Youngs, "How the Border Crisis Shattered Biden's Immigration Hopes," *The New York Times*, January 30, 2024.

289 *But nearly 80 percent*: "How Americans View the Situation at the U.S.-Mexico Border, Its Causes and Consequences," Pew Research Center, February 15, 2024.

289 *New York mayor Eric Adams*: Jeffrey C. Mays, "Mayor Adams Criticizes Biden in Rare Public Rebuke over Migrant Crisis," *The New York Times*, April 19, 2023; Emma G. Fitzsimmons, "In Escalation, Adams Says Migrant Crisis 'Will Destroy New York City,'" *The New York Times*, September 7, 2023.

290 *The reasons for this massive*: Alex Nowrasteh, "The U.S. Labor Market Explains Most of the Increase in Illegal Immigration," Cato Institute, November 16, 2023, Cato.org.

SIXTY-ONE

293 *Poland also shares*: Michal Kranz, "How the Russia-Ukraine Crisis Is Turning Poland into a Strategic Player," *Foreign Policy*, February 23, 2022.

294 *Polish families brought*: Elisabeth Zerofsky, "Poland's War on Two Fronts," *The New York Times Magazine*, April 4, 2023.

294 *Duda said Biden*: See also "In White House Visit, Polish President Pushes NATO to Ramp Up Spending, Calls on U.S. to Fund Ukraine," Associated Press, March 12, 2024.

295 *A month earlier*: Andrzej Duda, "NATO Members Must Raise Their Defense Spending to 3 Percent of GDP," *The Washington Post*, March 11, 2024.

295 *At a campaign rally*: Edward Helmore, "Trump Says He Would Encourage Russia to Attack NATO Allies Who Pay Too Little," *The Guardian*, February 11, 2024.

295 *Trump replied*: Ibid.

295 *Duda took a more*: Duda, "NATO Members Must Raise Their Defense Spending to 3 Percent of GDP."

295 *Notably, most of the NATO*: Derek Hawkins, "See Which NATO Countries Spend Less Than 2 Percent of Their GDP on Defense," *The Washington Post*, February 12, 2024.

297 *That evening, April 17*: Jill Colvin and Monika Scislowska, "Poland's President Becomes the Latest Leader to Visit Donald Trump as Allies Eye a Possible Return," Associated Press, April 18, 2024.

298 *After the dinner with Duda*: @realDonaldTrump, "Why isn't Europe giving more money to help Ukraine? Why is it that the United States is over $100 Billion Dollars into the Ukraine War more than Europe, and we have an Ocean between us as separation! Why can't Europe equalize or match the money put in by the United States of America in order to help a Country in Desperate need? As everyone agrees, Ukrainian Survival and Strength should be much more important to Europe than to us, but it is also important to us! GET MOVING EUROPE! In addition, I am the only one who speaks for "ME" and, while it is a total mess caused by Crooked Joe Biden and the Incompetent Democrats, if I were President, this War would have never started," 1:55 p.m., April 18, 2024, TruthSocial.com.

298 *"We have to remember"*: "Remarks by President Trump to the People of Poland," The White House, July 6, 2017, Trumpwhitehouse.archives.gov.

299 *Biden directed his team to*: See also Liz Goodwin, Yasmeen Abutaleb, and Tyler Page, "Aid to Ukraine Seemed Dead. Then Secretive Talks Revived It," *The Washington Post*, April 24, 2024; See also Vivian Salama, "Why Donald Trump Didn't Sink Mike Johnson's Ukraine-Aid Bill," *The Wall Street Journal*, April 22, 2024.

300 *As the House voted*: Mary Clare Jalonick, Stephen Groves, and Farnoush Amiri, "Senate Overwhelmingly Passes Aid for Ukraine, Israel and Taiwan in Big Bipartisan Vote," Associated Press, April 23, 2024.

300 *The bill then*: Ibid.

300 *Biden signed the bill*: "Remarks by President Biden on the Passage of H.R. 815, the National Security Supplemental," State Dining Room, April 24, 2024, Whitehouse.gov.

SIXTY-TWO

302 *Hamas later publicly posted*: Ibrahim Dahman and Eyad Kourdi, "Hamas Releases Video of Hostage Hersh Goldberg-Polin in Proof He Survived Oct. 7 Injuries," CNN, April 25, 2024.

302 *Hamas militants had entered*: Emily Mae Czachor, "Abigail Mor Edan, the 4-Year-Old American Held Hostage by Hamas, Is Now Free. Here's What to Know," CBS, November 27, 2023.

303 *Now Abigail*: Michelle Stoddart, Justin Gomez, and Fritz Farrow, "Biden Says Meeting with 4-Year-Old Girl Orphaned and Held Hostage by Hamas a Reminder of Work Needed to Free Remaining Hostages," ABC, April 25, 2024.

SIXTY-THREE

304 *According to Daleep Singh*: Walter Pincus, "Russia Sanctions 101—Via a Top White House Advisor," *The Cipher Brief*, June 4, 2024.

305 *Putin was also having to source*: See Yoonjung Seo and Helen Regan, "North Korean Factories Making Arms for Russia Are 'Operating at Full Capacity,' South Korea Says," CNN, February 28, 2024.

305 *Putin's autobiography*: Vladimir Putin, *First Person* (New York: PublicAffairs, 2000), p. 7.

306 *"A dog senses when"*: Ibid., p. 168.

SIXTY-FOUR

307 *Parlatore, who had represented Trump*: "Trump's Former Lawyer in the Docs Case Explains Why He Left," *Politico*, June 16, 2023; Kaanita Iyer, "Former Key Trump Attorney Says He Left Because of Legal Team Infighting," CNN, May 20, 2023, cnn.com.

308 *On May 30, 2024*: "Donald Trump Found Guilty on All Counts in N.Y. Hush Money Trial," *The Washington Post*, May 30, 2024.

308 *Trump and his campaign*: Philip Bump, "Trump Insists His Trial Was Rigged . . . Just Like Everything Else," *The Washington Post*, March 31, 2024.

309 *In the 24 hours*: Shane Goldmacher, "Trump Announces Nearly $53 Million Fund-Raising Haul After Guilty Verdict," *The New York Times*, May 31, 2024.

309 *"I'm a very innocent man"*: Sarah Burris, " 'I'm A Very Innocent Man': Trump Attacks Rule of Law After 'Rigged' Guilty Verdict," *RawStory*, May 30, 2024.

SIXTY-FIVE

310 *"They're trying to"*: Hunter Biden interview with Moby, *Moby Pod*, December 2023.

311 *Hunter Biden, 54*: "Read the Full Hunter Biden Indictment over Federal Gun Charges," PBS, September 14, 2023; "Grand Jury Returns Indictment

Charging Robert Hunter Biden with Three Felony Tax Offenses and Six Misdemeanor Tax Offenses," Department of Justice, December 7, 2023.

312 *In his memoir*: Hunter Biden, *Beautiful Things* (New York: Gallery Books, 2021), p. 145.

SIXTY-SIX

313 *President Biden's frustrations*: For other examples: Michael Hirsh, "From 'I Love You' to 'Asshole': How Joe Gave Up on Bibi," *Politico*, March 22, 2024.

313 *Netanyahu was destroying*: "The IDF Is Accused of Military and Moral Failures in Gaza," *The Economist*, April 11, 2024.

314 *Before October 7*: Raf Sanchez, "Israeli Leaders Lash Out at Biden's Criticism as Judicial Overhaul Plan Sparks a Rare Public Rift," NBC News, March 29, 2023; Patrick Kingsley, "The Netanyahu Trial, Explained," *The New York Times*, February 8, 2021.

314 *But after*: Kevin Liptak, "Biden Hints Netanyahu Is Dragging Out Gaza War for Political Survival," CNN, June 4, 2024.

315 *Netanyahu expanded Israel's military assault*: Bilal Shbair et al., "Carnage and Contradiction: Examining a Deadly Strike in Rafah," *The New York Times*, June 14, 2024.

315 *By the end of May 2024*: "Gaza Death Toll: How Many Palestinians Has Israel's Campaign Killed," Reuters, May 14, 2024.

316 *"Unfortunately, Mr. Netanyahu"*: Jake Lapham, "Israeli War Cabinet Minister Benny Gantz Quits Emergency Government," BBC, June 9, 2024.

316 *In June, Israel's military*: Mohammad Jahjouh, Jack Jeffery, and Kareem Chehayeb, "How an Israeli Raid Freed 4 Hostages and Killed at Least 274 Palestinians in Gaza," Associated Press, June 10, 2024.

SIXTY-SEVEN

317 *Trump was using the southern border*: "Speech: Donald Trump Holds A Political Rally in Conway, South Carolina," February 10, 2024, rollcall.com.

317 *Trump's language was becoming*: See also Jake Traylor, "What Trump Is Promising Supporters He'd Do In A Second Term," NBC News, February 18, 2024.

SIXTY-EIGHT

319 *Media coverage had recognized*: See also Jeffrey Goldberg, "The Patriot: How General Mark Milley Protected the Constitution from Donald Trump," *The Atlantic*, November 2023.

319 *"Things may look unsteady"*: Bob Woodward and Robert Costa, *Peril* (New York: Simon & Schuster, 2021), p. xiii.

319 *Milley also testified*: Phil Stewart and Patricia Zengerle, "Under Fierce Republican Attack, U.S. General Milley Defends Calls with China," Reuters, September 28, 2021.

319 *But Trump referred*: Brian Klaas, "Trump Floats the Idea of Executing Joint Chiefs Chairman Milley," *The Atlantic*, September 25, 2023.

320 *"So disloyal!"*: Mark Esper, *A Sacred Oath* (New York: William Morrow, 2022), p. 474.

321 *Milley and Esper advised*: Ibid., p. 474.

322 *"Can't you just shoot them?"*: Ibid., p. 1.

322 *"We're going to send in the troops"*: Bob Woodward, *The Trump Tapes: Bob Woodward's Twenty Interviews with President Donald Trump* (New York: Simon & Schuster, 2022), p. 329.

322 *In another interview*: Ibid., pp. 341–342.

323 *Milley and Esper only narrowly*: Woodward and Costa, *Peril,* pp. 89, 99–100; Esper, *A Sacred Oath*, pp. 333–340.

323 *"I want you to be in charge"*: Esper, *A Sacred Oath,* p. 338.

323 *Milley threw his hands up*: Ibid.

323 *"We look weak"*: Ibid.

323 *"We seemed on the verge of crossing"*: Ibid., p. 5.

323 *"What would happen, I wondered"*: Ibid., p. 6.

324 *For instance, Trump's proposed solution*: Isaac Arnsdorf, Nick Miroff and Josh Dawsey, "Trump and Allies Planning Militarized Mass Deportations, Detention Camps," *The Washington Post*, February 21, 2024.

324 *"If I thought things were"*: "Read the Full Transcripts of Donald Trump's Interviews With TIME," *TIME*, April 30, 2024.

324 *"These aren't civilians"*: Ibid.

324 *Esper warned that*: Esper, *A Sacred Oath*, p. 5.

324 *Former secretary of defense James Mattis*: Bob Woodward, *Rage* (New York: Simon & Schuster, 2020), p. 76.

325 *"If he shoots, he shoots"*: Woodward, *The Trump Tapes: Bob Woodward's Twenty Interviews with President Donald Trump*, p. 62.

SIXTY-NINE

326 *By June 2024*: See Anne Linskey and Siobhan Hughes, "Behind Closed Doors, Biden Shows Signs of Slipping," *The Wall Street Journal,* June 4, 2024.

327 *Former special counsel Robert Hur*: "Report on the Investigation Into Unauthorized Removal, Retention, and Disclosure of Classified Documents Discovered at Locations Including the Penn Biden Center and the Delaware Private Resident of President Joseph R. Biden, Jr.," February 5, 2024, Justice.gov.

327 *A transcript of Biden's interview*: See "Transcript of President Joe Biden's Interview With Special Counsel Robert Hur," March 12, 2024, CNN.

327 *Twice Biden struggled*: See also Charlie Savage, "How the Special Counsel's Portrayal of Biden's Memory Compares With the Transcript," *The New York Times,* March 12, 2024.

327 *Hur listed among his reasons*: "Report on the Investigation Into Unauthorized Removal, Retention, and Disclosure of Classified Documents Discovered at Locations Including the Penn Biden Center and the Delaware Private Resident of President Joseph R. Biden, Jr.," February 5, 2024, Justice.gov., p. 220.

327 *"I'm well-meaning"*: "Remarks by President Biden," Briefing Room, February 8, 2024, Whitehouse.gov.

328 *In late February*: Kevin O'Connor, D.O, RAAFP, "Memorandum: President Biden's Current Health Summary," February 28, 2024, Whitehouse.gov.

328 *Dr. O'Connor noted in his public report*: Ibid.

329 *President Biden's State of the Union*: "Remarks by President Biden in State of the Union Address, U.S. Capitol," March 7, 2024, Whitehouse.gov.

329 *At a Silicon Valley fundraiser*: Zach Montague, "Biden Courts Wealthy Donors on West Coast Fund-Raising Trip," *The New York Times*, May 10, 2024.

332 *Polling indicated*: "Cross-Tabs: February 2024 Times/Siena Poll of Registered Voters Nationwide," *The New York Times*, March 2, 2024.

333 *"He didn't slash defense"*: See "Department of Defense Releases the President's Fiscal Year 2024 Defense Budget," March 13, 2023.

333 *A hallmark of*: "Remarks by President Biden and NATO Secretary General Jens Stoltenberg Before Bilateral Meeting," June 17, 2024, Whitehouse.gov.

334 *Biden visited two active war zones*: Peter Baker and Michael Shear, "Biden's Surreal and Secretive Journey into a War Zone," *The New York Times*, February 20, 2023; David Sanger and Peter Baker, "Biden Faces Risks in Wartime Visit to Israel," *The New York Times*, October 16, 2023.

SEVENTY

335 *"We have a thousand trillionaires"*: "Biden-Trump Debate Transcript, CNN, June 28, 2024.

336 *"I really don't know what he said"*: Ibid.

336 *Even before the debate was over*: "Political h-bomb': Trump-Biden debate scored by Bob Woodward, legendary Pulitzer-Watergate reporter," MSNBC, June 28, 2024.

336 *At first Biden shrugged*: "Read the Letter President Biden Sent to House Democrats Telling Them to Support Him in the Election," Associated Press, July 8, 2024.

SEVENTY-ONE

338 *Several minutes into*: See also Renée Rigdon, Amy O'Kruk, Marco Chacon et al., "Minute-by-minute: Visual Timeline of the Trump Assassination Attempt," CNN, July 26, 2024, cnn.com.; Michael Levenson, "What we Know about the Assassination Attempt Against Trump," *The New York Times*, July 30, 2024.

339 *After 10:30 in the evening on July 19*: "Read the Transcript of Donald J. Trump's Convention Speech," *The New York Times*, July 19, 2024.

340 *On Sunday, July 21*: See, @JoeBiden, 1:46 p.m. July 21, 2024, Twitter.com.; Katie Rogers, Michael Shear, Peter Baker and Zolan Kanno-Youngs, "Inside the Weekend When Biden Decided to Withdraw," *The New York Times*, July 21, 2024.

SEVENTY-TWO

341 *ISIS-K was responsible*: Jessie Yeung, "Who Are ISIS-K, the Group Linked to the Moscow Concert Hall Terror Attack?" CNN, March 26, 2024.

341 *The U.S. embassy in Moscow*: "Security Alert: Avoid Large Gatherings Over the Next 48 Hours," U.S. Embassy & Consulates in Russia, March 7, 2024; Guy Faulconbridge, "US Embassy Warns of Imminent Attack in Moscow by 'Extremists,'" Reuters, March 8, 2024.

342 *A month after the Moscow*: Josh Campbell, "Eight Tajikistan National Arrested In Los Angeles, New York and Philadelphia. Some May Have ISIS Ties, Sources Say," CNN, June 12, 2024.

343 *Going back to last year*: Graham Allison and Michael J. Morrell, "The Terrorism Warning Lights Are Blinking Red Again," *Foreign Affairs*, June 10, 2024.

SEVENTY-THREE

346 *At a rally in Charlotte*: "Fact-Checking Donald Trump's Rally in Charlotte, N.C.," PolitiFact, July 24, 2024.

346 *At a National Association of Black Journalists*: Daniel Dale, "Fact Check: Trump's Lie that Harris 'All of a Sudden' Embraced A Black Identity," CNN, July 31, 2024.

347 *Harris's late mother*: Ibid.

347 *Trump was hit*: Stephen Fowler, "Trump Attacks Kamala Harris' Racial Identity at Black Journalism Convention," NPR, July 31, 2024.

347 *The vice president barely*: Ibid.

SEVENTY-FOUR

354 *At a press briefing*: Aamer Madhani, "Watch: Harris Outlines Steps in Gaza Ceasefire Proposal After Meeting with Israel's Netanyahu," PBS News, July 25, 2024.

SEVENTY-FIVE

359 *During the presidential debate*: "Read: Biden-Trump debate Transcript," CNN, June 28, 2024.

361 *Trump's war was the coronavirus pandemic*: Bob Woodward, *Rage* (New York: Simon & Schuster, 2020).

361 *"Oh, I have a plan, Bob"*: Bob Woodward, *The Trump Tapes* (New York: Simon & Schuster, 2022), p. 276.

361 *"You will see the plan, Bob"*: Ibid., p. 397.

SEVENTY-SIX

363 *Israel had taken out*: Ronan Bergman, Adam Rasgon, Euan Ward et al., "Israel Says It Killed Hezbollah Commander in Airstrike Near Beirut," *The New York Times*, July 30, 2024.

363 *"Hezbollah crossed the red line"*: "Israel Says Its Beirut Strike Killed Hezbollah's Top Military Commander, Who It Blames for Golan Heights Attack," CNN, July 30, 2024.

363 *Israel had planted*: Ronan Bergman, Mark Mazzetti and Farnaz Fassihi, "Bomb Smuggled Into Tehran Guesthouse Months Ago Killed Hamas Leader," *The New York Times*, August 4, 2024.

SEVENTY-SEVEN

366 *In* The Commanders: Bob Woodward, *The Commanders* (New York: Simon & Schuster, 1991), p. 34.

367 *"That is not on the table"*: John Wagner and Ashley Parker, "Biden Says U.S. Ground Troops 'Not on the Table' for Ukraine," *The Washington Post*, December 8, 2021.

367 *When the war came*: Joseph R. Biden Jr., "President Biden: What America Will and Will Not Do in Ukraine," *The New York Times*, May 31, 2022.

367 *"The United States and our allies"*: "Remarks by President Biden on Russia's Unprovoked and Unjustified Attack on Ukraine," The White House, February 24, 2022, Whitehouse.gov.

Photography Credits

AFP via Getty Images: 19
Amanda Andrade-Rhoades (for *The Washington Post*): 15
Associated Press: 8
Loay Ayyoub (for *The Washington Post*): 21
Arthur Bondar (freelance photographer): 10
Jabin Botsford (*The Washington Post*): 3, 4, 11, 25, 26
Andrew Caballero-Reynolds (Getty Images): 27
Demetrius Freeman (*The Washington Post*): 9
Wojciech Grzedzinski (for *The Washington Post*): 14
Andrew Harnik (Associated Press): 24
Haiyun Jiang (*The Washington Post*): 6
Nicholas Kamm (Getty Images): 23
Heidi Levine (for *The Washington Post*): 13
Jacquelyn Martin (Associated Press): 16
Jonathan Nackstrand (Associated Press): 5
Alexey Nikolsky (AFP via Getty Images): 12
Adam Schultz (Official White House Photo): 20
Adam Schultz (Official White House Photo via Associated Press): 7
Patrick Semansky (Associated Press): 1
Brendan Smialowski (AFP via Getty Images): 2
Trump Campaign Office Handout (Anadolu via Getty Images): 28
Megan Varner (Getty Images): 29
Evan Vucci (Associated Press): 17, 18
Alex Wong (Getty Images): 22

Index